ECONOMIC DEVELOPMENT
OF COMMUNIST CHINA

AN APPRAISAL OF THE FIRST FIVE YEARS
OF INDUSTRIALIZATION

Publications of the
Bureau of Business and Economic Research
University of California

ECONOMIC DEVELOPMENT OF COMMUNIST CHINA

An Appraisal of the First Five Years
of Industrialization

BY

CHOH-MING LI

UNIVERSITY OF CALIFORNIA PRESS

BERKELEY AND LOS ANGELES

1959

UNIVERSITY OF CALIFORNIA PRESS

BERKELEY AND LOS ANGELES

CALIFORNIA

❖

CAMBRIDGE UNIVERSITY PRESS

LONDON, ENGLAND

LIBRARY OF CONGRESS CATALOG CARD NUMBER: 58-13330

TO
SYLVIA, WINSTON, JEAN,
AND TONY

Preface

This work is neither a general survey nor a historical study of the Chinese economy, but an economic analysis of its growth from 1952 to 1957. Virtually all quantitative and qualitative information was derived from Chinese-language sources published in Peiping up to the last quarter of 1957. The data were checked for reliability and consistency, and the statistical concepts were carefully examined before they were used. Interpretation was based on the facts thus established, and every effort was made to maintain objectivity and to provide an accurate appraisal of the economic transformation in Communist China during the period of her First Five Year Plan.

The manuscript was completed in March, 1958. The preliminary statistics for 1957 have since become available. According to them, the gross agricultural value product fell below expectations while the gross industrial product went beyond. This development strengthens the observations and conclusions in the text. However, in order to bring the data up to date, an addendum to the Statistical Appendix has been prepared, showing the preliminary figures for 1957 as well as the planned quota for 1958.

This work may also be taken as a case study of economic development of a low-income, agricultural country which has adopted a program of rapid and concentrated expansion of heavy industry. Both the mechanism of the industrialization process and the ramifications of change should be of interest. But the importance of the case goes beyond its instructive value. Steel production in Communist China in 1957 is now estimated to be 5,240,000 metric tons as against 1,350,000 tons in 1952. It was 21,000,000 tons in the United Kingdom in 1956. At the end of the First Five Year Plan, the chairman of the State Planning Commission in Peiping declared before the All-China Labor Congress that the country would be expected to surpass the United Kingdom by the end of the Fourth Five Year Plan (1972) "probably in steel production with about 40,000,000 tons, and certainly in the output of coal, lathes, cement, and chemical fertilizers." This, in fact, was a decision taken *by the Central Committee of the Chinese Communist party in the winter of 1957. Since then, the party drive to overtake the oldest industrialized country of the West in industrial output within the next fifteen years has become a national effort. If China succeeds, the impact on the rest of the world will be considerable. Her economic, political, and social development during this period demands special attention. Incidentally, to promote interest in this important field the Center for Chinese Studies has been set up at the University of California at Berkeley.*

In the preparation of this volume I have incurred indebtedness to many of my colleagues on this campus. Professors Walter Galenson and Gregory Grossman read a preliminary and the final drafts of the manuscript and offered many fruitful suggestions from their store of experience in Soviet economic studies. Grossman placed his knowledge of Soviet economic statistics and Russian language at my disposal, and the acknowledgments made in the text are not adequate to indicate the extent of his assistance. Professors J. B. Condliffe and A. G. Papandreou read the entire manuscript, and Professor Howard S. Ellis read several chapters, especially chapter vi. Their suggestions resulted in improving the exposition.

Research for this study was supported by the Bureau of Business and Economic Research, and at one time also by the Institute of Industrial Relations. Chancellor Clark Kerr, now president of the University, and Dean E. T. Grether of the School of Business Administration gave me constant encouragement. Professor Frank Kidner, director of the bureau, aside from taking an active interest in this work, was especially helpful in expediting its publication. Dr. Elizabeth Huff, head of the East Asiatic Library, extended to me many courtesies.

C. M. Li

Berkeley, California

Contents

I. *Introduction*   1
   1. Nature of Source Data
   2. The First Five Year Plan
   3. Socialization of the Economy
   4. Commodity and Factor Markets
   5. Current Prices

II. *Industrial Development* 29
   1. The Pace of Industrialization
   2. The Development of Producer- and Consumer-
      Goods Industries
   3. New Industrial Location

III. *Agricultural Development* 53
   1. Gross Agricultural Value Product
   2. Agricultural Development in Physical Terms
   3. Concluding Observations

IV. *National Product: Structure and Growth, 1952–1957* .   75
   1. The Concept of National Income
   2. Some Global Calculations
   3. Reconstruction of the National Income Account,
      1952–1957
   4. Summary of Estimates and Some Observations on
      the Net National Product

V. *Net Capital Formation, 1952–1957* 112
   1. Net Capital Formation, Accumulation, and
      Basic Construction Investment
   2. Estimate of Net Capital Formation
   3. Summary of Estimates and Some Observations

VI. *Internal Financing* 141
   1. The State Budget
   2. Note Circulation, Credit Expansion, and
      Budgetary Balance
   3. Summary

VII. *External Financing and Export Drive* 169
   1. Soviet Economic Aid
   2. Foreign Trade and Balance of International
     Payments
   3. Concluding Remarks

VIII. *Prospects: Some Strategic Factors of Growth* 196
   1. Population Growth
   2. Consumption
   3. Conclusion

Statistical Appendix 223
   Introduction
   Tables
   Addendum

Bibliography 261

Index 275

TABLES IN THE TEXT

   I. The State Investment Plan, 1953–1957 9
   II. Planned Increase in Annual Productive Capacity upon Completion of 694 Industrial Projects Initiated under the First Five Year Plan 10
   III. Socialization of Trade, Industry, Transportation, and Agriculture, 1950–1956 16
   IV. Wholesale and Retail Price Indices of Urban Areas, 1950–1957 25
   V. Some Indicators of Industrialization, 1952–1957 . . 31
   VI. Gross Industrial Value Product at 1952 Prices, by Sectors, 1952–1957 38
   VII. Development of Producer- and Consumer-Goods Industries at 1952 Prices, 1952–1957 40
   VIII. Production of Major Industrial Products, 1952–1957 . 44
   IX. Location of Factory Industry, According to Value Product at 1952 Prices, 1952–1956 50
   X. State Total and Agricultural Investment at Current Prices, 1952–1957 54

XI. Nature of the Agricultural Year and the Gross Agricultural Value Product at 1952 Prices, 1952–1957, and Composition of the Value Product, 1952–1956 . . . 58

XII. Some Indicators of Agricultural Development, 1952–1957 60

XIII. Farm Animals and Collectivization, 1956 70

XIV. Exports and Consumption of Food Grains and Soybeans, 1953–1957 72

XV. Some Global Calculations, based on Official Data of September, 1956, of the Domestic Material Product at 1952 Prices, 1952–1956 82

XVI. Certain Basic National Income Data, with Their Sources 86

XVII. Estimate of Net Agricultural Value Product at 1952 Prices, 1952–1957 88

XVIII. Estimate of Net Factory Value Product at 1952 Prices, 1952–1957 91

XIX. Estimate of Net Handicraft Value Product at 1952 Prices, 1952–1957 94

XX. Summary of Estimates of Net Industrial Value Product at 1952 Prices, 1952–1957 94

XXI. Estimate of Net Domestic Material Product at 1952 Prices, 1952–1957 96

XXII. Net Value Product per Worker in Construction, Transportation and Communications, and Trade, at 1952 Prices, 1955–1956 96

XXIII. Labor Force and Net Product of Construction, Transportation and Communications, and Trade, at 1952 Prices, for Selected Years 98

XXIV. Estimate of Net National Product at 1952 Prices, 1952–1957 104

XXV. Summary of Estimates (Based on Official National Income Data) of Net National Product and Its Components at 1952 Prices, 1952–1957 106

XXVI. India and Communist China: Relative Importance of Different Sectors in the Net National Product for Selected Years 110

XXVII. Basic Construction Investment at Current and at 1952 Prices, 1952–1957 117

XXVIII. Estimate of State Capital Investment in Machinery and Equipment, Housing and Other Construction, at 1952 Prices, 1952–1957 122

XXIX. Estimate of Working Capital Investment by Factory Industry at 1952 Prices, 1952–1957 128

XXX. Agricultural Credit and Sales of Producer Goods in Rural Areas at Current Prices, 1952–1956 132

XXXI. Estimate of Net Capital Formation in Agriculture at 1952 Prices, 1952–1957 134

XXXII. Summary of Estimates of Net Capital Formation at 1952 Prices, 1952–1957 136

XXXIII. State Budget: Planned and Realized Total Receipts and Expenditures, Net of Carryovers, 1950–1957 . . 143

XXXIV. Sources of Internal Financing of the State Budget, 1950–1957 148

XXXV. Taxes, Profits and Depreciation Reserves of State and Joint Enterprises, and Government Bond Proceeds, 1954–1957 149

XXXVI. Government Bonds: Issues, Terms, and Actual Proceeds, 1949–1957 152

XXXVII. Budgetary Expenditures, by Categories, 1950–1957 . 153

XXXVIII. Total Bank Deposits of the Public, 1949–1956 . . . 155

XXXIX. Composition of Social Purchasing Power, 1956 . . . 158

XL. Estimated Volume of Note Circulation, 1949–1957 . 160

XLI. Budgetary Balance, Note Circulation, Basic Construction Investment, Industrial Working Capital, Agricultural Credit, and Gross Agricultural and Industrial Product, 1950–1957 164

XLII. Total Trade, Imports, and Exports, 1950–1957 . . 178

XLIII. Estimate of Servicing Payments on National Debt and Foreign Borrowing, 1952–1957 181

XLIV. Estimate of Major Items in the Balance of International Payments, 1953–1957 184

XLV. Geographical Distribution of Total Foreign Trade, 1950–1956 186

XLVI. Communist China's Export and Import Trade with the Free World, by Areas, 1953–1956 189

XLVII. Rural and Urban Population of Census, and Population subject to "Planned Supply" of Food Grains, 1953–1957 201

XLVIII. Effect of Agricultural Year on the National Economy, 1952–1957 220

TABLES IN THE STATISTICAL APPENDIX

Table 1. Gross Agricultural and Industrial Product at 1952 Prices, 1949–1957 227

Table 2. Industrial Production at 1952 Prices by Sectors, 1949–1957 228

Table 3. Industrial Product at 1952 Prices: Producer and Consumer Goods, 1949–1957 229

Table 4. Socialization of Industry, by Sectoral Value Product at 1952 Prices, 1949–1957 230

Table 5. Operation of Private Factory Industry by Value of Production at 1952 Prices, 1949–1955 231

Table 6. Structure of Industry by Number and Size of Establishments, 1949–1955 232

Table 7. Structure of Industry by Employment, 1949–1955 . . 233

Table 8. Distribution of Factory Industry between Inland and Coastal Areas, by Value of Production, 1949–1956 . . 234

Table 9. Mechanization of Industrial Production: Fixed Capital Assets per Worker in State-operated and State-private Jointly-operated Establishments of Various Industries, 1952–1955 235

Table 10. Development of Railway, Highway and Air Transportation, and of Post and Telecommunications, 1950–1957 236

Table 11. Development of Water Transportation (Steam Barges and Ships), 1950–1956 237

Table 12. Socialization of Transportation by Freight Carried, 1952–1956 238

Table 13. Wholesale and Retail Trade (Sales Volume), 1950–1956 239

Table 14. Development of "Supply and Selling" Coöperatives, and Consumers' Coöperatives, 1949–1954 240

Table 15. Development of Institutionalized Internal Trade by Number of Agencies, Operating Personnel, and Trade Volume, 1950–1955 241

Table 16. Geographical Distribution of Internal Trade, 1955 .   242
Table 17. Composition of Gross Agricultural Value Product at
          1952 Prices, 1952–1956   242
Table 18. Socialization of Agriculture by Farming Households,
          1950–1956   243
Table 19. Development of Agricultural Producers' Coöperatives,
          1950–1956   244
Table 20. Cultivated Land and Crop Area, 1949–1957   245
Table 21. Agricultural Production, 1949–1957   246
Table 22. Yield per Unit of Crop Area for Selected Crops, 1949–
          1957   247
Table 23. Livestock on Farms and Ranches, 1949–1957   248
Table 24. Ownership of Livestock, 1956   249
Table 25. Development of State-operated Farms (Mechanized and
          Nonmechanized), 1950–1955   249
Table 26. Development of State-operated Mechanized Farms,
          1950–1956   250
Table 27. Development of State-operated Tractor Stations, 1953–
          1956   250
Table 28. Population Census of the Mainland, June 30, 1953 . .   251
Table 29. Student Enrollment, 1949–1957   252
Table 30. College Student Enrollment in Specialized Fields, 1949–
          1957   253
Table 31. Polytechnical Student Enrollment in Specialized Fields,
          1949–1956   254
Table 32. Conversion Rates between Yuan and Certain Foreign
          Currencies, as of December, 1957   254
Table 33. Foreign-Exchange Rates (Telegraphic Transfer) of the
          People's Bank for Certain Currencies, as of March, 1957   255
Addendum: Estimated and Realized Data for 1957, and Planned Quota
     for 1958:
Table 34. Industrial Development   256
Table 35. Agricultural Development   257
Table 36. Financing   258

I

Introduction

This volume is an attempt to evaluate the economic development of Communist China during the First Five Year Plan from 1953 through 1957. The term "economic development" is used in the neutral sense: while it may denote an increase in per-capita national product, it need not imply an increase in per-capita consumption. The appraisal is based on an examination of industrial and agricultural production, a reconstruction of the national income account, an estimate of net capital formation, an estimate of currency in circulation in relation to internal financing, and an investigation of Soviet aid and of the balance of international payments in relation to external financing. It concludes with an evaluation of the prospects for further growth of the economy in terms of population increase, per-capita consumption, and agricultural development.

The discussion will be largely confined to the development during these five years, with 1952 as the point of departure. Whether 1952 is a good base year for the measurement of growth will be discussed later in this chapter. The final results for the last year of the period will not be known for some time, but the expected outcome as announced by Peiping in the latter half of the year seems close enough to reality to serve the purpose at hand. (But see Addendum.) No attempt will be made to compare this period with the 1930's or 1940's before the Chinese Communists came to power; nor will there be any discussion of what Peiping calls the period of rehabilitation from 1949 to 1952. Treatment of this subject is readily available elsewhere.[1]

---

[1] See, for example, D. K. Lieu, *China's Economic Stabilization and Reconstruction*, New Brunswick, 1948; Cheng Yu-Kwei, *Foreign Trade and Industrial Development of China*, Washington, D.C., 1956; W. W. Rostow, *et al.*, *The Prospects for Communist China*, Boston, 1954; and Wu Yuan-li, *An Economic Survey of Communist China*, New York, 1956. Lieu deals with industrial development in the 1930's and the early 1940's, while Cheng's is the only English publication that gives production data up

The draft proposal of the Second Five Year Plan has been made public in the form of a broad outline of targets to be attained. Although it will certainly be revised, the pertinent data will be introduced in order to show the aspirations of the planning authorities.[2]

1. NATURE OF SOURCE DATA

In this undertaking the statistics published in the Chinese mainland must be used, which leads to certain difficulties. The first problem is availability. For its own planning purposes Peiping requires comprehensive statistics, and it is true that we have now much more statistical information about the mainland economy than before. However, much information is withheld from the public, especially on banking and finance, foreign trade and the balance of international payments, and market prices of various categories of commodities. The published data, on the other hand, have not been given in a systematic fashion. For example, the official release that comes close to what may be called a statistical abstract of the country consists of but twenty-three short tables. But additional data are contained in the speeches, statements, and reports made by high officials, in the communiqués of the State Statistical Bureau, and in editorials and feature articles of newspapers and periodicals. Unsatisfactory as all these data are, they constitute the primary sources.

Because of the fragmentary nature of the data two other difficulties appear. One is that certain data may be given for one year but for some reason withheld the next year: there is no assurance of a continuous time series.[3] The other is the much more serious problem of finding out the exact meaning of the available statistics. When tables are presented, hardly any technical notes are appended. What constitutes "the gross agricultural value product"? What is the definition of a "factory" for statistical purposes and

---

to 1948. Although both Rostow's and Wu's volumes are out of date so far as the economic data pertaining to the First Five Year Plan period are concerned, they are still readable for different reasons. Rostow and Alexander Eckstein (who is responsible for the economic part) take a balanced point of view in judging the development since the 1930's. Wu's study of the rehabilitation period deserves attention, although his judgment of the prospects seems severe. S. Adler, *The Chinese Economy*, New York, 1957, is principally a restatement of the First Five Year Plan with enthusiastic and uncritical running comments, based almost exclusively on English-language materials released by Peiping.

[2] The draft is in fact proposed by the Chinese Communist party.

[3] Hence, the sign "..." is used to indicate data not available in the tables presented in this study. Other signs are: "– – –" for "negligible"; "——" for "not applicable"; and square brackets for my estimates.

in what way does a "large" factory differ from a "small" one? How is "modern factory" defined? The precise meaning of all such concepts and terms so generally used in the official statistics has to be discovered—if discoverable at all—from sources unrelated to the presentation of data. The difficulty is multiplied when the data are found in reports or editorials with no clear indication as to what the figures really mean. A case in point is the production data for cotton cloth. Does the figure given refer to factory production alone? Does it include handicraft production? Or, does it mean both factory production and that part of handicraft production that makes use of machine-made yarn? Moreover, for many years cloth production had been given in terms of "bolts" of indefinite length; then for 1956 it was given in terms of meters. To what extent are these figures comparable? Such difficulties have rendered the Peiping statistics open to the charge of inconsistency and even to the suspicion that they are fabricated. However, examination will reveal that as long as the meaning of a given figure can be ascertained, it often does fit into a consistent series.[4] This means that every figure has to be carefully scrutinized.

The question of reliability and accuracy of the data may be raised in three ways. First is the possibility of falsification. As far as I could see, there is no evidence of deliberate fabrication. But the degree of reliability depends much more on the technical competence of the personnel collecting the data from the field than on the policy of the authorities giving out the information. Since the establishment of the State Statistical Bureau in late 1952, the quality of statistics has evidently been improved, and the amount of published information has greatly enlarged. Nevertheless, the shortage of trained people for statistical work is severe for such a large country, and the data are therefore suspect. This is the second possible source of unreliability and unlike the first presents a real problem which, besides, varies among different types of data. For instance, the production statistics of industry are much more reliable than those of agriculture, partly because the industrial data are more precise, not subject as much to personal estimates as those of agriculture, and partly because the reports come from factory managers who are better trained for the purpose than either the peasants or the field statistical workers. This relative reliability of the industrial statistics does not mean that they are necessarily accurate. In fact, being more sophisticated, the factory manage-

---

[4] This of course is not always true. See, e.g., the explanatory notes to Table 11 on the development of water transportation in the Statistical Appendix.

ment may not be averse to manipulating the data in the interest
of fulfilling the quota or even of black-market activities.[5] How
extensively such practice exists on the Chinese mainland is not
known at the present.

The third consideration affecting reliability stems from the very
process of statistical development in a country. The faster the statistical service improves, the more comprehensive the statistical
coverage becomes, the less comparable the earlier data will turn
out to be, and the more difficult it will be to tell how much of
the change in the series is due to the technical improvement. The
semblance of a national statistical system was not set up on the
Chinese mainland until 1954. As a result statistics for 1952 through
1954 have been subject to extensive revision, thus rendering unusable practically all data published before August, 1955. As we
will see, the question remains as to whether it was possible for the
bureau to make sufficient corrections for those early years, particularly 1952, the base year used in the First Five Year Plan. In any
case this development makes it meaningless and misleading to compare the production statistics of recent years with those of, say,
1949 or 1936, as the Peiping authorities are prone to do. For this
reason the present study makes no attempt to carry the discussion
back to those years.[6]

The last two sources of error apply, of course, with equal if not
greater force to almost all other underdeveloped countries today.
Unless one is willing to work without statistics, it is necessary to
use their data, knowing the pitfalls and limitations.

This study is based on materials in Chinese, all published in
Peiping unless otherwise stated.[7] *The direct quotations from the
Chinese texts are my translations.* The value data are expressed
in yuan, and no attempt is made to convert them into the American

[5] This point is familiar to students of Soviet industrial statistics.

[6] However, the tables in the Statistical Appendix do present available figures for
1949 through 1951—as a matter of general interest. Their questionable comparability
with those of the later years should always be kept in mind.

[7] The two most frequently cited sources are the *Jen-min jih-pao (People's Daily)*
and the *Hsin-hua pan-yueh-k'an (New China Semi-Monthly)*, both official publications of the Chinese Communist party. Henceforth they will be cited without the
corresponding English titles. The *Daily* is meant to be studied, not read, on the
mainland, and contains the current government policy statements, economic reports,
and statistical releases. The *Semi-Monthly*, which used to be the *Hsin-hua yueh-pao
(New China Monthly)* until the end of 1955, is mainly a repository of important
government directives and selected articles from the periodical literature of the
country, including provincial newspapers and publications that would not otherwise
be accessible to the general public; it also contains a bibliography of the literature
classified into Politics, Economics, Culture, and International Relations.

dollar equivalent. The yuan is the new monetary unit introduced by Peiping on March 1, 1955, to take the place of the old *Jen-min-pi (People's currency)*, with a conversion rate of 10,000 old units to one yuan.[8] Although the official exchange rate to the American dollar notes is 2.355 yuan (2.343 buying against 2.367 selling), no meaning can be attached to the foreign-exchange equivalent of the yuan values because of the insulation of the Chinese mainland from international price effects.[9]

2. THE FIRST FIVE YEAR PLAN

The Chinese Communists took over the whole of Manchuria in the latter part of 1948 and set up the central government in Peiping about one year later. By the end of 1952 the government announced that the period of rehabilitation was coming to an end and that the First Five Year Plan for development of the national economy would begin in 1953. However, the final plan was not drafted until February, 1955, and five months later a detailed version of it was made public for the first time.[10]

[8] Strictly speaking, the yuan is also "people's currency," and the only way to differentiate the new from the old is to identify them as *Hsin jen-min-pi* and *Chiu jen-min-pi (new people's currency* and *old people's currency)*. This clumsy way of identification has been dispensed with in official and common usage on the Chinese mainland by calling the new uit "yuan." Of course, "yuan" has long been the Chinese generic name for the dollar. The introduction of the new yuan was originally scheduled for 1953. For the reason of its postponement to 1955, see chapter vi, section Note Circulation and Internal Financing.

[9] There is no official rate for remittances in American dollars. The official rate quoted by the Peiping banks operating in Hong Kong is 2.345 yuan per American dollar note and 0.427 yuan per Hong Kong dollar. In October, 1957, the average open-market rate for yuan notes in Hong Kong was 0.6787 yuan per Hong Kong dollar—a "depreciation" of 59 per cent from the official rate. To show further the futility of converting yuan values into foreign-exchange equivalent: for the week ending October 31, 1957, the open-market remittance rate *to* mainland China from Hong Kong was 57.5 yuan per 100 Hong Kong dollars as compared to the official rate of 42.70 yuan—a "depreciation" of 34.7 per cent of the yuan. At the same time, the unofficial remittance rate *from* the mainland to Hong Kong was 143 Hong Kong dollars per 100 yuan against the official rate of 234.19 Hong Kong dollars—a 63.8 per cent "depreciation." The tight control of traveling, the government monopoly of foreign trade, and the rationing of essential daily necessities on the part of Peiping authorities—all this makes even an interpretation of "depreciation" difficult. For exchange quotations in Hong Kong, see *Far Eastern Economic Review* (Hong Kong), xxiii: 18, p. 573, October 31, 1957, and other October issues.

[10] According to the editorial of *Jen-min jih-pao*, April 5, 1955, the planning work began in the spring of 1951. The basic document of the plan is the *Chung-hua-jen-min-kung-ho-kuo fa-chan kuo-min-ching-chi ti-i wu-nien-chi-hua (The First Five Year Plan for Development of the National Economy of the People's Republic of China)*, August 1955, 238 pp. Hereafter, it will be cited as the *First Five Year Plan*. An English version of the Plan was published by the Foreign Language Press, Peiping, but reference will be made to the Chinese text.

Why was it put into operation two years ahead of its final formulation? Officially the time was considered opportune in 1953 because Soviet assistance in the form of ninety-one industrial plants was committed in May, and the Korean war came to an end in July of that year.[11] Since both events occurred in the middle of the year, there would have been more reason to postpone the launching of the plan to 1954. In retrospect, perhaps the Korean war did help rush it into operation.

To operate a national plan of this nature it was necessary for the central authorities to have the major sectors of the economy under firm control from the beginning. Had it not been for the war, Peiping might have had to proceed cautiously on this path in order not to alienate private enterprises too soon, particularly since they were hailed as allies of the working class in the society of the "new democracy." The war provided both the opportunity and the necessity of widening control.

In 1950 and 1951 the government, devoting 41.5 and 42.5 per cent of the state budget (inclusive of Soviet aid) to national defense, was in serious financial difficulty.[12] Inflation threatened the price- and financial-control machinery set up in March, 1950.[13] Thus came the "five anti" campaign of 1952, which, economically interpreted, was a move to impose a capital levy on private enterprises, partly as a fund-raising and anti-inflationary device, and partly as a means of reducing their economic power.[14] By the end of the year private enterprises accounted for only 36 per cent of the total wholesale trade, 58 per cent of retail trade, and 39 per cent of factory production, as compared to 76 per cent, 84 per cent, and 52 per cent in 1950.[15]

---

[11] Chairman of the State Planning Commission Li Fu-ch'un, "Report on the First Five Year Plan," *Jen-min jih-pao*, July 8, 1955. This was the first full statement of the Plan.

[12] Yang Pei-hsin. "The Problem of Accumulation of Funds for the First Five Year Plan." *Ching-chi yen-chiu (Economic Research)*, 4: 12–35, October, 1955.

[13] For price control, see later sections in this chapter. For financial control, see chapter vi.

[14] The campaign started in October, 1951, and was brought to a conclusion about the middle of 1952. It was ostensibly a movement against bribery, tax evasion, fraud against the government, theft of state properties, and leakage of state economic secrets and was accompanied by the "three anti" campaign against corruption, waste, and bureaucratism among government workers—evils attributed to the temptations provided by the middle class. In two cities the private industrial firms were found to have illegally gained an income equivalent to 38.6 per cent of their liquid assets and therefore were subject to heavy penalties. See Chao I-wen, "The Process of Socialist Transformation of China's Capitalist Industry," *Hsin-hua pan-yueh-k'an*, 2: 62–66, January, 1957.

[15] For details and sources, see Statistical Appendix Tables 4 and 13.

As a result, the general economic situation became so depressed that the government, not as yet in a position to absorb all private enterprises into the public sector, had to make a nationwide effort to revive industry and trade, not for the sake of the private interests but for the health of the economy as a whole. This was the situation when the program of industrialization, with large state investment, was put into operation in 1953.

Care must, therefore, be exercised in using 1952 as the base year for evaluating the later developments in industry and trade. Just as the year preceding the First Five Year Plan has been taken as the base year for appraising the rate of growth of Soviet Russia (1927) or India (1950–51), so 1952 is generally chosen for China. All targets under Peiping's First Five Year Plan are established with 1952 as the point of reference. But the "five anti" movement had so depressed private industry and trade in that year that the measurement of growth from that level would result in an exaggerated rate.[16] Agriculture was apparently not affected by the movement, but the analysis presented in the next chapter shows that 1952 is not a satisfactory base from which to determine the agricultural rate of growth either.

Underlying the First Five Year Plan is the long-range objective of establishing a socialist society through "socialist industrialization," which consists of industrialization on the one hand and of socialization of industry, trade, handicrafts, and agriculture on the other.[17] Industrialization means "the marshalling of all efforts and resources for the development of heavy industry so as to lay down a foundation for an industrialized state and a modernized national defense."[18] Although improvement in consumers' welfare is often mentioned, it has a secondary place in the scheme of things, and is promised either as a distant goal or as a natural consequence of the process of industrialization. The planners expect that it will take three five-year plans to realize the socialist society, by which time the country will be sufficiently industrialized and able to produce all machinery and equipment needed for further economic development. In the meantime, chiefly with the help of the rehabili-

---

[16] For evidence of the arrested development of private industry and trade in 1952, see Statistical Appendix, Tables 4 and 13.

[17] Editorial, *Jen-min jih-pao*, April 5, 1955.

[18] Li Fu-ch'un, "The First Five Year Plan," *Ta-kung-pao (Impartial Daily)*, Tientsin, September 16, 1953. According to Peiping usage the term "heavy industry" is synonymous with producer-goods industries, including mining, iron and steel, nonferrous metals, electric power, petroleum, machine making, chemicals, and construction materials. By the same token, consumer goods are identified with "light industry." For further discussion, see chapter ii, section 2.

tated industries in Manchuria, half of the capital goods needed
for industrialization would be manufactured at home during the
first five years and 70 per cent during the second.[19]

Specific goals are laid down for industry in terms of its relative
importance in the economy. Industry is composed of "modern"
factories, handicraft factories, handicraft coöperatives, and individual handicraft operators not engaged in agriculture.[20] The "modern" component is the most important and its production was to
increase from 27 per cent of the total gross value product of industry and agriculture in 1952 to 36 per cent in 1957 and to 60 per
cent in 1967.[21] Moreover, factory production, that is, the output of
both "modern" and handicraft factories, is expected to double
in value (at constant prices) in each of the two five-year periods
during the first ten years.[22] This development is intended to increase, in relative terms, the production of producer goods at the
expense of consumer goods. Hence, according to the plan, the output of heavy industry would rise from 40 per cent of the total value
of factory production in 1952 to 45 per cent in 1957 and 50 per
cent in 1962, with a corresponding decline in the relative importance of light industry.

Mechanization of agriculture as a part of the industrialization
process is expected to develop much more slowly. It will possibly
take twenty to twenty-five years to mechanize the farming operations on the 65 per cent of the cultivated area considered suitable
for such a development.[23] And, in contrast to factory production,

---

[19] Chi Fu, "The Rate of Economic Development under the Second Five Year Plan,"
Hsin-hua pan-yueh-k'an, 24: 40–42, December, 1956.

[20] In 1952 the relative importance of the four in the gross industrial value product
was as follows: modern, 64.2 per cent; handicraft factories, 14.5 per cent; handicraft
coöperatives, 0.7 per cent; individual handicraft operators, 20.6 per cent. I have not
been able to determine the exact definition of "modern" factories or "modern" industry, but from the above classification it may be surmised that it means factories
operating with mechanical power. See Statistical Appendix, Table 2.

[21] Report of Li Fu-ch'un, *Jen-min jih-pao,* September 29, 1955. The reason given
for setting the share of "modern" industry at 60 per cent for 1967 is that only after
industrial production attained 70 per cent of the gross social value product in the
Soviet economy did Russia regard itself as industrialized. There has been some discussion as to whether a country like China needs to go that far before being considered industrialized. See Wang Si-hua, "The Rapid Development of China's Socialist
Industrialization," *Ching-chi yen-chiu (Economic Research),* 4: 11–22, August, 1956.

[22] That is, an increase of 98.5 per cent in the first five years and 100 per cent in the
second. All data on the Second Five Year Plan are given in the draft of the Second
Five Year Plan adopted by the Chinese Communist party in September 1956, *Jen-
min jih-pao,* September 29, 1956.

[23] Chao Hsueh, "Mechanization of Chinese Agriculture," *Chi-hua ching-chi
(Planned Economy),* 4: 16–18, April, 1957.

the gross agricultural value product is expected to increase about 23 per cent in the first five years and 35 per cent in the second.

The crucial part of the First Five Year Plan lies in the investment program undertaken by the state. Out of a total of 76,640 million yuan of current and capital expenditures to be used in

TABLE I

THE STATE INVESTMENT PLAN, 1953–1957

Field of investment	Amount		Number of projects	
	In millions of yuan	In per cent	Large	Small
1. Industry (including mining, electric power)	26,400	61.8	694	2,300
2. Agriculture, water conservation, forestry	2,680	6.2	252 ⎫	
3. Transportation, communications	7,310	17.1	220 ⎪	
a. Railways	*5,670*	*13.3*	⎪	
b. Others	*1,640*	*3.8*	⎬ 3,700	
4. Education, culture, public health	3,070	7.2	156 ⎪	
5. Municipal utilities	1,600	3.7	118 ⎪	
6. Trade, banking, commodity reserves	1,220	2.9	⎪	
7. Working capital, extensive repair, etc.	460	1.1	⎪	
8. Others			160 ⎭	
Total	42,740	100.0	1,600	6,000
To be completed within 5 years	42,740	100.0	1,271	6,000

Note: For definition of "investment" see text and Net Capital Formation (chapter v); for definition of "large" and "small" investment projects, see text.
Sources: (1) On investment: The itemization differs from the *First Five Year Plan*, pp. 22–26, which gives figures classified according to the government ministries making the investment. The above re-classification according to fields of investment is based on information by Yang Pei-hsin, "The Problem of Accumulation of Funds for the First Five Year Plan," *Ching-chi yen-chiu (Economic Research)*, 4: 12–35, October, 1955, and Wei I, "The Problem of Agricultural Investment under the First Five Year Plan," *Jen-min jih-pao*, August 19, 1955. (2) On investment projects: Ta Kung Pao Editorial Board, *Ti-i wu-nien-chi-hua chiang-hua (Talks on The First Five Year Plan)*, 1955, and Fang Wei-chung, *Ti-i-ko wu-nien-chi-hua chieh-shuo (Explanations of the First Five Year Plan)*, 1955.

the five years for economic and social development, 48,040 million was for "basic" development, including 42,740 million for "basic construction investment." However, not all the investment went into addition to the capital stock, because of many incidental expenditures, such as surveying, training, and even compensation paid to the original occupants for removal from areas of construction.[24] Table I summarizes the distribution of the net investment.

The large share of investment in industry is not surprising, but the small amount for agriculture is out of all proportion, being

---

[24] *The First Five Year Plan*, p. 23n. For discussion of the concept of "basic construction investment," see discussion in chapter v.

even less than the allocation for the building of schools, workers' clubs, and hospitals. The Plan states that the farming households were expected to invest from their own resources a total amount of 10,000 million yuan (net of depreciation and replacement), of which 60 per cent would be for fixed capital and 40 per cent for working capital.[25] Even if this were true, the total would still be disproportionate to the importance of the agricultural sector in the economy.

TABLE II

PLANNED INCREASE IN ANNUAL PRODUCTIVE CAPACITY UPON COMPLETION OF 694
INDUSTRIAL PROJECTS INITIATED UNDER THE FIRST FIVE YEAR PLAN
(Capacity in thousands of metric tons except for trucks)

Product	Total increase in annual productive capacity	Percentage of Increase owing to 156 Russian-aid projects
1. Pig iron	5,750	92.1
2. Steel	6,100	82.8
3. Rolled steel	4,440	90.4
4. Coal	93,100	22.7
5. Crude oil	3,500	51.4
6. Metallurgical equipment	190	50.3
7. Electric generating equipment	800	45.0
8. Chemical fertilizers	910	28.5
9. Trucks (units)	9,000	100.0

Note: Chemical fertilizers refer to nitric and phosphorous compounds.
Source: Huang Chen Ming and Huang Jun-t'ing, *Ts'ung chung-su ching-chi ho-tso k'an chung-su jen-min wei-ta yu-i (Looking at the Great Sino-Soviet Friendship through Sino-Soviet Economic Coöperation),* pp. 10–11.

Seventy-nine per cent of the capital investment went to industry and transport. The development of transport was mainly in the building of railways. Of the investment in industry, 88.8 per cent was to be made in heavy industry, leaving only 11.2 per cent for light industry. If the amount for heavy industry is added to that for railways, 70 per cent of all capital investment during these five years went into the development of a heavy-industry complex.

The core of this complex consists of 156 engineering projects to be built with Russian aid. For them, Soviet assistance means not only detailed planning, but also the supply and installation of machinery and equipment, the operation of the plants when completed if necessary, and the training of personnel both on the job and in the Soviet Union.[26] However, only 145 of them were to

[25] See chapter v.

[26] Fifty of these were agreed upon on February 14, 1950, chiefly for the rehabilitation of the iron and steel complex left by the Japanese and the Russians in Man-

be under construction during the first five years, including 45 that were to be completed and put into operation before the end of 1957. The projects include the construction of new plants and the modernization and expansion of the existing industrial enterprises. Among them are seven for the iron and steel industry (including one each for the three heavy-industry complexes at Anshan, Wuhan, and Paotou), 27 for the coal industry, 24 for electric power generation, scores for metallurgical and machine-making industries (such as heavy-machine-making plant, automobile and tractor plants), many in nonferrous industries, chemicals, and petroleum, and several for light industry (such as flax textile, papermaking, and pharmaceutical industries).[27] Table II indicates their importance to the industrialization program.

The total investment in the 145 projects comes to 11,000 million yuan, equal to 41.7 per cent of the investment in industry as a whole. Moreover, an additional investment of 1,800 million was to be made during the five years for the establishment of 143 "large basic construction units" ancillary to the Russian-aid projects.[28]

churia; another 91 (plus 21 machine shops) on September 15, 1953; and an additional 15 on October 12, 1954. On April 7, 1956, 49 more (not including six nonindustrial items) were added, principally for the Second Five Year Plan. How these projects are financed will be discussed in chapter vii.

[27] Huang Chen Ming and Huang Jun-t'ing, *Ts'ung chung-su ching-chi ho-tso k'an chung-su jen-min wei-ta yu-i (Looking at Sino-Soviet Great Friendship through Sino-Soviet Economic Cooperation)*, Peiping, October, 1956, 39 pp.; reference on p. 9. The reference for electric power generatioin is based on *Ta Kung Pao*, Editorial Board, *Ti-i wu-nien-chi-hua chiang-hua (Talks on The First Five Year Plan)*, 1955, p. 27.

[28] It is important here to clarify the term "large basic construction unit," so often encountered in the literature from Peiping. "Basic construction" refers to an addition to fixed capital in physical terms; in principle, extensive repair does not constitute basic construction. A "basic construction unit" is any net capital investment project that involves both integrated planning for all its parts and a complete, unified budget. Thus an industrial basic construction unit may comprise a number of machine shops, transportation, power generation, housing, and educational facilities for the workers, and some of them may be constructed on separate locations.

The "large" or "small" unit is in fact a loose translation of the Chinese term "above limit" or "below limit," having reference to a standard amount of investment. When the capital investment is larger than the standard amount, the basic construction unit concerned is "above the limit" and therefore subject to the direct control of the state (that is, the State Economic Commission). If the investment is "below the limit," the unit comes under the direct control of the various ministries, provincial governments, governments of autonomous regions, or those of the Special Cities (Peiping, Tientsin, and Shanghai). Thus, the distinction is a device for division of control. The "limit" varies with different fields of investment. In general, 5 million yuan is the limit for heavy industry and 3 million for light industry. In some cases no limit applies and all investment projects come under the direct control of the state; examples are power stations, coal mines, oil refinery, railways, highways, river and sea ports, and tractor stations. But beginning in 1957, a "limit" has also been set

Around this core with its subsidiary plants would be built some 400 "large" and 2,300 "small" industrial basic construction units. From the total of 694 "large" industrial investment projects, 472 were to be located inland, with only 222 in the coastal areas, where the bulk of the Chinese industry used to be found.[20] Thus the state investment program embodies not only the policy of concentrated development of heavy industry, but also that of shifting the balance of industrial location.

3. SOCIALIZATION OF THE ECONOMY

While the investment program concerns only the state enterprises and the joint enterprises that the state has practically taken over from private interests, the production targets laid down in the First Five Year Plan relate to the total production of the country, including that of the private firms, coöperatives, individual operators, and peasants. These five-year targets serve as a guide to the determination of the yearly quotas at the beginning of the year on the basis of the performance of the previous year as well as on the prospects of the current year. Thus the nature of these targets and quotas, and the constant drive for their overfulfillment, make the complete socialization of the various sectors of the economy inevitable. This is the only way to render the planning effective and to assure the fulfillment of the goals.

Interestingly, the Plan, when finalized as late as February, 1955, envisaged only a moderate rate of socialization during the five-year period. In the important factory-industry sector private firms would still be allowed to exist in such numbers by the end of 1957 as to produce about 12 per cent of the sector product. Only few individual handicraft operators and one-half of all private trading shops and traveling merchants existing in 1952 would be organized in coöperatives. In agriculture only one-third of the farming households would be drawn into the so-called primary producers' coöperatives in which the income of a member depends on the con-

for each of them—as a move to relegate more enterprises to the control of the local governments.

For convenience, the "above limit" and "below limit" units will be called large and small ones in this study. All Russian-aided projects are large basic construction units.

See Peng Yung-ch'uan, "Tabulation Forms for Basic Construction Planning," *Chi-hua ching-chi (Planned Economy)*, 5: 29–33, May, 1957.

[20] According to D. K. Lieu, more than 90 per cent of China's factory industry (in terms of employment) was situated in the coastal areas. See his *China's Economic Stabilization and Reconstruction*, New Brunswick, 1948, p. 13.

tribution he makes to the common pool, including labor and land which is still considered his private property. There is no mention of collectivization of farms in the Plan.

These targets relating to the speed of socialization were clearly designed to make the Plan acceptable to the people at the time of its publication in July, 1955, especially in order to avoid disruption of the forthcoming autumn harvest that promised to be the largest on record. Soon after the harvesting season, a nationwide movement of transforming the entire private sector along socialist lines began. This radical change in the tempo of socialization may be best appreciated by reviewing briefly the transformation that had been taking place since 1950.

The process started in March, 1950, when the state set up a trading apparatus to deal in such daily necessaries as food, edible oil, and cloth, in such strategic raw materials as fuel, cotton, and industrial supplies, and in imports and exports.[30] This control enabled the state to restrict the operation and the gross revenue of the large private commercial and industrial concerns, for the supply was allocated to them only under contract for specific purposes. For example, as far as the controlled commodities were concerned, the wholesalers, retailers, and the manufacturing concerns in the private sector could operate only as agents of the state trading companies, receiving a fee or a predetermined margin as compensation for the services rendered.[31] Moreover, their net revenue was to be

---

[30] The apparatus consists of a network of state-operated commercial agencies and of "marketing" coöperatives, the latter being made up of consumers' coöperatives in the urban areas and, more important, the "supply and selling" coöperatives in the countryside. For details, see next section.

[31] In the circumstances, private wholesalers were rapidly reduced (see Table III); they were partly absorbed into the state commercial network. In foreign trade, private firms, operating entirely for the state commercial companies, accounted for only 8 per cent of the total imports and exports in 1953. Private factories, or what remained of them in the process of transformation, produced increasingly for the state rather than for the market. The percentage distribution of their production between these two channels was as follows:

	1949	1950	1951	1952	1953	1954	1955
State	12	29	43	56	61.8	78.5	81.7
Market	88	71	57	44	38.2	21.5	18.3

See Statistical Appendix, Table 5, for absolute figures and sources.

As to the situation of foreign private enterprises operating on the Chinese mainland, it was illustrated in the 12th annual report (1953) of the directors of the (British) Shanghai Worsted Mill, Ltd. It says in part, "We have fallen from all notions of 'dominating the market,' of equipping the Mill with the latest technical advances, or of producing the best yarn and cloth in the country. . . . We have large cash balances in Shanghai but the Government have given orders that dividends

divided among taxes, interest, dividend, and workers' welfare fund, in accordance with government regulations.[32]

These arrangements, applicable to both trade and industry, constituted the primary form of state capitalism, a transitory stage to the developed form, known as state-private joint operation. There were two variants of joint operation—by enterprise and by trade. In the joint enterprise the state was a partner, participating in investment and management.[33] The private share of the net revenue was further reduced. Interest on capital and wages of management together must not exceed one-quarter of the net revenue after deducting income taxes; of the remainder, a small part was used for workers' welfare, but a large part went to the state as reserve for further expansion of the enterprise or for investment in other joint enterprises. The joint enterprises were originally large private firms, whose services met the needs of the state and who showed "capacity for transformation."[34] Banking and shipping (steamers) were among the first to be put on joint operation in 1950, while factory industry was drawn into this form of transformation rapidly after 1953.[35]

By the fall of 1955, only small private firms were left, mostly with less than 15 employees, not adaptable to joint-enterprise operation. This gave rise to joint operation "by the whole trade." In retailing and motor transport, the private firms in the same line of business were reorganized into one large unit either by amalga-

cannot be paid without their consent, which, so far, has been withheld.... Eighty per cent of our production was sold to the state-operated China General Goods Company. In the future the whole of our production will be sold to the state-operated Company. In other words, we are simply working on commission account." *Far Eastern Economic Review* (Hong Kong), 15: 348–349, September, 1954.

[32] Net revenue, or net profit as called by Peiping, is the gross revenue minus depreciation and cost of production, which, however, does not include interest on capital. According to the regulation proclaimed in December, 1950, the net revenue, after deducting income taxes and previous losses, was to be divided as follows: (1) at least 10 per cent for reserve against future losses or for expansion, (2) not more than 8 per cent for interest on capital, (3) about 55 per cent for wages of management, and (4) about 27 per cent for workers' welfare and awards. Found to be too liberal during the "five anti" movement in 1952, it was soon amended, whereby the net revenue would henceforth be divided into four roughly equal parts, namely, taxes, interest on capital, dividend, and the welfare fund. It may be noted that this revised regulation did not provide for a reserve for expansion.

[33] The state share of investment might take the form of the unpaid penalties imposed on the private firm during the "five anti" movement. "A Survey of the Development of State Capitalism in Industry in China," *Hsin-hua pan-yueh-k'an*, 2: 66–70, January, 1957; reference on p. 68.

[34] Provisional Regulation on State-private Joint Enterprises adopted by the State Council on September 2, 1954, *Jen-min jih-pao*, September 6, 1954.

[35] For socialization of banking and the state banking system, see chapter vi.

mation or on a coöperative basis. In manufacturing, those producing the same type of products (for example, pens and pencils) in
the same locality were organized into a "special company," operating under the supervision of the Industrial Bureau of the local
government concerned. The company, supported financially by
the member firms, took over from them the management function,
with authority to determine the operating plan and the personnel
policy for each member. While the technical staff remained employed after the reorganization, the private investors and owners
were to be paid off by the company out of the net revenue of the
members, with 5 per cent annual interest on their original investment until 1961.[36] When the private interests are paid off, the enterprise will become state-owned, and therefore will have advanced
from the state-capitalist to the socialist form—the final stage in the
process of transformation.[37]

Table III shows the speed at which private interests disappeared
in trade, industry, transport, and agriculture. It will be observed
that the process of socialist transformation had been going on
since 1950 and that the tempo was greatly quickened the year after
the publication of the First Five Year Plan.[38] Aside from those
items shown in the table, socialization was also vigorously pushed
in 1956 to encompass all individual operators, for whom state-
private joint operation was not feasible. They were organized into
"coöperatives" with collective ownership, wherever feasible, of the

[36] According to the regulation proclaimed in February, 1956, the private investors
were to be paid from 1 to 6 per cent, depending on the nature and size of the business. But it was changed to a uniform 5 per cent four months later. See Chen Yun,
"Problems of State-private Joint Enterprises," *Jen-min jih-pao*, June 19, 1956. The
total amount of private investment, together with that in joint enterprises, was 2,200
million yuan in 1956. See *Shih-shih shou-ts'e (Handbook of Current Events)*, December 25, 1956. This paying off the private investors applies equally to the joint
enterprises. For the subject of Special Companies, see Wang Hung-ting, "The Nature
of Special Companies for Joint Operation," *Hsin chien-she (New Construction)*, 2:
12–16, February, 1957.
[37] The literature on socialist transformation of industry and trade is sizable. In
addition to those already cited, the following have been found helpful for the discussion: (1) Liu Shao-ch'i, "Political Report to the National Congress of Representatives of the Chinese Communist Party," *Jen-min jih-pao*, September 17, 1956; (2) Chen
Yun, "On Industry and Commerce," *ibid.*, July 1, 1956; (3) Sun Chung-ta, "The
Several Forms of State-Capitalist Trade," *ibid.*, May 15, 1955; (4) Wu Tsiang, "The
Development of State Capitalism in the Initial Stage of the Transition Period,"
Ching-chi yen-chiu (Economic Research), 1: 84–116, February, 1956, and also his
"Transition from Capitalist Economy to State-Capitalist Economy," *ibid.*, 2: 54–99,
April, 1956; and (5) Kuan Ta-t'ung, "The Problems of Peaceful Transformation of
Capitalist Enterprises," *ibid.*, 2: 40–53, April, 1956.
[38] For the growth of joint enterprises and collectives, see Statistical Appendix,
Table 4, 12, 13, and 18.

means of production. By the end of the year, 92 per cent of all individual handicraftsmen were drawn into the "handicraft cooperatives"; 77 per cent of the animal-powered wheelbarrow operators and 95 per cent of the wooden junks became members of

TABLE III

SOCIALIZATION OF TRADE, INDUSTRY, TRANSPORT AND AGRICULTURE, 1950–1956
(In per cent)

Economic sectors	1950	1952	1955	1956	1957 target
1. Wholesaling volume: Share of private sector	76.1	36.3	4.4	....	....
2. Retailing volume: Share of private sector	83.5	57.8	17.5	3.0	....
3. Gross industrial product: a. Share of private factory	48.7	30.7	13.2	} 1.3 {	10.0
b. Share of individual handicraftsmen	23.0	20.6	16.1		11.1
4. Water transport (steamships and barges only): Share of private sector	....	31.2	1.8	} 5.0 {	....
5. Motor transport: Share of private sector	....	49.5	18.0		....
6. Agriculture: Percentage of farming households organized in: a. Primary producers' coöperatives	– – –	0.1	14.2	8.0	33.3
b. Collectives	– – –	– – –	– – –	88.0	0

Notes: (1) The 1957 target is that of the First Five Year Plan. (2) Lines 1 and 2 refer to institutionalized trade only, not including trade conducted outside the regular commercial channels, such as that carried on by individual peasants. (3) The figures for agriculture (line 6), except those for 1956, refer to the farming households that had been in coöperatives long enough to participate in the autumn harvest of the year, whereas those for 1956 refer to the situation at the end of the year. Since the organization drive usually takes a spurt after autumn harvest, the number of farming households organized into coöperatives or collectives is less at the end of the autumn harvest than at the end of the same year.

Sources: Based on absolute figures given in Statistical Appendix, Tables 4, 12, 13, and 18. These tables should be consulted for details concerning the development of state-operated enterprises, various non-farm coöperatives and collectives, state-private joint enterprises, and seasonal and all-year mutual-aid teams in agriculture.

"transport coöperatives"; and an overwhelming majority of the individual peddlers, fishermen, salt miners, and human carriers were organized into coöperatives.[39] As in joint operation, their management is in the hands of the Communist party workers.

However, the transformation of agriculture in 1956 was the most drastic, as Table III shows. Instead of going through the stage of

[39] State Statistical Bureau, "Communiqué on the Results of the 1956 Plan," *Jenmin jih-pao*, August 2, 1957. A part of the 95 per cent of wooden junks referred to was put on joint operation. For the tonnage of wooden junks and the number of other means of "native" transport, see Statistical Appendix, Table 12.

being organized into primary producers' coöperatives, the farms were collectivized, that is, turned into what Peiping prefers to call the "developed" type of agricultural producers' coöperatives, where land, farm tools, and draft animals are collectively owned, and the members paid according to the number of their workdays with the coöperative. No compensation was made to the previous owner of the land, although for the farm tools and animals an amount to be decided upon by the coöperative might be paid to him in installments within a period of generally not over three years. Each member household was allowed to retain a small lot of land for its own use, the amount not to exceed 5 per cent of the per-capita land area of the coöperative.[40] With the party workers in charge of the collectives, the state thus gained complete control of the broad agricultural base of the economy.

To summarize: Through joint operation by enterprise or by trade, through collectivization of agriculture and other individual operators, and through organization of coöperatives, the whole economy was, for all practical purposes, completely socialized in 1956, a few months after the publication of the Plan. This result can justifiably be claimed as having surpassed the targets in the published version of the First Five Year Plan. Consolidation of these gains was one of the major tasks in 1957.

4. COMMODITY AND FACTOR MARKETS

Although commodity control started off the process of socialist transformation in March, 1950, it was imposed for the immediate purpose of curbing price inflation that threatened to get out of hand.[41] Since then, the widening and tightening of commodity con-

---

[40] See the revised regulations on agricultural producers' coöperatives, *Jen-min jih-pao*, July 1, 1956. A recent study based on fragmentary information from various parts of the country shows that the amount of retained land varies from 0.0083 to 0.045 acre per household, with 0.025 acre as the mode. See Sung Hai-wen, "The Problem of Retained Plot in Agricultural Producers' Coöperatives," *Ching-chi yen-chiu (Economic Research)*, 4: 7–17, August, 1957. In June, 1957, at the suggestion of Premier Chou En-lai, the National Congress of People's Representatives amended the regulation so that the retained land per member household was to be increased to not more than 10 per cent of the per-capita land area of the collective, the exact size depending upon the number of pigs raised by the household (*Hsin-hua pan-yueh-k'an*, 14: 153, July, 1957).

[41] For example, the market price for a composite commodity unit in Peiping rose steadily from 101 "old" yuan in April, 1949, to 6,409 in March, 1950—an increase of 64 times. The commodity unit was designed for insuring the value of bank deposits of the public; its composition varied according to different cities. In Peiping, it consisted of one-half of a kg. each of wheat flour and corn flour and one-third of a meter of cotton cloth. For market (wholesale) quotations of various commodity units for different cities, see *1952 Jen-min shou-ts'e (People's Handbook for 1952)*, pp. 298–299.

trol on the one hand and socialization of the economy on the other
have reinforced each other. Discussion of the socialization process
will not be complete without going further into the subject of commodity control and the operation of the market system.

Among the emergency economic and financial control measures
adopted by Peiping in March, 1950, was the establishment of eight
state companies for internal trade whose task was "to take a com-
manding position in the domestic market and to regulate national
and local supply and demand" by buying up the lion's share of
the supply of the essential commodities.[42] The eight companies
dealt in food grains, cotton, yarn, cloth, general supply (that is, daily
necessaries), salt, coal and construction materials, and indigenous
products.[43] To assist these companies, a network of "supply and
selling coöperatives" was set up all over the countryside. Ostensibly
voluntary organizations of the peasants, they are actually an arm
of the state companies, receiving priority in supply allocation and
favorable financial terms from the state in order to induce the
peasant to sell and therefore to secure a sufficient supply of food
grains and other agricultural products for the operation of the state
companies.[44]

The state commercial network had to compete, of course, with
private interests in obtaining the supply in the open market. For
a while, up to the end of 1951, private as well as foreign merchants
were encouraged to join the state commercial agencies in making
purchases in the rural area so that none of them would bid up
prices against one another. In the urban areas the state commercial
agencies maintained official retail prices at a level where private
merchants would be able to make reasonable profit.[45] Given these

[42] For a full statement of the policy measures, cf. *T'ung-i-kuo-chia ts'ai-cheng kung-
tso (National Unification of Financial and Economic Operations)*, Hankow, May, 1950.
121 pp. The quotation is on p. 26. For discussion of the financial measures, see chapter vi.

[43] At the same time, six companies were established for foreign-trade operations,
namely, bristles, export of indigenous products, fats and oils, tea, mineral products,
and general imports. *Ibid.*, pp. 26–30.

[44] For the history of the coöperatives, see Ch'eng Tzu-hua, "The Development of
Supply and Selling Coöperatives in the Past Five Years," *Ta Kung Pao (Impartial
Daily)*, Tientsin, September 24, 1954. For the operations of these coöperatives, see
Ch'u Ch'ing and Chu Chung-chien, "Variations in the Commodity Turnover in
China's Rural Markets," *Ching-chi yen-chiu (Economic Research)*, 3: 100–126, June,
1957.

[45] See the instructions issued by the Ministry of Trade regarding the purchase of
food grains, in State Council, Financial and Economic Commission, ed., *Chung-yang
ts'ai-ching cheng-ts'e fa-ling hui-pien (Collection of Laws, Regulations and Statements concerning the Fiscal and Economic Policies of the Central Government)*, II
(June, 1951), 876–877. Hereafter, it will be cited as *Collection of Laws* ...

rather favorable circumstances, private trade (wholesale, in particular) rapidly grew to a point where either its growth had to be severely checked or the state would lose control of the market. One of the consequences of the "five anti" movement, as shown in Table II, was to reduce the share of private trade from 76 per cent of the total wholesaling volume in 1950 to 36.3 per cent in 1952 and from 83.5 per cent of the total retailing volume to 58 per cent.[46]

Nevertheless, by the end of 1952, although the number of state trading companies increased to eleven, the open market price mechanism remained very much in operation. Price stabilization was to be achieved through the control of the supply of selected producer and consumer goods and the selling of them at official prices. However, such a scheme leaves one gap wide open. After the state had made its purchase, the remaining supply in the hands of the producers would be made available on the open market at high prices if the state supply was not enough to meet the market demand. Private trade could grow again, as indeed it did in the first half of 1953. Commodity and market control would have to be tightened.

This took place in the latter half of the first year of the First Five Year Plan. The first to be affected were producer goods. Heretofore, industrial supplies produced by the state-operated factories and raw materials handled by the state companies were sold either to other state enterprises or to private firms at the same market price. In 1953 a dual pricing system was introduced, one for the state-operated enterprises and the other for the market (chiefly private firms and handicrafts). The former, much lower, was an ex-factory cost price.[47] In fact, transactions between state enterprises did not go through any marketing channel, because the said supplies and raw materials were subject to allocation by the State Economic Commission, the related ministries or the local governments. The market price, on the other hand, was determined by the state commercial companies on the basis of ex-factory cost,

---

[46] At the same time, the total number of private commercial agencies was reduced from 4.5 million in 1951 to 4.3 million in 1952, and the total number of people so engaged from 7.4 million to 6.8 million. Many private wholesalers who were thus forced to liquidate their businesses were employed by the state commercial network. See Yang Po, "A Preliminary Analysis of the Process of Socialist Transformation of Private Trade in China," *T'ung-chi kung-tso t'ung hsin (Statistical Bulletin)*, 15: 7–10, August, 1956.

[47] The transport cost was paid either by the producing factory or by the buying unit. See Chang Shih, "An Important Problem in the System of Rationalized Transport of Coal," *Chi-hua ching-chi (Planned Economy)*, 10: 24–25, October, 1957.

plus transport, warehousing and handling charges, and a high margin of profit.[48] Thus the market supply of industrial materials was reduced to the high-price products handled by the state trading companies and the output of private factories and handicraftsmen.[49] This dual price system was in operation until the private sector disappeared in 1956. Since then, the whole industry has been brought into the allocation scheme with a one-price system.

The broadening of state control over consumer goods began in November, 1953, when food grains and edible vegetable oil and its raw materials were placed under a scheme known as "planned purchase and planned supply."[50] Raw cotton and cotton cloth (machine- and hand-made) have been brought into it since September, 1954. The state sets up an annual quota of purchase that has to be fulfilled before the producers are allowed to sell the remainder—and to do so only, not on the open market, but through the state commercial network.[51] The objective is clearly to reduce the retained portion in the hands of the peasants to the minimum and therefore to obtain a maximum supply for the state.[52] The purchase quota tends to be so high as to leave little "surplus" for the farming household.[53] As far as these commodities are concerned, there must be no open market and no supply for an open market.

[48] See Lin Shui-hua, "An Exploration of the Problem of Delegating Authority to the Lower Levels Regarding the Government Supply of Centralized-Control Commodities," *Chi-hua ching-chi (Planned Economy)*, 8: 22–23 and 29, August, 1957.

[49] There was a third set of prices, applicable to the agricultural producers' coöperatives and collectives, that probably were lower than the "market" prices. See Nan Ping and Soh Chen, "The Pricing Problem of Producers' Goods," *Ching-chi yen-chiu (Economic Research)*, 2: 12–24, April, 1957.

[50] This scheme was first introduced in 1950, when wolfram, aluminum and tin ores and ingots were to be purchased, supplied, or exported by the state companies only. At the same time, bristles were placed under "planned supply" for both the domestic and the foreign market, and soybeans could be exported only by the state companies. *Collection of Laws . . .* , I (August, 1950), 413–414, and II (June, 1951), 905. The purpose was to control essential exports.

[51] In January, 1951, cotton yarn was placed under "planned purchase," whereby the entire output must be sold to the state. Up until 1953 this was perhaps the only major product important to domestic consumption, in which the state had explicitly excluded private merchants from dealing. But there might well have been other products falling under the same method of control. The fact that cotton yarn was so treated had not been made known until it was reported by the official news agency on October 15, 1954. *1955 Jen-min shou-ts'e (People's Handbook for 1955)*, Tientsin, pp. 456–458.

[52] Editorial, *Jen-min jih-pao*, November 12, 1954. The remark in the text, of course, excludes machine-made cloth and factory-processed edible oil, for both of which the planned purchase quota is the entire output.

[53] For food grains, the quota was so high in 1954 that what was left for the peasant

The "planned supply" part of the scheme means some form of rationing in accordance with availabilities, based partly on consumers' needs, and partly on the state's requirements for export and for commodity reserves. The quota, therefore, is revised annually, but subject to change at any time when the state finds itself unable to meet it.[54] The rationing of edible oil has been chiefly confined to cities and industrial and mining areas, whereas cloth has been rationed nationwide from the beginning.[55] These two rationed commodities are sold, of course, through the state commercial network, with coupons issued for the purpose. The selling price may be raised in order to discourage the use of the coupons.[56]

With regard to staple food (that is, food grains in the villages and processed food grains in others), the "planned supply" is more complicated. At first, rationing was confined to urban areas where purchase permits were issued, without which no resident could buy food.[57] Private merchants who used to operate between rural and urban areas were no longer permitted to trade in food; in other words, all open markets for food grains were abolished. To take their place, thousands of new food markets were established by the state all over the countryside to facilitate the exchange of grains among peasants and especially to provide an outlet for their re-

---

was not even enough for his household consumption, let alone seed and animal-feed requirements. As a result, the purchase quota had to be scaled down the following year, and the government has since adopted the policy of announcing before the planting season the expected production quota, the expected purchase quota, and the expected government-supply quota for every village. *Jen-min jih-pao,* March 9, 1955.

[54] For example, the quota for cloth was reduced by one-half in the second quarter of 1957. Cf. Ministry of Trade, "Report on the Problem of Cotton Cloth Supply in 1957," *Hsin-hua pan-yueh-k'an,* 10: 112–113, May, 1957; and editorial, *Jen-min jih-pao,* April 20, 1957.

[55] The way in which cloth has been rationed is of interest. Until recently, the ration per capita was highest in big cities, declining continuously along the scale to medium-sized cities, small cities and towns, and finally the villages. And, within any geographical area, the ration for workers, cadres, and students of higher education was higher than that for the general population. However, beginning in 1957–58—the year for cloth ration starts in September—all these gradations were abolished, except that the ration for big cities and industrial areas remains a little higher than for the rest. This change was made "as a result of dissatisfaction on the part of the rural population." Ministry of Trade, "Report on the Supply of Cotton Cloth for Civilian Use during the Fourth Year of 'Planned Supply,'" *Jen-min jih-pao,* August 20, 1957.

[56] For example, the price for edible oil was raised on April 20, 1957. The raise of the selling price may also be due to an increase in the government-purchase price for stimulating production. *Jen-min jih-pao,* April 30, 1957.

[57] That this was done in virtually all urban and industrial areas is attested by an instruction issued by the State Council on April 28, 1955, to all local governments, requesting them "to check, household by household, the food-purchase permits" in accordance with the actual size of the household. *Jen-min jih-pao,* April 29, 1955.

tained portion. The immediate consequence was the rise of black markets.[58] Finally, the state was compelled to institute a nationwide food-rationing system in August, 1955, from cities down to the village household level.[59] This is the system still in operation, and is not likely to change. However, there have been persistent reports of black-market activities.[60] To tighten the control of food grains, even the state-directed food markets were abolished altogether in October, 1957.[61]

Side by side with the "planned purchase and planned supply" scheme is another, introduced since the middle of 1953, and known as "centralized purchase"—a term for "planned purchase," as explained above, without "planned supply." It embraces a large number of chiefly agricultural products, to be used in industry as raw materials and for consumption and exports.[62] It differs from the other scheme only in that the commodities are sold by the state commercial agencies at official prices without rationing. The adjustment of the official prices is relied upon for restriction of consumer demand.

[58] Cf. Liang Ming and Ts'ao Yen, "A New Type of Food Market," *Jen-min jih-pao*, February 5, 1955. According to Kang Wei-chung, some 30,700 new food markets were established during the first half of 1954, but the number declined at the following autumn harvest when the state commercial agencies were engaged in making "planned purchases." In the spring of 1955, the number of markets recovered to about 30–50 per cent of the 1954 level. The reason for this slow recovery was that many cadres operating in the rural area were under the apprehension that the growth of new markets would imply their own ineffectiveness in getting all the retained portion of food grains out of the hands of the peasants. The cadres began to issue food-purchase permits to the peasants, requiring them to register every sale and purchase. Again, as a result, "black markets flourished in many areas." See Kang's "Why Must State-directed Food Markets Be Established in Rural Areas?" *Jen-min jih-pao*, March 19, 1955. The rural food markets were managed by representatives of the local governments, and of the Ministries of Industry, Trade, and Food.

[59] The per-capita ration, to be reviewed monthly, varies according to age and the nature of profession, and for a rural household, also according to its animal feed and seed requirements. For full detail of the schedule, see *Jen-min jih-pao*, August 25, 1955.

[60] See also discussion on current prices in the next section.

[61] In addition, the "planned purchase" quota will be raised for those agricultural collectives that are able to increase food-grains production. Only green vegetables and animal feeds are allowed to be grown on the plots retained by the peasants. See instruction issued by the State Council on the planned purchase and planned supply for food grains, *Jen-min jih-pao*, October 13, 1957.

[62] The list of products has grown through the years even without explicit legal authorization. The consumer goods include sugar and paper made by craftsmen, oil seeds not otherwise included, citrus fruits, aquatic products produced in production centers, tea, and meat. Industrial raw materials are cured tobacco, jute and hemp, sugar cane, silkworms, hides and skins, wool, tung oil, timber from production centers, and scrap metals. Some of these products are for export. In addition, live animals, such as pigs, cows, and sheep, are included.

The operation of these two schemes has resulted in the elimination of an open market for the controlled commodities. Private merchants in the business were in the early stage either absorbed into the state trading apparatus or encouraged to go into industrial ventures. Commodities not subject to control—chiefly by-products of agriculture—make up what is left of the open market.

In the middle of 1956 when inflation threatened the economy again, the authorities permitted the peasants to sell on the open market the remaining portion of their output after the state had filled its purchase quota under either scheme. This was done to stimulate production. Henceforth, the open market was widened to encompass about 20 per cent of the total value of marketable commodities.[63] But because of this "reopening of a free market" many peasants withdrew from agricultural collectives in order to engage in the trading of indigenous products, subsidiary food, general daily supplies, and even the controlled commodities before the state had completed its purchase.[64] Thus the "free market" was closed in September, 1957. Since then, the open market has been restricted again to the commodities not subject to "planned purchase and planned sales" or to "centralized purchase."[65]

The status of the commodity market since 1953 may be briefly summarized. As far as manufactured products are concerned, the open market, as distinct from that provided by the state trading network, had been made up of the supply (other than cotton cloth, processed food, and edible oil) produced by private factories and individual handicraftsmen. Because a large part of private factory production was for the state, the market was in fact very limited. When the private sector was socialized in 1956, the joint factories and the handicraft collectives were still permitted to produce and sell the uncontrolled products without going through the state commercial agencies. Hence, an open market for manufactured goods still exists. As to the market for agricultural products, it has been confined to some of the by-products of agriculture, chiefly poultry and green vegetables raised on the minute retained lot of the farming household. From the middle of 1956 to September, 1957, the market was broadened. But since then it has been further

[63] Chao Chin-hsien, *op. cit.*
[64] Editorial, *Jen-min jih-pao,* November 22, 1956.
[65] Moreover, the number of controlled commodities has been increased to include 38 varieties of herbs, and the state trading companies are under instruction to purchase "an appropriate proportion" of the goods not subject to control. See the State Council's decision on commodities allowed to enter the free market, *Hsin-hua pan-yueh-k'an,* 18: 207–208, September, 1957.

reduced from what it used to be before the "reopening of the free market." As for food grains, the state-directed markets established all over the countryside since the end of 1953 were eliminated in October, 1957. The tight control imposed on major agricultural products has not been effective in preventing the rise of widespread black markets.

A word should be said about the factor market. Legally, no restriction on the private sale and purchase of land had been imposed after the land reform, although a great amount of persuasive pressure was exerted by the party workers to discourage such practices. Collectivization of farms in 1956 eliminated the land market altogether. The movement of unskilled labor within the urban areas does not seem to have been restricted, as is evidenced by the general practice among the state-operated enterprises of taking in a large number of "temporary" workers at the last quarter of every year in order to fill or exceed the annual production quota.[66] The continuous migration of labor from the rural to the urban areas was subject only to periodic check whenever the number became too big for the cities and towns to absorb. However, since the beginning of 1957, there has been a more or less planned movement of population from the urban to the rural areas.[67]

But skilled or trained workers have been very much under state control since 1953. Although their own shift from factory to factory is sometimes reported, the practice apparently has not been general. The decline and disappearance of private industry have helped to make the control effective. As the core of the labor force for industrialization, the workers have been deployed from such old industrial centers as Shanghai and Tientsin to the expanding or new industrial sites, mostly in the interior of the country. Finally, the institutionalized supply of capital and credit was centralized in the People's Bank in 1950.[68] On the whole, it may be said that no open market exists for various factors of production, except unskilled labor.

5. Current Prices

How did current prices behave during the process of socialist transformation of the economy? How effectively had the system

---

[66] See Statistical Appendix, Table 7.

[67] See later discussion on population growth in chapter viii.

[68] For the functions of the bank, see chapter vi. As brought out in the discussion of producer goods, the capital goods produced by the state-operated enterprises were subject to allocation by the state—a system that discriminated against the private sector.

of commodity control worked in terms of price stability? Although price data are very limited, an attempt should be made to answer these questions.

Aside from these considerations, there is another important reason for discussing current prices in this introduction. In this study, the gross agricultural value product, the industrial value product and the national income are all valued at 1952 prices. This is the way in which the basic data are given in the official statistics;

TABLE IV

WHOLESALE AND RETAIL PRICE INDICES OF URBAN AREAS, 1950–1957

(1952 = 100)[a]

Year	Wholesale[b]	Retail[c]
1950	84.7	88.6
1951	99.8	99.1
1952	100.0	100.0
1953	98.7	103.7
1954	99.1	104.1
1955	99.7	105.5
1956	99.2	105.8
1957, Jan.-June	99.9	108.1

[a] Conversion from the original series with 1950 as the base.
[b] The number of cities covered: 15 in 1950; 25 in 1951; 47 in 1952; 44 in 1953; 42 in 1954; 37 in 1955. The number for 1956 and for the first half of 1957 has not been stated.
[c] Only eight cities are included: Peiping, Tientsin, Shanghai, Wuhan, Canton, Chungking, Sian, and Shenyang (Mukden).
Sources: (1) Wang Chien-chen, "Evaluation of People's Living Conditions through Price Indices," *Ta Kung Pao (Impartial Daily)*, September 24, 1957. (2) State Statistical Bureau, "Economic Statistical Abstract," *Hsin-hua pan-yueh-k'an*, 17: 14, September, 1956.

no series at current prices is available. To obtain the proper perspective of the changes in the economy during the period under study, a picture of the current price situation is necessary.

The official price indices are presented in Table IV. No information is available regarding the commodities chosen and the weight assigned to each, the weights given to the prices of each city, the formula by which the index numbers are computed, and, finally, the reasons for varying the number of cities in the wholesale series. Taking the indices as they are, certain characteristics stand out. In contrast to typical price behavior, the wholesale prices are "sticky" and stable, whereas the retail prices show a continuous rise. Only during the first two years when state control operated through the open market mechanism did both price series behave in the normal manner. Moreover, as the retail prices took a record jump from 1952 to 1953 (the first year of the Plan), the wholesale prices displayed the heaviest drop of all the years shown in the table. Finally, when both the actual wholesale and retail prices were authentically reported to have taken a steep climb since the middle of 1956, such rises were only mildly reflected in the retail series and hardly at all in the wholesale.[69] If the index numbers have not been manipulated to show price stability, the explanation must lie in the choice of commodities and price quotations.

The wholesale indices are made up of prices of eight groups of commodities: (1) industrial supplies, (2) construction materials, (3) fuel, (4) food grains, raw or milled, (5) "subsidiary foods"—that is, foodstuffs other than grains, such as meat, vegetables, eggs, (6) cotton yarn and cloth, (7) indigenous products (mainly for export), and (8) miscellaneous items. "All the quotations are prices announced by the state-operated commercial companies."[70] In view of the rapid decline of the private sector's share in the national wholesaling volume from 36.3 per cent in 1952 to 4.4 per cent in 1955 (see Table III), the wholesale price series based on official quotations presumably should be quite representative of the actual market condition. The following official comment on the price situation in 1956, therefore, comes as a surprise: "As the state-operated companies were unable to supply sufficient quantities of certain commodities to meet the market demand, no transactions took place at official prices, with the result that the market prices rose. . . . Hence, the wholesale price index for 1956 was lower than the *actual market level*."[71] Since the economy had been virtually socialized by the middle of 1956, what could have constituted the "actual market"? Did the "reopening of the free market" between July, 1956, and September, 1957, have the effect of reviving *private wholesale* as well as retail trade? What was the size of the "actual" market relative to that of the "official" market? If the official series did not reflect the actual market situation in 1956, how good was it in describing the situation for the earlier years? It is difficult to get definite answers to these questions.

---

[69] The price rises since the middle of 1956 have been widely reported. See, e.g., Minister of Finance Li Hsien-nien's budget message of 1957, *Jen-min jih-pao*, June 30, 1957.

[70] Editorial section, *T'ung-chi kung-tso t'ung-hsin (Statistical Bulletin)*, "A Survey of Market Prices in China for 1956," *Hsin-hua pan-yueh-k'an*, 10: 114–115, May, 1957; quotation on p. 114. The *Bulletin*, an official publication of the State Statistical Bureau, has not been made available to foreign circulation until recently; it is an important source of statistical information. In 1957, the title of the publication was changed to *T'ung-chi kung-tso (Statistical Work)*.

[71] *Ibid.*, p. 114. Italics mine.

The retail price series is composed of at least six categories of goods: (1) milled food grains, (2) subsidiary foods, (3) general daily supplies, (4) educational supplies, (5) household utensils and other similar supplies, and (6) tobacco, tea, and beverages. The major commodities in these categories such as staple food, cloth, fuel oil and fats, tobacco and beverages, and pork "are all catered for by the state-operated commercial companies, which hold the sources of supply in hand, and therefore exercise virtually complete control over their market prices. Their sales represent over 70 per cent of the total retailing volume" in the eight cities.[72] The weights assigned to these commodities in the computation of the index number are not known. But there is no doubt that the various categories of goods in the series include many more commodities than those over which the state companies have complete control. This means that the retail price indices are better than the wholesale price series in reflecting the actual market situation.

Nevertheless, the retail price series is still, for two reasons, far from describing the real situation. First, the commodities chosen are admittedly not representative enough. Second, and more important, when both official and actual market prices obtain for the same commodity, the former is invariably used for the computation. Thus, in 1956 and 1957, "the prices of those commodities which the state companies fail to supply sufficiently have risen fast in the free market. Particularly beginning with the fourth quarter of 1956, the market prices of many items of daily necessaries have greatly outdistanced the official quotations."[73] This phenomenon was not reflected in the retail price series "because of the choice of commodities"—and, it may be added, the choice of quotations. The price behavior of the 30 per cent of the retail market must have been disrupting enough for the authorities to reverse sharply their policy in curbing the free market operations in September, 1957.

Since the retail price index did not represent the actual market situation for the last two years of the period under study, the question raised in connection with the wholesale price series may again be asked: How good was it for the earlier years? An adequate answer must be based on facts which are lacking. A glimpse of the current price picture may be had from a report on the living conditions of an urban worker's family. One and a half kilograms of

---

[72] *Ibid.*, p. 115.

[73] *Ibid.* As an example, the official retail price for a half kilogram of green ginger in Peiping was 0.30 yuan when the market price was 0.90 yuan.

cabbage and two squares of beancurds—the daily food of the people, besides rice or flour—cost 8 cents in 1951, 12 cents in 1954 and 24.5 cents in February, 1957.[74] Thus, it is almost certain that the official retail-price index, though showing a continuous but very gradual rise throughout the period, has greatly understated the actual rate of increase.

Available data have restricted the foregoing discussion to the official- and open-market prices at wholesale and retail. There is no information about "black markets," which "had not been non-existent even before the reopening of the free market" in the middle of 1956.[75] Two reasons may be advanced to support the belief that black-market activities have been rampant. The stability of the official wholesale prices and the continuous, gradual rise of the official retail prices imply that the price at which the state trading companies purchase the supply from the producers is low and out of line with the market situation, and that the profits made by the state from trading are high.[76] The incentive for the producers to engage in black-market activities must have been strong. In addition, the fact that the state commercial companies have failed to meet the market demand with adequate supply might have induced the authorities to half-tolerate the existence of black markets.[77] Of course, how consistently the state companies have failed to meet the demand depends on the supply under their control on the one hand and the aggregate purchasing power in the hands of the public on the other. The discussion on internal financing of economic development in chapter vi attempts to throw some light on this situation.

[74] Yeh Chien-yun, "Changes in the Living Conditions of an Industrial Worker's Family," *Jen-min jih-pao*, April 20–21, 1957.

[75] Chao Chin-hsien, "A Preliminary Study of the Opening of the Free Market under State Direction," *Ching-chi yen-chiu (Economic Research)*, 3: 78–99, June, 1957; quotation on p. 82. Cf. also discussion in the preceding section.

[76] According to Chao, *op. cit.*, the differential between purchase and sales prices is usually about 40 per cent. The stability of the wholesale prices should not be construed to mean that no change in the government-purchase price has been made. In fact, price has been taken as an indispensable instrument for adjusting agricultural production as well as regulating the demand for the unrationed commodities. The periodic variation of the relative prices between food grains and raw cotton in order to encourage production of one or the other is a good example. A recent example is the raising of the purchase price for live pigs by 14 per cent in March, 1957. The stability of the wholesale price index since 1952 has been made possible by a continuous decline in the prices of industrial supplies and construction materials—prices largely applicable only to the state-operated enterprises.

[77] In fact, their existence has been implicitly given as one of the reasons for the reopening of the free market in 1956. See Chao, *ibid.*

II

Industrial Development

Although the First Five Year Plan called for a total of 42,740 million yuan of "basic construction" investment, the actual amount that had been spent for this purpose in the first four years (36,622 million) plus the planned investment for 1957 came to the sum of 47,722 million.[1] This increase of 11.6 per cent of investment was chiefly caused by the construction of 131 more "big basic industrial projects" than originally planned, making a total of 825 projects.[2] It is expected (at the time of writing) that by the end of 1957, 448 of them would have been completed during the five years as against 455 scheduled in the Plan, the reason for the lag being that some of the projects had been enlarged while the others had been making slow progress.[3] As far as the Russian-aid industrial projects are concerned, the original 156 had been increased to 205 in April, 1956; and by the end of 1957, 56 would have been completed during the five years, with 102 still under construction.[4]

The direct effect of investment on industrial production depends, of course, on the gestation period, which is usually longer for heavy than for light industry.[5] During the five-year period there was a close correlation between the *variation* of investment and change in output of producer-goods industries in the same year, excepting the iron and steel industry where the investment effect

---

[1] It should be kept in mind that "basic construction" investment is larger than what is usually defined as net capital formation. This will be discussed in chapter v.

[2] For definition of "big basic projects," see chapter i, section 2.

[3] Po I-po, "Report on the Results of the 1956 Plan and on the Plan for 1957," *Jen-min jih-pao*, July 2, 1957.

[4] Li Fu-ch un, "Economic Progress from 1953 to 1956," *Jen-min jih-pao*, June 19, 1956; and, State Planning Commission, "Results of the First Five Year Plan," *Jen-min jih-pao*, October 1, 1957.

[5] The common scene in Russia where (according to Professor Gregory Grossman) the construction of a light-industry factory is dragging on for years because of lack of allocated materials or funds has not been reported in China.

took about two years to work itself out.[6] During the first year or two of the Plan, the investment effect might well have been over-shadowed by the rehabilitation effect of the industries in Man-churia where they began to recover three or four years previously.

1. THE PACE OF INDUSTRIALIZATION

Industry by definition includes mining and electric-power genera-tion as well as manufacturing. The pace of industrialization in the First Five Year Plan was conceived in terms of the growing relative importance of industry in the whole economy, and in terms of the rising output of producer goods in particular. The development during the five-year period is shown in Table V, which also gives the number of cotton spindles and power looms and the mileage of railways and highways to indicate the speed of industrialization. The development of the cotton textile industry, so important in many other underdeveloped countries at least in their first stage of industrialization, has been subsidiary in the industrialization process in Communist China.

The table shows that the gross industrial value product at 1952 prices has been growing much faster than the gross agricultural and industrial value product, even though both had overreached the 1957 target one year earlier; that the importance of industry in the economy has been rising as indicated by industry's contribu-tion of well over one-half of the total production in the last two years of the period as compared to only 41.5 per cent in 1952; and that the composition of industrial output has been rapidly changed in favor of producer goods as planned. Has the country actually been so rapidly industrialized as to make agricultural production secondary to industrial output—and this within a period of five years? How do we interpret the average annual rate of industrial growth of 16.3 per cent with 1952 as the base or 13 per cent with 1953 as the base?

Industry vs. Agriculture.—In attempting an answer it is impor-tant to understand the issues in the statistical measurement. The gross industrial value product is the sum total of the output at current ex-factory prices of each enterprise during a given period, after elimination of any intraenterprise duplications in the com-putation.[7] However, the global values released annually are given

[6] Chi Ch'ung-wei, "How to Make China's Industry Develop Evenly," *Chi-hua ching-chi (Planned Economy)*, 7: 4–8, July, 1957.

[7] Yueh Wei, "The Method of Computing National Income," *Ching-chi yen-chiu (Economic Research)*, 3: 48–66, August, 1956. The concept was first adopted in 1950

TABLE V

SOME INDICATORS OF INDUSTRIALIZATION, 1952–1957

(Indices for value figures are based on real data given at 1952 prices)

Item	Unit	1952	1953	1954	1955	1956	1957 est.	1957 target	1962 target
A. Gross agricultural and industrial product..........	Value index	100.0	114.4	125.3	133.5	155.5	161.4	151.1	256.3
B. Gross industrial product..........	Value index	100.0	130.2	151.8	159.9	205.0	212.6	190.3	381.6
1. As percentage of A..........	Per cent	41.5	47.2	50.3	49.7	54.7	54.1	52.3	61.8
2. Composition:									
a. Producer goods..........	Per cent	35.6	....	....	42.5	....	....	38.0	50.0
b. Consumer goods..........	Per cent	64.4	....	....	57.5	....	....	62.0	50.0
C. Cotton spindles, operating..........	Thousands	5,660	5,860	6,300	6,410	6,810	....	7,550	....
D. Power looms..........	Thousands	89	....	....	111	180	....	143	....
E. Railways, trunk and branch lines......	Thousand km.	24.2	24.7	25.4	26.9	29.1	30.0	....	38.5
F. Highways in service..........	Thousand km.	129.6	138.6	142.4	162.5	227.0	228.1	....	244.6

Notes: (a) The target refers to that of the Five Year Plan. (b) The 1957 target for railways is an increase of 4,000 km. of trunk lines over that of 1952. The target for 1962 is originally given as an increase of 8,000–9,000 km. over the mileage in 1957. For convenience, an average has been taken of the range, and added to the estimated mileage for 1957 in order to arrive at the 1962 target. (c) For highways, the target for 1962 is originally given as an increase over 1957 of 15,000–18,000 km. The same procedure has been used to arrive at the figure given in the table as in the case of railways. (d) According to Ching Wei (see below), the estimated number of spindles in 1957 was 7.5 million; but it is doubtful if they were all in operation.

Sources: (1) For A and B, see Statistical Appendix, Table 3. (2) For E and F, see Statistical Appendix, Table 10. (3) For C and D, (a) Ching Wei, "The Problem of Textile Production in 1957," *Chi-hua ching-chi (Planned Economy)*, 5: 5–7, May, 1957; (b) News dispatches, *Jen-min jih-pao*, September 10, 1954, and December 20, 1956; (c) Tung Hsin, "China's Achievements in Industrial Production," *Kung-jen jih-pao (Workers' Daily)*, September 13–14, 1957; (d) Wang Ching-yu, "Six and Sixty Years—the Past and Present Development of the Textile Industry," *Jen-min jih-pao*, July 13, 1956; (e) Li Fu-ch'un, "Achievements in the First Three Years of the First Five Year Plan, *Jen-min jih-pao*, September 29, 1955; and (f) Chen Wei-chi, "Report on the Progress and Condition of the Textile Industry," *Jen-min jih-pao*, March 9, 1954.

at 1952 prices; no current price lists are available, although some have evidently been published.[8] From the standpoint of measurement, this concept of industrial value product at constant prices, as applied to the Chinese scene during the First Five Year Plan, comprises two elements—the 1952 constant prices and the "grossness"—each of which has operated to exaggerate the relative importance of industry to agriculture. The exaggerations are so serious as to have called forth open discussion among the statisticians and planning authorities in Peiping.[9]

The 1952 prices at which all value product series have been given are actually the average "official" prices during the third quarter of that year for several thousands of commodities. They are weighted averages, to be applied nationally.[10] As may be recalled, it was in the third quarter of 1952 that the "five anti" campaign against private industry and trade was brought to a conclusion and that the first bumper crop since 1950 was in sight. In other words, it was a period of unusually low agricultural prices relative to industrial prices and also one of lower prices for light-industry products than for heavy-industry products.[11] Thus, the ratio between the industrial and agricultural product for 1955 would have been 44.9 to 55.1 at 1956 prices, as compared to the ratio of 49.7 to 50.3 at 1952 prices.[12] It must be pointed out that the use of the 1952 constant prices, having already misrepresented the relative importance between industry and agriculture for the base year, would not have aggravated the distortion any further for the following years.

Further distortion of the relationship between the two sectors

---

from Russian usage, with very little modification. See "Materials on Methods of Computing the Gross Industrial Value Product," *T'ung-chi kung-tso t'ung-hsin (Statistical Bulletin)*, 17: 2–5, September, 1956.

[8] For instance, publication was announced in July, 1956, of price lists to be used by state enterprises for drawing up budgets regarding basic construction investment. None of these is as yet accessible.

[9] "Several Problems of Computing the Gross Industrial Value Product," *T'ung-chi . . . (Statistical Bulletin)*, 17: 1–2, September, 1956, and following issues.

[10] The number of commodities represents the majority of output. For products not covered by the national constant price list, the 1952 prices are to be determined locally by the government authorities or by the management according to some formula. Each enterprise is required to report, at least annually, its production at constant prices. See State Statistical Bureau, Department of Industry, "Explanations of Certain Problems arising from the Computation of 1957 Constant Prices for Industrial Products," *T'ung-chi kung-tso (Statistical Work)*, 9: 11–13, October, 1957.

[11] "Diverse Opinions on the Methods of Computing the Gross Industrial Value Product," *T'ung-chi kung-tso t'ung hsin (Statistical Bulletin)*, 24: 5–10, December, 1956. Private industry produced chiefly consumer goods.

[12] *Ibid.*, p. 6.

comes from the grossness of the industrial value product. If an enterprise (say, a factory with independent management, operating on its own account) consists of two machine shops, the value of the semifinished materials passing from one shop to the other must not be counted in the gross value product of the enterprise. But all materials coming from outside the enterprise will enter in full value into the gross product. A cotton-yarn factory value product includes the cost of raw cotton, while the weaving-factory product includes the cost of yarn, and the dyeing-factory product includes that of cloth.[13] Although the gross agricultural value product also contains a certain amount of duplication, the extent of grossness is far less. It has been computed that double counting in the sense described accounted for 22.7 per cent of the agricultural value product but 61.8 per cent of the industrial value product in 1954.[14]

It is then easy to see the reason for such a rapid rise in the importance of industry relative to agriculture as shown in Table V. More than 40 per cent of industrial output is based on agricultural raw materials, whose value enters into the gross industrial product together with transport costs.[15] The more industrialized the country, the greater the industrial consumption of agricultural raw materials, the more serious the factor of double counting in the gross industrial value product, and the faster the growth of industry in relation to agricultural in the total product—especially if agriculture remains unmechanized. This has largely been the situation in Communist China during the five years under study. It has been estimated that if all duplications *within* industry as a whole were eliminated for 1955, the ratio between the industrial and the agricultural value product (at 1952 prices) would be 41.9 to 58.1 instead of 49.7 to 50.3; and that if only the "values added" were compared, the ratio would have been 32.8 to 67.2.[16]

There are other reasons that have made the gross concept especially problematical for China. Handicraft production, still accounting for about one-third of the gross industrial product,

[13] Liao Chi-lih, "Accelerating Agricultural Development—a Condition for Accelerating the Development of Heavy Industry," *Chi-hua ching-chi (Planned Economy)* 8: 4–6, August, 1957.

[14] "Several Problems . . . ," p. 1

[15] In 1955, 41 per cent of the gross industrial product were manufactures of agricultural raw materials. See "Several Problems of China's Socialist Industrialization," *Hsin-hua pan-yueh-k'an*, 1: 67–71, January, 1957.

[16] "Diverse Opinions on the Methods of Computing the Gross Industrial Value Product," *T'ung-chi . . . (Statistical Bulletin)*, 24: 5–10, December, 1956.

requires simple transformation of raw materials into finished products, such as food processing, tailoring, and the like, and the double
counting thus entailed is in many cases higher than 90 per cent.[17]
Also, industrial enterprises are so numerous and mostly so small
that a product usually has had to pass through a number of them
before it has reached finished form.[18] This accentuates double counting. Finally, a change in industrial organization also affects the
gross product. On the one hand, the merger of small enterprises
into a number of larger ones during the socialization process may
have reduced the extent of double counting. But as the height of
socialist transformation was reached in 1956, the gross product
for the year was reduced only 1 per cent.[19] On the other hand,
when the definition of "enterprise" was changed from a group of
coal mines under one control bureau to individual mines in 1956,
the effect was to increase the gross value product of the coal industry by 10 per cent.[20]

It is, therefore, clear that while the 1952 constant prices have
distorted the relationship between agriculture and industry from
the beginning, the element of grossness has seriously exaggerated
the relative growth of industry during the following five years.
Calculated in terms of "value added" at 1956 prices, agriculture
would have accounted for 71.3 per cent of the total net product
in 1955.[21] If so, agriculture would still have been twice as important
as industry in terms of the net value product (at 1956 prices) by
the end of the first five years.[22] This is perhaps much nearer to the

[17] "Diverse Opinions . . . ," p. 6. When the butchers were organized into coöperatives as a part of industry in 1954, the gross industrial product was significantly
affected.

[18] For example, in 1954, 136,440 industrial enterprises out of a national total of
167,630 were classified as "small," each employing less than 16 men if mechanical
power is used, or less than 31 men if it is not used. For a fuller definition of "size"
and for the development of industry by number and size of establishments, see Statistical Appendix Table 6.

[19] "Diverse Opinions . . . ," p. 6.

[20] *Ibid,* p. 6.

[21] *Ibid.,* p. 8.

[22] This is estimated by comparing the net values calculated for 1957 at 1952 prices,
as given in chapter iv. It may be pointed out that the use of "value added" to gauge
the relationship between agriculture and industry is not without its problem. The
major elements in "value added" are wages, taxes, and profit; the two latter are
much heavier proportionally to the net value of industrial product than to that of
agricultural product. Moreover, the "profit" of the state-operated and joint enterprises is set down in the annual plan and is automatically deducted from their gross
revenue by the state bank, irrespective of their actual production or sales. Unlike in
Soviet Russia, taxes are levied on producer goods as well as on consumer goods. See
"Diverse Opinions . . ."

real situation than the ratio (54.1 per cent for industry) calculated on the basis of gross value at 1952 prices, as shown in Table V.

The problems arising from the application of the gross concept at 1952 prices are of practical importance. The annual quota for each enterprise had been established in those terms. As a result, a strong preference had generally developed among the industrial enterprises to manufacture products that required a large amount of materials and a small amount of labor, with little incentive to economize in the consumption of raw materials. Therefore, it is no surprise that for the Second Five Year Plan the constant prices to be applied will be those of 1957 instead of 1952, and that serious consideration is being given (a) to use "net value" instead of "gross value" to determine the interrelationships of the different sectors in the economy, and (b) to adopt criteria other than the gross value product with which to judge the annual performance of the industrial enterprises.[23]

Rate of Industrial Growth.—The problem of measuring industrial growth is quite different. Since the gross concept has been consistently applied throughout the period for the computation of the industrial value product, the rate of industrial growth would not have been affected by the "gross" factor, especially for such a short period as five or six years, provided that the effect of decentralization of enterprise (such as coal mines) has been balanced by that of amalgamation of small enterprises. By the same token, it may be argued that no matter what constant prices are used, those of 1952 or of 1957, as long as they have been consistently applied to the output throughout the period, the rate of growth will be the same. This, of course, is not true, particularly for a country under rapid industrialization.[24] Until more current price data are available, it is difficult to estimate at this time the effect on the industrial growth rate from 1953 through 1957 if 1957 prices were used in the place of 1952 prices.

Nevertheless, taking the series of gross industrial value product at 1952 prices as it stands, we see that the pricing of numerous new products manufactured for the first time each year in the five years greatly affects the growth rate calculated from the series.[25] These

[23] Hsieh Mu-ch'iao (director of the State Statistical Bureau), "Our Experience in Statistical Work during the First Five Year Plan Period and Our Future Tasks," *T'ung-chi kung-tso (Statistical Work)*, 21: 1–21, November, 1957; State Statistical Bureau, Department of Industry, "Explanations . . ."; and "Diverse Opinions . . ."
[24] This is a problem well investigated by scholars of the Russian economy.
[25] This is also familiar to scholars of the Russian economy. See A. Gerschenkron,

new products range from fine industrial instruments to heavy electric generators and motors, trucks, and jet airplanes.[26] Their production costs at the beginning must be very high, only to decline
as the volume of output grows.[27] How have they been priced in the
constant-price scheme?

According to the provision set forth by the State Statistical Bureau, they have been priced at the "test-manufacturing" expenses,
with some allowance for the prospective decline in cost when regularly produced, and these expenses are converted to 1952 prices
by a factor applicable to the current prices of similar products
already on the constant-price list.[28] But "because of the difficulty
in forecasting at the time what the cost level will be after production takes place, the constant prices of new products have been too
high in most cases—far exceeding even the actual prices."[29] As
hundreds of important new products appeared every successive
year during the period, each being priced close to the "test-
manufacturing expenses," the gross industrial value product must
have been unduly inflated every year, with an exaggerated rate

---

A Dollars Index of Soviet Machinery Output, 1927/28–1937, Santa Monica, 1951; and
A. Nove, " '1926/7' and All That," *Soviet Studies*, ix: 2: 117–130, October, 1957, esp.
pp. 118–121.

[26] New products include new manufactures under the same general commodity
label. For example, whereas only some 180 types of crude steel and 400 types of rolled
steel could be made in the country in 1952, they increased to more than 370 and 3,000
types, respectively, by the end of 1957. Some 200 new types of lathes (including four-
axis automatic lathes) were being produced for the first time during the five-year
period. Other outstanding "innovations" include 1,000-cu.m.-high furnaces and 185-
ton furnaces for steel, 12,000-kw. electric generating equipment, complete sets of
15,000-kw. hydraulic power generating equipment, coördinated coal-mining machinery, drills for geological survey, high-efficiency steam locomotives, and other
machinery. See State Planning Commission, "The Results and Achievements of the
First Five Year Plan," *Jen-min jih-pao*, October 1, 1957. According to observations
by various Western journalists and travelers, these claims seem authentic. On the
production of jet airplanes, see the *New York Times* dispatch of July 30, 1957 (p. 3)
concerning the observations of a group of retired Japanese army and navy com-
manders who had just made an extensive visit to China at the invitation of Peiping.
One member of the group said he believed the jets operated by the Chinese air force
were made in China, "but by the Russians." If so, the manufacturing plant must be
one of the 156 Russian-aid projects.

[27] Fan Jo-i, "The Pricing Policy of Products of Heavy Industry," *Ching-chi yen-
chiu (Economic Research)*, 3: 54–67, June, 1957. He gives an example of the pricing
of a 6,000-kw. engine for steamships. It cost 1,320,000 yuan in 1955 when first produced, but only 380,000 yuan the following year.

[28] Test-manufacturing denotes the final stage of developing successfully a new
product. It is done before production takes place.

[29] State Statistical Bureau, Department of Industry, "Explanations . . ."; quotation
on p. 13.

of industrial growth as a result.[30] In fact, the problem is serious enough for the State Statistical Bureau to have decided upon changing the basis, for the second five-year period, of pricing new products to actual cost or ex-factory price during the first month or quarter of production.[31]

It may be concluded that during the period of the First Five Year Plan the annual rate of industrial growth must have been less than the 16.3 per cent (with 1952 as the base) or the 13 per cent (with 1953 as the base) as calculated from the data given in Table V. Most of the new products pertain to heavy industry, and their "test-manufacturing" costs are high. However, information is lacking for a quantitative estimate of the effect of their pricing on the industrial value product, and, therefore, for an estimate of a realistic average annual rate of industrial growth for the period.

Development of Different Sectors within Industry.—Reference has been made to the fact that handicraft production is included in the gross industrial value product. The growth of handicraft production is, of course, not an indicator of industrialization. Moreover, even factory production consists of the output of both "modern" and handicraft factories.[32] It is important, therefore, to investigate the changing relationship among the different sectors within industry and the development of each sector during the period of the First Five Year Plan. The pertinent data are summarized in Table VI.

The table shows that modern factory output has been growing at the rate of 18.7 per cent (1952 base) or 15.7 per cent (1953 base). This development is chiefly responsible for the doubling of the gross industrial value product during the five years. The relative importance of total handicraft production has steadily declined, and in both relative importance and absolute growth it has fallen short of the target set forth in the Plan. Because production is

---

[30] The First Five Year Plan calls for a total of 3,350 major new products. The list has not been made known, but most of them are heavy industrial commodities. On the basis of scattered information, it seems the goal has on the whole been achieved.

[31] "Explanations . . . ," p. 13.

[32] As indicated before, the definition of "modern" is not clear, but presumably a "modern" factory is one that employs mechanical power. It is reported that beginning with the Second Five Year Plan, the distinction between "modern" and handicraft factories and between "large" and "small" industrial enterprises will be eliminated in statistical tabulation. See State Economic Commission, Bureau of Planning, Department of Methodology, "Major Changes in the Tabulation Forms for National Economic Planning for 1958," *Chi-hua ching-chi (Planned Economy)*, 8: 24–27, August, 1957.

TABLE VI
GROSS INDUSTRIAL VALUE PRODUCT AT 1952 PRICES, BY SECTORS, 1952–1957

Sector	1952	1953	1954	1955	1956	1957 est.	1957 target
	(In per cent of total)						
A. Sectoral composition							
1. Factory product.........	78.7	79.6	79.7	81.6	83.4	84.0	82.0
a. Modern factory.........	*64.2*	*64.5*	*65.2*	*67.6*	......	*72.1*	*68.7*
b. Handicraft factory.....	*14.5*	*15.1*	*14.5*	*14.0*	......	*11.7*	*13.3*
2. Individual handicrafts...	20.6	19.3	18.5	16.0 }	16.6	16.2	11.0 }
3. Handicraft coöperatives...	0.7	1.1	1.8	2.4 }			7.0 }
4. Total gross industrial product.....	100.0	100.0	100.0	100.0	100.0	100.0	100.0
	(Base year 1952)						
B. Value index							
5. Gross industrial product......	100.0	130.2	151.8	159.9	205.0	212.6	190.3
6. Modern factory product......	100.0	130.6	154.1	168.2	......	235.6	203.6
7. Total handicraft product (including A.1.b, 2, and 3).........	100.0	129.4	147.5	144.9	......	163.7	166.4

Sources: Computed from data in Statistical Appendix, Table 2.

carried on in the modern factory sector with a much higher degree of division of labor *among* enterprises than in the handicraft sector, the total handicraft value product is less conducive to double counting than the modern-factory product. Furthermore, the problem of pricing new products arises exclusively in the modern-factory sector. Thus its relative importance to the handicraft sector must have been overstated. The growth of the modern sector may be stated in another way: its product accounted for 39 per cent of the estimated gross agricultural and industrial product in 1957 as compared to 26.7 per cent in 1952 and 30.5 per cent in 1953. How much of this growth is due to new-product pricing remains indeterminate.

The modern-factory sector is composed chiefly of state-operated and joint enterprises. In these enterprises the average amount of mechanical power at the command of each worker increased from 2.1 kw. in 1952 to 3 kw. in 1955, and the amount of fixed capital assets per worker from 5,656 to 6,835 yuan.[33] Such mechanization of production is more rapidly developed in heavy industry than in light industry, where, as represented by the cotton textile industry, the fixed capital assets per worker had increased only 6 per cent as compared to from 25 to more than 100 per cent in many producer-goods industries.

In summary, with no allowance made for new-product pricing, and calculated from the gross value product series at 1952 prices, the industrial growth rate during the five-year period has been 13 per cent per year (1953 base). Chiefly responsible for such growth is the modern-factory sector, whose gross value product, computed on the same basis, has been increasing at the rate of 15.7 per cent. In relative terms, handicrafts in various forms have played a declining role in industry. Modern factory production is being rapidly mechanized. Therefore, it is beyond doubt that the country has been on its way to industrialization. Yet, by the end of the First Five Year Plan, agriculture, measured in net value terms, was still probably twice as important as industry.

2. The Development of Producer- and Consumer- Goods Industries

Rates of Growth.—In the definition adopted by the State Statistical Bureau, an industrial product is classified according to its major use as a producer good or a consumer good, and the producer-goods and consumer-goods industries are identified as heavy and light

---

[33] See Statistical Appendix, Table 9, for details.

TABLE VII

DEVELOPMENT OF PRODUCER- AND CONSUMER-GOODS INDUSTRIES AT 1952 PRICES, 1952–1957

Industry	1952	1953	1954	1955	1956	1957 est.	1957 target
A. Factory product (value index)	100.0	131.7	153.7	165.6	217.1	223.4	198.3
1. Producer goods:							
a. In per cent of A	39.7	41.2	42.4	46.0	49.7	51.6	45.4
b. Value index	100.0	136.7	164.0	191.8	271.9	290.1	226.6
2. Consumer goods:							
a. In per cent of A	60.3	58.8	57.6	54.0	50.3	48.4	54.6
b. Value index	100.0	128.4	147.0	148.4	181.1	179.4	179.6
B. Machine-making industry product:							
1. In per cent of A	5.2	6.1	6.4	6.8	9.7	9.1	.....
2. Value index	100.0	154.0	188.7	216.3	411.1	391.9	.....
C. Value product indices of some other heavy industries:							
1. Iron and Steel	100.0	136.0	170.0	211.0	302.0	.....	.....
2. Metal fabricating (other than machine-making)	100.0	157.0	193.0	208.0	337.0	.....	.....
3. Construction materials (other than lumber)	100.0	148.0	160.0	163.0	240.0	.....	.....
4. Lumber (logging and manufacture)	100.0	128.0	151.0	129.0	149.0	.....	.....
D. Individual and coöperative handicraft product (index)	100.0	124.7	144.5	138.5	160.0	160.0	161.0
1. Producer goods (in per cent of D)	20.4	.....	.....	27.1	.....	.....	4.3
2. Consumer goods (in per cent of D)	79.6	.....	.....	72.9	.....	.....	95.7

Sources: The indices and percentages for A, B, and D and their subdivisions are computed from actual data given in the Statistical Appendix, Table 3. The value-product indices for C are given by Chi Ch'ung-wei, "How to Make China's Industry Develop Evenly," *Chi-hua ching-chi* (*Planned Economy*), 7:4–8, July, 1957. Absolute data for C are not available.

industries.[34] Such a definition makes for inconsistencies. For example, a good part of the output of what has been formally classified as light industry (e.g., paper) and of handicrafts (e.g. simple agricultural implements) belongs to the category of producer goods, and, indeed, is classified as such in official statistics. There is no reason to identify the output of producer goods with that of heavy industry.[35] Definitional difficulties of this kind, so familiar to students of industrial statistics, are mentioned in order to clarify one point. In the official statistics, the output of producer goods includes, but is larger than, that of heavy industry. In view of the basic objectives of socialist industrialization, the development of heavy industry is paramount. Unfortunately, the output of heavy industry is not differentiated from that of producer goods. The output of producer goods in the factory sector is closest to that of heavy industry, but it must be kept in mind that the factory sector comprises both modern and handicraft factories.

Table V showed that producer goods had increased from 35.6 per cent of the gross industrial product in 1952 to 42.5 in 1955, which was already far above the 38 per cent called for by the First Five Year Plan. Table VII presents a detailed picture of the divergent development of producer- and consumer-goods industries. It will be observed that in the factory sector the producer-goods industries have been growing at a rate of 20.7 per cent (1953 base) against a rate of 8.7 per cent for the consumer-goods industries.[36] By the end of the First Five Year Plan, producer goods constituted, for the first time, more than one-half of the factory product as compared to 40 per cent in 1952. Among the producer-goods industries, the machine-making industry developed fastest, with an increase in its value product by four times in as many years. As a matter of fact, the metal-working industry had grown faster than machine-making in the first two years of the Plan, only to be caught up and surpassed by the latter in the last three years. Thus, despite definitional difficulties in the official statistics, it is heavy industry that has been developing fastest.

---

[34] State Statistical Bureau, "Diverse Opinions . . . ," p. 8. As shown in chapter i, heavy industry comprises: iron and steel, nonferrous metal, electric power, coal mining, petroleum, machine making, chemicals, and construction materials. The components of light industry are textiles, food processing, paper, pharmaceuticals, furs and hides, printing, and other industries that manufacture daily necessities.

[35] On the other hand, the products of heavy industry which are used either for military use or for consumption (such as coal and kerosene), cannot be wholly identified as producer goods.

[36] With 1952 as base, the growth rates would have been 23.8 per cent and 12.4 per cent, respectively.

It may be argued that the price structure may have discriminated against consumer goods and therefore reduced their relative importance in favor of producer goods. That the country is at the first stage of industrialization would lead one to expect the relative prices of producer goods to be much higher than in the West. Not only is this true, but both the relative and absolute prices are also much higher now than before in China herself. In terms of the present value of the yuan, the price index of producer goods had gone up five times from 1936 to 1956 when the general price index had increased only about three times.[37] But such a relative price structure at home may well reflect as much the relative scarcities in the mind of the planning authorities as the high production cost of producer goods resulting from the inevitable disregard (at least in the short run) of the law of comparative advantage under the industrialization program. The relatively high price of producer goods is the result of the natural course of events.

The pertinent question is whether there are any elements in the data that may have distorted the relationship between the two components and their respective rates of growth. Two factors seem to have operated in favor of consumer-goods industries. The gross factor, though present in the value products of both components, figures prominently in that of consumer goods.[38] Moreover, the rate of taxes and profits combined is much higher for consumer goods than for producer goods.[39] Counterbalancing, at least in part, the effect of these two factors is the use of the 1952 constant prices where the prices of consumer goods as well as agricultural products were abnormally depressed in relation to those of producer goods. If the net effect has been the enhancement of the relative importance of consumer-goods industries, it would not have worked progressively to their advantage during the five-year period, because the tax structure and the composition of consumer-goods output have remained comparatively stable. If this is true, a further

[37] During the same period, the prices of agricultural products doubled. See Fan Jo-i, "The Pricing Policy of Products of Heavy Industry," *Ching-chi yen-chiu (Economic Research)*, 3: 54–67, June, 1957.

[38] In 1955, 93.1 per cent of the gross value product of consumer-goods industries in the factory sector came from output in which agricultural raw materials were directly or indirectly used. See "Several Problems of China's Socialist Industrialization," *Hsin-hua pan-yueh-k'an*, 1: 67–71, January, 1957.

[39] From 1952 through 1955, the taxes and profits paid by light industry to the national treasury amounted to 14.4 per cent of the total state budgetary revenues, but those paid by heavy industry came to 10.1 per cent. "Several Problems of China's Socialist Industrialization," *ibid.*

implication would be that the growth rate of either component in the factory sector has not been affected by any of the factors mentioned.

However, two other elements are at work. One is the growing practice of organizing individual handicraftsmen or handicraft co-operatives into either handicraft factories or even modern factories.[40] Since the bulk of their production consists of consumer goods, the effect would have been to increase the growth rate of consumer-goods industries. Of course, socialization has also brought about amalgamation of some small production units, thus reducing double counting and therefore the gross value product, but, as indicated earlier, this process has not gone far enough to be statistically significant. The other element is the pricing of new products, which chiefly concerns the value product of producer-goods industries. It clearly introduces a progressive bias in their favor both in relation to consumer-goods industries and in their own growth rate. However, it is difficult to determine whether the effects of these two factors on the relationship between the two industrial components neutralized each other.

The conclusions reached thus far may be briefly stated. As measured by the gross value product at 1952 prices, the relationship between the two components in the factory sector has not been distorted nearly as much as that between agriculture and industry. But the growth rate of consumer-goods industries may have been inflated by changing industrial organization, and that of producer goods, by new product pricing. Nevertheless, it seems clear that producer-goods industries have been growing about twice as fast as consumer-goods industries.

Table VII shows further that the policy of concentrated development of heavy industry has also resulted in an increasing relative importance of producer goods in the output of individual handicraftsmen and handicraft coöperatives. In the light of the 1957 target, the original plan must have been for the factory sector to absorb those handicrafts that engaged in manufacturing producer goods, leaving the others to produce consumer goods. Whether the absorption failed to take place or another reason was responsible, the fact remains that by 1955 more than one-quarter of the output of the handicraft sector (exclusive of handicraft factories) were producer goods as compared with only one-fifth in 1952, and with

[40] See Statistical Appendix, Table 7, for changing structure of industry by employment, 1949–1955.

TABLE VIII

Production of Major Industrial Products, 1952–1957

Product	Unit	1952	1953	1954	1955	1956	1957 est.	1957 target	1962 target
I. Heavy Industry									
1. Pig iron	Thousand tons	1,929	2,234	3,114	3,872	4,777	5,554	4,674	....
a. Factory	Thousand tons	1,900	2,175	2,962	3,630	....	....	4,610	....
b. Handicraft	Thousand tons	29	59	152	242	....	....	64	....
2. Steel	Thousand tons	1,349	1,774	2,230	2,853	4,465	4,987	4,120	11,250
3. Rolled steel	Thousand tons	1,110	....	1,176	2,505	3,921	4,478	3,045	....
4. Coal	Million tons	63.5	66.6	79.5	93.6	105.9	117.3	113	200
5. Crude oil	Thousand tons	436	622	789	966	1,163	1,500	2,012	5,500
6. Electric power	Billion kw. hr.	7.3	9.2	11	12.3	16.6	18.9	15.9	41.5
7. Lathes	Thousand units	13.7	20.5	16.1	13.7	26	22.6	12.7	62.5
8. Power-generating equipment	Thousand tons	16.3	24	22.8	....	....	....	29.3	....
9. Electric generators	Thousand kw.	30	53	55	108	288	284	227	....
10. Electric motors	Thousand kw.	639	....	....	....	1,069	1,251	1,048	....
11. Locomotives	Units	20	1	52	98	184	....	200	....
12. Freight cars	Units	5,792	4,500	5,446	9,258	7,122	7,000	8,500	....
13. Trucks	Units	0	0	0	0	1,654	....	4,000	....
14. Double-wheeled ploughs	Thousand units	5	3	60	523	1,793	....	689	....
15. Alkali	Thousand tons	192	223	311	405	446	478	476	....
16. Ammonium sulfide	Thousand tons	181	226	298	324	658	499	504	....
17. Chemical fertilizers	Thousand units	194	263	343	425	....	755	578	3,150
18. Tires	Thousand tons	417	488	701	593	....	....	760	....
19. Cement	Thousand tons	2,861	3,877	4,600	4,503	6,393	6,807	6,000	13,500
20. Lumber	Million cu. m.	10	....	....	20.5	20.6	25.1	20	32.5
a. Factory	Million cu. m.	....	....	....	12.5	10.7	....	13.9	....
b. Handicraft	Million cu. m.	....	....	....	7.9	9.9	....	6.1	....
II. Light Industry									
1. Paper (including paper board)	Thousand tons	539	....	846	849	....	....	892	1,550
a. Factory	Thousand tons	372	427	556	589	746	....	655	....
b. Handicraft	Thousand tons	167	....	290	260	....	....	237	....
2. Cotton yarn	Thousand bales	3,618	4,104	4,598	3,968	5,246	4,635	5,000	8,500

Item	Unit								
3. Cotton cloth									
a. Factory and all handicrafts	Million bolts	137.9	154.2	182.5	144.9	163.7	...	178.7	247.5
b. Factory	Million m.	4,158	5,002	5,541	4,510	5,860	5,000	...	...
	Million bolts	89.3	107.8	122.3	103.2	...	...	...	...
	Million m.	...	...	...	3,485	4,600	...	...	...
c. All handicrafts	Million bolts	48.6	46.4	60.2	41.7	...	...	...	...
d. Factory and those handicrafts using machine-made yarn	Million bolts	111.6	...	...	...	...	...	...	...
4. Flour	Thousand tons	2,995	3,390	3,724	4,530	5,020	5,030	...	4,670
a. Factory	Thousand tons	...	...	...	...	4,310	...	...	...
b. Handicraft	Thousand tons	...	...	...	...	710	...	...	...
5. Sugar	Thousand tons	451	638	693	717	807	874	1,100	2,450
a. Factory	Thousand tons	249	298	347	410	518	...	686	...
b. Handicraft	Thousand tons	202	340	346	307	289	...	414	...
6. Salt	Thousand tons	4,945	...	...	5,900	4,900	7,000	7,554	10,500
a. Factory	Thousand tons	3,460	...	...	...	3,832	...	5,932	...
b. Handicraft	Thousand tons	1,485	...	...	...	1,068	...	1,622	...
7. Edible vegetable oil	Thousand tons	983	...	900	900	862	...	1,794	...
8. Cigarettes	Thousand cases	2,650	3,552	3,720	3,567	3,907	...	4,700	3,150

Notes: (a) When handicraft production is not indicated, the data pertain to factory production only. (b) The original 1962 targets given in the draft of the Second Five Year Plan are in terms of a range (*e.g.*, for steel, 10,500,000–12,000,000 metric tons). For brevity, they have been reduced to averages (thus for steel, 11,250,000 tons). (c) A bale of cotton yarn equals 400 lbs. Although a bolt of cotton cloth is formally defined as having 40 yards, it varies between machine-made and hand-made cloth; and from the data given in the table, it appears that a bolt of machine-made cloth has 33⅓ yards while a bolt of hand-made cloth has 24.26 yards. A case of cigarettes contains 10,000 cigarettes.

Sources:
1) Unless otherwise stated, the sources are:
a) For 1952 through 1955: (i) "A General Survey of Socialist Industrialization in China," *Hsin-hua pan-yueh-k'an*, 2:54–62, January, 1957; (ii) State Statistical Bureau, "Economic Statistical Abstract, *Hsin-hua pan-yueh-k'an*, 17:41, September, 1956; (iii) State Statistical Bureau, "Communiqué on the Results of the 1954 Plan," *Jen-min jih-pao*, September 24, 1955; and "Communiqué on the Results of the 1955 Plan," *ibid.*, June 15, 1956.
b) For 1956 and 1957 (estimated): (i) Po I-po, "Report on the Results of the 1956 Plan and on the Plan for 1957," *Jen-min jih-pao*, July 2, 1957; (ii) State Statistical Bureau, "Communiqué on the Results of the 1956 Plan," *Jen-min jih-pao*, August 2, 1957. When the bureau's data differ from those given by Po, the former are adopted.
c) For 1957 and 1962 targets: (i) The *First Five Year Plan*; (ii) Chinese Communist Party, "Draft Proposal of the Second Five Year Plan," *Jen-min jih-pao*, September 28, 1956.
2) For 1956 production of electric generators, electric motors, and freight cars, Tung Hsin, "China's Achievements in Industrial Production," *Kung-jen jih-pao (Workers' Daily)*, September 13–14, 1957.
3) For 1952 through 1956 production of double-wheeled ploughs and chemical fertilizers, Lin Chung-fan, "The State Assistance to Peasants," *Kung-jen jih-pao (Workers' Daily)*, September 21, 1957.
4) For 1956 production of alkali, Kao Kuang-chien, "Recent Development of the Chemical Industry," *Kung-jen jih-pao (Workers' Daily)*, September 30, 1957.
5) Lumber: for 1955, Chen Yun, "The Problem of Increasing Production and Economizing," *Hsin-hua pan-yueh-k'an*, 7:15–18, April 10, 1957; for 1956 and 1957 (estimated), from a reference appearing in *ibid.*, 6:42, March, 1967.
6) Handicraft paper production for 1954 and 1955, Tung Chih-fu, "Why Has Handicraft Paper Production Declined?" *Jen-min jih-pao*, November 11, 1956.
7) Flour production for 1956, a preliminary estimate by the State Statistical Bureau, cited in editorial, *Jen-min jih-pao*, January 1, 1957.
8) Salt (total) for 1956, from editorial, *Jen-min jih-pao*, February 26, 1957.

only 4 per cent called for by the First Five Year Plan. Moreover, consumer goods produced in the handicraft sector increased only 26.8 per cent from 1952 to 1955, when producer goods increased 84.2 per cent. Finally, in 1952 the handicraft sector accounted for 26.3 per cent of the total output of consumer goods in industry as a whole; it declined to 23.4 per cent in 1955. It is therefore incorrect to say, as has been done, that the relatively slow development of consumer-goods industries in the factory sector has been more than made up by the output in the handicraft sector.

Production of Major Commodities.—The conclusions reached above on the divergent development of producer- and consumer-goods industries are further supported by Table VIII, which presents the physical production data of certain major industrial products from 1952 through 1957, together with the targets set forth for them in the First and Second Five Year Plans. The commodities are chosen as much because of their importance as because of the comparative completeness of data for all years indicated.

In interpreting the table, two points should be kept in mind. First, since the final Plan was not drafted until as late as February, 1955, the 1957 targets must have been set about that time, when the fulfillment of the Plan certainly was more likely than if the targets had been determined in 1952. In fact, the Plan received a big boost during its first year of publication from an exceptionally good harvest, the best since 1949. Hence, it is not the fulfillment or overfulfillment of the Plan in certain lines of production that should receive special attention, but the failure to meet the targets in others. Secondly, the drive to exceed annual quotas has, in many cases, resulted in the deterioration of the quality of output. This is particularly true of multiproduct enterprises, for which the quotas are set forth in terms of gross value product at 1952 prices.[41] In addition, production is often carried on for the mere purpose of filling the quota, with no attention being paid to market-demand conditions or any incentive to introduce product varie-

---

[41] See discussion in last section, above. The following statement made by the chairman of the State Economic Commission Po I-po may be cited: "To exceed the quota or even to obtain overfulfillment awards, many enterprises have been resorting to an increase in personnel, in the number of shifts, or to other improper means. This not only wastes manpower and materials, but adversely affects the quality of construction, product, and work" (*Jen-min jih-pao*, July 2, 1957). It will be observed that these "improper means" would not help if the enterprises had not regularly built up illegal reserves of basic materials—a practice widespread among all enterprises, leading not only to quality deterioration but also to high cost of production. On illegal material reserves, see editorial, *Jen-min jih-pao*, May 21, 1955 and January 31, 1957.

ties or new products (except those called for by the Plan).[42] There was a time when even the state enterprises preferred to buy producer goods from private factories than from other state firms because of quality and price considerations.[43] Hence, the filling of a quota need not mean that the output is uniform in quality or in line with market demand.

These considerations notwithstanding, heavy industry has made great strides. It constitutes, of course, the field in which the heaviest investment has been made. The results are the pride of the new regime. Reference has already been made to the new products manufactured in the country for the first time. Cotton textile and paper-making machinery and equipment that China used to import are now searching for export markets. Even the progress in the building of railways, highways, and dams—which many people have considered to be but a continuation of pre-1949 efforts—does not match this development.

However, the development of heavy industry has already run into the bottlenecks of the supply of power and basic industrial materials. Coal and metal mining, crude oil and electric power have failed to grow rapidly enough to meet the demand of all other industries, while the production of iron, steel, and construction materials are unable to keep up with the rising demand of the metal-working and machine-making industries. This is especially evident in the last two years of the five-year period, despite the fact that the output of coal, iron, steel, and electric power exceeded the 1957 target one full year ahead of schedule. The situation reveals a lack of integration and coördination in planning and must have been the primary reason for the government to set up the State Economic Commisison in May, 1956, to be responsible for determining the current quotas for each year, thus leaving to the State Planning Commission (established in November, 1952) the task of over-all long-term planning and coördination.

On the whole, the heavy industries have more than filled the quotas of the First Five Year Plan. Among the few important items in this category that did not reach the goals are crude oil, which is limited by the lack of developed resources, double-wheeled

---

[42] Writing about "The Problems of Textile Production in 1957," *Chi-hua ching-chi (Planned Economy)*, 5: 5–7 and 19, May, 1957, Ching Wei recommends *"taking stern measures against enterprises producing blindly with no regard to market conditions, or manufacturing excessively with no regard to quality."* Quotation on p. 19; italics in original.

[43] See reference to this development in 1954 by Fan Jo-i, *op. cit.*

ploughs, and such transportation equipment as locomotives, freight cars, and ships for civilian use."

The development of the light industries presents a contrasting picture. Paper, the only important product in this category that has exceeded the quota, has grown fastest, mainly because of the development of industrial paper manufacturing. The remaining light industries have performed poorly. Cotton cloth, wheat flour, sugar, and matches as well as cigarettes are not expected to fill the 1957 quota. Cotton yarn exceeded it in 1956 but fell behind again in 1957 because of a poor crop. Salt and edible vegetable oil not only failed to meet the quota of the Plan but had fallen below the 1952 level in 1956. It is significant that all these are daily necessities of the population."

Although so many major products of light industry are not expected to meet the 1957 target, yet according to Table VII, both the gross value product of consumer-goods industries in the factory sector (see line A.2.b) and that of the handicraft sector (line D) are expected to do so. The explanation perhaps lies, first, in the organizational shift from the handicraft to the factory sector as already mentioned and, secondly, in the fact that the remaining handicrafts have been engaged more in the output of producer goods which command a higher price than consumer goods.

It will be recalled that according to the Plan only 11.2 per cent of the industrial investment funds was to go into consumer-goods industries. In June, 1956, the chairman of the State Planning Commission declared that for 1956 and 1957 the percentage would be raised to 12.5 per cent." Small as the change is, the decision would not have been made in view of the basic objectives of the industrialization program, if the need had not been pressing. It is not known whether the increase was put into effect. But the planned output of consumer goods in 1957 is expected to increase by 1.1 per cent over 1956 against an expected increase of 8 per cent for producer goods." This means that consumer-goods industries

---

" Chia To-fu, "Report on the Drafting of the 1957 Plan for the National Economy," *Chi-hua ching-chi (Planned Economy)*, 4: 1–9, April, 1957.

⁴⁵ For the listing of important consumer goods not expected to hit the 1957 target, see Chia To-fu, *op. cit.* See Table 34 in Addendum for confirmation, except for salt.

⁴⁶ Li Fu-ch'un "Economic Progress from 1953 to 1956," *Jen-min jih-pao*, June 19, 1956.

⁴⁷ Po I-po, "Report on the Results of the 1956 Plan and on the Plan for 1957," *Jen-min jih-pao*, July 2, 1957. The increases mentioned in the text refer to the output of that part of the factory sector that has been brought "into the state plan." According to Po's data, only 1.6 per cent of the total output of the factory sector was outside the state plan in 1956. No indication is given as to how much of the out-

are so tied up with agriculture for both raw materials and market outlets that their development does not depend so much on investment in themselves as on keeping pace with the investment and growth in agriculture.[48]

3. NEW INDUSTRIAL LOCATION

In the coastal areas were located, as late as 1952, more than 80 per cent of the productive capacity of the iron and steel industry, 80 per cent of the cotton spindles, and 90 per cent of the power looms.[49] The only heavy-industry center of the country was Anshan in Liaoning Province, originally developed by the Japanese. Various light industries were concentrated in Shanghai, Tientsin, and the provinces of Kiangsu and Kwangtung. The coastal areas claimed 73 per cent of the gross factory value product, leaving 27 per cent for the other 18 provinces and autonomous regions. The policy as manifested in the investment program of the First Five Year Plan is "to locate industries as close to sources of raw materials and fuel supply as to consumption centers, when the interest of national security is served."[50] Railways and highways have been developed with this principle in mind.

During the first three years of the First Five Year Plan, 55.3 per cent of the industrial investment was made inland, and 44.7 per cent on the coast, as compared to 50.2 and 49.8 per cent, in the previous three years of rehabilitation. Moreover, most of the investment made on the coast was for reconstruction of existing plants. From the total investment for new industrial enterprises, 73.9 per cent was made behind the coastal areas.[51] Thus by the end of 1955 the inland industries were able to account for 32 per cent of the factory value product.

put would remain outside the state plan in 1957. Because of the "high tide" of socialization in 1956, it stands to reason that by the end of 1957 the output remaining outside the state plan would be negligible. In other words, for the purpose of this study the 1957 output of the factory sector under the state plan is taken to be the whole output of the sector. On this basis, as shown in Table VII in the text, the planned output of consumer goods for 1957 would be 1 per cent less than in 1956, and that of producer goods, 6.7 per cent more.

[48] Po I-po has recently announced that the amount of investment in light industry will have to be reduced in 1958 for shortage of agricultural raw materials. See his "Problems of Setting the Planned Production Quotas for 1958," *Hsin-hua pan-yueh-k'an*, 17: 206–208, September, 1957.

[49] Sha Ying, "The Relationship between Coastal and Inland Industries," *Jen-min jih-pao*, November 24, 1956. By definition the coastal areas comprise the three special cities of Peiping, Tientsin, and Shanghai, and the seven provinces of Liaoning, Hopei, Shantung, Kiangsu, Chekiang, Fukien, and Kwangtung.

[50] The *First Five Year Plan*, p. 31.

[51] "The Scope and Development of China's Basic Construction Investment," *T'ung-chi kung-tso t'ung-hsin* (*Statistical Bulletin*), 18: 4–6, September, 1956.

During this three-year period, however, national security considerations predominated in the establishment of many industries inland when it would have cost much less to expand the existing capacities on the coast.[52] The building of such industries as cotton textile mills in the raw-material producing areas (away from the coast) seems logical and economically justified. But the coastal in-

TABLE IX

LOCATION OF FACTORY INDUSTRY, ACCORDING TO VALUE PRODUCT
AT 1952 PRICES, 1952–1956
(In per cent)

Location	1952	1955	1956 Jan.–June	1956
1. Inland..................	26.9	32.0	32.2	32.1
2. Coastal:..................	73.1	68.0	67.8	67.9
Shanghai...............	24.3	20.2	20.1	....
Tientsin...............	6.8	6.4	6.0	....
Peiping...............	2.8	3.1	3.2	....
7 Provinces.............	39.1	38.3	38.5	....

Note: The seven coastal provinces are Liaoning, Hopei, Shantung, Kiangsu, Chekiang, Fukien, and Kwangtung.
For sources and actual data from 1952 through 1956, see Statistical Appendix, Table 8.

dustrial capacity, especially for the production of consumer goods, was far from fully utilized, and the degree of utilization was much higher inland for the same type of industrial equipment.[53] Neglect of the coastal industries was carried to the extent that there was actually disinvestment in the old industrial center of Shanghai in 1955, when the gross industrial investment was equal to only 76 per cent of the depreciation of the fixed capital assets.[54] Thus the external economies afforded by the old industrial centers were

[52] The moving of existing industries from the coast was encouraged in 1950, when railway freight rates for transporting industrial equipment inland were reduced by one-half. *Jen-min jih-pao*, January 12, 1950.
[53] For example, among the local industries in the first half of 1955, the utilization rate (i.e., percentage of productive capacity used) was as follows:

	Rubber shoes	Printed cloth	Machine-made paper	Soap	Cigarettes	Machine-making
Coastal	33	53	71	28	20	34
Inland	58	56	73	36	31	38

SOURCE: "Several Problems of China's Socialist Industrialization," *Hsin-hua pan-yueh-k'an*, 1: 67–71, January, 1957.
[54] "Several Problems . . . ," *ibid.* Even so, the coastal industries produced about 70 per cent of consumer goods for the country. See editorial, *Jen-min jih-pao*, July 9, 1956.

deliberately sacrificed. In 1955, with 36 per cent of the capital assets of the country, the inland industries produced only 32 per cent of the gross factory product, and the productivity per worker per year was one-third less there than on the coast.[55] There is no reason why the old centers should not have been developed at comparatively low cost in order to help build up the new industries inland— except for security considerations.[56]

Beginning in 1956, as "the international situation became favorable,"[57] a new policy was initiated with the slogan of "balanced development" between the two areas.[58] The tide began to turn in the latter half of 1956, as may be seen from Table IX. At least, the one-sided development of the previous three years seems to have been checked. Whereas the factory product increased 13.9 per cent inland as against 4.7 per cent on the coast from 1954 to 1955, the corresponding increases were 31.5 and 30.9 per cent the following year.[59] Furthermore, from the 825 big industrial projects initiated during the five-year period, 530 (or 64 per cent) were located inland.[60] This is proportionately less than what the First Five Year Plan called for.[61]

The location of heavy industry, on the other hand, is dictated more by the sources of raw materials and fuel supply than by security considerations. Even during the Korean War, heavy investment was made in rehabilitating and expanding the iron and steel complex at Anshan. It happens that iron and coal are available

---

[53] Labor productivity is computed on the basis of gross factory value product with the exclusion of handicraft factories. It was 13,500 yuan per worker per year on the coast against 9,000 yuan inland. See "Several Problems . . ."

The comparison in the text is valid only if the industry mix is the same between inland and the coastal area, because the element of "grossness" varies greatly in the value product of different industries. The fact that in 1955 about 70 per cent of consumer goods were produced on the coast means the presence of a higher gross factor in the coastal factory value product than in the inland product. But the construction of new heavy-industry centers inland had not started in 1955, and heavy industry was weighted much more importantly in the coastal industrial mix than in the inland mix. Hence, the comparison stands as an approximation.

[56] Undoubtedly sentiment against the old locational setup was another potent reason.

[57] Sha Ying, *op. cit.*

[58] Chairman of the State Planning Commission Li Fu-ch'un, "Economic Progress from 1953 to 1956," *Jen-min jih-pao,* June 19, 1956.

[59] Calculated from real data given in Statistical Appendix, Table 8. The bumper crop in the fall of 1955 also helped the coastal consumer-goods industries.

[60] Yang Ch'ing-wen, "Two Problems of Industrial Location," *Chi-hua ching-chi (Planned Economy),* 8: 13–15, August, 1957.

[61] The Plan expects 472 projects from a total of 694 (68 per cent) to be located inland.

together in large quantities in several inland regions.[62] Thus the Plan required the building of two new centers for heavy industry, one at Paotou in Inner Mongolia and another at Wuhan in Central China. After a long period of surveying, construction started at Paotou in 1956 and at Wuhan in 1957.[63] The latter will be second in size and importance only to Anshan; upon completion of the first stage of construction in 1961, it will increase the present national output of iron and steel by about one-third. The Second Five Year Plan calls for the building of more heavy industry complexes of lesser size at Chungking in the Southwest and at the Sanmen Gorge area in Honan.[64]

It is clear that despite the principle laid down in the First Five Year Plan, the real, basic shift in the geographical balance of industrial location in the country results only from development of new centers for heavy industry.

[62] This study does not propose to deal with the natural resources of the country, a subject that will require separate treatment on a later occasion. At the present, only fragmentary information is available on the new discoveries of mineral reserves. Since the establishment of the Ministry of Geology in 1952, vigorous surveys of natural resources have been undertaken with reportedly significant results. For example the present estimate of iron ore reserves is 11,000 million metric tons as against the pre-1949 estimate of 3,000 million, and 3,600 million tons had been ascertained by the end of 1956. The possible coal reserve is now estimated to be as high as 1,200 billion tons, with a reserve of 20.1 billion tons already established. See Liu Ching-fan's statement before the National Congress of People's Representatives, in *Hsin-hua pan-yueh-k'an*, 17: 49–51, September, 1957. In addition to the oil center at Yumen, Kansu Province, a hugh oil field has been discovered at Karmi and its vicinity in Sinkiang Province, promising to be the largest in the country with an estimated reserve of more than 100 million tons—several times the reserve at Yumen. By September, 1956, 26 wells had been drilled, each producing oil in quantity. See editorials and dispatches in *Jen-min jih-pao*, July 12, September 5, and September 22, 1956. The hydraulic power potential that can be utilized has been estimated at 300 million kw. From the increase of two million kw. in electric power during the five-year period, 600,000 kw. is hydraulic. See Li Jui, "China's Water Power Potential and the Advantages of Building Hydraulic Power Stations." *Jen-min jih-pao*, December 12, 1955; and Yu Tsing-chuan's statement before the National Congress of People's Representatives, in *Hsin-hua pan-yueh-k'an*, 15: 16–17, August, 1957.

Although the authenticity of these pronouncements is hard to verify, the reported discoveries are not beyond the realm of possibility. For the purpose of this study, it suffices to keep in mind that China is endowed with certain basic mineral resources sufficient for its industrialization program. Of course, reserves need time to develop, and there are other basic resources of which the country is short, such as copper. More comment on the situation will be made in chapter vii.

[63] Cf. "Paotou under Construction," *Jen-min jih-pao*, July 27, 1956; and editorial, *ibid.*, April 9, 1957. It will be remembered that both come under the 156 Russian-aid projects.

[64] Sha Ying, *op. cit.*

III

Agricultural Development

Agriculture constitutes such a broad base of the Chinese economy that a full treatment of its development in its various aspects is beyond the confines of this study. The changes in its organization and in the marketing and disposal of farm products have been commented on in the introductory chapter.[1] This chapter will deal only with the development of agricultural production.

During the first four years of the First Five Year Plan, the total basic construction investment in agriculture, forestry, and water conservation amounted to 2,776 million yuan, to which may be added the planned investment of 970 million for 1957, thus making a total of 3,746 million for the first five years. (See Table X.) This is less than 8 per cent of the total investment by the state during the period, but about 40 per cent more than originally planned.

It will be observed, first, that in proportion to the total investment the state investment in agriculture and related fields was much higher during the rehabilitation period, as represented by 1952, than in any year during the First Five Year Plan. In fact, the proportion declined precipitously up to the end of 1954, to recover gradually to only two-thirds of its former relative importance in 1957. Secondly, and more important, the bulk of the investment in agriculture and related fields has been used for water conservation projects. From 1952 through 1955 two-thirds of such investment was so spent, and the investment in agriculture proper and forestry represented less than 3 per cent of the total state investment. The water-conservation projects serve multiple purposes. How much they have benefited agriculture will be discussed fully

---

[1] This socioeconomic change may be studied in a new series published by the Peiping Academy of Sciences, Institute of Economic Research, titled *Kuo-min ching-chi hui-fu shih-ch'i nung-yeh sheng-ch'an-ho-tso tzu-liao hui-pien, 1949–1952* (Collection of Materials on Agricultural Producers' Coöperation during the Period of Rehabilitation of the National Economy, 1949–1952), Peiping, June, 1957, 2 vols., 1214 pp. The materials concern primarily the various regions in the country.

54 *Economic Development of Communist China*

in the following pages. From the debate at Peiping, it seems apparent that the development of hydroelectric power is the primary aim in making the investment.[2] The allocation of investment funds between agriculture proper and forestry is not known. As shown in Table XII, afforestation has been developing very fast, overreaching the five-year goal by more than 63 per cent—obviously as a result of the severe shortage in construction lumber. The invest-

TABLE X

STATE TOTAL AND AGRICULTURAL INVESTMENT AT CURRENT PRICES, 1952–1957

Investment	1952		1953		1954	
	millions of yuan	per cent of A	millions of yuan	per cent of A	millions of yuan	per cent of A
A. Total basic construction investment	3,711	100.0	6,506	100.0	7,498	100.0
B. Investment in agriculture, forestry, and water conservation	517	13.9	652	10.0	363	4.8
1. Agriculture and foresty	186	5.0	276	4.2	144	1.9
2. Water conservation	331	8.9	376	5.8	219	2.9

Investment	1955		1956		1957 est.	
A. Total basic construction investment	8,212	100.0	13,986	100.0	11,100	100.0
B. Investment in agriculture, forestry, and water conservation	601	7.3	1,160	8.3	970	8.7
1. Agriculture and forestry	199	2.4	...	...	...	...
2. Water conservation	402	4.9	...	...	...	...

Sources: (1) For 1952 through 1955, State Statistical Bureau, "Economic Statistical Abstract," *Hsinhua pan-yueh-k'an*, 17:42. (2) For 1956 and 1957, Po I-po, "Report on the Results of the 1956 Plan and on the Plan for 1957," *Jen-min jih-pao*, July 2, 1957.

ment in forestry, therefore, must have been that much more than originally planned, and the amount left for agriculture proper far less than the undifferentiated total conveys.[3] Where the state has made its investment in agriculture will be discussed in connection with the agricultural development program.

[2] Cf. Wang Shu-ch'un, "The Question of Apportioning the Investment in Water Conservation," *Chi-hua ching-chi (Planned Economy)*, 5: 14–15, May, 1957; and Hsieh Shu-an, "An Opinion on the Question of Apportioning the Investment in Water Conservation," *ibid.*, 10: 23–24, October, 1957. The articles discuss the question whether the Ministry of Water Conservation should be entirely responsible for such investment, as it has been, or such other ministries as Railways and Electric Power should also participate in allocating funds for the purpose.

[3] Agricultural credit will be discussed in chapter v.

With so little state investment, how much has agricultural production been growing? What has been the development in agriculture? Has collectivization helped raise agricultural output? These are the question which we will attempt to answer.

1. GROSS AGRICULTURAL VALUE PRODUCT

According to official statistics, the gross agricultural value product at 1952 prices rose from 48.4 billion yuan in 1952 to 61.2 billion (estimated) in 1957—an average annual increase rate of 4.8 per cent. Does this rate reflect the actual agricultural growth? The question may be approached by examining the composition of agriculture and the problem of valuation.

Agriculture by definition consists of three activities—crop growing, animal raising, and subsidiary work of the farming household. The total valuation of the annual results of these activities is the gross agricultural value product. It is important, therefore, to study each activity. The following tabulation is presented for that purpose.[4]

I. Crop Growing:

  A. Major crops:

    1. Food grains: rice, wheat, coarse grains, sweet and Irish potatoes. Coarse grains include corn, millet, kaoliang, oats, buckwheat, various kinds of beans and peas (except soybeans), and others. In the First Five Year Plan, soybeans were included in the food grains and were so reported in official statistics through 1955; but since then they have been listed among the industrial crops. For the purpose of this study, food grains will not include soybeans, unless otherwise stated.

    2. Industrial crops: cotton, jute and hemp, tobacco, sugar cane, sugar beets, and oil-producing seed (chiefly groundnuts, soybeans, rapeseed, sesame seeds, and flax seeds).

    3. Other crops: tea, green vegetables, fruits, animal feed, flowers, green compost.

  B. Secondary products, such as straw, stalks, bran.

  C. Intermediate products in the process of production:

    1. Ploughing after autumn harvest;

    2. Seeding before the end of the year;

    3. Cultivation of fruits and trees requiring many years before harvesting.

---

[4] The classification is based on the following sources: Huang Meng-fan, "Agricultural Production Statistics," *T'ung-chi kung-tso t'ung-hsin* (*Statistical Bulletin*), 12: 30–33, June, 1956; Liao Hsien-hao, "Tabulation Forms for Agricultural Production Planning," *Chi-hua ching-chi* (*Planned Economy*), 4: 30–33, April, 1957; and Liao chi-lih, "Accelerating Agricultural Development—a Condition for Accelerating the Development of Heavy Industry," *Chi-hua ching-chi* (*Planned Economy*), 8: 4–6 August, 1957.

II. Animal Raising:

A. Products gained without slaughtering: milk, wool, eggs, bristles, honey, dungs, and the like. Slaughtering of animals is an industrial activity, and the value of the products so derived goes into the gross industrial value product.

B. Offspring of animals; and natural weight increase of animals.

C. Cultivation of aquatic products.

D. Silkworms.

III. Subsidiary Work of the Farming Household:

A. Hunting and the collection of natural products, such as herbs, fuel, minerals, fish.

B. Processing of own farm crops: rice milling, grinding flour, cotton ginning, shelling groundnuts, and the like.

C. Handicraft work for own household use: tailoring, shoemaking, etc.

D. Wages received for handicraft work done for other consumers who supply the raw materials.

The gross agricultural product is the valuation of the annual results of all activities listed above. Unlike manufactured goods, however, agricultural products are not valued at market prices. "The gross agricultural value product—irrespective of whether the produce involved is for self-consumption or for the market—is estimated by the statistical office according to the average of prices at the places of production."[5] Certain products, as we have seen, must be sold to the state, while others are permitted to be freely exchanged. Since the bulk of the products (in terms of value) is state-controlled, valuation is mostly based on government-purchase prices. Valuation for products not sold at the village level or used entirely on the farm (like vegetables and green compost), is based on "either the average market prices minus transport cost or on production costs or on the prices of similar products."[6]

The "average" of prices used in computing the gross value product is probably a national average, for the annual agricultural plan is framed in terms of value, issued by the central authority to all local governments "without taking into consideration any regional differences in price."[7] Moreover, the "average" is one of current prices, to be converted into 1952 prices in accordance with con-

[5] Huang Meng-fan, *op. cit.*, p. 33. Products for the market (or, briefly, "commercialized" products) are not only those sold for money, but also those used for barter and for payment of services, debts, and taxes.

[6] *Ibid.* Intermediate goods are recorded in terms of the net increase in labor and material costs between the beginning and the end of the year.

[7] Quotation from Liao Hsien-hao, *op. cit.*, p. 32.

version factors as explained earlier for the gross industrial value product.[8] It will be recalled that since agricultural prices were depressed in the third quarter of 1952, a comparison of the agricultural with the industrial value product at 1952 prices would distort the relationship between these two major sectors. But because of the nature of production, valuation at 1952 prices should not affect the growth rate of agriculture as it affects the rate of industry.

The "grossness" in the agricultural product is also far less than in the industrial product. The processing of own farm produce and the handicraft work for own household use lead to double counting. Since the product is usually finished by the household without division of labor among households, the raw materials are double-counted only once. Further duplication is found in the difficulty of differentiating between the food grown on the farm that will enter into the value of crops and the food used there for animal feed that will go into the valuation of animal raising.[9] Farm production with the assistance of tractor stations includes in value terms not only the farm output but also the tractor services received. This last duplication factor is increasingly important because of the growing number of tractors in operation.[10] It will entail an exaggerated effect on the growth rate of agriculture. Finally, the increasing use of chemical fertilizers as well as insecticides produces the same effect as tractor services (see Table XII, p. 60).

More serious than the gross factor in affecting the growth rate is the valuation of the various activities not amendable to measurement. Valuation of the intermediate products in the process of production is difficult enough, but how is the subsidiary work of the farming household to be estimated and valued? It certainly "cannot be estimated with any degree of accuracy."[11] How much of the agricultural value product is subject to this kind of guesswork is not known. Table XI presents, among other things, the available data pertinent to the question.

---

[8] According to Liao Hsien-hao, *ibid.*, the gross agricultural value product at current prices is used for computation of national income.

[9] Yueh Wei, "The Method of Computing National Income," *Ching-chi yen-chiu* (*Economic Research*), 3: 48–66, August, 1956.

[10] There has already been some serious discussion in Peiping of this double-counting problem. See Liao Hsien-hao, *op. cit.* The number of tractor stations increased from 11 in 1953 to 326 in 1956 with 9,862 tractors (in terms of 15 horsepower each). The area operated had also rapidly increased from 80,000 ha. in 1954 to 1,915,000 ha. in 1956, which was about 1.2 per cent of the total national cropping area. For development of tractor stations, see Statistical Appendix, Table 27.

[11] Liao Hsien-hao, *ibid.*, p. 32.

TABLE XI

NATURE OF THE AGRICULTURAL YEAR AND THE GROSS AGRICULTURAL VALUE PRODUCT AT 1952 PRICES, 1952–1957, AND COMPOSITION OF VALUE PRODUCT, 1952–1956

Item	1952	1953	1954	1955	1956	1957 est.	1957 target
I. Nature of agricultural year	Good	Normal	Poor	Best	Poor	Poor	.....
II. Area damaged by natural calamities (in million ha.)	6.7	8.7	12.0	6.7	15.3	.....	.....
				(Base year 1952)			
III. Value product							
A. Gross agricultural product	100.0	103.2	106.6	114.8	120.5	126.4	123.3
B. Food grains (including soybeans)	100.0	.....	.....	.....	.....	123.7	119.8
C. Cotton	100.0	.....	.....	.....	.....	115.1	125.5
				(In per cent of total)			
IV. Gross agricultural product	100.0	100.0	100.0	100.0	100.0	100.0	100.0
A. Crop growing	79.5	78.6	78.8	78.7	68.2 }	.....	.....
B. Animal raising	}				11.0	.....	.....
C. Subsidiary work	20.5	21.4	21.2	21.3	20.8	.....	.....
1. For own household	15.7	16.6	16.3	15.9	.....	.....	.....
2. For others	4.8	4.8	4.9	5.4	.....	.....	.....

Sources: (1) Nature of the agricultural year: description after Po I-po, "Report on the Results of the 1956 Plan and on the Plan for 1957," *Jen-min jih-pao*, July 2, 1957. Description for 1957 is based on current information. (2) Area damaged for 1952, 1954, and 1955, from Liao Chi-ih, "Accelerating Agricultural Development: A Condition for Accelerating the Development of Heavy Industry," *Chi-hua ching-chi (Planned Economy)*, 8: 4–6, August, 1957. For 1953, my interpolation based on Liao's data for 1952 and 1954 and data given by Minister of Internal Affairs Hsieh Chueh-tsai in his report to the National Congress of People's Representatives, *Jen-min jih-pao*, September 28, 1954. For 1956, from Chou En-lai, "Report on the Work of the Government," *ibid.*, June 27, 1957. (3) For III.A and C, see Statistical Appendix, Table 17. (4) For III. B and C, State Planning Commission, "Results and Achievements of the First Five Year Plan," *Jen-min jih-pao*, October 1, 1957. No absolute data are available for them.

The table shows that, of the three components in the gross agricultural product, crop growing is the most important, to be followed by subsidiary work and animal raising. Representing as much as one-fifth of the gross product, subsidiary work consists chiefly of work for the own household, which is three times the work done for others. The element of pure guess in the estimation is obvious. The problem is fully realized by the Peiping statisticians, who have decided to separate the estimate for subsidiary work from the gross agricultural value product beginning with the Second Five Year Plan.[12]

Aside from subsidiary work, there are many items included in crop growing and animal raising that cannot be accurately estimated. Data certainly could be more adequately collected when farms are collectivized than when they are mostly privately owned. This is equally true of estimating the food and industrial crops, and farm animals. When the gross product was first calculated for 1952, data on the secondary products of crop growing (like straw and bran) and the products of animal raising (like milk, eggs, bristles) were lacking. Estimates were made "on the basis of data collected from a few areas regarding the output of secondary products per unit-weight of the major crops and the output of products per farm animal. When these averages were multiplied by the national total of the respective crops and animals, the required estimates were reached."[13] Thus if the total crops and animals should have been inadequately recorded by a small percentage, the effect on the gross value product would be magnified. Furthermore, what could have been the method of, say, estimating the "other crops" and the "intermediate products"? The inadequacy of statistical coverage for agriculture as a whole during the early years of the First Five Year Plan is clear.

As socialization of farming progressed, the number of reporting units increased, and statistical coverage widened. One fact shown in Table XI is worth attention. The three years from 1952 through 1954 were successively good, normal, and poor agricultural years, and the annual increase in the gross value product was 3.2 per cent in 1953 and 3.3 per cent in 1954. The following three years also began with a bumper crop, followed by two poor crops, yet

---

[12] Hsieh Mu-ch'iao (director of the State Statistical Bureau), "Our Experience in Statistical Work during the First Five Year Plan Period and Our Future Tasks," *T'ung-chi kung-tso (Statistical Work)*, 21: 1–21, November, 1957.

[13] Yueh Wei, "On the Methods of Estimation and Interpolation," *T'ung-chi kung-tso t'ung-hsin (Statistical Bulletin)*, 18: 25–27, September, 1956; quotation on pp. 25–26.

TABLE XII

Some Indicators of Agricultural Development, 1952–1957

Indicator	Units	1952	1953	1954	1955	1956	1957 est.	1957 target
A. Cultivated area	Million ha.	107.9	108.5	109.4	110.1	111.9	113.2	110.5
1. Irrigated area[a]	Million ha.	23.4	24.0	24.8	26.1	32.8	34.5	...
B. Cropping area	Million ha.	141.3	144.0	147.9	151.1	159.3	160.0	151.6
1. Multiple cropping index	Per cent	130.0	132.7	135.2	137.2	142.3	141.3	137.2
2. Food grains	Million ha.	112.3	114.3	116.3	118.4	124.0	123.3	115.0
a. Rice	Million ha.	28.4	28.3	28.7	29.2	33.3	...	29.6
3. Cotton	Million ha.	5.6	5.2	5.5	5.8	6.3	5.8	6.3
C. Production:								
1. Food grains[b]	Million tons	154.4	156.9	160.4	174.8	182.5	191.0	181.6
a. Rice	Million tons	68.4	71.3	70.9	78.0	82.5	...	81.8
2. Soybeans	Million tons	9.5	9.9	9.1	9.1	10.3	...	11.2
3. Rapeseed	Million tons	0.9	0.9	0.9	1.0	0.9	...	...
4. Cotton	Million tons	1.3	1.2	1.1	1.5	1.4	1.5	1.6
D. Yield per hectare:[c]								
1. Food grains[b]	Kg.	1,375	1,373	1,379	1,477	1,472	1,549	1,579
a. Rice	Kg.	2,411	2,516	2,467	2,675	2,474	...	2,762
2. Soybeans	Kg.	815	803	718	797	...	...	885
3. Rapeseed	Kg.	500	527	515	414	...	...	...
4. Cotton	Kg.	234	227	195	263	231	259	276
E. Pigs	Million head	89.8	96.1	101.7	87.9	84.4	110.0	138.3
F. Afforested area: annual increase	Million ha.	...	1.1	1.2	1.7	3.3	3.0	6.3
G. Chemical fertilizers used	Thousand tons	295	555	808	1,175	1,620	1,650	5,156
H. Insecticides used	Thousand tons	1.7	15.3	41.3	67.4	160.0	...	139.0

a Cultivated area is divided into uplands and lowlands. An overwhelming part of the lowlands and about 7 per cent of the upland fields are irrigated. For details, see Statistical Appendix, Table 20.

b Food grains consist of rice, wheat, coarse grains, and potatoes; they do not include soybeans. Four kg. of potatoes is equivalent to one kg. of grain.

c Yield per hectare is the harvesting yield per hectare of cropping area. If the cropping area is damaged after planting but before harvesting, the unit-area yield as defined would be less than the harvesting yield per hectare of harvested area.

Sources: (1) For A, see Statistical Appendix, Table 20. (2) For A.1, Government of India, Ministry of Food and Agriculture, Report of the Indian Delegation to China on Agricultural Planning and Techniques, New Delhi, July–August, 1956, p. 92; Chen Cheng-jen, "The Problems of Agricultural Coöperation and Production," Jen-min jih-pao, March 15, 1957; and Lo Wen and Shang-kuan Chang-chun, "The Problem of Irrigation of Agricultural Fields," Chi-hua ching-chi (Planned Economy), 10: 15–17, October, 1957. The 1957 figure refers to the actual situation at the end of August. By the end of the Second Five Year Plan, the irrigated area is expected to increase to 46.7 million hectares. (3) For B, B.2, B.2.a, and B.3, see Statistical Appendix, Table 20. B.1 is obtained by dividing B by A. (4) For the whole of C, see Statistical Appendix, Table 21. (5) For the whole of D, see Statistical Appendix, Table 22. (6) For E, see Statistical Appendix, Table 23. (7) For F, Minister of Forestry Liang Hsi's report, in Jen-min jih-pao, September 25, 1954: State Statistical Bureau's annual communiqués on the results of the 1954, 1955 and 1956 plans in Jen-min jih-pao, September 23, 1955, June 15, 1956, and August 2, 1957; and Po I-po, "Report on the Results of the 1956 Plan and on the Plan for 1957," Jen-min jih-pao, July 2, 1957. (8) For G and H, see editorial section, "State Economic Support of the Agricultural Economy," Jen-min jih-pao, September 14, 1957; and editorial section, "Industrial Development Requires Simultaneous Development of Agriculture," Chi-hua ching-chi (Planned Economy), 10: 1–2, October, 1957.

the annual increase in the gross product was 5 per cent each in 1956 and 1957, precisely the years when collectivization of agriculture was achieved. Even if collectivization is conducive to increase in unit-area productivity, it requires time to take effect. Moreover, the fact that the transformation was not made smoothly is testified by the discontent expressed during the "free criticism" period in 1957.[14] If the data for 1956 and 1957 are not manipulated, a part of the increase must have been statistical rather than real.

In summary, the gross agricultural value product includes a large conjectural element that accounts for at least one-fifth of the product. This element grows larger for each year back to 1952. On the other hand, the broadening of statistical coverage as a result of collectivization in 1956 and 1957 has raised the product considerably.[15] For these two years, the gross factor, because of the development of tractor stations and use of chemical fertilizers and insecticides, has also contributed to the same effect. It may well be called into question whether the gross agricultural value product for the different years is homogeneous enough to constitute a statistical series in the proper sense of the term. In any case, the agricultural growth during the five-year period must have been far less than the average annual rate of increase of 4.8 per cent calculated from the official series.

2. AGRICULTURAL DEVELOPMENT IN PHYSICAL TERMS

Physical Data.—If the value data are so unsatisfactory, are the physical data any better for the purpose of evaluating the agricultural performance? Table XII presents the pertinent statistics. It shows, among other things, that the average annual rate of increase is 4.3 per cent for food grains and 2.9 per cent for cotton.[16] How reliable are such rates calculated from the physical series?

Obviously, apart from those items that have to be recorded in monetary terms, physical data furnish the basic materials for valuation. The accuracy of the gross value product is largely determined by the reliability of the physical data. How are they collected? The case of crop data provides a point of departure for discussion. Crop production is defined as the harvested amount within a year, recorded by its gross weight (that is, unhusked). Food crops are also

---

[14] The immediate effects of collectivization will be discussed in the next section.

[15] This will be examined further in the next section.

[16] In value terms at 1952 prices, the growth rates are the same, despite the fact that the gross value product of food grains includes soybeans. See Table XI, III—B and C.

added together to give the total production of food grains, in which potatoes are converted into a grain equivalent by a four-to-one weight ratio. The harvest of each crop is arrived at by multiplying the estimated harvested area by an estimated harvest per unit-area.[17] The source data for these estimates "are derived from the periodical reports of state-operated farms and agricultural producers' cooperatives, plus certain sample surveys."[18]

It may be observed, first, that because of the inevitable losses from moving the harvest to the barn, the barn crop may be less than the field harvest by as much as 10 per cent, as in Soviet agriculture.[19] Recording on the basis of harvest exaggerates the actual amount available for disposal; but this would not affect the growth rate so long as the percentage of loss remains stable each year, a proposition for which no information has been forthcoming. It is not certain, for example, whether socialization of agriculture, while making farming operations amenable to control by party workers, might not have stirred up resentment among the peasants with a higher percentage of loss as a result.

Secondly, the state-operated farms, totaling a little more than 2,000 in number and located all around the country, are much better equipped than peasant farms and agricultural coöperatives, even though the state farms operate mostly on newly reclaimed land.[20] How representative their unit-area productivity is for the country has not been made known.

Thirdly, sample surveys, when scientifically designed and properly conducted, could be expected to yield fairly accurate results. But apparently the sampling method, however conceived, has not been used in any significant way. We have at least the testimony of the Indian Food and Agricultural Delegation which spent three weeks in China in the summer of 1956 investigating agricultural planning and techniques. The delegation observes in its report, "the system of collection of agricultural statistics in China is com-

[17] Kung Chien-yao, "The Method of Computing the Harvest Rate," *T'ung-chi kung-tso t'ung-hsin (Statistical Bulletin)*, 6: 16–18, March, 1956.
[18] Huang Meng-fan, *op. cit.;* quotation on p. 31.
[19] N. Jasny, *The Socialized Agriculture of the U.S.S.R.*, Palo Alto, 1949, pp. 725–746.
[20] On the whole, they are still losing money for the state. See editorial, *Jen-min jih-pao*, March 11, 1957. Among them the number of mechanized farms (with tractors and harvesting combines) had increased from 50 in 1952 to 166. They are much more productive than the others. Presumably it is not the productivity of mechanized farms that affords a basis for estimating the area productivity for the country as a whole. For details on state-operated farms, see Statistical Appendix, Tables 25 and 26.

plete enumeration rather than sample survey."[21] Complete enumeration in connection with peasant farms is done much the same way as before 1949. "A trustworthy member of the village," states the Indian report, "is usually entrusted with the collection of relevant area and yield statistics. This person, however, does not undertake any field inspection as is done by the *patwari* in India. Because he lives in the village, many facts are supposed to come automatically to his knowledge and, if necessary, he also questions a few of the peasants concerned. And it is on the basis of this general observation that he supplies estimates of area and yield to the county statistical authority. There is thus no regular system of village maps and records or regular crop inspection, not to speak of crop cutting sample surveys, as is the practice in India."[22]

As the sampling method is not used, the accuracy of China's agricultural statistics must depend on the number of agricultural producer coöperatives making regular reports and on the quality of these reports. The number of farming households joining coöperatives grew from 57,000 in 1952 to nearly 17 million in 1955, and to 110 million in 1956.[23] Thus, during the five-year period under study, agricultural statistics have greatly broadened the coverage, presumably rendering the data for the later years more accurate and reliable than those for the earlier years. But the quality of these reports is another matter. Accountants in the coöperatives or collectives are responsible for reporting agricultural statistics. Particularly during the national drive for collectivization in 1956 and 1957 when an increase in output was strongly stressed by the central authorities as the inevitable result, the reporting field agencies were bound to overstate the results. In fact, such practice was already so arresting in its effect from 1953 to 1955 that the Indian delegation found it advisable not to make any direct comparison between the Chinese and the Indian agricultural data.[24] Thus the

[21] Government of India, Ministry of Food and Agriculture, *Report of the Indian Delegation to China on Agricultural Planning and Techniques, July–August, 1956,* New Delhi, 1956, p. 84. (Cited hereafter as Indian Delegation's report.)

[22] *Ibid.,* pp. 85–86. The *patwari* in India is generally the accountant for the village organization known as the *panchayat.*

[23] The number refers to those farming households which have joined the coöperatives or collectives long enough to participate in the autumn harvest of the year. For details, see Statistical Appendix, Table 18.

[24] The following remarks by the Indian Delegation are interesting: "But the important point to find out is how far the yield per acre is improving year by year as a result of various measures undertaken in India and in China. Here, unfortunately, the statistics are not strictly comparable because while in India the figures of yield of foodgrains are at present largely based on crop cutting sample surveys subject to

data during the five-year period have been affected not only by the widening coverage—which is all to the good—but also by a strong upward "psychological bias."[25]

According to official release, the change in agricultural data seems to have come in three stages. The first came in September, 1954, when the bureau released the revised figures for 1952 over those published a year earlier and also the presumably firm figures for 1953.[26] The revisions, however, were of minor importance. Then came the publication of the First Five Year Plan in August, 1955, in which the 1952 figures were substantially different from the previously revised ones. For instance, the total cropping area was increased by 6.8 per cent and food grain production by 2.4 per cent.[27] With this new revision the 1952 figures would have been acceptable as the bases to measure the rate of growth, if an indication of a third revision had not appeared two months later when the bureau made public for the first time something like a statistical abstract.[28] There not only were food production and crop acreage revised upward for 1953 (5.2 per cent and 1.1 per cent), but the food crop area given for 1954 already exceeded the target set for 1957 in the First Five Year Plan by more than one million hectares (see Table XII). This last point is especially significant, because it means the five-year target was set against what was known then to be the 1952 base and at a level high enough not to be

---

no psychological bias, in China they are determined by subjective valuation which must be quite appreciably influenced by the psychological climate prevailing there" (Indian Delegation's report, pp. 87–88). The psychological climate referred to is described as follows: "When the peasants and members of the coöperative farms, local agricultural officials as also local party members are told that yield of crops must be increased from year to year and that their work will be judged by their record in this regard and when there is a natural enthusiasm in the whole countryside for increasing yields and also outdoing others, it will be only human if instead of understating the yield they tend to overstate it" (p. 87). The delegation makes three other observations on statistics: (1) "Chinese data after 1952 are not strictly comparable with earlier data" (p. 86); (2) the authorities are concerned with the accuracy of data, and "if there is any overstatement, it must be at the primary level itself and not at any other level" (p. 88); and (3) "There is little doubt that the bulk of the increase in acreage and output is due to the various measures undertaken by the Chinese Government and the people and is not at all merely statistical increase" (p. 86).

[25] As for livestock, annual surveys are taken at the middle of the year. The method of survey "varies according to different economic types"—that is, according to whether the enterprise is state-operated, joint, coöperatively operated, collectively owned, or private. See Huang Meng-fan, *op. cit.*, p. 32. Thus, the observations on output and yield statistics are with equal force applicable to livestock data.

[26] State Statistical Bureau's communiqués on the fulfillment of the 1952 (revised) and 1953 plans, *Jen-min jih-pao*, September 28 and 15, 1954.

[27] It should be repeated that food grains do not include soybeans.

[28] *Hsin-hua yueh-pao*, 11: 181–189, November 1955.

reached until two or three years later. It turned out that the basis of the target—that is, the 1952 level—was too low. But since the 1952 data had already been published in the First Five Year Plan and any later change in such important figures would have thrown doubt on the validity of the statistics used in the entire document, they must have been left unrevised as they were given in the Plan. It is highly probable that the apparent increases over 1952 in production and acreage since 1954 are, at least in part, the result of statistical improvements.[29]

Thus the conclusion reached from analyzing the physical data reinforces the observations on the value product. It is no surprise that speaking as late as October, 1957, the director of the State Statistical Bureau admitted, "the survey of the quantity of agricultural output remains a very weak link in our statistical work."[30] If the quantity data on output are weak, those on other items included in agriculture must be weaker. If agricultural statistics remain unsatisfactory at the end of 1957, they must have been all the more so for each year back to 1952.[31]

Should the data for 1952 be properly revised, the rate of increase over the period under review for food grains—or, for that matter, the gross agricultural value product—would be reduced. However, it is impossible to propose any adjustment to the data without making drastic assumptions. One may take the 1956 figures as the best that Peiping could produce up to this time and work back to 1952 with certain assumptions of varying annual increases in accordance with the nature of each crop year. But this will result in abandoning altogether the available statistics for the early years. Hence, no attempt is made to adjust them in this study, although, as in industry, the question of the rate of increase in agricultural production during this five-year period remains open.

Agricultural Development Program.—What has been said should not be construed to mean that no development has taken

---

[29] Chong Twanmo has attempted to readjust the food production data of the 1930's to make them comparable to those of the 1950's. See his *Production of Food Crops in Mainland China: Prewar and Postwar*, Santa Monica, Calif., March, 1956, 79 pp. (mimeographed). In this preliminary study, the author is more concerned with adjusting the prewar data than with the inherent statistical difficulties in the postwar data.

[30] Hsieh Mu-ch'iao, *op. cit.*, p. 16.

[31] In October, 1957, a national conference on agricultural statistics convened in Peiping. One of the items on the agenda was "the adjustment of agricultural statistical materials for all the years." "A Brief Bulletin on the National Agricultural Statistical Work Conference," *T'ung-chi kung-tso (Statistical Work)*, 21: 21 and 23, November, 1957; quotation on p. 23.

place in agriculture. The development program may be simply summarized as consisting of expansion of cultivated area through reclamation, increase in cropping area through irrigation, and improvement in the unit-area yield by such various means as extension of irrigation, application of fertilizers, planting of high-yield crops, introduction of new implements, adoption of new technique in cultivation, soil improvement and conservation, and pest control.[32]

As the investment program under the First Five Year Plan has demonstrated, the state's direct participation in this development work is limited. Even in reclamation the state has played a very small role. The state-operated farms and ranches were responsible for less than 20 per cent of the increase of five million hectares of arable land for cultivation during the five-year period. The total increase averaged less than 1 per cent per year of the existing acreage.[33] Reclamation was found too slow and too expensive to meet the needs of the country, the amount of cultivated land per capita of the farming population having already declined 3.4 per cent from a little more than one-half of an acre in 1952 to about one-half of an acre in 1956.[34]

The development program, therefore, has centered on an increase in cropping area and in unit-area yield. According to official statistics, the multiple cropping index had increased from 130 in 1952 to 142 in 1956, and 141 (estimated) in 1957; as a matter of fact the five-year target was reached the very year when the Plan was published. What made this possible was the expansion of irrigated area by 11.5 per cent from 1952 to 1955 and 32 per cent from 1955 to 1957. For the five-year period, it amounts to a total increase of 11 million hectares, of which small irrigation projects undertaken by peasants accounted for 90.8 per cent, while large and

---

[32] Mao Tse-tung, "Draft Outline of Agricultural Development from 1956 to 1957," *Jen-min jih-pao*, January 26, 1956; Teng Tzu-hui's report at the National Conference of Model Agricultural Workers, *ibid.*, February 22, 1957; Chen Cheng-jen, "The Problem of Agricultural Coöperation and Production," *Hsin-hua pan-yueh-k'an*, 7: 22–26, April, 1957.

[33] Since we do not know how much of this increase is purely statistical, the figures should not be taken at their face value. This must always be kept in mind when official data are used for comparing 1952 with later years. The present discussion of the agricultural program is based on data presented in Table XII, plus the relevant tables in the Statistical Appendix.

[34] Sung Shao-wen, "The Principle of Diligence and Economy in Economic Construction," *Hsueh-hsi (Study)*, 11: 22–24, June, 1957. An editorial in *Jen-min jih-pao*, July 24, 1957, says that to reclaim one million hectares of land costs 1,500 million yuan. This includes expenditures for road building, housing, etc. (One hectare is equivalent to 2.45 acres.)

medium-sized projects undertaken by the state accounted for only
1.4 and 7.8 per cent.[35] Twenty-one large irrigation projects have
been initiated during the five years, each requiring two to four
years for completion; by the end of 1957 only a few had been completed—with poor results.[36] The peasants themselves had to pay
for 83 per cent of the cost of the small irrigation projects. For an
increase of every hectare of irrigated area by their effort, the state
gave them a subsidy of a little more than 10 yuan together with a
loan of about 50 yuan.[37]

The state's direct participation in the improvement of yield is
equally modest. The establishment of tractor stations, technique
popularization centers, and agricultural schools or institutes, and
the use of state-operated farms as experimental stations represent
its investment in this field.[38] Other related investment includes
afforestation and a network of veterinary and meteorological stations.[39] Improved farm implements (like double-wheeled ploughs)
and chemical fertilizers are sold to the peasants or collectives
through the "supply and selling coöperatives" mostly on agricultural credit.[40] But through the party workers, the state has spared
no effort in organizing emulative drives from time to time and in
urging peasants to plant high-yielding crops, especially rice. The
increase of 8 per cent in rice acreage from 1955 to 1956 indicates
the help given by collectivization to the expected shift in cultivation.[41]

[35] The large and medium-sized projects undertaken by the state correspond to the
"large and small basic construction projects" defined in chapter i, section 2.

[36] Lo Wen and Shang-kuan Chang-chun, "The Problem of Irrigation of Agricultural
Fields," *Chi-hua ching-chi (Planned Economy)*, 10: 15–17, October, 1957. "For those
few projects that have been completed," the authors observe, "they will not within
a short time, or can never, produce expected results, either because the area to be
irrigated is too large and the network of trenches too complicated, or because the
planning has been faulty" (p. 16). In Tsinghai Province, one project can only benefit
447,000 ha. instead of 933,000 ha. as planned. Another one in Hupei Province falls
short in irrigated acreage by 40 per cent.

[37] In contrast, an increase of a hectare of irrigated area by construction of "large
projects" requires a state investment of 480 yuan, which are reduced to 255 yuan if
the project is of medium size. Moreover, it takes only a year to complete a project of
medium size, and one season or less for small projects. See Lo and Shang-kuan, *ibid.*

[38] The Indian Delegation's report (pp. 141–146) gives a detailed account of the
operation of the technique-popularization stations, which had increased from 3,500 in
1954 to 10,000 by the summer of 1956 and, according to plan, would be 16,000 in 1957.

[39] In 1956 there were 1,377 meteorological stations. See State Statistical Bureau,
"Communiqué on the Results of the 1956 Plan," *Jen-min jih-pao*, August 2, 1957.
The number of veterinary stations is not known.

[40] This, of course, is not investment by the state. For discussion, see chapter v.

[41] Before collectivization, the state relied heavily on the government-purchase price
differential between food grains and cotton to make the desired shift.

Nevertheless, all such strenuous effort made to improve the yield
has not been able to produce the results expected by the First Five
Year Plan. The yield of major crops has not reached the target.
This is certainly true of food grains as a whole and cotton, and
probably of soybeans. The worst performance is found in the
yield of rapeseed (a major source of edible oil), which had declined
steadily since 1953 to far below the 1952 level in 1955, the very
year of record harvest. Edible oil has remained a commodity of
severely short supply. It seems that the land suitable for rice cultivation—and this is invariably the best land in any area—has been
increasingly used for it at the expense of such other important
crops as cotton and soybeans. And, until somewhat corrected in
1957, the pricing policy for government purchases discouraged the
planting of oil-bearing crops. Clearly, it is the drive for high-yielding food grains (rice, potatoes, and corn) that has become the paramount goal of the agricultural program.

Effects of Collectivization.—Producer coöperation has also been
stressed as an effective means to augment the unit-area yield and
therefore the total agricultural output.[42] Collectivization in 1956
and 1957 would have been a good test case, except for the fact that
the time is too early for an evaluation, and the two years happened
to be poor crop years following a good harvest in 1955. But certain
immediate effects may be noted. The consolidation of minute and
fragmented peasant holdings into collectives, thus eliminating the
waste in land utilization (like the numerous small paths necessary
under fragmentation), must have accounted for a large part of the
unusually large increase in cultivated area in those two years. According to the instruction issued by the Chinese Communist party
in 1957, a collective is to be composed generally of an entire village
with 100 farming households or more, in which every 20 households form a production team.[43] Thus the average size of an operating farm is about 50 acres, as compared to about two and a half
acres before, and the farm area is contiguous instead of being
parcelled out into numerous fragmented lots.[44]

---

[42] According to Hua Shu, a survey of the major producing areas in 1955 establishes
that producer coöperatives showed an increase of 10 per cent more rice per unit area,
7 per cent more wheat, 19 per cent more soybeans, and 26 per cent more cotton,
than the individual farmers. It will be recalled that "producer coöperation" includes
both producer coöperatives and collectives. See his "Has Agricultural Development
in China Been Rapid or Slow?" *Jen-min jih-pao,* January 8–9, 1957.

[43] See instruction issued by the Central Committee concerning management of production in collectives, *Jen-min jih-pao,* September 16, 1957.

[44] Consolidation of holdings has also been a feature in the agricultural program in
India.

But the success of collectivization lies primarily in the attitude of the peasants. Fully realizing the importance of this factor, the state poured three times as much agricultural credit into the countryside in 1956 as in 1955, as a means of insuring in increase in farm production and in the money income of the households.[45] The amount of investment by the state in agriculture, forestry, and water conservation also doubled from 600 million yuan in 1955 to 1,160 million in 1956 (see Table X). All this, however, did not prevent the decline in the relative importance of subsidiary work in the gross agricultural value product, as Table XI has shown. This decline is all the more significant, because in a poor crop year like 1956, subsidiary work, which usually accounts for about 30 per cent of the income of a farming household, should rise in relative importance as it did in 1953 and 1954.[46]

Another immediate effect of collectivization that may be taken as a manifestation of peasant sentiment is the failure of livestock to meet the goals of the 1956 plan (see Table XIII). Pigs, which are an important source of subsidiary income for the peasant household and at the same time the major source of fertilizers on the farm, had in fact started to decline precipitously from 1954 (Table XII), when the government-purchase quota for food grains left little feed for them.[47] The decline in water buffaloes, though slight, was significant because they are the most important draft animal on the farm. The reasons for this unfavorable turn in 1956, in the order given by the State Statistical Bureau, were (1) the refusal on the part of the collectives to accept old, weak and suckling animals and oxen and mules. (2) lack of experience on the part of collectives to raise animals coöperatively, (3) no time allowed by the collective to its members for attending to subsidiary work, (4) no allowance for animal feed in the distribution of food grains to the members, (5) high government-purchase quota for food grains, leaving little feed for young animals, (6) low government-purchase

[45] The amount of agricultural credit outstanding at the end of the year was 1,000 million yuan in 1955, but 3,030 million in 1956 and 3,300 million in 1957. The average amount outstanding from 1952 through 1954 was 600 million. For sources and further discussion, see chapter v. The State Statistical Bureau (as cited in n. 39), has reported that 75 per cent of the farming households had an increase in "income" in 1956. For discussion of peasant income, see chapter viii.

[46] Although valuation of subsidiary work is subject to a wide margin of error, its relative importance in the gross product certainly reflects the judgment of the State Statistical Bureau in the light of the real situation.

[47] For government-purchase quota, see chapter i, section 4.

prices for live animals, pigs in particular, and (7) widespread animal diseases.[48]

But more alarming than the decline in numbers is the changing
age structure among the draft animals. In 1956, one-third of them
were more than 15 years of age and one-half more than 10. Writing
in late 1957, an author observed, "The decline in the physical
power of draft animals is a rather common phenomenon all over
the country."[49] The rate of reproduction has also dropped. Among
the large farm animals in 1956, the sucklings constituted only 11.8
per cent of the total population, and owing to diseases 75 per cent
of the pregnant miscarried.[50] Such a result, of course, should not be

TABLE XIII
FARM ANIMALS AND COLLECTIVIZATION, 1956

Animal	1956 actual number in per cent of planned	1956 actual in per cent of 1955 actual
1. Pigs	65.0	96.0
2. Mules	88.2	99.2
3. Asses	88.6	95.1
4. Sheep	90.6	106.5
5. Horses	93.4	101.4
6. Buffaloes	94.1	99.4
7. Oxen	94.2	101.6
8. Goats	95.6	113.6
9. Camels[a]	105.6	104.8

[a] Camels strictly speaking are not farm animals.
Sources: "A National Survey of Animals for 1956," *Hsin-hua pan-
yueh-k'an,* 1: 88–90, January, 1957. For details, see Statistical Appendix,
Table 23. Animal censuses are those of July 1, 1955 and 1956.

entirely attributed to collectivization, but rather to the whole agricultural development since 1952. But, as indicated by the reasons
officially given, collectivization has aggravated the trend.

The events transpiring in the first two years of collectivization
must have been serious enough for the authorities to undertake an
extensive revision of the outline of the agricultural development
program from 1956 to 1967, originally put forth by Mao Tse-tung
himself in January, 1956.[51] Significantly, the revision, framed in

[48] "A National Survey..." On March 1, 1957, the government-purchase price for
live pigs was raised 14 per cent. *Jen-min jih-pao,* April 30, 1957.

[49] Hsiao Yu, "Proper Allocation of Agricultural Investment," *Chi-hua ching-chi*
(Planned Economy), 9: 5–8, September, 1957; quotation on p. 7. For draft animals,
those over 15 years of age are regarded as too old for farmwork.

[50] *Ibid.,* p. 7.

[51] Mao, *op. cit.*

more cautious language than the original, scales down many important goals.[52] For example, the arable land to be reclaimed by the state-operated farms during the twelve years will be six million instead of eight million hectares.[53] The expansion of cropping area for rice cultivation for the period is reduced from 21 million hectares to 16.7 million. By 1967, the yield of cotton per hectare is expected to be from 300 to 750 kg. instead of from 450 to 750 kg. The original draft urges each collective to keep one to two years' reserve of food grains (after meeting the government-purchase quota and taxes), but the revision calls for a reserve of three, six, nine, twelve, and eighteen months. In short, all changes signify that agricultural development will henceforth be more difficult than was thought at the beginning of collectivization.[54]

3. CONCLUDING OBSERVATIONS

For technical reasons we have rejected as too high both the annual over-all agricultural growth rate of 4.8 per cent calculated from the gross value product and the annual growth rate of 4.3 per cent for the physical output of food grains. The picture of agricultural development emerging from the foregoing discussion shows a desperate drive to increase the output of food grains, especially rice. All suitable land is used for them, and their meeting the targets of the Plan is made possible only by the arrested development of cotton and the probable failure of virtually all other industrial crops to reach their goals. Land resources are simply too scarce to permit agricultural advance on all fronts—a goal made all the more difficult to attain because of the lack of substantial investment. The high opportunity cost entailed in the food drive has further manifested itself in the fact that the productive capacity in the cotton textile industry is much larger than the domestic supply of raw cotton, a certain amount of which has to be imported in lieu of capital equipment.

At the same time, despite the increase in food production, farm animals—the other important branch of agriculture—have had to compete with the general population for food, resulting inevitably in their deterioration. Population is generally estimated to

---

[52] Chinese Communist Party, Central Committee, "Revised Draft Outline of Agricultural Development from 1956 to 1967," *Jen-min jih-pao*, October 26, 1957.

[53] It will be recalled that according to official data the increase in cultivated land during the First Five Year Period was 5.3 million hectares.

[54] Some other important changes in the revised draft will be discussed in the concluding part of this volume.

have been increasing at the rate of between 2 and 2.5 per cent per year, and the rate itself has been on the increase as well.[55] If the output of food grains had been growing at the rate of 4.3 per cent, there would have been no need to sacrifice the farm animals. That the rate of 4.3 per cent is too high is beyond question. Could it have been lower than the natural growth rate of population? That is not probable, because otherwise mass starvation would have resulted, which does not seem to have been the case.

TABLE XIV

EXPORTS AND CONSUMPTION OF FOOD GRAINS AND SOYBEANS, 1953–1957
(In terms of clean weight)

Item	1953–54	1954–55	1955–56	1956–57
1. Exports of grains and soybeans in per cent of production...................	1.1	1.4	1.4	1.4
2. Per cent of soybeans in exports of grains and soybeans...................	56.1	56.2	51.8	55.8
3. Per-capita consumption of grains and soybeans (in kg. per year).............	227.0	234.3	244.7	262.3
a. Urban..........................	284.8	279.1	278.4	282.4
b. Rural..........................	218.2	227.3	239.4	258.9

Notes: (a) Clean weight, in contrast to gross weight, is that of the food grains and soybeans already husked. (b) The food year begins on July 1.
Source: State Statistical Bureau, "The Basic Situation of Planned Purchase and Planned Supply of Food Grains in China," *T'ung-chi kung-tso* (*Statistical Work*), 19: 31–32 and 28, October, 1957. Food grains are not differentiated from soybeans in the absolute data.

Two possibilities are left: the growth rate of food grains has been either somewhat higher than the population increase or about the same. The former possibility seems plausible, because industrialization, exports, and the state's policy of keeping food reserves would require an increase in food output at a rate higher than that of the population increase.[56] Exports and consumption of food grains and soybeans are presented in Table XIV.

The proportion of soybeans in the figure for total export shows that the export of food grains alone fluctuated widely from year to year, rising, for example, steeply in 1955–56 after the record harvest. The continuous increase in per-capita consumption of food grains and soybeans was made possible by an increase in

[55] See discussion in chapter viii.

[56] Had the export of food grains maintained a constant percentage relation to output throughout the whole period, the annual rate of increase in food grain production could be the same as that of population increase without reducing per-capita consumption. The same would be true for food reserves, for which, unfortunately, no data are available.

rural rather than urban consumption. In contrast to the expectation of many economists who maintain that per-capita consumption of food must increase among the urban population as an inevitable result of industrialization, the per-capita urban consumption had declined. The official explanation that this decline was due to an increase in consumption of such subsidiary food as green vegetables, eggs, and meat cannot be accepted as satisfactory, because the consumers' choice has been restricted by rationing since 1953 and consumption did recover some lost ground in 1956–57.[57] The increase in per-capita consumption in the rural areas may be attributed to several reasons. The low government-purchase price might have induced a higher consumption in the peasant household than before. The major increase taking place in 1956–57 might well be due to collectivization, which had the effect, first, of raising the consumption of the hitherto poor peasants to the same level as the other members of the collective, and, second, more importantly, of completely eliminating the self-retained food in the peasant household so that per-capita consumption was much more accurately estimated than before. How much of the increase in per-capita rural consumption was real is difficult to determine.[58]

In view of the export requirements and the reduced per-capita urban consumption, and especially the rising rate of population growth, collectivization starting after the autumn harvest of 1955 may be interpreted as a move of vital importance to the state for it to obtain complete control of the entire food-grains output—a necessary sequel to the "planned purchase and supply" scheme instituted in the fall of 1953 for the purpose of getting the maximum of self-retained food from the peasant. Since rural consumption did increase a little, it seems reasonable to conclude that the average annual rate of increase in food production during the First Five Year Plan was very close to but perhaps somewhat higher than the natural rate of population increase.

Whatever the rate of increase for food grains, it must have been higher than the over-all agricultural growth rate. This conclusion follows because of the relative scarcity of land resources and the small capital investment in agriculture. If so, the growth of the agricultural value product at constant prices should be slower than that of the food-grains value product. But, according to official statistics (Table XI), the index (1952 base) of the agricultural value

---

[57] Soybeans are not important for daily consumption of the population.
[58] For further discussion see chapter viii, section 2.

product for 1957 is higher than the index for food grains (including soybeans). What could have accounted for this phenomenon? There is not enough information for a definite answer. It could not be those items that compete with food for land resources, nor could it be the animal-raising component. It must be either subsidiary work, tractor-station services, use of chemical fertilizers and insecticides, or the intermediate products of forest growth, or a combination of these. The last may be an important factor in view of the rapid development in afforestation. Thus, if those three items are omitted, the agricultural growth rate is likely to have been lower than the rate of increase in food grains.

IV

National Product: Structure and Growth, 1952-1957

1. THE CONCEPT OF NATIONAL INCOME

The First Five Year Plan makes no reference to the subject of national income. Only after the State Statistical Bureau had set up a national system of statistical reporting and investigation did an attempt to compute the national income begin in 1954. With the work on the accounts for 1952 through 1954 completed in early 1956, the bureau was in a position to bring them up-to-date by the middle of the year. The results have properly been regarded as preliminary, since they represent the country's first effort in this undertaking.[1]

The concept of national income adopted by the bureau is that of material product, net of depreciation, and the methodology falls generally into line with the Soviet practice.[2] The product for any one year is composed of the net contributions (values added) from industry, agriculture, construction, restaurants, freight transportation, and that part of trade and communications which serves the materially productive sectors. Omitted are not only passenger transportation, private use of communications, and pure service elements of trade, but also finance and insurance, public administration, army and internal security, education, public health, private housing, and all other professions that render services to the people. It follows from this definition, modified somewhat in actual application, as the discussion below will show, that the method used is what is generally known as the production approach instead of the income approach.

[1] This brief history is based on Yueh Wei, "The Method of Computing National Income," *Ching-chi yen-chiu (Economic Research)*, 3: 48–66, August, 1956.

[2] For an excellent summary of the Soviet practice and the criticism thereof, cf. M. C. Kaser, "Estimating the Soviet National Income," *Economic Journal*, lxvii: 83–104, March, 1957.

The net value of each materially productive sector is derived from its gross value product. It is essential, therefore, to find out how the gross and net value product of each sector is defined. The gross value products of industry and agriculture have been discussed in the two preceding chapters. There is no need to enumerate all the items to be deducted from the gross industrial value product in order to obtain the net product, for many of them are obvious enough. Some items, however, are worth mentioning. Depreciation concerns not only the fixed capital equipment used in production, but also such "nonproductive" assets as mess halls, workers' housing, and clubs. The net value product consists chiefly of wages, taxes and profits, insurance charges, and training expenses.[3] As to the net agricultural value product, it is the gross product net of "material consumption"—that is, the costs of seeds and sprouting grains, fertilizers, insecticide, animal feed, fuel and electric power, payments for transportation, communication expenses, and depreciation of farm implements and equipment and of draft animals and barns. Depreciation of peasant housing is not deducted.

Construction includes (1) the building of various structures (houses, factories, steel furnaces), highways, railroads, communication lines, and big dams; (2) drilling and dredging; (3) installation of equipment; (4) architectural services and geological surveys directly related to the project; and (5) extensive repairs.[4] But the building of roads, small dams, dikes, and the like "by means of mobilizing the masses" is not included, except perhaps the small amount of state subsidies given for the purpose.[5] In fact, the "construction" included in the national income account pertains almost

[3] Yueh Wei, *op. cit.*, p. 54. This article gives relatively the best account of the method used by the State Statistical Bureau. "Profits" include not only realized profits, but also those accrued to the increase in intermediate or unfinished products during the year.

[4] State Statistical Bureau, "The Basic Situation of China's Construction Enterprises," *T'ung-chi kung-tso t'ung-hsin (Statistical Bulletin)*, 24: 31–33, December, 1956; Peng Yung-ch'uan, "Tabulation Forms for Basic Construction Planning," *Chi-hua ching-chi (Planned Economy)*, 5: 29–33, May, 1957; Li Yung, "Tabulation Forms for the Planning of Construction and Installation," *ibid.*, 6: 28–31, June, 1957; and Yueh Wei, *op. cit.*

[5] State Economic Commission, "Major Changes in the Tabulation Forms for National Economic Planning for 1958," *Chi-hua ching-chi (Planned Economy)*, 8: 24–27, August, 1957; quotation on p. 25. The following reasons are given for the omission: (1) some of the work done is only for ordinary repair, (2) some is improvised without plan, and (3) most is done by mobilizing the people, which means that no single unit or person could be held responsible for the fulfillment of plan. Beginning in 1958, even the subsidies will be excluded.

entirely to the work done with state investment.[6] Its gross value product, while not including the value of machinery and equipment to have been installed, is made up of wages, costs of construction materials, the "user's costs" (in the Keynesian sense) and depreciation of construction equipment, transportation charges, and office expenses.[7] The value of all materials spent must be deducted, of course, in computing the net value, of which the chief component is wages.[8]

Probably resulting from the tight control of food in the urban areas since September, 1953, the restaurant business has been flourishing under the new regime. In contrast to the rapid decline of private trade from 1950 through 1955, privately owned restaurants had increased during the period by more than 10 per cent in number, employment, and capital and by more than 100 per cent in the volume of sales.[9] There were 183,600 privately owned restaurants employing 350,000 workers on the eve of the socialization drive which succeeded in transforming virtually all of them into state-private joint enterprises, coöperatives, or branches of the state-operated network.[10] The gross product is the value of sales, priced at retail, whereas the net value excludes materials used, fuel, electricity, ice, and depreciation of equipment.[11]

Freight transportation refers to all means of transportation, including carts and wheelbarrows pulled (or pushed) by men or animals. However, unorganized human carriers, so common a sight in the country, are not taken into consideration. The gross value product is "determined by the gross receipts of transportation enterprises from moving freight."[12] The net value is the gross product minus all material cost. Considering the large number of carts and wheelbarrows in the country, it is impossible to have an ac-

---

[6] Li Yung, *op. cit.* The author further indicates that "the construction work done by state security agencies themselves" is included.

[7] The gross value product of construction at 1952 prices had increased from 4,560 million yuan in 1952 to 14,400 million in 1956. See Yang Po, "An Understanding of the Proportion between Consumption and Accumulation in the Disposal of China's National Income," *Hsueh-hsi (Study),* 20: 24–26, October, 1957.

[8] Yueh Wei, *op. cit.,* p. 55.

[9] Yang Po, "A Preliminary Analysis of the Process of Socialist Transformation of Private Trade in China," *T'ung-chi kung-tso t'ung-hsin (Statistical Bulletin),* 15: 7–10, August, 1956.

[10] State Statistical Bureau, "Achievements in Socialist Construction and Socialist Transformation in the First Half of 1956," *T'ung-chi kung-tso t'ung-hsin (Statistical Bulletin),* 15: 5–6 and 26, August, 1956.

[11] Yueh Wei, *op. cit.,* p. 55.

[12] *Ibid.,* p. 53.

curate accounting of their value product unless they have become organized.[13] As in agriculture, statistical coverage grows with the development of socialization. It will also be noticed that passenger transportation is not included, because "it does not produce any material product."[14]

Trade includes government purchase and government supply on the one hand and wholesaling and retailing on the other.[15] Trade carried on outside the regular commercial channels (chiefly by peasants) is probably included, for statistics relating to it have been published.[16] But trading in used articles, for instance, serves no material sector and is excluded. The gross value product of trade is generally determined by the buying and selling price differential, from which the value added is obtained by deducting the material costs of doing business, such as loading and unloading, carting and carrying, spoilage, office expenses, and depreciation of fixed assets.[17] But those expenses not directly related to warehousing, packing and packaging, sorting, and breaking lots, are materially nonproductive, and are included neither in the gross product nor in the net product.[18]

Communication refers to post and telecommunications, both being government-owned enterprises. Its gross value product is equal to that part of gross revenue derived from serving the material sector. The value, for example, of personal mail service and of private and government use of telephones and telegraphs is not considered. Net value is arrived at in much the same way as for trade.[19]

According to the definition given earlier, these seven sectors constitute the entire source of the total material product. In this account, an important omission is found in the construction work done both by the peasants themselves and by mass mobilization. Proper valuation of it would doubtless raise the national product considerably. Moreover, as in the case of agriculture and handi-

[13] For data on the indigenous means of transportation, see Statistical Appendix, Table 12, explanatory note.

[14] "Is Passenger Traffic in Transportation Business a Part of the Material Product?" *Chi-hua ching-chi (Planned Economy)*, 6: 32, June, 1957. This is a questioin put to the editorial board of the journal, which is a joint publication of the State Economic Commission and State Planning Commission.

[15] For discussion of government purchase and supply, cf. chapter i, section 4.

[16] See Statistical Appendix, Table 13.

[17] Yueh Wei, *op. cit.*, p. 55.

[18] *Ibid.*, p. 52.

[19] *Ibid.*, p. 53. The development of post and telecommunications is given in the Statistical Appendix, Table 10.

crafts, socialization must have helped in widening the statistical coverage of transportation, trade, and restaurants.

Aside from the seven sectors discussed, it seems that another one has been added under the title of "a part of household labor."[20] Given without any explanation, it probably refers to hired domestic help in the urban households, although this is at variance with the material concept of national income. Since the beginning of the new regime, social prejudice had been very strong against any household (officials' households excepted) employment of domestic help, with the result that domestic servants rapidly declined in number. But beginning with 1957 the government authorities adopted a policy of encouraging service trades as a means of meeting the problem of unemployment.[21] Thus the revival of domestic help as a profession might have become significant enough to be considered by statisticians in the national income account.

The net products of the various material sectors are valued at current prices prevailing on the consumers' or users' level, except the net agricultural product which is valued, as may be recalled, at government-purchase prices in the place of production. For the sake of intertemporal comparability, the current-price valuation is then changed into valuation at 1952 prices according to the conversion factors designed by the State Statistical Bureau.

The total material product is net of depreciation of capital assets used in production. Data on depreciation are scarce, and this study does not propose to go into an estimation of the gross national product.[22] The material product is also net of "grossness" within the entire material sector. Although finance is not included in the material sector, interest charges and insurance premiums, not being deducted from the gross product, are a part of the net material product. So are the training expenses for workers. The nonmaterial sector does figure in the material product as far as the three items mentioned are concerned.

In sum, the net material product is composed of personal in-

---

[20] Ho Wei, "Discussion of the Economic Contradiction between the State and the Peasants," *Hsueh-hsi (Study)*, 12: 22–26, June, 1957; quotation on p. 23.

[21] For further discussion, see chapter viii, section 1.

[22] The discussion in the Chinese literature on depreciation has so far been in terms of principle. Clearly a straight-line method has been adopted. See Ch'ang Sun and Wang En-yung, "A Brief Discussion on the Fixed Assets of Industrial Enterprises and Their Depreciation," *Ching-chi yen-chiu (Economic Research)*, 5: 69–78, October, 1956; and Chang Wei-ta, "The Methods of Calculating the Depreciation Rate of Fixed Assets Employed in Production," *ibid.*, 3: 99–112, June, 1956. Depreciation schedules for industry are found in *Collection of Laws and Policy Statements ...*, II, 379–383.

come (chiefly wages), profits and taxes paid by enterprises in the material sector, and their payments in interest, insurance, and training.[23] No allowance is made at this stage for the balance in the international account, so that the national income (another name for the material product in Peiping usage) is actually what should be called the *net domestic material product.*

The net domestic material product, plus depreciation and the value of materials consumed by the material sector, becomes what is known as the *gross social value product.* It is, in fact, the sum total of the gross value products of the seven (or eight, if domestic help is included) components of the material sector discussed above.

From the standpoint of final disposal, the domestic product has to be adjusted in accordance with "the balance between international receipts and outpayments in order to arrive at the amount available for actual domestic use."[24] This *net national material product,* as it may be called, is then divided into "accumulation" and "consumption."[25] Accumulation is the part used for increasing fixed capital assets (productive and unproductive) in the entire economy, working capital (raw materials and intermediate goods) of the material sector, and commercial inventories and stockpiles of the state.[26] Consumption includes not only personal consumption and depreciation of private housing, but also the consumption of government agencies, armed forces, and all other nonproductive enterprises in the form of materials used, small repairs and depreciation of their fixed assets.[27] Thus per-capita consumption calculated from the national income account is different from what it is generally conceived to be.

Involved as the concept of national income is, this brief summary account will suffice for the purpose at hand, which is to obtain a picture of the macroeconomic changes during the period of the First Five Year Plan.

[23] Taxes paid by transportation enterprises regarding passenger traffic, by non-material sectors, and by the general population are not included.

[24] Yueh Wei, *op. cit.,* p. 64. Although it is not clear whether the reference is to the current account alone or to both the current and capital accounts in the international balance, the last few words "the amount available for actual domestic use" seem to imply that the entire international account is taken into consideration.

[25] Presumably this division is exhaustive. But according to Yueh Wei's tabulation (*op. cit.,* p. 60), a part of the net national material product may be used for "making up losses," a phrase not explained in his discussion. Perhaps this refers to losses which occurred after production during the course of the year.

[26] See chapter v.

[27] Yueh Wei, *op. cit.,* pp. 61–64.

2. SOME GLOBAL CALCULATIONS

How has China's national income account changed during the five-year period? The first and up to the present the only comprehensive report on the results of the computation was given by the chairman of the State Economic Commission in September, 1956.[28] It reveals that on the basis of the planned production for 1956 the domestic product at 1952 prices had increased 43.8 per cent, with an average annual increase of 9.5 per cent and that the amount of accumulation, growing at a rate of 19.9 per cent a year, rose from the equivalent of 15.7 per cent of the domestic product in 1952 to 22.8 per cent in 1956. No global totals were given, not to mention the breakdowns. However, the domestic product was said to bear certain percentage relationships with the state budgetary receipts. The details are presented in Table XV, Part I.

At that time, the realized budgetary data for the years before 1954 had not been made known, the available figures being "expected results."[29] Moreover, the budgetary receipt which bears the definite relationship to national income is not defined in the official statement as to whether it is the current receipt, or current receipt plus preceding years' surplus, or some other construction.

Nevertheless, using available data on current budgetary receipts, the Secretariat of the Economic Commission of Asia and the Far East has made a calculation in accordance with the percentage relationships officially given. The result is presented in Table XV, Part II. The Secretariat omits the figure for 1952, apparently because with it the series would give an increase higher than officially claimed. The missing number is here supplied by using approximately the same type of budgetary data that the Secretariat employs. Apart from overstating the increase, the calculated series gives a larger domestic product for each year than the official computation. According to information made available in the early part of 1957, the product for 1954 is 78,000 million yuan instead of 81,700 million as calculated by the Secretariat.[30]

What could have accounted for the discrepancy, especially as

---

[28] Po I-po, "The Correct Disposition of the Relationship between Accumulation and Consumption," *Jen-min jih-pao*, September 20, 1956. Originally delivered as a speech, it has been officially translated as "How Much to Invest, How Much to Consume," *People's China*, November 1, 1956.

[29] See chapter vi, section 1.

[30] Wu Ching-ch'ao, "A New Approach to the Chinese Population Problem," *Hsin Chien-she (New Construction)*, 102: 1–9. March, 1957. The statement made in the text implies no criticism of the Secretariat, for the information was not available at the time of its calculation.

TABLE XV

SOME GLOBAL CALCULATIONS, BASED ON OFFICIAL DATA OF SEPTEMBER, 1956, OF THE DOMESTIC MATERIAL PRODUCT AT 1952 PRICES, 1952–1956

Item	1952	1953	1954	1955	1956 est.
I. Official Data:					
A. Budgetary receipt as per cent of national income	27.6	29.2	32.4	31.9	31.5
B. National income: index	100.0	......	......	......	143.8
1. Accumulation					
a. In per cent of national income	15.7	18.3	21.6	20.5	22.8
b. Index	100.0	......	......	......	206.5
2. Consumption					
a. In per cent of national income	84.3	81.7	78.4	79.5	77.2
b. Index	100.0	......	......	......	129.7
II. ECAFE Calculation:					
A. Domestic product (million yuan)	[63,600]	74,300	81,700	85,700	94,500
B. Index	100.0	116.8	128.5	134.8	148.6
III. Alternative calculation:					
A. Domestic product (million yuan)	61,740	73,000	78,250	80,080	93,930
B. Index	100.0	118.2	126.8	129.7	152.1
IV. Gross agricultural and industrial product:					
A. Value (million yuan)	82,720	94,610	103,540	110,420	125,910
B. Index	100.0	114.4	125.2	133.5	152.2

Notes and Sources: (1) For Part I, see text. (2) For Part II, ECAFE, *Economic Survey of Asia and the Far East, 1956*, Bangkok, 1957. p. 85. The product for 1952 as well as the index are not given in the original. See text. (3) For Part III, see text for method of calculation. The budgetary current receipts minus foreign-loan proceeds are given in chapter vi, section 1. (4) For Part IV, State Statistical Bureau, "Economic Statistical Abstract," *Hsin-hua pan-yueh-k'an*, 17: 39, September, 1956. The figure for 1954 has since been revised, but the official data, given in the table, obviously relate, among others, to the unrevised figure. This is the only occasion in this volume where an unrevised figure is used.

the budgetary receipt for 1954 is known and definite? As we have seen, national income is defined as the domestic product. Since the current budgetary receipts include foreign-loan proceeds, such relationships of the budgetary receipts with the national income as given in the official statement must be based on the current revenue minus foreign loans. When this alternative procedure is adopted for computation, the result is a series in which the 1954 product, when rounded to the billion, is exactly the same as the reported total. (See Table XV, Part III.) But, if the product for 1954 is right, that for 1956 must be wrong. Had the latter been right, the increase during the four years would be far larger than the official claim. Based on estimated budgetary receipt and planned production data, the 1956 figure must be considered as too preliminary to be of value. The remaining four totals for 1952 through 1955, being based on realized data, may well be taken as approximating closely the actual results of the official calculation *made in the latter part of 1956.*

But close as they may be to the official results, the validity of these four totals is also subject to serious doubt. Among the seven or eight sectors that contribute to the domestic product, industry and agriculture are the most important. Together they account for about three-fourths of the domestic product, as we shall see. It is, therefore, reasonable to expect that both the domestic product and the gross agricultural and industrial value product should fluctuate closely together. Yet, as is shown in Table XV, the domestic product takes a yearly course unrelated to that of the gross product.[31]

The conclusion can be drawn that the official data released in September, 1956, in the form of percentages and indices, represent only the results of the first and preliminary calculation by the State Statistical Bureau. There must have been recalculations since with different results. Thus this set of official data and all later reported results *based on it* should no longer be used.

3. RECONSTRUCTION OF THE NATIONAL INCOME ACCOUNT, 1952–1957

For the purpose of this study it is important to find the sector products as well as the global totals for the five-year period and to see how each of them has changed over time. It is also important to estimate the amount of capital formation and to relate it to the

---

[31] This point will be further demonstrated on p. 95 below.

net national product—not the net domestic material product or net national material product—in order to have some basis on which to judge the over-all performance of the industrialization program and its prospects. For most countries the rate of capital formation is computed from the national product rather than the material product. International comparison of any statistical magnitude is, of course, full of pitfalls, and a purist's advice would properly be not to make any. But despite this, a comparison is made simply because of its challenging interest. For example, although a comparison of the rate of capital formation between China and the United States hardly makes much sense, one between China and India may not be devoid of meaning. No matter how rough the basic data are, such a comparison does give some idea of the difference in the extent of abstaining from consumption of the current output between two peoples under their industrialization programs. Only for this reason will an attempt be made to obtain a rough estimate of the net national product.

An estimate of capital formation will be presented in the next chapter. As to the national product, it seems that neither the quality nor the quantity of the data available warrants at this stage an independent estimation that bypasses the results of the official computation. From what was said in the last three chapters, especially with the "five anti" movement, 1952 is hardly the year for which an elaborate effort should be made to estimate the national product. The year 1956 or 1957 would be a better choice because of improved statistical coverage. But such an estimate, useful as it is, would not serve the present purpose of studying changes over time. Official statistics being what they are, as long as the computation by the State Statistical Bureau is made without any evidence of manipulation, estimates based on its results will serve the purpose.

Thus the present attempt is to reconstruct the national account on the basis of official results reported fragmentarily in the accessible literature. Since the official data released in September, 1956, and all further reported results based on them cannot be used, the data available for the reconstruction are those published in the latter part of 1957.[32] However, they pertain only to 1952 and 1956; for the other years, only a few figures are available for 1953 and 1955. Moreover, the data relating to 1956 are based on the expected (not realized) production for the year. It is, therefore, necessary to

---

[32] The data used are those published between June and the end of August, 1957.

find out, among other things, the expected 1956 production data used by the bureau for computing the national income of that year. With a few exceptions, the data are given in relatives with 1952 as the base. These few exceptions furnish the basis for our construction of the account for 1952 and 1956 (expected). With these results, the method of interpolation is used to estimate the account for 1953 through 1956 (realized) and also for 1957 (planned). Hence, the entire operation is not so much a reconstruction as an estimation based on available official national income data.

The national account so estimated will be the *net domestic material product* by origin, not by use, for the information relating to the latter is not satisfactory. From the domestic material product will be estimated the *net domestic value product* to include the net contribution of the service sectors. Information on China's balance of international payments is very scarce. All available data, however, point to the proposition that the net balance of currently earned income from abroad over that of foreign citizens living on the Chinese mainland—probably in China's favor because of immigrant remittances—is too small to be significant.[33] Thus the net domestic value product becomes the same as the *net national product*.

Some Basic Data for Reconstruction of Account.—Before we proceed with the details of computation, certain basic data may be appropriately indicated to avoid unnecessary repetition of references. They are shown in Table XVI together with the sources of information.

It is worth repeating that all data for 1956 are based on expected, not actual, results. Without knowing exactly the magnitude of the expected gross value products for the year on the basis of which the official calculations were made, we will not be able to make use of the results thus tabulated. In the first source of information given in the table, the State Economic Commission states that the expected gross agricultural value product for 1956 was 58,030 million yuan, and the expected gross factory value product, 57,136 million. As to the gross industrial value product, it had increased, according to Niu, 98.9 per cent from 1952 to 1956. Since the actual gross industrial value product for 1952, as given in official statistics, was 34,326 million yuan, the expected product for 1956 would be 68,274 million.

---

[33] The subject of China's balance of payments will be discussed in chapter vii, section 2.

It may be further deduced that as the net agricultural product for 1956 was 48 per cent of the national income (that is, the domestic material product), the latter would be 88,937.5 million yuan—a result consistent with Ma's remark that the national income for 1956 "is close to 90,000 million yuan." Then, 26 per cent of it, or 23,125 million yuan, would be the net industrial value product for the year (expected).

TABLE XVI

CERTAIN BASIC NATIONAL INCOME DATA, WITH THEIR SOURCES

Item	1952	1956 expected	Sources
A. Agricultural net product (million yuan)..........	36,950	42,690	Ma Yin-ch'u, "A New Theory of Population," *Hsin-hua pan-yueh-k'an*, 15: 34–51, August 10, 1957. Data supplied by the State Economic Commission.
B. Factory net product (million yuan)..........	11,572	19,567	*Ibid.*
C. National income (per cent)			Ho Wei, "A Discussion of the Economic Contradiction between the State and the Peasants," *Hsueh-hsi (Study)*, 12: 22–26 June, 1957.
1. Agriculture..........	......	48	
2. Industry...........	......	26	
3. Others.............	......	26	
D. National income (index based on 1952)..........	100	145.2	Niu Chung-huang, "Accumulation and Consumption in China's National Income," *Hsueh-hsi (Study)*, 16: 20–23, August, 1957.
1. Agriculture..........	100	118.0	
2. Industry...........	100	213.2	
3. Construction........	100	272.6	
4. Transportation and communications.....	100	156.2	
5. Trade..............	100	143.0	

Estimate of the Net Value Product of Agriculture.—The gross agricultural value products for 1953 and 1956 (expected) were 49,915 million and 58,030 million yuan. According to the State Economic Commission, the net products for these two years were correspondingly 36,950 million and 42,690 million yuan. Hence, the ratio of net product to gross product in agriculture was 74.03 per cent for 1953 and 73.56 per cent for 1956. On the basis of Niu's statement that the net agricultural product had increased 18 per cent from 1952 to 1956, the net product for 1952 must be 36,180 million yuan. Since the gross product for that year was 48,392 million, the ratio of net to gross product was 74.77 per cent. Thus we have three ratios of net to gross product; 74.77 per cent for 1952, 74.03 per cent for 1953, and 73.56 per cent for 1956.

The ratio declines over a period of time for several possible reasons. As was brought out in chapter iii, subsidiary farm work is little more than the use of labor time for collection of products of nature or for handicraft. If it grows in relative importance in the total agricultural product, the ratio of net to gross product would drop, because the value added by such work is proportionately (to its gross value) less than the value added by crop production or by animal raising. But, according to Table XI, the subsidiary work component was 20.45 per cent of the gross agricultural product in 1952, 21.44 per cent in 1953, 21.16 per cent in 1954, 21.26 per cent in 1955, and 20.8 per cent in 1956. Its rising importance from 1952 to 1953 might have been an important factor accounting for the decline in the ratio of net to gross agricultural product during those two years. But the relative stability of this component in the gross product from 1953 through 1955 with a slight decrease in 1956 could not have caused the decline in the said ratio.

The slight decline in the ratio could also have been due to the increasing importance of animal raising which requires animal feed. Livestock did increase from 1952 to 1954, when it began to decrease. Thus the cause of the change in the ratio since then must be found elsewhere.

The increasing use of fertilizers (chemicals as well as oil cakes) and insecticides might have been an important factor contributing to the decline of the said ratio during the period under consideration. One farm study reports that the costs of production in collectivized farms are, in the order originally given, seeds, fertilizers, and labor, followed by animal labor, insecticides, and depreciation of tools and implements.[34] As shown in Table XII, the use of chemical fertilizers increased rapidly and steadily from 295,000 tons in 1952 to 1,620,000 in 1956 (actual), and to 1,650,000 in 1957 (planned). Oil cakes were used in several times the amount of chemical fertilizers; there were also green compost and night soil. Although data are not available for them, it can be seen from the chemical-fertilizer statistics that the use of various kinds of fertilizers had grown steadily in a more or less straight line from 1952 through 1956, with a pause in 1957.

[34] Ta Sun, "The Meaning and Method of Studying Comparative Prices for Agricultural Products," *Ta Kung Pao (Impartial Daily)*, August 18, 1957.

TABLE XVII

ESTIMATE OF NET AGRICULTURAL VALUE PRODUCT AT 1952 PRICES, 1952–1957

Item	1952	1953	1954	1955	1956 exp.	1956 actual	1957 est.
1. Gross product (million yuan)............	48,392	49,915	51,566	55,544	58,030	58,290	61,150
2. Ratio of net to gross product (per cent)...	74.77	74.03	73.87	73.71	73.56	73.56	73.56
3. Net product (million yuan)...............	36,180	36,950	38,090	40,940	42,690	42,880	44,980

This last observation furnishes the basis for interpolation. We will assume that the ratio of net to gross product had declined steadily from 1953 through 1956, and that no change of the ratio took place in 1957. On this basis, the net agricultural value product for 1952 through 1957 is calculated. The results are presented in Table XVII.

Estimate of the Net Value Product of Factory Industry.—We have seen that the net factory value product was 11,572 million yuan for 1953 and 19,567 million for 1956 (expected). Since the gross factory value product for these two years was 35,577 million and 57,136 million (expected), the ratio of net factory product to gross factory product was 32.53 per cent in 1953 and 34.25 per cent in 1956 (expected). The reason for such an increase in the ratio clearly lies in the growing importance of producer goods, which constitute a higher "value added" per unit than consumer goods do.

The gross factory product of 35,577 million yuan for 1953 consists of 14,670 million yuan worth of producer goods and 20,907 million of consumer goods. (See Statistical Appendix, Table 3.)

The expected gross factory product of 57,136 million yuan for 1956 may be taken as being composed of producer and consumer goods in the same proportion as found in the actual gross factory product for that year. In that event, the expected gross value of producer goods was 28,413 million and that of consumer goods, 28,723 million. Given the gross and net factory value products for 1953 and for 1956 (expected), the ratios of net to gross value products for producer-goods industries and for consumer-goods industries may be computed by simultaneous equations as follows:

Let x be the ratio of net to gross value product of producer-goods industries, and
y be the ratio of net to gross value product of consumer-goods industries.

Then,

$$14,670x + 20,907y = 11,572$$
$$28,413x + 28,723y = 19,567$$

Solving for x and y, we find

$$x = 0.444 \text{ and}$$
$$y = 0.242$$

In other words, for both 1953 and 1956 the ratio of net to gross value product was 44.4 per cent for producer goods and 24.2 per cent for consumer goods. These may be compared to those of India.[85] When India's registered factories are reclassified according to Peiping's definition of heavy and light industries, the ratio of net to gross value product for 1950 was 38.6 per cent for producer-goods industries and 24.98 per cent for consumer-goods industries. The similarity between the Chinese and Indian ratios for light industries is striking. The difference between the ratios for heavy industries is due to the absence from this category for India of such industries as electric power, coal mining, petroleum refining, transport machinery and vehicles, etc.

However, the Chinese ratio for consumer-goods industries thus discovered is at variance with the observation that "in China at the present the value created by labor in the light industry is about 20 per cent of the gross value product, the other 80 per cent being values transferred chiefly from agriculture in the form of raw materials."[86] If the 20 per cent is applied to the expected production of consumer goods in 1956, the ratio of net to gross factory product for producer goods would be 48.65 per cent. And if the 20 per cent is applied to the actual production of consumer goods in 1953, the ratio for producer goods would be 50.38 per cent. The decline of the ratio for producer-goods industries over these years was a reasonable result of increasing mechanization, while an unchanged ratio for consumer-goods industries was equally reasonable in view of the little change in mechanization in light industry.[87]

We may then assume that the ratio of net to gross factory value product for consumer-goods industries was 20 per cent from 1952 through 1957, and that the ratio for producer-goods industries had steadily declined, because of increasing mechanization, from 50.38 per cent in 1953 to 48.65 per cent in 1956, forming a straight line with a negative slope of 0.5767. Thus for producer-goods industry in the factory sector, the ratio of net to gross value product was 50.96 per cent for 1952, 50.38 per cent for 1953, 49.8 per cent for 1954, 49.23 per cent for 1955, 48.65 per cent for 1956, and 48.07 per cent for 1957.

In comparison with the ratios obtained by simultaneous equations, the present results, while possibly underestimating the con-

---

[85] Government of India, Ministry of Commerce and Industry, Directorate of Industrial Statistics, *Report on the Seventh Census of Indian Manufacturers, 1952*, New Delhi, 1955.

[86] Hsiao Kung-yu, "The Principles of Wage Increases," *Hsueh-hsi (Study)*, 15: 17–18, August, 1957; quotation on p. 18.

[87] See discussion in chapter ii and Statistical Appendix, Table 9.

TABLE XVIII

ESTIMATE OF NET FACTORY VALUE PRODUCT AT 1952 PRICES, 1952–1957

Item	1952	1953	1954	1955	1956 exp.	1956 actual	1957 est.
1. Producer goods:							
a. Gross value (million yuan)	10,730	14,670	17,598	20,578	28,413	29,170	31,130
b. Ratio of net to gross value (per cent)	50.96	50.38	49.80	49.23	48.65	48.65	48.07
c. Net value (million yuan)	5,468	7,391	8,764	10,131	13,823	14,191	14,964
2. Consumer goods:							
a. Gross value (million yuan)	16,284	20,907	23,935	24,170	28,723	29,490	29,210
b. Ratio of net to gross value (per cent)	20	20	20	20	20	20	20
c. Net value (million yuan)	3,257	4,181	4,787	4,834	5,745	5,898	5,842
3. Total factory value product (million yuan):							
a. Gross value (1.a. + 2.a.)	27,014	35,577	41,533	44,748	57,136	58,660	60,340
b. Net value (1.c. + 2.c.)	8,725	11,572	13,551	14,965	19,568	20,089	20,806

tribution of light industry and overestimating that of heavy industry, are much more in line with the fact of increasing mechanization of producer-goods industries. The net factory value product, in terms of producer-goods and consumer-goods industries, is presented in Table XVIII.

Estimate of the Net Value Product of Individual and Coöperative Handicrafts.—Estimation of the net contribution by handicraft coöperatives and individual handicraftsmen is difficult because of the lack of available information. Like the factory industry, their output of producer goods almost doubled between 1952 and 1955, with an increase of nearly 27 per cent in the output of consumer goods. But no data have been made available concerning the composition of the handicraft value product for the other years. As in the factory sector, handicrafts must have had a continuous increase in the ratio of their net to gross value product as more and more producer goods were made.

In order not to make too arbitrary an assumption concerning the ratio of net to gross product for handicrafts, we have to make use of the earlier calculation of national income for 1956 (expected) in accordance with the data given by Ma and Ho. There we have found that the net product of industry as a whole was 23,125 million yuan. Since, according to our calculation, the net product of factory industry was 19,568 million, then the net product of handicrafts for 1956 (expected) would be 3,557 million, which was 31.94 per cent of their gross product of 11,138 million.

According to Niu, the net product of industry as a whole had increased 113.2 per cent from 1952 to 1956 (expected). As the net product for 1956 was 23,125 million, it would be 10,846 million for 1952. The net product of factory industry having been calculated to be 8,725 million for 1952, the net product of handicrafts would be 2,121 million, which was 29 per cent of their gross product of 7,312 million.

These two ratios, 29 per cent for 1952 and 31.94 per cent for 1956, furnish the only basis for estimating the net product of handicrafts. From the composition of handicraft output in 1952 and 1955, we have seen that the producer-goods component had grown steadily. The rise of the ratio of net to gross product is a reasonable phenomenon. However, with an actual absolute decline in the gross value product from 1954 to 1955, the composition of the gross value product could not have been very different between the two years. In other words, the ratio rose steadily from 1952 to 1954 and then leveled off in 1955, only to rise again in 1956. As for 1957, the chairman of the State Economic Commission has stated that little change in handicraft production was expected.[38] Thus it may be assumed that the ratio remained the same for 1957 as for 1956.

Applying the series of ratios of net to gross product thus obtained gives the results shown in Table XIX.

Summary of the Net Industrial Value Product.—The sum of the net factory value product and the net handicraft value product is, of course, the net industrial value product. It has been reported that during the five-year period the net industrial product "has been in the neighborhood of one-third of the gross product."[39] This serves as a check on the results of the estimates of the net factory and net handicraft products. Table XX brings out a relationship between the net and the gross industrial product that answers the description. It will be remembered that the continuous rise of the ratio of net to gross product was basically due to the growth of producer-goods industries.

Estimate of the Net Domestic Material Product.—We have estimated earlier that the net domestic material product for 1956 (expected) was 88,937.5 million yuan. According to Niu, it had increased 45.2 per cent from 1952 (Table XVI). Thus the domestic material product for 1952 was 61,252 million, of which, according to our estimate, 36,180 million (or 59.1 per cent) was the net agricultural product and 10,846 million (or 17.7 per cent) was the net industrial product. For 1956 (expected), as given by Ho, 48 per cent of the domestic material product was from agriculture and 26 per cent from industry. In other words, the ratio of net agricultural and industrial product to the material product had declined from 76.8 per cent for 1952 to 74 per cent for 1956.

Such a result is consistent with the report that "during the period of the First Five Year Plan about three-fourths of the national income are derived from agriculture and industry."[40] It should be pointed out that different results also appear in the Peiping literature. For example, a publication (dated November, 1956) of the State Statistical Bureau indicated that industry contributed 20.2 per cent to the national product in 1952.[41] A few months later, an-

[38] Po I-po, "Report on the Results of the 1956 Plan and on the Plan for 1957," *Jen-min jih-pao*, July 2, 1957.

[39] Niu Chung-huang, "Accumulation and Consumption in China's National Income," *Hsueh-hsi (Study)*, 16: 20–23, August, 1957.

[40] *Ibid.*, p. 20.

[41] "A General Survey of Socialist Industrialization in China," *Hsin-hua pan-yueh-k'an*, 2: 54–62, January, 1957. It originally appeared in *T'ung-chi kung-tso t'ung-hsin (Statistical Bulletin)*, November, 1956.

TABLE XIX

ESTIMATE OF NET HANDICRAFT VALUE PRODUCT AT 1952 PRICES, 1952–1957

Item	1952	1953	1954	1955	1956 exp.	1956 actual	1957 est.
1. Gross value (million yuan).............	7,312	9,119	10,566	10,128	11,138	11,700	11,700
2. Ratio of net to gross value (per cent).......	29	29.74	30.48	30.48	31.94	31.94	31.94
3. Net value (million yuan).............	2,121	2,712	3,221	3,087	3,557	3,737	3,737

TABLE XX

SUMMARY OF ESTIMATES OF NET INDUSTRIAL VALUE PRODUCT AT 1952 PRICES, 1952–1957

Item	1952	1953	1954	1955	1956 exp.	1956 actual	1957 est.
1. Gross product (million yuan).............	34,326	44,696	52,099	54,876	68,274	70,360	72,040
2. Net product (million yuan).............	10,846	14,284	16,772	18,052	23,125	23,826	24,543
3. Ratio of net to gross product (per cent).........	31.60	31.96	32.19	32.90	33.87	33.87	34.07

other publication reported the industrial contribution to be 18.9 per cent for the same year instead.[42] These two figures, at variance with each other, are both larger than the 17.7 per cent that we have computed on the basis of information released in June and August, 1957. The 20.2 per cent must have been the original calculation which provided the preliminary results that the chairman of the State Economic Commission made public in September, 1956. Later revision has produced different results. It will also be recalled that several net value figures for certain years were quoted in the discussion of the gross industrial value product in chapter ii. Different from our present results, they were all published at the end of 1956. Perhaps the data on which our estimates are based represent the latest official results.

This is a convenient place to bring back for further comment the results of estimating the material product on the basis of early official data released in September, 1956. (See Table XV, line III.A.) The results were rejected as being inconsistent with the gross agricultural and industrial product. Now after having estimated the net agricultural and industrial value product, we are in a better position to see the difficulty with those results. The ratio of the net agricultural and industrial product to the national income computed with the early official data is as follows: 76 per cent for 1952, 70 per cent for 1953 and 1954, 74 per cent for 1955, and again 70 for 1956 (estimated). That the relative importance of the net agricultural and industrial product in national income should have fluctuated so widely over these years and been so low for 1953, 1954, and 1956 is not only unreasonable, but also contradicted by the information given by Niu and Ho.

The report that the net agricultural and industrial product constituted about 75 per cent of the national income through the First Five Year Plan provides the basis for estimating the material product. As has been brought out, this ratio had actually declined from 76.8 per cent in 1952 to 74 per cent in 1956. Such a decline is expected as the natural consequence of the growing importance of the other material sectors in the economy, like construction, transport and communications, and trade. For lack of any other information, it is necessary to assume a linear decline up to 1956, so that the share of the net agricultural and industrial product in national income would be 76.8 per cent for 1952, 76.1 per cent

---

[42] Chang Hsing-fu, "The Road and Method of China's Industrialization," *Kung-jen jih-pao (Worker's Daily)*, May 23, 1957.

TABLE XXI

ESTIMATE OF NET DOMESTIC MATERIAL PRODUCT AT 1952 PRICES, 1952–1957

Item	1952	1953	1954	1955	1956 exp.	1956 actual	1957 est.
A. Net agricultural and industrial product (million yuan)	47,026	51,234	54,862	58,992	65,815	66,708	69,523
B. A as per cent of net domestic product	76.8	76.1	75.4	74.7	74.0	74.0	74.0
C. Net domestic product (A ÷ B), (million yuan)	61,252	67,325	72,761	78,792	88,938	90,146	93,950
D. Net product of other material sectors (C − A), (million yuan)	14,226	16,091	17,899	19,800	23,123	23,438	24,427

TABLE XXII

NET VALUE PRODUCT PER WORKER IN CONSTRUCTION, TRANSPORT AND COMMUNICATIONS, AND TRADE AT 1952 PRICES, 1955–1956

(In yuan)

Item	1955	1956 exp.
1. Construction	838	936
2. Transport and Communications	1,528	1,950
3. Trade	2,491	2,499

Source: Niu Chung-huang, "Accumulation and Consumption in China's National Income," *Hsüeh-hsi (Study),* 16: 20–23, August, 1957.

for 1953, 75.4 per cent for 1954, 74.7 per cent for 1955, and 74 per cent for 1956. As far as 1957 is concerned, it was in fact a year of curtailment of "unproductive" construction and consolidation of the 1956 gains.[43] Hence, the share of the net agricultural and industrial product in national income may be assumed to have been the same between the last two years of the Plan.

Given these ratios and given the net agricultural and industrial products for 1952 through 1957, the net domestic material product would be obtained. Moreover, the difference between the net material product thus obtained and the net agricultural and industrial product would be the net product of the other material sectors (construction, transport and communications, trade, restaurants, and hired domestic labor). The results are shown in Table XXI.

Estimate of the Net 'Value of Other Material Sectors.—The preceding section has already given the annual totals of the net product for all material sectors other than agriculture and industry. The present task is to estimate the net product of the components of these "other sectors." However, data are available only for construction, transport and communications, and trade, and these only for 1952, 1955 and 1956 (expected).

The data for the increase in the net value of these three components (in relatives) between 1952 and 1956 were shown in Table XVI, line D—3, 4 and 5. These relatives cannot be utilized unless actual figures are found for either one of these years. None have been made available in the accessible literature published since June, 1957. However, some useful actual figures were published in May, 1957, by the same author who three months later made public some of the basic data which we have used for estimation.[44] Although it is possible that these data presented in May were later revised, we are left with no choice but to take them as a basis for calculation. They are given in the form of net product per worker (including staff) for 1955 and 1956, and may best be shown as in Table XXII.

The net product of each of these three components for those two years can be calculated by applying the net product per worker to the labor force so engaged. Statistics of labor force are also full of difficulties. Technical problems aside, the annual surveys are usually taken of the situation at the end of September. But, because of the drive for filling or exceeding the quota, the increase in em-

---

[43] Po I-po, "Report on the Results ..."

[44] Niu Chung-huang, "The Problems of Calculating Labor Productivity and Wage Levels," *Hsueh-hsi (Study)*, 9: 5–6, May, 1957.

TABLE XXIII

LABOR FORCE AND NET PRODUCT OF CONSTRUCTION, TRANSPORT AND COMMUNICATIONS, AND TRADE AT 1952 PRICES, FOR SELECTED YEARS

	Labor force (in thousands)		Net product (in millions of yuan)			
	1955	1956	1952	1955	1956 exp.	1956 actual
A. Original estimate:						
1. Construction	1,430	2,170	745	1,199	2,031	2,059
2. Transportation and communications	1,120	1,300	1,623	1,711	2,535	2,569
3. Trade	6,132	6,482	11,327	15,275	16,199	16,420
4. Total	8,682	9,952	13,795	18,185	20,765	21,048
5. "Other material sectors" (Table XXI)			14,226	19,800	23,123	23,438
6. Discrepancy (5 − 4)			431	1,615	2,358	2,390
B. Official data (December, 1957):						
7. Construction			1,872	......	5,078	5,147
8. Transportation and communications			2,495	......	3,991	4,045
9. Trade (including restaurants)			9,859	......	14,054	14,246
10. Total (Table XXI)			14,226	19,800	23,123	23,438

ployment during the last quarter of the year has invariably been very substantial (see Statistical Appendix, Table 6). This is particularly true of construction. It is therefore necessary to adjust the survey data with other available information in order to obtain the total employed at the end of the year. Such an adjustment is possible for 1955, but with information available at the present, not for 1956. However, since the data on net product per worker were published in May, 1957, it is likely that the calculation was made on the basis of employment at the end of September, 1956, as well. In any case, we have no other choice than to use the available data for 1956 without adjustment.[45] The results of the calculation show in Table XXIII, Part A. The net products of the three components for 1956 (actual) are computed on the assumption that their relative importance is the same as for 1956 (expected).

The table shows that the difference between the total net value product of "all other material sectors" and those of the three components under discussion widens considerably from 1952 to 1956. The residue certainly does not represent the growth of restaurants, for we have already indicated that the volume of restaurant business had doubled from 1950 to 1955. It is possible that the labor force data used for calculation are faulty, so that the net products of the three components are underestimated for 1955 and 1956. But the results for 1952 are computed by applying the given index numbers to the 1956 data: whatever labor force data are used, the difference between lines 5 and 4 in Table XXIII would grow in the same degree. Another possible explanation is that the residue includes the net value product of both restaurants and "a part of domestic labor services." However, since restaurant business had only doubled from 1950 to 1955 (and in all probability it could not have increased that much from 1952 to 1955), the hired domestic help would have had to have a tremendous increase over these years before the residue could be accounted for. If that had been a fact, comments would have been found in various publications.

We are then left with only one plausible explanation. The hired

---

[45] The sources of data on labor force for 1955 and 1956 are (1) State Statistical Bureau, "A National Survey of the Composition and Distribution of the Labor Force in 1955," *Hsin-hua pan-yueh-k'an*, 2:87–88, January, 1957; (2) "A Survey of the Labor Force and Wages in 1956," *ibid.*, 10: 115–116 and 74, May, 1957; (3) "The Basic Situation of China's Construction Enterprises," *T'ung-chi kung-tso t'ung-hsin (Statistical Bulletin)*, 24: 31–33, December, 1956; and (4) "A Survey of the Development of China's Commercial Network and of the Situation in 1955," *ibid.*, 18: 7–10, September, 1956.

domestic help must have been omitted altogether for 1952. This is likely because no mention of it was made in the comprehensive essay on the method of computing national income written in August, 1956, by a responsible official in the State Statistical Bureau.[46] In all accessible literature, the reference to "a part of domestic labor services" has been made only once, and that was in June, 1957.[47] If the omission of it for 1952 is true, the fact is of great importance for the interpretation of the rate of increase in national income during the period under study.

The foregoing estimate is not satisfactory, because the data used were published before June, 1957, because the net value for construction is too small, and because the results show a discrepancy too great to be explained away. Fortunately, additional data were released at the end of 1957, giving the percentage shares of various material sectors in the domestic material product for 1952 and 1956 (expected).[48] The shares of agriculture and industry are, 59.2 per cent and 18 per cent for 1952, and 48.1 per cent and 26.4 per cent for 1956 (expected). They may be compared with our estimates of 59.15 per cent for agriculture and 17.81 per cent for industry in 1952 and 48.03 per cent and 26 per cent, correspondingly, in 1956 (expected). The results are therefore strikingly close. As for the "other material sectors," however, the relatives given by Niu (Table XVI, Part D, lines 3, 4, and 5) have again been revised. According to the new data, the shares of construction, transportation and communication, and trade (including restaurants) in the domestic material product are 3 per cent, 4 per cent, and 15.8 per cent for 1952, and 5.6 per cent, 4.4 per cent, and 15.5 per cent for 1956 (expected). A new estimate is therefore necessary. For consistency, the percentages have to be recalculated, not as percentages of the domestic product, but as percentages of the net product of "all other material sectors." The results are given in Part B of Table XXIII. It will be noted that restaurants are grouped together with trade, and that no mention is made of hired domestic help. Has the latter been taken into account at all? Until further information is available, the question cannot be answered.

Estimate of the Gross Social Value Product.—Before proceeding to estimate the net national product, we may digress to find the magnitude of the gross social value product and to see how it has

[46] Yueh Wei, *op. cit.* This remains the only authoritative essay on method.
[47] Ho Wei, "Discussion of . . . ," p. 23.
[48] Yang Po, "On the Distribution of National Income in China," *Ching-chi yen-chiu (Economic Research)*, 6:1–11, December, 1957; reference on p. 3.

changed. It will be recalled that it is defined either as the net domestic material product plus all the materials consumed (including depreciation of capital assets) during the process of production or, which is the same thing, the sum total of the gross value products of all the material sectors.

The basic data for the calculation are also given by Niu.[49] According to this source, the average gross value product per man in all material sectors except agriculture was 6,222 yuan for 1956 (expected) while the average net product was 2,766 yuan. This is another way of saying that the total gross value product except agriculture was 2.249 times (i.e., 6,222 ÷ 2,766) the total net value product with the same exception.

Since the expected domestic material product (exclusive of agriculture) for 1956 has been estimated to be 46,250 million yuan (Table XXI, line C and Table XVII, line 3), the expected gross value product (exclusive of agriculture) would be 2.249 times that amount, giving a total of 104,000 million. The expected gross agricultural product being 58,000 million yuan (Table XVII, line 1), the gross social value product for the year 1956 (expected) therefore amounted to 162,000 million. The ratio of net domestic material product to gross social value product was then 54.9 per cent. This is in complete agreement with the report that "under the present conditions in China, national income is 55 per cent of the gross social value product, the other 45 per cent being materials consumed."[50] When the ratio is applied to the actual domestic material product for 1956 (Table XXI, line C), the gross social value product for 1956 (actual) becomes 164,200 million yuan.[51]

It is further stated by Niu that the gross social value product had increased 60.6 per cent from 1952 to 1956 (expected). Thus the gross social value product for 1952 was 100,900 million yuan. Since the domestic material product for the year was 61,250 million (Table XXI, line C), it was 60.7 per cent of the gross social value product.

That the ratio of net material product to gross social product should have declined from 60.7 per cent in 1952 to 54.9 per cent in 1956 is, of course, a natural consequence of industrialization. The value added by agriculture is about three-quarters of its gross value product, whereas the value added by industry is about one-

---

[49] Niu Chung-huang, "Accumulation and Consumption . . ."

[50] Niu, *ibid.*, p. 21

[51] It may also be estimated that the total labor force in all material sectors numbered 16,700,000 in 1956 (expected).

third. The increasing relative importance of industry (and construction) will result in a larger and larger consumption of raw materials included in the gross social value product.[52]

Estimate of the Net National Product.—Estimating the net national product is the most speculative of all calculations undertaken in this study. For while the national income account in terms of net domestic material product is estimated with the data released by Peiping, the net national product can be estimated only by reviewing the results of estimation by others for different situations Employment and wage data are too fragmentary and too scarce for the purpose.

The present task requires an estimate of the net value of all service items not included in the net domestic material product but normally found in the national income account of most other countries. The most important of these service items are (1) finance and insurance—services, (2) housing—services, (3) liberal professions (teachers, doctors, etc.), (4) government administration, and (5) defense and internal security. Others include (6) transport and communications—personal use, (7) trade—services, (8) communal services, and (9) municipal utilities, electric power generation and transmission excepted.[53]

Perhaps the most important omission of all—one that generally does not appear in the national income account of the Western countries but should have been included in the Chinese account— is the labor services used for the building of dams, earth works, roads, and the like. This work is done either by conscription of the masses for big projects or voluntarily by the peasants themselves in their own villages. Unfortunately, no estimate of it is possible without the relevant quantitative data.

All estimates of national income for pre-1949 China are based on incomplete data. However, their results may serve as a point of departure for discussion. In the most detailed estimate that was ever made of the national income of prewar China, Ou Pao-san

---

[52] Depreciation is another factor. If agricultural development keeps even pace with industrial development, the relative importance of industry would not rise, and the statement in the text would not apply. Moreover, while the decline in the ratio is regarded as a natural consequence under the circumstances, the *rate* of decline is different. It is a subject for statistical measurement, for which, as we have shown in the last two chapters, the official data are not satisfactory.

[53] Electric power generation and transmission, whether municipal or otherwise, are under the central control of the Ministry of Electric Power Industry, and presumably are regarded as a part of the material sector. See Ku To-ching, "Tabulation Forms for Municipal Utilities," *Chi-hua ching-chi (Planned Economy)*, 7: 31–33, July, 1957

finds that public administration, housing, liberal professions, and finance accounted for 9.7 per cent of the national income for 1936 while trade (including restaurants) accounted for 10 per cent.[54] According to the findings of another study undertaken by T. C. Liu, modern financial institutions, government, trade, education, and other liberal professions contributed 27 per cent to the average gross national product from 1931 through 1936.[55] In this study, no breakdown for the trade sector alone is given; but if it is assumed that trade's share of the national product was about 10 per cent as given by Ou, then the other service sectors would have contributed about 17 per cent. Using Liu's results, Kuznets attempted to make China's national income account comparable to that of the United States.[56] His results bring out the point that the entire service sector accounted for 16.6 per cent of China's gross national product during the period from 1931 to 1936.

Bergson, in estimating the gross national product of Soviet Russia for 1937, finds that 15.63 per cent of the product is omitted from the Soviet definition of national income.[57] This percentage apparently need not be applicable to the Chinese situation because Soviet Russia even in 1937 was already on a higher level of economic development than China is today. But the close similarity of the percentage to those mentioned above is striking.

In terms of the stage of economic development China is much closer to India than to Russia, and India's experience should be instructive. In India, the four major service sectors—liberal arts and professions, government administration, domestic services, and house property—accounted for 15.6 per cent of the net national product in 1950–51, and 15.7 per cent in 1955–56, and are expected to contribute 15.6 per cent in 1960–61.[58] The stability of the percentage should be noted, and deserves attention because separate estimates were made for each of the four service sectors indicated. Finance is not included in these sectors. According to another official Indian calculation, organized banking and insurance con-

[54] Ou Pao-san and others, *Chung-kuo kuo-min-so-te (China's National Income)*, 2 vols., Shanghai, 1947; reference at I, 19.

[55] T. C. Liu, *China's National Income, 1931–36: An Exploration Study*, Brookings, 1946, 91 pp.

[56] S. Kuznets, "National Income and Industrial Structure," *Econometrica*, 17: supplement, 205–241, July, 1949.

[57] A. Bergson, *Soviet National Income and Product in 1937*, New York, 1953, pp. 143–145.

[58] Government of India, Planning Commission, *Second Five Year Plan*, New Delhi, 1956, p. 73.

TABLE XXIV

ESTIMATE OF THE NET NATIONAL PRODUCT AT 1952 PRICES, 1952–1957

Item	1952	1953	1954	1955	1956 exp.	1956 actual	1957 est.
A. Domestic material product (Table XXI), (million yuan)	61,250	67,330	72,760	78,790	88,940	90,150	93,950
B. Net national product (119.05 per cent of A)	72,920	80,155	86,620	93,800	105,900	107,300	111,800
C. Net product of service sectors (B − A), (million yuan)	11,670	12,825	13,860	15,010	16,960	17,150	17,850
D. Indices of A or B	100.0	109.9	118.8	128.6	145.2	147.2	153.4

tributed 0.7 per cent to the net national product in 1950–51, and this, when added to the net value of the other four major service sectors mentioned above, would account for 15.8 per cent of it.[59] Hence, it may be surmised that for 1955–56 these five sectors together may have accounted for some 16 per cent of the net national product.

In summary, the findings bear out the significant fact that the relative importance of the service sectors in the national product (whether gross or net) is very similar between China of 1931–1936, Russia of 1937, and India of the 1950's, and that the relative weight of these sectors has been surprisingly stable in India.

Regarding the situation in China of the 1950's, we may remember that until 1955 or 1956 when the problem of employment became pressing in the urban areas, the number engaged in pure service trades had been declining because of "social prejudices" against them.[60] The size of the national defense force may also have been reduced according to various official pronouncements. Although no information is available on the forces for internal security, it must be of considerable size. Public health, education, and government activities have been developing rapidly.[61] In short, the Chinese service sector as a whole during the period under study cannot be smaller than in India of today or in China of the 1930's. If anything, it is likely to be larger.

These considerations seem to justify the adoption of a ratio of at least 16 per cent, which is derived from India's experience, for estimating the net national product from the net domestic material product. This in fact is a conservative measure, for the 16 per cent according to India's tabulation covers only a limited number of the missing items in the Chinese national account, omitting particularly the labor services for "mass mobilization" projects. However, whether it should be 16.6 per cent as Kuznets suggests or higher, only an independent estimate based on sufficient reliable data can determine. Thus, taking the conservative figure, we estimate that the domestic material product is 84 per cent of the net national product. The annual variation of this ratio, according to India's experience, is not more than 0.1 per cent, a variation too small to be taken into consideration in our estimate. (See Table XXIV.)

[59] Government of India, Ministry of Finance, Department of Economic Affairs, *Final Report of the National Income Committee, February, 1954*, New Delhi, 1954, p. 106, Table 28.

[60] Sung Ping, "The Problem of Employment," *Hsueh-hsi (Study)*, 12: 25–28, June, 1957.

[61] For development of education, see Statistical Appendix, Tables 29–31.

TABLE XXV

Summary of Estimates (Based on Official National Income Data) of Net National Product and Its Components at 1952 Prices, 1952–1957

(Source tables in Roman numerals)

Item	1952	1953	1954	1955	1956 exp.	1956 actual	1957 est.
I. Net product (in billions of yuan):							
A. Agriculture (XVII)	36.2	37.0	38.1	40.9	42.7	42.9	45.0
B. Industry and mining (XX)	10.9	14.3	16.8	18.1	23.1	23.8	24.5
1. Factory industry (XVIII)	8.8	11.6	13.6	14.9	19.5	20.1	20.8
a. Producer goods (XVIII)	5.5	7.4	8.8	10.1	13.8	14.2	15.0
b. Consumer goods (XVIII)	3.3	4.2	4.8	4.8	5.7	5.9	5.8
2. Handicrafts (XIX)	2.1	2.7	3.2	3.0	3.6	3.7	3.7
C. Construction (XXIII—B)	1.8	16.1	17.9	18.8	5.1	5.2	24.4
D. Transport and communications (XXIII—B)	2.5				4.0	4.0	
E. Trade (XXIII—B)	9.8				14.0	14.3	
F. Domestic material product (XXI)	61.2	67.4	72.8	78.8	88.9	90.2	93.9
G. Service sectors (XXIV)	11.7	12.8	13.8	15.0	17.0	17.1	17.9
H. Net National product (XXIV)	72.9	80.2	86.6	93.8	105.9	107.3	111.8
II. Indices of F or H (XXIV)	100.0	109.9	118.8	128.6	145.2	147.2	153.4

Notes: (a) Figures for 1956 (expected) are estimates made on the basis of such expected production data for the year as adopted by the State Statistical Bureau for a preliminary computation of the domestic material product. (b) Figures for 1956 (actual) are based on actual production data for the year, but the estimates are made in the same way as those for 1956 (expected). (c) Figures for 1957 (estimated) are computed on the basis of estimated production data for the year. (d) Net value figures may differ slightly from those given in the source tables because of rounding.

It will be noticed that the net national product has not taken into account the net balance (positive or negative) of currently earned income from abroad over that of foreign citizens living in China. This omission is made on the assumption that the balance of currently earned income in the international account is too small to be taken into the estimate. The subject will be discussed in chapter vii, section 2.

4. Summary of Estimates and Some Observations on the Net National Product

The estimates of the net domestic material product and the net national product are summarized in Table XXV.[62] Figures for 1956 (expected) are shown because they have played an important part in the whole estimation process. In the following discussion, however, references to 1956 are made to 1956 (actual) only.

The table shows that while the average annual rate of increase of the net national product is 9.8 per cent from 1952 to 1956, it is 8.9 per cent from 1952 to 1957. The biggest yearly increase (14.4 per cent) took place in 1956, and the smallest (4.2 per cent) in 1957. If 1953 should be taken as the base instead of 1952, the average rate of increase to 1957 was 8.7 per cent.

Is such a rate of increase realistic? The answer is definitely in the negative. We have seen that in industry the pricing of new products has increasingly inflated its gross and net product. This inflationary effect, however, manifests itself in a much stronger degree in the net product than in the gross product. For, the net product being the difference between the gross value product and the value of materials consumed, the inflationary effect of new product pricing bears a much smaller proportion to the gross product than to the net product. Suppose that a new product representing a total material cost of 50 yuan should have been properly

---

[62] After this calculation was completed, a publication arrived, giving the real figures for the domestic material product for 1952 and 1956 (expected) as 61,100 million and 88,700 million yuan. See Yang Po, "An Understanding of the Proportion between Consumption and Accumulation in the Disposal of China's National Income," *Hsueh-hsi (Study)*, 20: 24–26, October, 1957.

According to an official publication (dated December 9, 1957) of the State Economic and Planning Commissions, the national income for 1957 has been computed to be "not over 94,000 million yuan." This may be compared with our estimate of 93,950 million. (It may be noted that in this study while the estimate of national income for 1952 and 1956 (expected) is based on index numbers found in the literature, the estimate for other years including 1957 is based on a set of assumptions.) Editorial, "Carry Through the Principle of Diligence and Economy in National Construction," *Chi-hua ching-chi (Planned Economy)*, 12: 1–3, December, 1957.

priced at 100 yuan, but is actually priced at 120 yuan. The net product should have been 50 yuan instead of 70 yuan as it stands. Thus the gross value is overpriced by 20 per cent, while the net value is inflated by 40 per cent. It is clear that the net national product is much more seriously inflated by new product pricing than is the gross industrial value product.[63]

By the same reasoning, the depressed pricing of agricultural products at the base period has a much greater effect on the net agricultural value product than on the gross product. This is tantamount to assigning a much smaller weight to agriculture in the composition of net national product (at constant prices) than the gross agricultural value product would suggest, let alone the proper weight that agriculture should have had. Since agriculture is a sector with a relatively slow rate of growth, its small weight in the net national product would have enabled the latter to grow at a much faster rate than if agriculture had been given its proper weight. In other words, the greater is the weight given to the component with a low rate of growth, other things being equal, the slower must be the rate of growth of the net national product, which is none other than the average (weighted) rate of growth of all its components.

For these reasons alone, the growth rate of the net national product at 1952 prices must have been unduly exaggerated. But we have also seen that in agriculture, aside from the effect of the growing use of chemical fertilizers and tractors, the gross value product is understated for the earlier years of the period under study while for the later years it receives the full impact of improved statistical coverage and "psychological bias." If it had been increasing at a rate not much higher than the rate of population increase, the growth of the net national product would be substantially less than is shown in Table XXV. Furthermore, it is not clear whether hired domestic help had been omitted for the earlier years in the national income account and included for the later years. If that is the case, the growth of the net national product has been inflated all the more.

Possibly counteracting somewhat the effect of all these factors is the construction work done by the masses that has not been recorded. The small projects undertaken by the peasants themselves are likely to be on the whole regular in nature, so that their

[63] This point has been forcefully brought out by N. Jasny, "Intricacies of Russian National Income Statistics," *Journal of Political Economy*, IV: 299–322, August, 1947. I am indebted to Grossman for a profitable discussion of this point.

omission does not affect the growth rate of the national product. But if "mass mobilization" projects should have been undertaken in *increasing* magnitude throughout the period, their omission would make the statistical rate of growth lower than the real rate.[64] It is, however, quite certain that their inclusion could not have appreciably reduced the exaggerated effect of all those factors mentioned above on the growth rate of the net national product.

Table XXV also shows the relative importance of the various sectors in the economy. It must be recognized that the net product of each sector does not necessarily reflect its real importance. In addition to what has been said, other effects of pricing on the net product may be noted. The net products of all material sectors are valued at current market prices, except the net agricultural product which is valued at government-purchase prices at the village level. The low level of government-purchase prices relative to current prices renders the share of the agricultural sector in the national product smaller than if it were valued on a basis more or less similar to the others.

Even among those sectors whose net products are valued at current prices, their relative importance to one another is closely related to state policy. Most current prices are official prices. State pricing policy with regard to nonagricultural products is based very much on the predetermined quota of taxes and profits assigned to each commodity or industry. Construction is a case in point. In spite of the feverish activity in this field, its share in the net national product as well as the net product per worker has remained relatively small, "owing to the state's deliberate policy to encourage capital investment by setting a low rate of profit and taxes for construction enterprises".[65] Finally, the fact that current prices include indirect taxes exaggerates the relative importance of industry and trade on which the taxes principally fall in the first instance.[66] Thus the net product of each sector does not represent its "actual" contribution to the national product.

Nevertheless, the *changes* in the relative importance of different sectors have not been distorted as much as their relative position in any one year. Table XXV shows a rapid relative decline in agriculture and increase in construction and industry throughout

---

[64] Of course, if the volume of construction fluctuates widely from year to year with no net increase over the period, the effect of its omission in the national income account would not be important for the growth rate.

[65] Niu Chung-huang, "The Problem of Calculating Labor Productivity and Wage Levels," *Hsueh-hsi (Study)*, 9: 5–6, May, 1957; quotation on p. 6.

[66] For discussion of profit and taxes, see chapter vi.

the period. If agriculture's contribution should be adjusted upward for the base period, the growth of the net national product would have been slower, and the relative decline of agriculture would have probably been less. But its decreasing importance is real and substantial. Similarly, if it is possible to correct the inflationary effect of new product pricing, the net product for factory industry would have been smaller, the net national product would have grown slower, and the relative increase of industry would have

TABLE XXVI

India and Communist China: Relative Importance of Different Sectors in Net National Product for Selected Years
(In per cent)

Economic sector	India (at 1952–53 prices)		China (at 1952 prices)		
	1950–51	1955–56	1952	1956	1957 est.
A. Agriculture...............	48.9	48.4	49.7	40.0	40.3
B. Industry and mining........	15.4	16.5	15.0	22.1	21.9
1. Factory..................	7.3	8.7	12.1	18.7	18.6
2. Handicrafts..............	8.1	7.8	2.9	3.4	3.3
C. Construction..............	2.0	2.0	2.4	4.8	21.8
D. Trade, transport, and communications...............	18.1	17.4	16.9	17.1	
E. Professions and services.....	15.6	15.7	16.0	16.0	16.0
Total......................	100.0	100.0	100.0	100.0	100.0

Note: For discussion of definitions and comparability, see text. On line E, the Chinese percentage is based on the Indian percentage; they should not be compared.
Sources: (1) For India, computed from data given in Government of India, *Second Five Year Plan*, 1956, p. 73, and *Final Report of the National Income Committee*, February, 1954, pp. 68–73. (2) For Communist China, computed from data in Table XXV.

probably been less. In any case, the change in the relative importance of the other material sectors, construction in particular, is understated. Thus the economic structure of the country is being transformed rapidly.

Despite all the distortions, it may still be of interest to compare the change in the Chinese economic structure with the change in India during the period of their First Five Year Plans.

In India, agriculture is defined in much the same way as by Peiping, except that the value product is priced at the median of harvest-period market prices at the state level, and that handicraft work for own household use is probably not included.[67] Factory

[67] Government of India, *Final Report of the National Income Committee*, February, 1954, pp. 24–60. "State" here means province.

industry in India includes large and medium-sized factories, and has been adjusted through a national sample survey to take into account electric power generation and transmission.[68] It differs from the Chinese definition mainly in the exclusion of "small" factories. Handicrafts are given in Indian statistics as "small establishments" a large part of which "is carried on in households."[69] Probably the corresponding establishments are classified by Peiping mostly under factory indutsry with the remainder under subsidiary work in agriculture. On the whole, the totals for industry and mining are more comparable than the component parts. Whether construction can be directly compared is not certain, for the Indian definition is not clear. In the statistics of both countries, restaurants are classified as a part of trade.

Thus, keeping also in mind all that has been said about the effect of pricing on the net product and all the statistical difficulties with the Chinese data, we should compare, at best, the *changes* over time within each country rather than comparing the numbers as given in the table for any other year, although their close similarity in the base year is of interest. The changes in the relative importance of agriculture and industry from the base year to the end of the First Five Year Plan in each country are very different. The transformation in the national economic structure (as distinct from socialization) has been much more rapid and profound in China than in India. Difference in the basic objectives of industrialization between the two countries accounts for such diverse development.

As a matter of common interest, mention may be made of the fact that the percentage of net national product passing through the state budget had increased from 23 in 1952 to 28 in 1956 and 27 in 1957.[70] This may be compared to 37 per cent for 1937 in Soviet Russia and 17 per cent for the same year in the United States.[71] Of course, such a percentage is no index of the pervasive role of Peiping, as the virtually complete socialization of the economy demontsrates.

---

[68] Government of India, *Second Five Year Plan.*

[69] Government of India, *Final Report* . . . , p. 71.

[70] This is computed on the basis of current budgetary receipts, net of foreign-loan proceeds, at 1952 or 1955 prices. See discussion and source data in chapter vi, section 1.

[71] These percentages relate to the gross national product, and are given by A. Bergson, *op. cit.*, p. 93. Bergson's comments on this point regarding Soviet Russia are almost entirely applicable to Communist China.

V

Net Capital Formation, 1952-1957

1. NET CAPITAL FORMATION, ACCUMULATION, AND BASIC CONSTRUCTION INVESTMENT

Net capital formation may be defined for the purposes of this study as the net investment in producer durables (machinery, equipment, implements), in construction of housing units, non-residential buildings (factories, hospitals, schools) and other permanent structures (railways, big dams), and in the intermediate goods in the process of production (unfinished products, materials). It does not include maintenance, repair, and replacement. The definition is designed to measure the potential of increasing the total physical output of an economy as a result of net expansion in its fixed capital assets. Improvement of education and health, for example, when coupled with net capital formation, raises the potential significantly, but expenditures for such purposes are generally regarded as current developmental rather than investment. Residential building is a part of capital formation because of its relative permanency. Intermediate goods, necessary in the process of production and frequently identified as working capital, are included only so far as there has been a net increase from one accounting period to another (say, one year).[1] The rate of net capital formation relates the amount of net capital investment to the net national product.[2]

Which items in the Chinese national income account come close to this definition? It has been indicated in the discussion of the concept of national income that for final disposal, the domestic material product, after having been adjusted to the net balance in the international account and probably also to losses (if any) sub-

---

[1] Hence, by definition an increase in cash or bank balances of an industrial enterprise is not considered as capital formation.

[2] These elementary definitions are given only to clarify the meaning of the terms in the following discussion. There is no intention here to go into capital theory.

sequent to production during the year, is divided into accumulation and consumption, each of which is defined in a special way.[3] Accumulation seems to come close to net capital formation. It is chiefly derived from the state's collection of taxes, profits, and depreciation reserves (above current replacement).[4] Also contributing to it are various types of coöperatives and collectives (agricultural, handicraft, marketing, transport) which are required to keep a certain percentage of their annual earnings as reserves for expansion. Private investment and individual savings deposits and purchase of government bonds make up the rest. Thus the state is the major investor and how much of the annual accumulation is net capital investment depends on the uses to which accumulation is put.

As mentioned in the preceding chapter, accumulation is used for three types of investment. The most important is what has been known as "basic construction investment"—investment in fixed capital assets in both the materially productive and nonproductive sectors.[5] A fixed capital asset is defined as one with at least one year's life and a minimum cost of 500 yuan.[6] Investment will result in a *net* increase in fixed capital assets because maintenance and current replacement in the productive sector have already been taken into account in the gross social value product while those in the nonproductive sector are considered as a part of current "consumption." Included in the investment, however, are all such expenditures ancillary to the process of fixed capital formation as geological survey and exploration, constructural engineering serv-

[3] See chapter iv, section 1.

[4] Only a part of this collection is classified as accumulation. For discussion of internal financing, see next chapter.

[5] Livestock of working age are considered among the fixed capital assets in agriculture. See Yueh Wei, "The Method of Computing National Income," *Ching-chi yenchiu (Economic Research)*, 3: 48–66, August, 1956; reference on p. 63. But the young are probably regarded as a part of working capital.

[6] Yen Ts'ui-yu, "The Standard of Fixed Assets and the Authority of the Enterprises," *Chi-hua ching-chi (Planned Economy)*, 6: 23, June, 1957. According to Yen, this 500-yuan standard is set in accordance with Soviet practice of fixing 200 rubles as the rule. The standard is important for an enterprise because no fixed capital asset thus defined can be acquired without approval from above. It is not clear whether the 500-yuan limit was initiated for the first time in 1957 for all state-operated and joint enterprises or had been in use for some years. According to another source, the situation in 1956 was as follows: "Managers of state-operated enterprises have authority to spend up to 200–500 yuan, depending on the size of the enterprise. The limit for joint enterprises is even smaller; and for those that have newly become a joint operation, no authority is given." Chang Shih-hung, "The Need for Self-governing Authority in Enterprises," *Jen-min jih-pao*, November 6, 1956. Thus the definition given in the text should be taken with these reservations in mind.

ices and architectural planning, scientific testing and research, workers' training, and compensation to the original occupants of the land on which new construction takes place.[7]

The second type of investment serves to increase the working capital for the productive sector, working capital being so defined as to include raw materials and industrial supplies, unfinished goods in the process of production, assets of short life or low value, and projects under construction.[8] The third and last form of investment is found in the increase in inventories of commercial organizations and the stockpiles of the state.[9] The annual increase in the unused part of military supplies has also been regarded as an item of accumulation, and presumably comes under the category of stockpiles.[10]

Among these three types of investment, basic construction takes the lion's share of accumulation, accounting for 41.3 per cent in 1952 and 52.3 per cent in 1955.[11] The rate of accumulation—the ratio of accumulation to the net material product—becomes a matter of vital concern to the central authorities, for the speed of industrialization depends on it, and there has been open discussion as to how high the rate should be under the present circumstances in the country.[12] It has been reported that at 1952 prices the rate had increased from 18.2 per cent in 1952 to 25.3 per cent in 1956 (expected), while at current prices it was 21.4 per cent in 1953, 22.3 per cent in 1954, 20.9 per cent in 1955, and 22.5 per

[7] The *First Five Year Plan*, p. 23n. According to an editorial in *Jen-min jih-pao*, July 1, 1956, the last item (compensation) is very small.

[8] Yueh Wei, *op. cit.*, p. 63, and Yen Ts'ui-yu, *op. cit.* It is not explained why the last item should not be included under the first type of investment, except perhaps for administrative reasons.

[9] Finance Minister Li Hsien-nien in his report on the 1957 budget (*Jen-min jih-pao*, June 30, 1957) stated that the regular commodity reserves for the commercial departments of the government amounted to 20–30 billion yuan. That is the total reserve, not the annual increase.

[10] Chu Cheng-ping, "Production and Consumption under the First and Second Five Year Plans," *Hsin-chien-she (New Construction)*, 101: 1–6, February, 1957. The author states that the most important component of the annual national defense budgetary expenditures is the procurement of military equipment and supplies, the unused part of which is "classified under accumulation according to the present method of computation" of national income.

[11] State Statistical Bureau, "The Scope and Development of China's Basic Construction Investment," *T'ung-chi kung-tso t'ung-hsin (Statistical Bulletin)*, 18: 4–6, September, 1956. These percentages, being unrevised results of first calculation, are given here merely as illustration.

[12] The inverse relationship between the rate of accumulation and the rate of consumption is considered as one of the "internal contradictions" to be resolved. See Mao Tse-tung, "Concerning the Correct Disposal of the Problem of People's Internal Contradictions," *Jen-min jih-pao*, June 19, 1957.

cent in 1956 (expected).[13] On the whole it has been about 20 per cent of the net material product at current prices during the five-year period.

In conclusion, it may be stated that basic construction investment, with the ancillary expenses deducted, is practically the same as "investment in producer durables and construction of housing units and nonresidential buildings and structures" given in the definition of net capital formation. The treatment of working capital investment is also not too different when proper adjustment is made of unfinished projects. Commodity and matériel reserves, however, are not included in our definition. The rate of net capital formation, therefore, must be lower than the rate of accumulation, partly because net capital formation is much narrower in scope than accumulation, and partly because the former rate is calculated from the net national product that is much larger than the net material product on which the latter rate is based.

2. ESTIMATE OF NET CAPITAL FORMATION

For the purpose at hand, the total amount of net capital formation in the entire five-year period is not as informative and interesting as the annual changes in the investment in producer durables (machinery and equipment in particular), residential housing, other construction, and working capital. Thus estimates have to be made of the investment in each of these components for all those years where some information is available.

The task would have been simpler if breakdowns of the annual accumulation into the three types of investment were given in official statistics. In fact, not even the total amount of accumulation for each year of the period is known. Data for basic construction investment are available, but they are broken down by fields of investment rather than by nature of investment. No official information has ever been released on working capital.

Therefore, estimation has to be made on the basis of qualitative as well as quantitative data. This will be done for each year from 1952 to 1957. The operation is rather speculative. Although maximum use will be made of whatever information is available for the purpose, the results must be regarded at best as a rough approximation to reality.

[13] Yang Po, "An Understanding of the Proportion between Consumption and Accumulation in the Disposal of China's National Income," *Hsueh-hsi (Study)*, 20: 24–26, October, 1957. These are revised official results. Note the difference between the rates at 1952 prices given above with those given in Table XV.

We will begin with an estimate of fixed capital formation by
the state in machinery and equipment, residential housing, and
other construction, to be followed by a discussion of fixed capital
formation by private industry. Then working capital will be estimated for (factory) industry as a whole. The question of private
investment in housing will have to be taken up. Finally, fixed
and working capital investment in agriculture will be discussed.
As for individual handicrafts, no separate estimate will be made,
because neither their fixed nor their working capital investment
could be large enough to figure significantly in the whole picture,
and also because after they had been organized into coöperatives
or collectives, any substantial fixed capital investment very probably would have been made from the state's basic construction
program. It may be recalled that factory industry includes handicraft factories.

Estimate of Fixed Capital Formation by the State.—The primary
data for estimating fixed capital formation by the state are found
in its basic construction investment which is summarized in Table
XXVII. The annual investment includes not only the amount that
falls within the state plan (annual), but also investment undertaken outside the plan.[14] The latter refers to either investment by
state-operated enterprises with their self-retained funds, which
cannot be used before approval from above, or investment by the
state in newly organized joint enterprises.[15] It should be realized
that like state-operated enterprises, concerns operating on a joint
basis are required to appropriate from their net revenue a reserve
for expansion, which together with depreciation reserve, taxes, and
a certain proportion of profits, is paid to the state.[16] Thus basic construction investment covers not only the state's share in joint enterprises, but also investment from their own funds.

Table XXVII (A and B) shows that official data on investment
are given at current prices—the prices used in setting up the state
budget for the year.[17] Obviously official rather than market prices,
they affect the valuation of investment mainly because official prices
for producer goods—industrial supplies and construction materials

[14] State Statistical Bureau, "The Scope and Development of China's Basic Construction Investment," *T'ung-chi kung-tso t'ung-hsin (Statistical Bulletin)*, 18: 4–6, September, 1956.
[15] For discussion of "retained" funds, see next chapter.
[16] Chen Yun, "The Problem of Internal Trade and Its Relationship with Industry,"
Jen-min jih-pao, July 1, 1956. For definition of net revenue, see chapter 1, section 3.
[17] See discussion on the problem of pricing for the 1956 and 1957 budgets in the
next chapter.

in particular—have declined since 1953.[18] Thus investment in 1955 amounted to 8,600 million yuan at current prices but to 8,200 million "at comparable prices." The latter, however, must be meant at prices comparable to those of 1954 rather than to those of "all the previous years" as the official explanation states.[19] In fact, the note appended to the official table continues to point out that prices for construction materials had been falling throughout the

TABLE XXVII

BASIC CONSTRUCTION INVESTMENT AT CURRENT AND AT 1952 PRICES, 1952–1957
(In millions of yuan)

Item	1952	1953	1954	1955	1956	1957 planned
A. Total investment at current prices except for 1955.........	3,711	6,506	7,498	8,212	.....	.....
1. Industry and mining.........	1,549	2,756	3,634	4,204	.....	.....
2. Construction...............	92	345	355	290	.....	.....
3. Agriculture and forestry.....	186	276	144	199	.....	.....
4. Water conservation.........	331	376	219	402	.....	.....
5. Railways...................	502	642	917	1,202	.....	.....
6. Other transport.............	229	354	445	452	.....	.....
7. Education and health........	320	767	771	689	.....	.....
8. Municipal construction.......	171	250	232	218	.....	.....
9. Others not included above....	331	740	781	556	.....	.....
B. Total investment at current prices.......................	3,711	6,506	7,498	8,632	13,986	11,100
C. Total investment at 1952 prices	3,710	6,210	7,210	8,170	13,230	10,250

Notes and sources: (1) For A and the subitems, State Statistical Bureau, "Economic Statistical Abstract," *Hsin-hua pan-yueh-k'an,* 17: 42, September, 1956. Investment in 1955 is given at "prices comparable to other years." See discussion in text. Data for 1956 and 1957 (planned) are not available, except that investment in agriculture, forestry, and water conservation was 1,160 million in 1956 and 970 million planned for 1957. See Po I-po, "Report on the Results of the 1956 Plan and on the Plan for 1957," *Jen-min jih-pao,* July 2, 1957. (2) For B, in addition to the source for A, Li Hsien-nien, "Report on the Final Accounting of the 1956 Budget and on the Budget for 1957," *Jen-min jih-pao,* June 30, 1957. (3) For C, see text.

period. Only an unusually heavy drop in such prices in 1955 called for an adjustment. Unfortunately, no information is available concerning the exact changes in the prices of producer goods from year to year. It has been reported for 1956 that wholesale prices had fallen 2.1 per cent for industrial supplies and 2.5 per cent for construction materials from the 1955 level, while prices for fuel had increased 0.2 per cent.[20]

Measurement of investment under these circumstances is a com-

[18] See discussion on current price indices in chapter i, section 5.
[19] See State Statistical Bureau, "Economic Statistical Abstract."
[20] State Statistical Bureau, "A Survey of Market Prices in China for 1956," *Hsin-hua pan-yueh-k'an,* 10: 114–115, May, 1957.

plicated index-number problem. When measured *in money spent,* a given amount of investment for, say, 1953 will become a smaller total at 1952 prices (which are higher than 1953 prices). But when measured *in terms of results*—that is, in what the amount of investment fund can do, an identical amount of investment will produce more results if spent at lower prices than if it is spent at high prices. That explains why investment in 1955 was 8,600 million yuan at current prices but 8,200 million at 1954 prices. Thus basic construction investment at 1952 prices understates the results of investment actually attained. Yet if investment is valued at current prices, the problem of intertemporal comparability arises. The technical difficulties involved in measurement are such that the State Statistical Bureau has called for assistance of Soviet experts.[21]

For the present purpose, since the domestic material product and net national product have been estimated at 1952 prices, it is necessary to adjust basic construction investment to the same basis. The question may be raised as to whether this procedure will not result in understating the *rate* of net capital formation. Take 1956 for instance. Since investment at 1952 prices is smaller than at current prices and since basic construction investment accounts for more than one-half of accumulation, one would expect that the rate of accumulation would be lower at 1952 prices than at current prices. But the reverse is true: we have seen that the rate of accumulation for 1956 was 25 per cent at 1952 prices in contrast to 22 per cent at current prices. The reason for this unexpected result is the fact that both agricultural and consumer-goods prices were unusually depressed in the base period.[22] The material product for 1956 was therefore larger at current than at 1952 prices. Thus at current prices, both the amount of accumulation and the material product for 1956 were larger, but the latter increased more than the former, giving thereby a smaller rate of accumulation at current prices than at 1952 prices. In other words, the rate of net capital formation will be larger instead of smaller when both the national product and the amount of net capital formation were valued at 1952 prices.

Basic construction investment at 1952 prices is given in Table XXVII, line C. The series is computed from indices presented in an official publication of the State Economic and Planning Com-

---

[21] The call for assistance was mentioned by Hsieh Mu-ch'iao, "How to Strengthen and Improve Statistical Work on Basic Construction," *T'ung-chi kung-tso t'ung-hsin (Statistical Bulletin),* 6: 7–9, March, 1956.

[22] See chapter ii, section 1.

missions.[23] In the original source, the indices were given without any explicit mention of whether the changes in basic construction investment as represented by the indices were valued at current or 1952 prices. Comparison with the indices of investment at current prices proves that the author must mean investment at constant prices. In fact, he uses the indices to correlate with changes in the output of various producer-goods industries valued at 1952 prices. Calculation of the amounts of basic investment according to his indices produces for the whole period a series that does not deviate too much from the current-price investment series.[24]

The course of those price changes that had affected the valuation of investment may be traced. The ratio of investment at 1952 prices to investment at current prices was, of course, 100 for 1952. Thence it fell to 95.43 in 1953, recovered a little to 96.13 the following year, only to dip further to 94.61 in 1955 and 94.60 in 1956, and finally stood at 95.38 in 1957 (planned). This shows that while the prices of investment goods were lower throughout the First Five Year Plan than in 1952, their decline had not been steady and continuous as officially reported.[25] In view of the more than 2 per cent decline in prices of industrial supplies and construction materials from 1955 to 1956, the virtually identical ratios between the two years can be explained only if fixed capital formation accounted for a smaller proportion of basic investment in 1956 than in 1955. As we will see presently, this indeed was the case.

Having determined the amount of annual basic construction investment at 1952 prices, we have to estimate how much of it went into fixed capital formation each year during the whole period. The First Five Year Plan anticipated that for the five years 84.5 per cent of the total investment would result in fixed capital assets, the other 15.5 per cent being expenditures ancillary to basic construction.[26] According to the State Statistical Bureau, 86 per cent of basic construction investment in 1955 and 75 per

[23] Chi Ch'ung-wei, "How to Make China's Industry Develop Evenly," *Chi-hua ching-chi (Planned Economy)*, 7: 4–8, July, 1957.

[24] Another series of indices given by a Soviet advisor to the State Planning Commission shows the changes in basic construction investment from 1952 through 1956. The indices for the first two years were clearly based on current values; but those for the next three years were not, and differed from the indices based on current values too much to be explainable by the known price changes. See "Certain Problems in Basic Construction Work," *Chi-hua ching-chi (Planned Economy)*, 6: 8–9 and 33, June, 1957.

[25] For inflation in 1956, see next chapter.

[26] The *First Five Year Plan*, p. 26.

cent in 1956 wer turned into such assets.[27] No similar figures were
given in the bureau's annual communiqués for early years. However, in his budget message for 1956, the finance minister disclosed
that fixed capital assets had increased in 1955 by 16 per cent (at
current prices) over 1954 as a result of investment.[28] With this information it can be readily computed that 85.3 per cent of the
investment in 1954 went into fixed capital assets. It will be noticed
that the percentages for 1954 and 1955 (85.3 and 86) were not far
apart. What could have been the percentage for 1953? Very likely
it was not as high as in 1954, and probably was slightly lower,
because the ratio increased from 1954 to 1955. Since the final draft
of the Plan was done early in 1955, the 84.5 per cent given there
might well have been determined by the experience in 1953. Thus
in the absence of any other information we may take that percentage to represent the portion of investment made in 1953 that
resulted in fixed assets.

Source data are totally lacking for estimating the amount of
fixed capital formation in 1952. There is no reason to project the
percentage given in the Plan to the investment in that year, because
it was the last year of rehabilitation rather than one of construction. In 1952, 65.7 per cent of the investment was for rehabilitation
and reconstruction of existing enterprises, while 32.7 per cent was
for construction of new ones; the corresponding proportions for
1955 were 36.3 per cent and 57.4 per cent.[29] Moreover, the costs of
extensive repairs during the period of rehabilitation were most
probably regarded as a part of basic construction investment. Even
in the First Five Year Plan they are so listed.[30] Thus the percentage
of investment in 1952 that resulted in net capital formation must
be much smaller than in any one of the following three years.

It may be taken as a rough approximation that the percentage
of basic construction investment resulting in net capital assets is
directly related to the percentage of the investment in machinery
and equipment. As will be recalled, the two major components
of basic investment are construction and machinery. Investment
in livestock is probably too small to be significant.[31] For a country
embarking on industrialization, investment in producer durables
has to go together with new construction. Even reconstruction and

---

[27] *Jen-min jih-pao*, June 15, 1956, and August 2, 1957.
[28] *Jen-min jih-pao*, June 16, 1956.
[29] State Statistical Bureau, "The Scope and Development . . ."
[30] See Table I, above.
[31] See discussion in chapter iii, section 2.

expansion of existing plants require both types of investment. Construction includes housing, most of which is for workers. Not only hospitals, schools, public buildings, and workers' clubs, but new transportation lines and big dams (for hydroelectric power) are built in direct relation to industrialization. The proposition stated above is therefore in reasonable accord with the real situation. For a country rich in capital resources, the situation will be different. Housing activities, for example, may surge in a certain phase of the building cycle ahead of investment in plant and equipment. But certainly this does not apply to China at the present. If this reasoning is correct, the proposition may be used for estimating the net capital formation undertaken by the state.

According to the State Statistical Bureau, 25.3 per cent of the basic construction investment in 1952 and 33.2 per cent in 1955 were for machinery and equipment.[32] Since new fixed capital assets accounted for 86 per cent of the investment in 1955, investment in fixed capital assets was 2.59 times the amount used for acquiring new machinery and equipment.[33] Applying this number to the percentage of investment in machinery and equipment in 1952, we find that new fixed capital assets took 65.5 per cent of the basic investment for that year.

For lack of any definite data on state investment for 1957, we had originally decided to omit making any estimate of it. But information has become available for one item (residential building). However rough the estimate will be, it seems desirable to make an attempt. Table XXVII, line C, shows that basic construction investment for 1957 at 1952 prices was almost exactly one-half of the total amount of investment for the previous two years. That furnishes the basis for assuming the amount of fixed capital investment by the state to be also one-half of the total amount for 1955 and 1956. The sum of 8,470 million yuan is thus obtained, equivalent to 82.6 per cent of the basic construction investment planned for 1957. When compared with the corresponding percentages for 1953 through 1955 (84.5, 85.3 and 86), the 82.6 per cent may be an underestimate, though it is much higher than the 75 per cent for 1956.

The estimate of net fixed capital formation undertaken by the state from 1952 through 1957 is summarized in Table XXVIII, Part B.

How did the components of fixed capital investment change

---

[32] "The Scope and Development . . ."
[33] That is, 0.86 ÷ 0.332.

TABLE XXVIII

Estimate of the State's Capital Investment in Machinery and Equipment, Housing and Other Construction, at 1952 Prices, 1952–1957

Item	Unit	1952	1953	1954	1955	1956	1957 est.
A. Basic construction investment (Table XXVII)...............	Million yuan	3,710	6,210	7,210	8,170	13,230	10,250
B. Fixed capital investment:							
1. Per cent of A in fixed assets...............	Per cent	65.5	84.5	85.3	86.0	75.0	[82.6]
2. Investment (B.1. × A.)...............	Million yuan	2,430	5,250	6,150	7,030	9,920	8,470
C. Investment in machinery and equipment:							
1. Per cent of A in machinery and equipment .	Per cent	25.3	32.6	32.9	33.2	29.0	[32.0]
2. Investment (C.1 × A.)...............	Million yuan	940	2,020	2,370	2,710	3,840	3,280
D. Investment in construction (B.2. − C.2.):.....	Million yuan	1,490	3,230	3,780	4,320	6,080	5,190
1. Housing:							
a. Area built...............	Million sq. m.	.....	12	13	14	25	16
b. Investment (at 53.3 yuan per sq. m.).....	Million yuan	290ᵃ	640	690	750	1,330	850
2. Other construction (D. − D.1.b.)...........	Million yuan	1,200	2,590	3,090	3,570	4,750	4,340

ᵃ Amount originally given in official data, obviously at 1952 prices. That was the appropriation or investment actually used. Measured in terms of area built at average prices, the result would be larger than it really was. Strictly speaking, it should be reduced to an average-price basis; that is not done because of lack of data on the area built. However, if at average prices the investment in housing should be smaller, as is likely, then the investment in "other construction" would be larger. The amount of investment in total construction would not be affected.

throughout these years? An estimate has to be made of investment in machinery and equipment, housing, and other construction. Information is available for estimating the first two; the residue will be considered as the amount of investment for the third.

For machinery and equipment, the percentage of basic construction investment used for this purpose was, according to official data, 25.3 per cent in 1952 and 33.2 per cent in 1955. By means of the proposition suggested earlier, it can be readily estimated, for example, that with 84.5 per cent of the basic investment going into fixed assets in 1953, the percentage of the investment for acquiring machinery and equipment was 32.6 per cent.[34] Using the same procedure, we will find that it was 32.9 per cent in 1954 and 29 per cent in 1956. For 1957, however, the assumption must be made again that the investment in machinery and equipment amounted to one-half of the total amount for 1955 and 1956, and therefore came to 3,280 million.

The estimate of the amount of investment in machinery and equipment from 1952 through 1957 is summarized in Table XXVIII, Part C. It should be pointed out that the estimate is at variance with the expectation of the First Five Year Plan. According to the minister of supervision, the Plan anticipates the use of 38 per cent of basic construction investment for acquisition of machinery and equipment, to be made up as follows: 40 per cent of investment in industry, 17 per cent in agriculture, forestry, and water conservation, and 10 per cent in education and culture.[35] This part of the Plan obviously had not been realized.

The amount of investment for construction is the difference between investment in fixed capital assets and in machinery and equipment. (See Table XXVIII, line D.) Construction has to be separated into "housing" and "other construction."

The amount of investment in housing was 286 million yuan in 1952.[36] The annual communiqués of the State Statistical Bureau give the following figures for the volume of new residential construction from 1953 through 1956: 12 million square meters in 1953, 13 million in 1954, 14 million in 1955, and 25 million in 1956.[37] The volume of housing construction increased substan-

---

[34] That is, 0.845 ÷ 2.59.

[35] Ch'ien Ying, "Report to the National Congress of People's Representatives [on Production Waste and Corruption]," in *1956 Jen-min shou-tse (People's Handbook for 1956)*, pp. 228–229.

[36] Jui Mu, "The Development of Civil Legislation since 1949," in *1956 Jen-min shou-tse (People's Handbook for 1956)*, pp. 334–339; reference on p. 337.

[37] *Jen-min jih-pao*, September 16, 1954; September 23, 1955; June 15, 1956; and August 2, 1957.

tially in 1956, reflecting the urgency of the housing situation. However, there are other reports on the volume for the same year that do not agree with the bureau's data. According to a national housing survey of 166 cities, the amount of residential construction from 1953 through 1955 came to 35 million square meters (four million less than the national total given by the bureau), and was only 13 million in 1956.[38] In July, 1957, the minister of communications stated that from 1953 through 1956 a total of 61 million square meters of residential construction had been completed.[39] If 49 million had been built from 1953 to 1955, the amount for 1956 should be 21 million. However, since the bureau's figure was released at a later date, it is adopted for our purpose.

Thus the total volume of residential construction by the state amounted to 64 million square meters from 1953 through 1956. For 1957, it may be gauged from the report that the total volume came to 80 million during the First Five Year Plan.[40] The volume for 1957 therefore was 16 million, higher than the level of 1953 to 1955, but much lower than that of 1956. This is in accord with the investment policy for the year to cut down all nonproductive construction from 22.4 per cent of basic construction investment in 1956 to about 20 per cent.[41]

The volume of residential construction has to be translated into values at constant prices. It has been reported that mainly because of the lowering of housing standards, the cost of housing construction per square meter had fallen from 83 yuan in 1953 to 45 yuan in 1956.[42] The cost in 1952 must have been higher than in 1953. If the unit cost in 1952 were known, could it be applied to the volume of construction for each of the following years in order to find out the cost at 1952 prices? In view of what we have said about the problem of measuring investment, the procedure would be illegitimate. It would mean measurement by results rather than by the amount of appropriation for the purpose. A given amount of appropriation will produce more square meters of housing space

---

[38] Cheng Sung-shen and Lo Lai-yuen, "The Present Problems of Urban Housing in China," *Ta Kung Pao (Impartial Daily)*, March 3, 1957.

[39] Chu Hsueh-fan, "Report on the Improvement of Workers' Welfare," *Hsin-hua pan-yueh-k'an*, 16: 51–54, August, 1957.

[40] Ts'ao Yen-hsing, "Municipal Construction in Accordance with the Principle of Diligence and Economy," *Chi-hua ching-chi (Planned Economy)*, 12: 4–9, December, 1957.

[41] Po I-po, "Report on the Results of the 1956 Plan and on the Plan for 1957," *Jen-min jih-pao*, July 2, 1957.

[42] I Lin, "The Problem of Maximizing the Results of Industrial Investment," *Chi-hua ching-chi (Planned Economy)*, 6: 5–7 and 15, June, 1957.

at lower prices than at higher prices; but to value at higher prices the volume of construction actually attained with a given amount of appropriation would give a total amount of investment larger than the actual appropriation.

For the sake of consistency, the volume of construction has to be valued at an average price of the period. Since prices for construction were declining during the period, valuation at an average price also has the effect of understating the amount of appropriation (investment) for the early years when current prices were higher and of overstating the amount for the later years when current prices were lower than the average price. Such a valuation, however, neither exaggerates the rate of growth of housing construction nor inflates the five-year aggregate as much as valuation at 1952 prices does.

The average price per square meter of housing construction during the five-year period is found in two different sources. One is the national survey of urban housing already referred to. There the joint authors took an average price of 50 yuan per square meter from 1949 through 1956, exclusive of expenses for construction outside the buildings, for purchase of land and for compensation to the original occupants of the land.[43] The other source is found in the comprehensive report on municipal construction during the five-year period, where an average price of 53.3 yuan is given to include the auxiliary but necessary construction outside the housing units.[44] These two prices agree very well. Since the latter is more inclusive, it is adopted for calculation.

The estimate of residential construction by the state is given in Table XXVIII, line D. 1. The difference between the investment for construction as a whole and for housing is the investment for "other construction." This is given in the same table, line D. 2. Since housing is valued at average prices while the annual appropriation for all construction is valued at 1952 prices, "other construction" therefore is also priced on an average basis.

Fixed Capital Investment by Private Industry.—It is almost certain that private industry up to its virtual disappearance at the end of 1955 had not made any appreciable net investment in fixed capital. On the subject of investment the First Five Year Plan makes only a passing reference to private enterprises to the effect that besides the joint enterprises they "will also have some funds

[43] Cheng and Lo, *op. cit.*
[44] Ts'ao, *op. cit.*

to invest in basic industrial construction."[45] Written in early 1955 with some two years of experience behind it, the Plan gives no estimate of their investment even though it does go into some detail in assessing private investment in agriculture. Apparently it regards private investment in industry as insignificant.

There is no need to go over again the ground covered in the discussion of socialization of private industry in chapter i. Certain facts may be recalled. The regulations on private enterprises, revised in the latter part of 1952 upon the conclusion of the "five anti" campaign, did not even require them to keep any reserve for expansion. Beginning in 1953 when practically all industrial materials were under government control, the great majority of private firms had to operate under various types of contract with the state enterprises, whereby the government was in a position to regulate and restrict their revenues. Private industry operated for the state to the extent of 56 per cent of its output in 1952, 61.8 per cent in 1953, 78.5 per cent in 1954, and 81.7 per cent in 1955. In the meantime, industrial plants of any important size were rapidly brought into joint operation, and the remaining private industry consisted of very small firms with total capital assets of less than 20,000 yuan each by the end of 1954.[46]

It is true that shortly after the "five anti" campaign private industry did recover during the first half of 1953. Comparing with 1952, private industry employed 8 per cent more workers in 1953, produced 25 per cent more output, had 14 per cent more funds, and gained 146 per cent more profit.[47] But the number of private factories had increased only from 149,570 in 1952 to 150,275 in 1953, and there was an extensive amalgamation of factories employing less than 15 people.[48] Thus even in the best year for private industry during the five-year period, any evidence of its net expansion in capital investment can hardly be found. As indicated by the revision of the regulations in 1952, it was not the state's policy to encourage the development of private interests. In fact, by 1954 "the amount of accumulation was generally very little" among private factories, and private industry was on its way to extinction.[49] Whereas private factory industry accounted for 14.8 per cent

[45] The *First Five Year Plan*, p. 24.

[46] Wu Tsiang, "The Transition from Capitalist Economy to State-Capitalist Economy," *Ching-chi yen-chiu (Economic Research)*, 2: 54–99, April, 1956.

[47] "A Survey of the Development of State Capitalism in Industry in China," *Hsin-pan-yueh-k'an*, 2: 66–70, January, 1957.

[48] Statistical Appendix, Table 6.

[49] Wu Tsiang, *op. cit.*, pp. 58–59.

of the fixed capital assets in industry in 1952, it could claim only 4 per cent in 1955.[50]

Hence, facts are not violated by leaving out altogether any fixed capital investment by private industry during the period under study.

Estimate of Working Capital Investment in Factory Industry.— Working capital has been defined as the intermediate goods in the process of production, including raw materials and industrial supplies, and assets of short life or low value. Thus private industry, as long as it was operating, had to have a certain amount of working capital, just as did the state and the joint enterprises.

Information on working capital is extremely scarce. The only basis for estimation is derived from a report that the working capital of all factory industries (except private firms) amounted to 5,730 million yuan in 1955.[51] This amounted to 15.29 per cent of their gross value of production. For lack of any other data, this percentage will be used to determine the amount of working capital of the entire factory industry with the private firms included. It stands to reason that the amount of working capital required is closely related to output. However, because of the prevailing practice among state enterprises of storing up raw materials and industrial supplies, working capital was probably larger than officially reported. The 15.29 per cent is indeed low in comparison with 36 per cent in India for 1952.[52] Such a wide discrepancy is probably due to underreporting on the part of the Chinese factories and to inclusion of cash balances on the part of the Indian factories. Thus to estimate working capital requirements on the basis of 15.29 per cent of gross value output is a conservative procedure.

From the annual working capital requirements so obtained, the yearly net increase in working capital investment can be readily computed. The results are summarized in Table XXIX. It will be observed that a heavy increase in working capital took place in 1956. This induced much criticism from the planning authorities. A survey was therefore made of 175 state enterprises operating directly under six industrial ministries of the central government.

---

[50] "A General Survey of Socialist Industrialization in China," *Hsin-hua pan-yueh-k'an*, 2: 54–62, January, 1957.

[51] Wu Ching-ch'ao, "A New Approach to the Chinese Population Problem," *Hsin chien-she (New Construction)*, 102: 1–9, March, 1957.

[52] Computed from data given by Government of India, Ministry of Commerce and Industry, Directorate of Industrial Statistics, *Report on the Seventh Census of Indian Manufactures*, New Delhi, 1955, pp. 8–15.

The result showed that working capital was 21.1 per cent more than necessary, this being caused partly by overstocking of materials and low-cost assets and partly by an increase of unfinished goods in the process of production.[53] It will be further observed that the net increase from 1953 through 1957 (planned) totaled 5,100 million yuan. Although this represented the increase for the entire factory industry, including private firms, it may be compared with the amount of 6,900 million yuan provided in the First

TABLE XXIX

Estimate of Working Capital Investment by Factory Industry
AT 1952 Prices, 1952–1957
(In millions of yuan)

Item	1951	1952	1953	1954	1955	1956	1957 planned
A. Gross product..	20,210	27,014	35,577	41,533	44,748	58,660	60,340
B. Working capital (15.29 per cent of A)............	3,090	4,130	5,440	6,350	6,840	8,970	9,230
C. Annual increase	———	1,040	1,310	910	490	2,130	260

Note: By the same method of calculation, the increase in working capital was 500 million yuan in 1950 and 940 million in 1951.

Five Year Plan as working capital for all state and joint enterprises, including industrial, commercial, handicraft, and others.[54] Our estimate falls within reasonable proximity to the figure given in the Plan.

Private Investment in Housing.—The net addition to residential building in the public sector consists of dormitories and houses attached to factories, mines, and schools.[55] How much investment has there been in private housing? The answer may be found in a report on the use of lumber in 1954.[56] In that year 63 per cent of the lumber was used in basic construction (chiefly by industry), 17 per cent in railways, 12 per cent in fuel industry (chiefly coal mining), 4 per cent in telecommunications and highways, 3 per cent in paper manufacturing, and, finally 1 per cent for general requirements of the public. The report probably refers to the lum-

[53] Sung Shao-wen, "Several Problems of the Movement for Increasing Industrial Production and Economizing," *Kung-jen jih-pao* (*Workers' Daily*), February 26, 1957.
[54] The *First Five Year Plan*, p. 22.
[55] Peng Yung-ch'uan, "Tabulation Form for Basic Construction Planning," *Chi-hua ching-chi* (*Planned Economy*), 5: 29–33, May, 1957.
[56] Director of the Lumber Production Control Bureau Chang Tzu-liang. "Report on the Lumber Industry," *Jen-min jih-pao*, May 31, 1955.

ber from the state-operated forests and factories, generally located in inaccessible areas.[57] But lumber produced in production centers of any size has been subject to "planned purchase" by the state since 1953.[58] Although no data are available concerning the sales of lumber, it may be surmised from the shortage of construction materials even for basic construction projects that very little was left for the use of the public.

It is therefore hardly conceivable that the small amount of lumber supply for the public could have been sufficient to maintain all existing private houses in the urban and rural areas, let alone new construction. And the supply had become shorter year after year. Furthermore, construction workers had been organized since 1952 in increasing numbers for building activities in the state sector; labor shortage must also have multiplied the private owners' difficulties.

All this is confirmed by a housing survey of 166 cities where the major construction undertaken by the state has taken place. Observing that "everywhere is found a large number of private houses out of repair," the report sets forth the reasons for this situation in the following order: (1) the fear of confiscation of the property, (2) the difficulty of obtaining construction materials, (3) the difficulty of getting temporary construction workers, and (4) the fear of removal or demolition of the property in favor of industrial and public needs.[59] According to the survey, general disrepair is only one part of the picture. In some cities as much as 20 per cent of the original houses have been razed to make way for industrial development, public buildings or road construction, and despite some new houses having been built there by the state, there is a net decrease in housing area.

Thus, while the housing situation in the rural areas is unknown, it is probable that there has been a net disinvestment in residential building at least in the urban areas, overbalancing the new housing investment by the state. Without making any allowance for this fact because of lack of sufficient quantitative data, the estimate of fixed capital formation arrived at in this chapter may be overstated.

---

[57] Liu Wen, "Drive for Overfulfillment of the Lumber Production Plan for 1957," *Chi-hua ching-chi (Planned Economy)*, 5: 8–9, May, 1957.

[58] Chapter i, section 4.

[59] Cheng Sung-shen and Lo Lai-yuen, *op. cit.* The extent of disrepair is illustrated by the fact that one day of heavy rain in 1954 resulted in the collapse of more than 3,000 houses in Peiping.

Estimate of Capital Formation in Agriculture.—The First Five Year Plan gives an estimate "according to the planned increase in the gross agricultural value product and in the peasants' buying power for producers' goods" that the total *net* investment on the part of farming households and agricultural producer coöperatives for the five-year period would be 10 billion yuan, of which 60 per cent would be in fixed capital and 40 per cent in working capital.[60] Fixed capital investment consists of equipment and implements for farm and subsidiary work, livestock, and construction of nonresidential building, housing, and small dams.[61] Working capital includes all intermediate goods defined in chapter iii, section 1, among which are seeds, animal feed, fertilizers, insecticides, raw materials for subsidiary work, young farm animals, and costs of planting trees.

The estimated amount of 10 billion yuan of net capital formation for five years is equivalent to nearly 4 per cent of the gross agricultural value product per year. This is far above a previous estimate made on the basis of a sample survey in the late 1920's, giving only 2 per cent of the gross value product as the rate of *gross* capital formation on the farm.[62] It has been officially stated that the land redistribution program, concluded at the end of 1952, had the effect of raising the income of the farming household. This may be true in respect of money income and perhaps even of gross real income. But such increase has to be balanced against (1) the agricultural tax and surtax and the purchase of government bonds, all of which from 1953 to 1956 had increased by 30 per cent per capita of the agricultural population;[63] (2) the discriminatory pricing policy;[64] and, (3) most important, the rapid increase in rural population due to a high birth rate with a declining death rate.[65]

All this notwithstanding, it is not difficult to accept the proposition that a certain amount of net capital formation did take place on the farm before collectivization in 1956. As may be recalled,

[60] The *First Five Year Plan*, p. 26n. See also Wei I, "The Problem of Agricultural Investment under the First Five Year Plan," *Jen-min jih-pao*, August 19, 1955.

[61] According to the discussion given in the preceding two chapters, probably small dams are limited to those requiring state subsidies.

[62] J. L. Buck, *The Chinese Farm Economy*, New York, 1930, p. 65.

[63] Per-capita outlay for the agricultural tax and surtax and government bonds increased from 5.6 yuan in 1953 to 7.2 yuan in 1956. This is based on data furnished by the State Economic Commission for Ma Yin-ch'u, "A New Theory of Population," *Hsin-hua pan-yueh-k'an*, 15: 34–41, August, 1957.

[64] See next chapter.

[65] See chapter viii.

the bulk of agricultural produce had been placed under the government "planned purchase and planned supply" and "planned purchase" schemes.[66] Whether the purchase was arranged before or after harvest, the sales proceeds were subject to the government's manipulation as to the manner in which they should be spent. Generally a part of the proceeds was required to be used for producer goods supplied by the "supply and selling" coöperatives, which were at the same time the state's agent in making the purchase of farm produce. Often the peasant was compelled to accept equipment not adaptable to his needs, a practice so widely prevalent that Peiping had to call publicly for its rectification.[67] Thus the peasants were for the first time forced to make regular investment in tools and implements and perhaps barns and warehouses, in addition to the various kinds of small irrigation and soil-improvement projects that the peasants were organized to carry out from time to time by the party workers.

Furthermore, the state has also relied upon the extension of agricultural credit as a measure of encouraging peasants to make capital investment. The amount of credit outstanding at the end of the year from 1952 through 1957 (planned) is given in Table XXX, line A.1. The credit generally runs for one year, although it may be as long as three, five, or ten years. Acting on behalf of the state bank for this operation are the credit coöperatives organized by the peasants under the leadership of the party workers.[68] The use of agricultural credit is supervised by these coöperatives. The amount of credit outstanding usually reaches the peak in June (just before the planting season), when freight rates for agricultural producer goods on railways and highways are reduced and the interest rates charged to the peasants by either the state bank or the credit coöperatives are lowered by one-half.[69] Since the pri-

---

[66] See chapter i, section 4.

[67] In some cases, the situation was serious enough for the state to buy back the equipment. See the various reports on agriculture by Deputy Premier Teng Tzu-hui, Minister of Agriculture Liao Lu-yen, and Deputy Premier and Minister of Commerce Chen Yun.

[68] Credit coöperatives, developed along the lines of the old Chinese institution of credit societies for mutual aid, perform chiefly the following functions: (1) encouraging savings deposits by the peasants, (2) extending agricultural credit on behalf of the People's Bank or later the Agricultural Bank, and (3) lending money to members for consumption purposes. In early 1956, they had been established in more than 80 per cent of the villages in the country, with more than 70 million members. At the end of 1955, the total of share capital and deposits stood at 800 million yuan. Cf. Tseng Ling, "The Rural Market in the Surging Tide of Agricultural Collectivization," *Ching-chi yen-chiu (Economic Research)*, 2: 1–29, April, 1956.

[69] Tseng Ling, *op. cit.*, p. 7.

TABLE XXX

Agricultural Credit and Sales of Producer Goods in Rural Areas at Current Prices, 1952–1956

Item	Unit	1952	1953	1954	1955	1956
A. Agricultural credit:						
1. Outstanding at year's end[a]	Million yuan	438.0	569.6	758.7	1,000	3,030
2. Net annual increase	Million yuan	139.9	131.6	189.1	241	2,030
B. Sales of producer and consumer goods:						
1. Sales of producer goods:						
a. Agricultural credit outstanding as per cent of sales[b]	Per cent	....	25.0	26.1	32.3	81.4
b. Sales volume	Million yuan	....	2,280	2,910	3,100	3,720
2. Sales of both types of goods:						
a. Sales of producer goods as per cent of total sales	Per cent	....	14.5	14.4	12.1	16.0
b. Total sales volume of both types	Million yuan	....	15,720	20,210	25,620	23,250
C. Sales of selected items as per cent of producer goods sales:[b]						
1. Chemical fertilizers	Per cent	....	38.0	33.9	35.9	33.2
2. Insecticide and equipment	Per cent	....	0.8	1.8	2.1	3.9
3. Irrigation equipment	Per cent	....	....	0.5	1.0	3.7
4. Outdated implements	Per cent	....	23.0	20.5	17.1	12.8
5. Construction materials	Per cent	....	....	7.3	11.8	11.0
6. Livestock, wheelbarrows, and materials for subsidiary work	Per cent	....	36.7	23.4	23.3	22.8
7. Others not specified	Per cent	....	1.5	12.6	8.8	12.6
D. Sales of capital equipment:						
1. Per cent of producer goods sales in capital equipment (C.3 through C.6)	Per cent	....	59.7	51.7	52.2	50.3
2. Sales volume of capital equipment	Million yuan	....	1,320	1,500	1,620	1,890
E. Sales in physical units:[c]						
1. Double-wheeled ploughs	Thousand units	0.4	7.7	17.8	368.3	1,070
2. Chemical fertilizers	Thousand tons	295	555	808	1,175	1,620
3. Insecticides	Thousand tons	1.7	15	41	67	160

Notes and sources: (a) Tseng Ling, "The Rural Market in the Surging Tide of Agricultural Collectivization," *Ching-chi yen-chiu* (*Economic Research*), 2: 1–29, April, 1956; Li Hsien-nien, "Report on the Final Accounting of the 1956 Budget and on the Planned Budget for 1957," *Jen-min jih-pao*, June 30, 1957. According to Tseng, the amount outstanding was 80.4 million yuan at the end of 1950 and 298.1 at the end of 1951. According to Li, the amount outstanding at the end of 1957 was expected to be 3,300 million. Finance Minister Li's report shows that the amount of agricultural credit outstanding each year includes credit extended for disaster relief. (b) Ch'u Ch'ing and Chu Chung-chien, "Variations in the Commodity Turnover in China's Rural Markets," *Ching-chi yen-chiu* (*Economic Research*), 3: 100–126, June, 1957. The percentage of 81.4 given on line B.1.a. is not actual, but planned. According to the authors, all percentages were computed by the "supply and selling cooperatives." (c) Editorial section, "State Economic Support of the Agricultural Economy," *Jen-min jih-pao*, September 14, 1957. These data on sales are different from production data as given in Table XII in chapter iii. The domestic production of chemical fertilizers, for example, had been much less than sales. From 1953 through 1957, the total imports of chemical fertilizers amounted to more than four million tons at a cost of 700 million yuan. Wang Hsing-fu and Nan Chien-chao, "Develop the Chemical Industry," *Chi-hua ching-chi* (*Planned Economy*), 10: 11–15, October, 1957.

mary purpose of agricultural credit is for the purchase of producer goods, the loans have usually been made in kind. This again has led to many abuses, such as compelling peasants to accept unusable equipment and in some cases even to accept unwanted credit.[70]

Table XXX presents a comprehensive picture of agricultural credit expansion and the sales of producer goods in the rural areas from 1952 through 1956. It shows that agricultural credit had been playing an increasingly important part in the sales of producer goods, rising from 25 per cent of the sales in 1953 to more than 80 per cent in 1956 (planned). Although the volume of sales had increased from 2,280 million yuan to 3,100 million between 1953 and 1955, its relative importance in total retail business had declined from 14.5 per cent to 12.1 per cent. Only collectivization was able to make the peasants buy more capital goods out of their total expenditure in 1956. In the sales of producer goods, the share of capital equipment had also decreased from 60 per cent in 1953 to 50 per cent in 1956; in absolute terms, however, the sale of capital equipment did increase from 1,320 million yuan to 1,890 million. While a good part of this sale of capital equipment must be for replacement and did not represent a net addition to the capital stock on the farm, the sales volume does lead one to believe that a substantial amount of investment did take place.

This discussion thus far indicates that the estimate given in the First Five Year Plan on the basis of "the planned increase in the gross agricultural value product and in the peasants' buying power for producers' goods" may not be unrealistic. The problem remains of estimating the amount of net capital investment for each year.

A nationwide agricultural survey of coöperatives and collectives for 1955, undertaken after the publication of the Plan, shows that the savings for net investment among the primary producer coöperatives amounted to 0.90 yuan per *mou* of cultivated land.[71] If this estimate were taken as the national average for 1955, the total net savings would equal 2.7 per cent of the gross agricultural product, instead of the 4 per cent suggested in the Plan. But peas-

---

[70] Policy directives issued by Peiping against such practices are found almost every year since 1953. See, for example, the State Council's instruction of July 7, 1956, against the high-handed methods in extending credit by the Agricultural Bank and the credit coöperatives, in *1957 Jen-min shou-tse (People's Handbook for 1957)*, pp. 538–539.

[71] This is a survey of some 26,700 coöperatives and 200 collectives all over the country except Tibet and Chang-tu Autonomous Area. It was found that 5.2 per cent of the current gross receipts was saved for net investment by the coöperatives as compared to 8.7 per cent by the collectives. See *Hsin-hua pan-yueh-k'an*, 24: 63–65, December, 1956. Fifteen *mou* make a hectare, or 6.12 *mou* an acre.

ant households outside the coöperatives and collectives would certainly have saved less.[72]

However, in the latter part of 1957 writers in Peiping agreed that the rate of accumulation had generally been 3 per cent among independent farming households and between 5 and 8 per cent among coöperatives and collectives.[73] Apparently this conclusion was reached after recalculation of the national income account. But

TABLE XXXI

Estimate of Net Capital Formation in Agriculture at 1952 Prices, 1952–1957

Item	1952	1953	1954	1955	1956	1957 est.
A. Gross value product (million yuan).........	48,400	49,900	51,600	55,500	58,300	61,200
B. Net capital investment						
1. In per cent of A.......	3	3	3	3	5	5
2. Total in millions of yuan (A. × B.1.).......	1,450	1,500	1,550	1,670	2,920	3,060
C. Fixed capital investment in millions of yuan (60 per cent of B.2.)...........	870	900	930	1,000	1,750	1,840
D. Increase in working capital (40 per cent of B.2.), (million yuan).........	580	600	620	670	1,170	1,220

what is meant by the rate of accumulation in this connection? The answer may be found in a study of collectives in 1957. Summarizing the experience of collectives in various areas, the author estimated that out of the gross value product of a typical collective in that year, 20 per cent was used to pay for production costs and depreciation, 10 per cent for agricultural tax, 5 per cent for accumulation.[74] Thus the rate of accumulation is calculated on the basis of gross agricultural value product.

With these findings, we may estimate that since independent

---

[72] Wang Si-hua, "Mutual Adjustment between Industrialization and the Agricultural Coöperative Movement in the Transition Period," *Ching-chi yen-chiu (Economic Research)*, 1: 5–18, February, 1956.

[73] Niu Chung-huang, "Accumulation and Consumption in China's National Income," *Hsueh-hsi (Study)*, 16: 20–23, August, 1957; and Yang Po, "An Understanding of the Proportion between Consumption and Accumulation in the Disposal of China's National Income," *Hsueh-hsi (Study)*, 20: 24–26, October, 1957.

[74] Li Po-kuan, "Income Distribution among Members of Agricultural Collectives," *Hsin chien-she (New Construction)*, 7: 1–5, July, 1957. The remaining 65 per cent was for consumption.

farming was predominant until 1956, the amount of net capital investment was 3 per cent of the gross value product from 1952 through 1955 and 5 per cent for 1956 and 1957. And, in accordance with the suggestion made in the Plan, 60 per cent of the investment would be in fixed capital with the other 40 per cent in working capital. Table XXXI summarizes the estimate.

The table shows that for the entire period of the First Five Year Plan the amount of fixed capital investment was 6,420 million yuan and the increase in working capital 4,280 million, making a total of 10,700 million. This seems to tally with the official statement, "During the five years from 1953 through 1957, net capital investment undertaken by farming households with their own funds is estimated to have exceeded 10,000 million yuan."[75]

3. Summary of Estimates and Some Observations

The estimates of the various components of net capital investment during the period from 1952 through 1957 (with figures rounded to the nearest 100 million) are summarized in Table XXXII, where the rate of fixed capital formation and of fixed and working capital formation are also given.

The total amount of fixed and working capital investment is shown on line III in the table. The low level of investment in 1952 reflects the effect of the Korean war, the needs for rehabilitation and the disruption of the "five anti" campaign. It increased by 63 per cent in the first year of the Plan, and the level was then kept rather steadily upward at an annual increase of 8 per cent until 1956 when another 63 per cent increase took place, followed by a drop of 21 per cent in 1957. This behavior of total investment makes an average annual rate of increase of 19.2 per cent from 1952 to 1957 or of 10.2 per cent from 1953 to 1957 meaningless.

The cause of this behavior of net investment was agricultural output. The most important yearly increase in investment took place in 1953 and 1956, both poor agricultural years themselves but each following a bumper-crop year. This stands to reason; the harvest comes in the late fall, enabling the country in the ensuing year to expand its industrial activity and increase its imports of producer goods. Thus a correlation between net capital formation and good harvest with a one-year lag clearly exists. The

---

[75] Editorial, "Industrial Development Requires Simultaneous Development of Agriculture," *Chi-hua ching-chi (Planned Economy)*, 10: 1–2, October, 1957.

poor crop in 1956 was perhaps the chief factor responsible for the absolute decline in net investment in 1957.

Such strong influence of agriculture upon net investment raises an interesting question regarding the application of the concept

TABLE XXXII

SUMMARY OF ESTIMATES OF NET CAPITAL FORMATION AT 1952 PRICES, 1952–1957
(Source table in Roman numerals)

Item	1952	1953	1954	1955	1956	1957 est.
I. Fixed capital investment:	(In billions of yuan)					
A. State investment (XXVIII):						
1. Machinery and equipment......	0.9	2.0	2.4	2.7	3.8	3.3
2. Construction other than housing	1.2	2.6	3.1	3.6	4.8	4.3
3. Housing*.....................	0.3	0.6	0.7	0.7	1.3	0.9
4. Total state investment.......	2.4	5.2	6.2	7.0	9.9	8.5
B. Agriculture: private and collective (XXXI)..................	0.9	0.9	0.9	1.0	1.8	1.8
C. Total fixed investment......	3.3	6.1	7.1	8.0	11.7	10.3
II. Working capital investment:						
D. Industry and mining: state and private (XXIX)..............	1.0	1.3	0.9	0.5	2.1	0.3
E. Agriculture: private and collective (XXXI)..................	0.6	0.6	0.6	0.7	1.2	1.2
F. Total working capital investment	1.6	1.9	1.5	1.2	3.3	1.5
III. Fixed and working capital investment (C + F)....................	4.9	8.0	8.6	9.2	15.0	11.8
IV. Net national product (XXV).......	72.9	80.2	86.6	93.8	107.3	111.8
	(In per cent of net national product)					
V. Rate of fixed capital formation.....	4.5	7.7	8.2	8.7	10.9	9.2
VI. Rate of capital formation.........	6.7	10.0	9.9	9.8	14.0	10.5

ª See note to Table XXVIII.

of the incremental capital coefficient to a country like China. While industrial output depends largely on agriculture for raw materials, agricultural production itself fluctuates with the nature of the crop year. An important part of the increase in the national product is not due to net capital investment, and the capital coefficient concept therefore loses much of its meaning and significance. It may be argued that the concept would be meaningful if investment were centered on agriculture rather than industry. But the idea that an increase in investment, wherever placed, will result, with a proper time lag, in an expansion of output seems to overlook the fact that any sizable increase in investment is made possible only by a good harvest (barring massive foreign borrowing).

Nevertheless, it is not devoid of interest—or, even of usefulness—to compare the Chinese capital coefficient with that of India. Because of the one-sided emphasis on the development of heavy industry, the Chinese marginal capital-output ratio should have been much higher than the Indian coefficient during the period of the First Five Year Plan for each country. In fact, it is 1.3 for China against 1.8 for India.[76] Why is the Chinese coefficient so much lower? Underestimating the amount of Chinese capital formation for the period is one possibility. But full use has been made of official data on basic construction investment and of the official estimate of private and collective investment in agriculture. While the estimate of net increase in working capital for each individual year may be questioned, the five-year total does not seem to be out of proportion in the entire picture of net investment. The omission of mass mobilization projects occurs in the estimate of both net capital formation and net national product; it is not likely that a proper adjustment would affect the coefficient.

An important explanation of the difference between the two national ratios is found in the definition of net capital formation. The one used in India includes a *part* of what has been treated in this study as current developmental expenditures, such as social services (besides housing). Moreover, sizable amounts of investment in "village and small scale industries" and in increases in commercial inventories are also included, items entirely omitted in the estimate for China.[77]

Thus with proper allowance for the difference in definition, the two national coefficients would not be so different as they appear.

[76] The Chinese ratio may be derived in two ways: (1) Calculated from the total net investment from 1953 through 1957 and the net increase in the net national product from 1952 through 1957, the ratio is 1.35; and, (2) calculated from the five-year average rate of capital formation and the average annual rate of increase in the net national product from 1952 through 1957, the ratio is 1.25. The difference is probably due to averaging. Therefore, the coefficient is estimated to be 1.3.

The coefficient for India is given in Government of India, Planning Commission, *Second Five Year Plan*, pp. 8–9.

[77] Government of India, *op. cit.*, pp. 51–52 and 56–57.

However, even if they were close to each other, the Chinese co-efficient is still too low to reflect accurately its investment policy. In this connection, the official comments given by the Indian Planning Commission on the coefficient are of interest. Originally, according to plan, the Indian ratio was expected to be about three. The favorable result of a much lower ratio is, as explained by the commission, due to a relatively small investment in capital-intensive heavy industries, to good monsoons, and finally to utilization of heretofore unutilized industrial capacity.[78] Difficult as it is to compare the degree of utilization of idle industrial equipment, perhaps the situation was not too different on the whole between the two countries. During the five-year period China had one record crop in 1955 and a normal harvest in 1953, the other three being poor agricultural years. And investment in heavy industry was certainly much more in relative terms in China than in India. All this implies that if the marginal coefficient was 1.8 in India, it should have been much higher in China.

We are again led to the conclusion that the Chinese net national product must have been either underestimated for the early years or overestimated for the later years, or both. All distorting factors brought out in the preceding three chapters enter into the picture. As a *hypothetical example,* if it is assumed that during the five-year period the average rate of net capital formation was 12.5 per cent (according to the Indian definition) in China with a capital coefficient of 1.8, the average annual increase in the Chinese national product would have been 7 per cent instead of nearly 9 per cent as now shown in the official data. And if the coefficient had been 2.5, the average increase in national product would be only 5 per cent. We are of course in no position to estimate a realistic rate of increase in the Chinese net national product during the First Five Year Plan, but this discussion confirms the conclusion reached earlier that the rate of increase in net national product has been overstated in the official data.

During the First Five Year Plan, the average rate of capital formation was 11 per cent, which may be compared to 6 per cent in India during the entire five years of its First Plan.[79] In China the rate had hardly changed from 10 per cent in the first three years, with in fact a slight downward tendency, and it was the substantial increase in 1956 that pushed the average rate up to 11

[78] *Ibid.,* pp. 8–9.
[79] *Ibid.,* p. 10. Although the rates are not directly comparable, it appears that the Chinese rate is definitely higher.

per cent. This course of change may be checked against the official data on the rate of accumulation cited earlier in this chapter. At current prices the latter rate was 21.4 per cent in 1953, rose to 22.3 per cent in 1954, but dropped to 20.9 per cent in 1955, only to rise again to 22.5 per cent in 1956. The fact that during the four years it did drop to the lowest level in 1955 is also reflected in the rate of capital formation at constant prices. At 1952 prices, the accumulation rate rose from 18.2 per cent in 1952 to 25.3 per cent in 1956 (expected), while the rate of capital formation increased from 6.7 per cent to 14 per cent between the two years. As has been said, the wide discrepancy between the two rates in 1952 is mainly due to the inclusion of rehabilitation expenditures in the accumulation account. For the whole period the average rate of accumulation at current prices is about 20 per cent whereas the rate of capital formation is about 11 per cent. Considering the composition of accumulation and the difference between the domestic material product and the national product, our estimate of the rate of capital formation to be about one-half as much as the rate of accumulation does not seem unreasonable.

It will be further observed from the table that for the whole period of the Plan, 15 per cent of fixed capital investment or 20 per cent of total investment was made in agriculture. This was undertaken entirely by individual peasants and agricultural collectives without direct participation by the state. The latter's share is accounted for under the items "machinery and equipment" (such as tractors) and "construction" (such as big dams, granaries). There is no way of breaking down the estimate of fixed capital investment by peasants and collectives. A part of it might well have been in housing, but in view of what has been said, the amount must be small. The work on small dams and dikes must have been equally small, for very probably it was brought into the estimate only so far as state subsidies were involved.[80] The data on sales of producer durables in the rural areas (Table XXX, Part D), when compared with the estimate of fixed capital investment in agriculture, seem to indicate that a predominant part of the investment was for acquisition of new tools and equipment.

Another feature of the investment situation is the small amount allocated for residential construction, accounting for only 8 per cent of the total investment during the five-year period. If the entire fixed capital investment in agriculture is considered to be

---

[80] See chapter iv, section 1.

in tools and implements, investment in machinery and equipment would be 4.2 per cent of net national product, construction 4.7 per cent, and working capital 2.1 per cent. This may be compared with the situation in the United States from 1869 to 1898 when 2.2 per cent of the national product was invested in producer durables, 10.2 per cent in construction and 2.8 per cent in inventories.[81] The comparison brings home the point that a capital-scarce country like China has to economize as much as possible on construction in order to build up its industrial base quickly. And the way to do so is not to reduce nonresidential building activities which are a necessary part of industrialization, but to go slow in building workers' dormitories and even to allow general disinvestment in private housing.[82]

The role of the state may again be noted. Although the state-operated and joint industrial and commercial enterprises operate on their own under a system known in China as "economic accounting"—a translation of the Russian term "khozraschët," all their fixed capital investment is made by the state. When agriculture is brought into the picture, it remains true that for the five-year period the state undertook 85 per cent of fixed capital investment and 70 per cent of total capital investment in the country. How the state managed to finance such a program of investment is the concern of the next chapter.

----

[81] Simon Kuznets, "Proportion of Capital Formation to National Products," in *Proceedings* of the American Economic Association, May, 1952, pp. 507–526. It is the relative magnitude of the different rates that should be compared, not the absolute magnitude.

[82] See also chapter viii, section 2.

VI

Internal Financing

How has the state managed to finance such a massive capital investment program in a country noted for its low level of per-capita income? This question may sound strange for a totalitarian economy in which the state is supposed to be in a position to predetermine the resource allocation between capital formation and consumption. But the problem of internal financing is as real as it is for other economies.[1] As was brought out in the introductory chapter, the state had to rely heavily on pricing to stimulate production and to regulate demand. This means that while resource allocation between investment and consumption is predetermined as a goal, its realization—or, more accurately, its full realization—depends upon the restriction of the public's spending to a level commensurate with the quantity of consumption goods available. Otherwise repressed or open inflation will occur with perhaps flourishing black-market activities. Taxation in various forms and limitation of wage increases can be effective if they are not carried too far in dampening the incentive of the people to work or inviting outright resistance. Here lies the core of the internal financing problem.

However, the following discussion will be confined to the sources of internal financing by the state budget, credit expansion and the currency in circulation.

1. THE STATE BUDGET

Budgetary Balance.—Available information is not sufficient for an extended analysis of the state budget and of the taxation system. As a matter of fact, the budgetary data are so confused that until recently we were not even sure of the global totals of receipts and

---

[1] See the interesting analysis of the problem in Soviet Russia by F. D. Holzman, *Soviet Taxation: The Fiscal and Monetary Problems of a Planned Economy*, Harvard University Press, 1955.

expenditures before 1954, let alone the subdivisions of the budget for every year of the period under study. The present treatment, therefore, is limited to determining the general nature of the budget from the standpoint of internal financing. Like the earlier discussion on current prices, the nature of the available data per- mits us to deal with the entire period from 1950 through 1957.

The primary source of information is the annual budget mes- sage which the finance minister delivered, before 1955, to the Political Committee of the government, and since then, to the Na- tional Congress of People's Representatives. This change of organi- zation receiving the report has produced an obvious improvement in the quality and informativeness of the budget. It has been the practice since 1955 for the finance minister to present in the mes- sage a final accounting of the receipts and expenditures for the preceding year and the planned budget for the current year, whereas before 1955 only the "expected results" of the previous year's budget together with the current planned budget were given.[2] Thus, the global totals of realized receipts and expenditures for the early years of the period have to be sought in other sources.

Table XXXIII presents the planned and realized budgetary re- ceipts and outlays, net of "surplus from previous years," from 1950 through 1957.[3] The figures are given at current prices, except those of 1956 and 1957. It seems probable that all appropriate items on the budget are based on prevailing official prices during the year. Among them are those of the producer goods manufactured by the state-operated factories, goods that are subject to state allocation

---

[2] Even so, there was no budgetary message published in 1951, probably because of the Korean war. Po I-po, the present chairman of the State Economic Commission, was finance minister from 1949 through 1953. He was succeeded by Teng Hsiao-ping. However, two days after his budgetary message was presented in 1954, Teng was removed from that office in favor of Li Hsien-nien, who has held the ministership up to the present.

[3] As indicated in the table, the data from 1950 through 1955 are from Wang. The same data for 1950 through 1953 were given earlier by Wang in *Ta Kung Pao (Im- partial Daily)*, Tientsin, January 27, 1955, and also cited by Yang Pei-Hsin, "The Problems of Accumulation of Funds for the First Five Year Plan," *Ching-chi yen-chiu (Economic Research)*, 4: 12–35, October, 1955. However, a different set of data was given by Ko Chih-ta, "The Nature of China's National Budget and Its Role in the Transition Period," *ibid.*, 3: 67–80, June, 1956. Ko's data were gross of "surplus," but when the "surplus" was deducted from each year's total, the result did not jibe with Wang's. Thus there was no certainty about which set of data was correct, until the budget message of 1957 (*Jen-min jih-pao*, June 30, 1957) appeared, which proved Wang to be correct.

After the 1957 planned budget was presented, the Congress of People's Representa- tives approved it with an addition of 101 million yuan to the receipts and to the expenditures. These are not shown in the table.

among the other state enterprises. In 1956 the prices of many items of these producer goods were lowered, and the realized budget for 1956 and the planned budget for 1957 were given at these "new" prices. The total receipts and expenditures for these two years presented in the table have been adjusted to 1955 prices.[4]

However, the adjustment does not make the budgetary receipts and expenditures for all the years from 1950 through 1957 strictly

TABLE XXXIII

STATE BUDGET: PLANNED AND REALIZED RECEIPTS AND EXPENDITURES,
NET OF CARRY-OVERS, 1950–1957

(In millions of yuan)

Year	Planned budget			Realized budget		
	Receipts	Expenditures	Balance	Receipts	Expenditures	Balance
1950	4,361	4,938	−677	6,519	6,808	−289
1951	6,070	6,950	−880	12,967	11,902	+1,065
1952	13,885	15,886	−2,001	17,560	16,787	+773
1953	20,344	23,350	−3,006	21,762	21,488	+274
1954	23,188	24,946	−1,758	26,237	24,632	+1,605
1955	28,050	29,737	−1,687	27,203	26,727	+476
1956	29,732	30,743	−1,011	29,703	31,560	−1,857
1957	30,093	29,493	+600			

Note: See text.
Sources: (1) For 1950 through 1955, Wang Tzu-ying, "The Experience and Lessons Gained from Compiling and Administering the 1956 National Budget," *Hsin-hua pan-yueh-k'an*, 5: 91–93, March, 1957 (2) For 1956 and 1957, see text.

comparable to one another. In the first three years of this period, no official prices were set for the producer goods subject to state allocation among the state-operated enterprises, and their prices, reflected in the budget, were market prices, which rose rapidly from year to year.[5] When the official prices were introduced in 1953, they were in fact slightly higher than the market prices; and they remained stable for the next two years, with a downward

[4] The adjustment is made by applying the relatives, given in the 1956 realized budget, to the appropriate items in the 1956 planned budget which was framed in "old" prices. In the 1956 realized budget, two sets of relatives of "new" to "old" prices were given, one referring to the 1955 realized budget and the other to the 1956 planned budget. When applied, these two sets of relatives produce somewhat different results. After careful checking, I adopted the set of relatives referring to the 1956 planned budget. For the 1956 budget message, see *Jen-min jih-pao*, June 16, 1956. For the 1957 message, see *ibid.*, June 30, 1957.

[5] Fan Jo-i, "The Pricing Policy of Products of Heavy Industry," *Ching-chi yen-chiu (Economic Research)*, 3: 54–67, June, 1957. According to Fan, the price index of 33 items of metallic products in Shanghai, with 1949 as the base, rose to 197 in 1950 and 278 in 1952.

adjustment of the prices of a few items.[6] Hence, comparability is much higher between the budgetary figures for 1953 through 1957 as adjusted than between them on the one hand and those for 1950 through 1952 on the other.[7]

Table XXXIII shows a budget surplus every year from 1951 through 1955. As a matter of fact, except for the planned budget of 1957, each of the previous budgets from 1951 onward carried over a large item of "surplus from preceding years" as a part of the current year's receipts available for spending. But the surplus had already been spent. While formally the surplus was deposited at the state's account with the People's Bank and could be used to retire the note issue, it had in fact been entirely used for credit expansion by the bank to finance the operations of the various economic enterprises of the country.[8] In his budget message of 1955, the finance minister stated, "For the past few years, the accumulated annual surpluses had been the chief source of funds for the People's Bank to finance the working capital requirements of the state-operated enterprises."[9] Thus, should the state need the preceding years' surplus for current outlay, the bank would either have to recall the loans, thereby disrupting the whole economy, or to resort to an increase in note issue.[10] According to Wang, these surpluses had not been used for budgetary expenditures from 1951 through 1955;[11] the transfer of 2,159 million yuan in 1954 and 2,418 million in 1955 from the surplus account to the bank was

[6] Fan, *op. cit.* As may be recalled, from 1953 to 1955, in addition to the official prices for these goods, there was another set of prices to be applied to their sales to private factories. These latter prices were much higher than the former which were applicable only to state-operated and joint enterprises. In 1956 when private industry virtually disappeared, only one price—the official price—prevailed for these producer goods. For the stability of the official prices, see the discussion of current prices, both wholesale and retail, in chapter i.

[7] The income and outlay of the "workers' insurance fund" (a form of workmen's compensation insurance against sickness and disabilities) were entered into the state budget regularly from 1951 through 1955, but since then have been relegated to the All-China Labor Union and the various enterprises concerned. However, the size of this item was small in the total budget, and its elimination in 1956 does not significantly affect comparability. The planned budget for 1957 indicated that there was an item of "working reserve" of 784 million yuan in the 1956 budget, but it was not found in the realized budget for 1956, presumably because after the money was spent it was charged to other items in the budget.

[8] Except that a small amount of 307 million yuan in 1954 and 201 million in 1955 was used to set up a "working reserve for local governments." Again, this had already been used by the bank long before the budgetary allocation from the surplus account.

[9] *Jen-min jih-pao*, July 10, 1955.

[10] Ko Chih-ta, *op. cit.*, and Wang Tzu-ying, *op. cit.*

[11] Wang Tzu-ying, *op. cit.*

only a matter of legal recognition of what had already been done. In order to determine the exact budgetary situation each year, it is important, therefore, to deduct from the expenditures these legalistic transfers and also from the receipts the preceding years' surplus.[12] For the first time, an item of "fund for the Bank's credit operations" (600 million yuan) appeared in the planned budget for 1957. This item is also deducted from the expenditures for 1957 in Table XXXIII, not only for the sake of consistency and comparability, but, more important, because its inclusion carries a dubious implication that the bank's credit expansion would be restricted to the amount stipulated.

The People's Bank, operating on its own profit-and-loss account as an independent unit, performs functions much broader than those of a central bank. It undertakes (1) to regulate the currency in circulation, (2) to make disbursements and keep deposits for the national economy, (3) to supply credit to all economic enterprises that operate on their own account, (4) to organize and operate the clearing for domestic exchange, and (5) to be the custodian of foreign-exchange reserves (including gold and silver) and to settle international balances.[13] Dependent on the bank for the supply of working capital are all state-operated and joint enterprises, agricultural, handicraft and other producer coöperatives, and private economic units.[14] The resources with which the bank operates consist of the bank deposits of the public, the idle balances of various government and public organizations and enterprises, and, above all, the note issue.[15] We have seen that in fact the chief resource for the bank had been the budgetary surplus. How far the bank

---

[12] For the same reason the appropriations for the "working reserves for local governments" have to be deducted.

[13] Wu Ch'ing-yu, "Is the Socialist State Bank a Government Agency or an Enterprise?" *Hsueh-hsi (Study)*, 2: 8, January, 1957. Interestingly, the author's answer to the question is that the People's Bank is a government agency, not an economic enterprise. Indeed, it operates as an agency directly under the jurisdiction of the State Council.

[14] Presumably all state-operated enterprises have a certain amount of "retained" funds at their own disposal. Whether this had been so during the period under study is uncertain, for in the budget message for 1957 the finance minister remarked, "We are considering a change from the present practice of requiring the enterprises to surrender their entire revenue to the government, with all of their expenditures separately appropriated, into a practice of permitting them to retain a certain share of the profits to be used for their own investment or other outlay." This means that the "retained" funds had been more of a fiction than a reality. In fact, whatever funds the enterprises have must be deposited at the state bank and cannot be used without approval from above. See also chapter v, section 1.

[15] See the message on the 1957 planned budget.

had to resort to note issue for its credit operations is a subject for exploration in the next section of this chapter.[16]

Another interesting feature of Table XXXIII is the persistent deficit in the planned budget up to 1955, resulting partly from an equally persistent underestimation of actual receipts for these years, and partly from an overestimation of expenditures of 1953 through 1955. For 1956, the situation was reversed—a deficit in the realized budget. Only for 1957 was the planned budget in balance. The main explanation lies in the fact that from 1952 on the preceding year's surplus had been considered as a part of current revenue for budgeting purpose until the experience of 1956 finally convinced the government authorities of the fault in such a procedure. Another explanation is that for most years under consideration both the tax-collecting agencies and the spending units each operated with a high safety factor in budgeting so as not to be caught falling behind the annual quota at the end of the year or short of funds during the course of the year.[17]

---

[16] In addition to the People's Bank, two banks have been established for special purposes. Starting operation on October 1, 1954, the People's Construction Bank, organized by the Ministry of Finance, was designed (1) to handle both the funds allocated from the state budget for basic construction to various enterprises and government agencies and the latter's "retained" funds, (2) to supervise them for the use of these funds, and (3) to extend to the state-operated enterprises short-term credit in accordance with a loan plan to be approved by the state. Directly operating under the People's Bank is the Agricultural Bank, created on March 25, 1955, whose functions are (1) the extension of long- and short-term credit to state-operated agriculture and stock-farming, and to the mutual-aid teams and producer coöperatives in agriculture, stock farming, fishery, and forestry; (2) the handling and supervision of the use of the basic construction funds allocated from the state budget for agriculture, forestry, and water conservation; (3) assistance given to the credit coöperatives; and (4) the institution of facilities to handle the time and demand deposits of the rural residents, the agricultural coöperatives and collectives, and the state-operated agricultural and water conservation enterprises. See *Jen-min jih-pao*, September 10, 1954, and March 27, 1955. The exact relationship between the Construction Bank and the People's Bank is not clear, but it may be surmised that the funds which the former can operate for short-term credit extension are only the idle balances of the enterprises and government agencies, and that when the Construction Bank has exhausted its operating resources for the purpose, either the bank itself or the enterprises must resort to the People's Bank. The Construction Bank has no authority to issue paper money. Thus, only the People's Bank can induce a net credit expansion for the country as a whole.

In 1950 and 1951 the private banks were organized into five state-private joint groups. Then in December, 1952, they, together with the trust companies and the "native banks" (*i.e.*, those not organized and operated as modern banks), were merged into one single state-private bank operating under the direction of the People's Bank. See *Ta Kung Pao (Impartial Daily)*, Tientsin, May 21, 1953.

All types of insurance business are operated by the People's Insurance Company as a state monopoly.

[17] Ko Chih-ta, *op. cit.*

Budgetary Receipts.—The budgetary receipts, net of carry-overs, include foreign-loan proceeds which must be deducted in order to determine the sources of internal financing.[18] Table XXXIV shows the changing importance of these sources from 1950 through 1957, with the exception of 1955 and 1956, for which comparable data are not available.

It will be observed that since 1952 the state-operated enterprises, the marketing and handicraft coöperatives, and the joint enterprises together have become the preponderant source of revenue for the government, and that among them the first group is the most important. The rate at which private enterprises had been socialized since the "five anti" movement in 1952 is clearly shown. Although no attempt is made in this study to discuss the taxation system, it is necessary to indicate the important taxes.[19] Applicable to various state, joint, coöperative, and private enterprises are the turnover tax, the income tax, the commodity tax (excise), the business tax (on volume), and the stamp tax; collectively, they are known as the taxes on industry and trade.[20] The

[18] In the budget message for 1957, Li Hsien-nien disclosed that the total Soviet loan receipts from 1950 through 1952 were 2,174 million yuan, and from 1953 through 1957, 3,120 million. At the same time, he gave the annual current receipts from 1953 through 1957, net of Soviet loan receipts, and at "old" prices. The Soviet loan receipts for 1956 and 1957 were separately given. Thus, the annual foreign-loan receipts for 1953 through 1955 can be adduced by comparing Li's figures, net of Soviet loans, with those given in Table XXXIII, which are gross of Soviet loans.
No information is available for separating the loan receipts of 1950 through 1952 into annual totals, except that those for 1952 may be estimated. It may be recalled that the first information on the national income account given by Po I-po in September, 1956, was in terms of a percentage relationship between the global total of the domestic product and the budgetry receipts, net of carry-overs and of foreign loans (see chapter iv, section 2). By applying Po's percentages to the budgetary receipts net of surpluses and foreign loans, the national income for 1953 through 1956 as given by Po may be obtained. According to *T'ung-chi kung-tso t'ung-hsin (Statistical Bulletin)*, 18: 4, September 1956, the national income for 1955 is 129.7 with 1952 as 100. Since the national income for 1955 so computed is 80,080 million, that for 1952 would be 61,740 million. And, according to Po, 27.6 per cent of it, or 17,040 million yuan, must be the budgetary receipts net of surplus and foreign loans for t,1at year. Thus, the foreign-loan receipts for 1952 is the difference between 17,560 million and 17,040 million—520 million yuan.
[19] The taxation system was established in 1950 when a successive series of laws and regulations was proclaimed. The system was somewhat revised on March 1, 1953. Although some changes have been made from time to time, especially regarding the schedules, the system has remained basically the same throughout these years.
[20] The turnover tax was introduced in March, 1953, to consolidate certain excise taxes previously levied, and has not taken the place of the other taxes mentioned in the text. The taxes on industry and trade are so numerous that it is not proposed even to name them all here. See the revised tax schedule for industry and trade, in *1953 Jen-min shou-tse (People's Handbook for 1953)*, Tientsin, 1953, pp. 290–292.

TABLE XXXIV

SOURCES OF INTERNAL FINANCING OF THE STATE BUDGET, 1950–1957

Item	1950	1951	1952	1953	1954	1955	1956	1957 planned[a]
A. Aggregates:	(In millions of yuan)							
1. Receipts, net of surplus of preceding year....	6,519	12,967	17,560	21,762	26,237	27,203	29,703	29,293
2. Soviet loan proceeds..........	1,654		520	438	884	1,657	117	23
3. Net internal receipts........	....	.....	17,040	21,324	25,353	25,546	29,586	29,270
B. Sources:	(In per cent of net internal receipts)							
4. State enterprises: taxes, profits, and depreciation reserves.....	34.08	49.35	57.98	65.40	65.24	....	....	79.2
5. Marketing and handicraft coöperatives: taxes	– –	– –	1.08		3.65	....	....	
6. Joint enterprises: taxes, state profits, and depreciation reserves.....	– –	– –	1.05	1.20	1.66	....	....	7.2
7. Private enterprises: taxes and bonds.........	32.92	28.66	21.19	16.90	13.34	....	....	1.1
8. Agricultural households and coöperatives: taxes and bonds.....	29.63	18.17	16.00	13.40	14.23	....	....	11.2
9. Others[b]........	3.37	3.82	2.70	3.10	1.88	....	....	1.3

[a] The 1957 planned receipts are given at "new" prices, because the percentages for the sources as originally given are so based.
[b] Other receipts include such items as payments into workmen's compensation insurance fund (until 1956), sales proceeds and rentals of public properties, various fees (on deeds, for example), penalties, and the purchase of government bonds by urban residents.

Sources: For 1953 and 1957, Li Hsien-nien's budget message for 1957, *Jen-min jih-pao*, June 30, 1957. For the other years, Yang Pei-hsin, "The Problem of Accumulation of Funds for the First Five Year Plan," *Ching-chi yen-chiu* (*Economic Research*), 4:12–35, October, 1955. The figures for 1950 and 1951 are the same as those given by Po I-po in his budget message for 1953, *Jen-min jih-pao*, March 16, 1953. The meaning and reliability of these early figures were clarified only in the 1957 message in which reference was made to the composition in 1953, which turned out to be virtually identical with that found in Yang.

income tax of state-operated enterprises is merged into their "profits" that have to be remitted to the state together with their depreciation reserves.[21] The agricultural tax is levied in kind on the farming household, generally according to its annual agricul-

TABLE XXXV

TAXES, PROFITS AND DEPRECIATION RESERVES OF STATE AND JOINT ENTERPRISES, AND GOVERNMENT BOND PROCEEDS, 1954–1957

Item	1954	1955	1956[a]	1957 planned[a]
A. Net internal receipts (million yuan)...	25,353	25,546	28,626	29,270
	(Per cent of net internal receipts)			
B. Taxes.................................	52.14	49.89	49.21	49.78
1. Industry and trade................	35.39	34.15	35.27	35.87
2. Agriculture.......................	12.93	11.96	10.36	10.22
3. Import and export dues, salt, and other.............................	3.82	3.78	3.58	3.69
C. Profits and depreciation reserves......	39.30	43.82	46.90	46.70
1. Industry..........................	.....	19.86	19.03	20.09
2. Railways, other transport, and tele-communications....................	.....	.....	7.45	7.74
3. Internal and external trade, and food grains..............................	.....	12.99	15.42	14.02
4. Others............................	.....	10.97	5.00	4.85
D. Government bond proceeds..........	3.30	2.42	2.12	2.05
E. Others[b]............................	5.26	3.87	1.77	1.47

[a] At "new" prices. They have not been converted according to "old" prices, because no details are given for the operation. Since the "new" low prices affect industry the most, the figures given on the table tend to understate somewhat industry's share relative to the others. The relative decline of the share contributed by trade (C.3.) was the result of certain contractual rearrangements in favor of industry (C.1.). See chapter i, section 3.
[b] Same as line 9 in Table XXXIV, except the purchase of government bonds by urban residents, which has been merged into line D above.
Sources: Budget messages of 1955, 1956, and 1957, *Jen-min jih-pao,* July 10, 1955, June 16, 1956, and June 30, 1957.

tural product calculated in terms of staple food grains or major commercial crops.[22] The relative importance of these payments, together with the government bond proceeds, is shown in Table XXXV.

[21] According to regulation, only a definite proportion of the profits is to be turned over to the state. But see discussion in the last section.
[22] The household is entitled to a minimum exemption, above which the tax rate advances either proportionally or progressively. The schedule varies according to different areas in the country. Although surtaxes levied by local governments were supposed to be abolished in 1953, they have not been eliminated, and Peiping has legalized the practice by limiting the surtaxes not to exceed 22 per cent of the tax proper. As a result of collectivization, the agricultural tax system is due for basic revision. See the budget message of 1957.

The total amount of taxes, and profits and depreciation reserves that the state and joint enterprises pay into the national treasury is known as "accumulation," and its rate is determined by the ratio of the total payment to the gross sales.[23] Taxes as well as depreciation reserves are considered as a part of production cost, and the profits are allegedly the difference between gross sales proceeds and production costs.[24] Although no separate data are available for the depreciation reserves, it may be visualized that for a country just embarking on industrialization these reserves must be making a growing contribution to the state budget, net of current replacement costs. As to profits, they cannot be any different from taxes because the selling prices of the products concerned are set and regulated by the state.[25] Table XXXV reveals that for its revenue the state relies almost as much on pricing policy as on tax collection.

This point is of great importance in understanding the sources of internal financing. Although the relative share of agricultural taxes has been gradually declining in the state budget, the burden of open and hidden taxes on the peasants need not in any sense be lightened. Aside from the payment of taxes, the farming household has to deliver the bulk of its produce to the state at official prices, while it buys industrial products through the "supply and selling" coöperatives again at official prices, the ratio between these two sets of prices being so set as to result in a high rate of accumualtion for industry and trade.[26] "An industrial product is subject to taxation many times from the point of production to the point of final sale, and some intermediate goods in the process of continuous production are also taxed."[27] Moreover, the accumulation rate has been higher in the consumer-goods industries than

[23] Wang Wen-ting and P'eng Wei-ts'ai, "Reform of the Taxation System Has to Be Taken in Two Steps," *Ta Kung Pao (Impartial Daily)*, August 11, 1957. According to them, accumulation is highest in spirits and tobacco, each with a rate of more than 80 per cent.

[24] Wang Cheng-yao, "The Incidence of China's Taxes during the Transition Period," *Ching-chi yen-chiu (Economic Research)*, 2: 62–79, April, 1957.

[25] The profit for each enterprise is predetermined at the beginning of the year on the basis of its gross-value-product quota and will be automatically deducted from its bank deposits in the course of the year, regardless of its actual production or sales. See chapter ii.

[26] Li Hsien-nien, "Price as an Instrument to Promote Production," *Jen-min jih-pao*, September 23, 1956. In this speech, the finance minister made it clear that the past pricing policy of depressing the purchased prices of agricultural produce too far was at fault, although he insisted that the ratio of industrial and agricultural prices had been narrowing.

[27] Wang Wen-ting and P'eng Wei-ts'ai, *op. cit.*

in the producer-goods industries.[28] Therefore, the total tax burden of the peasants is not reflected in the amount of agricultural taxes.[29]

Table XXXV also makes it clear that the sales proceeds of government bonds have not played an important part in internal financing. Bond sales take the form of a predetermined allotment to private enterprises, urban residents (including workers), farming households, and even armed forces, to be followed by a national drive to exceed the quota.[30] Bond issue is a device for forced saving and mopping up a certain amount of purchasing power in the hands of the public, for up to the present the servicing of the issues has been duly honored by the government. During the First Five Year Plan, four issues had been made, each to the amount of 600 million yuan. However, the annual amortization payments are growing, and whether the bond policy will be modified as the servicing outlay catches up with the proceeds of a new issue remains to be seen. It is not improbable that the amount of annual issues will be increased in which case the bond holders will be "urged" to reinvest their receipts. The issues since 1949, together with their terms and actual sales, are listed in Table XXXVI.

Budgetary Expenditures.—Budgetary expenditures are heavily weighted by those on economic and social development, accounting for more than two-thirds of the total (see Table XXXVII). This has been made possible by a sizable drop in the relative share devoted to national defense and a moderate decline in the share of administration throughout the years. These latter two items together have recently been stabilized at 28 per cent of the budget, and it does not seem likely that they could be appreciably reduced further in favor of economic and social development. Worthy of

---

[28] "Several Problems of China's Socialist Industrialization," *Hsin-hua pan-yueh-k'an*, 1: 67–61, January, 1957. According to this source, the amount of accumulation of the light and heavy industries as percentage of "total budgetary revenue of the state" is as follows:

	1952	1953	1954	1955
Light industry	13.3	13.0	15.3	15.5
Heavy industry	6.2	8.5	10.7	13.4

It is not clear whether the "total bugetary revenue" is gross or net of foreign-loan proceeds.

[29] Witness Deputy Premier Teng Tzu-hui's remark at the National Conference of Model Agricultural Workers (*Jen-min jih-pao*, July 22, 1957), "The important source of funds for state investment is derived directly or indirectly from agriculture—agricultural taxes and profits and taxes paid by light industry which depends on agriculture for 90 per cent of the supply of raw materials and which sells 70 per cent of its output to the peasants."

[30] The extent of overfulfillment had been inversely related to the rate at which private enterprises were socialized. See Table XXXVI.

special notice is the absolute reduction of the planned budgetary expenditures for 1957, with the impact being concentrated upon the item for economic development. Basic construction investment, of which net capital formation by the state is a part, had to be heavily scaled down from the level of the previous year. This sig-

TABLE XXXVI

GOVERNMENT BONDS: ISSUES, TERMS AND ACTUAL PROCEEDS, 1949–1957

Name of issue	Amount issued in millions of		Amount actually sold (in millions of yuan)	Terms
	Commodity units	Yuan		
1. 1949 Production Development Bond for the Northeast..................	20	...	[33]	....
2. 1950 Production Development Bond for the Northeast..................	30	...	[49.5]	5 years, 5%
3. 1950 First Victory Bond.............	100	...	[213.2]	5 years, 4%
4. 1954 Economic Development Bond...	...	600	836.13	8 years, 4%
5. 1955 Economic Development Bond...	...	600	619.3	10 years, 4%
6. 1956 Economic Development Bond...	...	600	606.54	10 years, 4%
7. 1957 Economic Development Bond...	...	600	......	10 years, 4%

Note: The first two issues, though local in nature, were serviced by the state budget. The commodity units for those two issues were each equivalent to the total of the market prices at Shenyang (Mukden) for 2½ kg. of kaoliang, 1 foot of cloth, 2½ kg. of salt, and 17 kg. of coal. The terms for the first issue, though unknown, may be reasonably assumed to be the same as those of the second. On the basis of scattered information, the amounts actually sold were not more than the original issues. The conversion of these commodity units into yuan is made at the rate of 1.65 yuan per unit. In the planned budget for 1950, given in commodity units, 0.1 per cent of the expenditures was for the servicing of the 1949 bond issue. The total expenditures were 4,937.7 million yuan. Assuming that 0.1 per cent of it, or 4.95 million yuan, was for the servicing of the national debt (2 million units of principal and 1 million units of interest), the worth of one commodity unit for the first two bonds was therefore 1.65 yuan.
   The commodity unit of the Victory Bond differs from that discussed above. It was quoted at the end of January, 1951, at 2.132 yuan. This is the conversion rate adopted.
   The actual sales proceeds of the last four bonds were duly reported in the state budget under "debt proceeds," from which the deduction of foreign-loan proceeds gives the net proceeds of bond issues.
   Sources: (1) For the first two bond issues, *1951 Jen-min shou-ts'e (People's Handbook for 1951)*, Tientsin, p. "shen" 15. (2) For the Victory Bond issue, *1955 Jen-min shou-ts'e, (People's Handbook for 1955)*, Tientsin, pp. 435–437. (3) For the last four issues, *Jen-min jih-pao*, December 10, 1953; December 21, 1954; November 11, 1955; and December 30, 1956.

nificant change will be examined together with consumption in the following chapter.

The state budget is national, covering both the central and the local governments. Generally, from 50 to 60 per cent of the national revenue is collected through the local governments.[31] It will be noted that the local share of the expenditures rose to 29 per cent in 1952, and then declined to 24 per cent during the first three years of the First Five Year Plan, only to rise again to some 29 per cent in 1956 and 1957. Probably the change up to 1955 was a political development when Peiping was forced after 1952

---

[31] See the budget messages for the planned budgets of 1955 and 1956.

TABLE XXXVII

BUDGETARY EXPENDITURES, BY CATEGORIES, 1950–1957

Category	1950	1951	1952	1953	1954	1955	1956[a]	1957 planned[a]
A. Total (million yuan)	6,808	11,902	16,787	21,488	24,632	26,727	31,560	29,493
				(Per cent of A)				
B. Current and developmental.[b]								
1. Economic	25.49	29.50	45.43	40.23	50.17	51.49	52.95	48.69
2. Social, cultural and educational	11.09	11.29	13.58	15.64	14.05	11.93	14.67	16.55
3. National defense	41.53	42.52	26.04	26.43	23.60	24.32	19.91	19.24
4. Administration	19.29	14.60	10.29	9.85	8.78	8.06	8.43	8.29
5. Others[c]	2.60	2.09	4.66	7.84	3.40	4.20	4.03	7.23
Total	100.00	100.00	100.00	100.00	100.00	100.00	100.00	100.00
C. Basic construction investment:[d]	.....	.....	22.11	30.28	30.44	32.30	44.32	37.64
D. Central and local:								
1. Central government	74.20	74.72	70.08	75.84	74.90	75.93	71.05	70.78
2. Local[e]	25.80	25.28	28.92	24.16	25.10	24.07	28.95	29.22
Total	100.00	100.00	100.00	100.00	100.00	100.00	100.00	100.00

[a] At 1955 prices, except that the percentages for basic investment are based on current prices and those for central and local governments are based on "new" prices.

[b] Sources: From 1950 through 1953, Yang Pei-hsin, "The Problem of Accumulation of Funds for the First Five Year Plan," Ching-chi yen-chiu (Economic Research), 4: 12–35, October, 1955, and Ko Chih-ta, "The Nature of China's National Budget and Its Role in the Transition Period," Ching-chi yen-chiu (Economic Research), 3: 67–80, June, 1956. From 1954 through 1957, annual budget messages, Jen-min jih-pao, July 10, 1955; June 16, 1956; and June 30, 1957.

[c] Other expenditures include payments for workmen's compensation (up to end of 1955), for veterans and militia, subsidies to minority regions, special reserve (for 1957), etc.

[d] At current prices; from Table XXVII.

[e] Local governments are those of the special cities, provinces, and autonomous regions. Sources: Annual budget messages of 1955 through 1957, and Wang Tzu-ying, "China's National Finance," Ta Kung Pao (Impartial Daily), Tientsin, January 27, 1955.

by circumstances to strengthen and centralize its authority.[32] But the increasing local share since 1955 is a matter of deliberate policy on the part of the central government to delegate more authority and to assign more economic enterprises to the local governments for management and operation.[33] How far this policy will be carried in the future remains to be seen.

The findings thus far indicate that the state had been able to finance the development program out of current revenue, with an annual surplus to spare, in four out of the five years of the First Five Year Plan. But could this achievement be apparent rather than real? Had not the working capital requirements been financed entirely outside the purview of the budget? How much had credit expansion and note issue contributed to the internal financing of the Plan? We will now attempt to answer these questions.

2. NOTE CIRCULATION, CREDIT EXPANSION AND BUDGETARY BALANCE

Bank Deposits and Note Circulation.—The discussion of current prices in the introductory chapter has shown that the wholesale and retail price indices, both based on official quotations, give no help in examining the monetary effects of internal financing of the economic development program. The problem may be approached by estimating the changes in the money in circulation. Although the subject is regarded as one of the top economic secrets of the country, enough information is available for a preliminary estimate.[34]

In March, 1950, when the emergency economic and financial

---

[32] The large and increasing share of the local governments from 1950 through 1952 was probably due to the semiautonomy of Manchuria under the rule of Kao Kang. He must have carried the autonomy too far by 1952, as evidenced by the sudden jump in the "local" share in that year, because he was recalled to Peiping under an order dated November 15, 1952, and later was accused of "making the Northeastern area his own independent kingdom since 1949," as the resolution of the Chinese Communist party was worded (*Jen-min jih-pao,* April 5, 1955). It was announced that he had already committed suicide before the resolution was passed.

[33] See the message on the planned budget for 1957. Although the percentages for the local governments in 1956 and 1957 are based on "new" prices, and therefore not strictly comparable to those for the early years, a rough estimate on the basis of "old" prices would reduce their share for each of these two years by only about one half of a percentage point. According to the budget messages for 1956 and 1957, 27.21 per cent of the local budgetary expenditures was for economic development and 36.80 per cent for social and educational development in 1955 (realized), while the corresponding percentages for 1957 (planned) were 32.71 per cent and 39.07 per cent.

[34] No attempt is being made here to undertake a thorough-going monetary analysis. The present analysis is intended only to ascertain the character of internal financing.

regulations were adopted, the most important monetary control measure was one that required all government agencies, armed forces, state-operated enterprises and coöperatives to deposit their cash balances (except petty cash) with the People's Bank. This measure, very strictly enforced, has since been extended to include public organizations and state-private joint enterprises. All transactions among the state-operated and joint enterprises themselves

TABLE XXXVIII

TOTAL BANK DEPOSITS OF THE PUBLIC, 1949–1956

(In millions of yuan)

End of year	Total	All cities	Rural area
1949....................	10	...	...
1950....................	132	...	...
1951....................	543	...	...
1952....................	861	740	121
1953....................	1,319	1,060	259
1954....................	1,640	1,278	362
1955....................	[2,066]	1,560	[506]
1956....................	3,034	2,235	779

Notes: (a) The deposits in the rural-area column include not only those of the individual peasants, but also those of the agricultural producer coöperatives. (b) The total deposits and those of the rural area for 1955 are not available. The figures in brackets are interpolations, based on the rate of increase of rural deposits from 1953 to 1954. (c) The total deposits are composed of demand and time deposits. The percentage of time deposits to the total was about 20 in 1951 and 50 in 1954. The average deposit period of the time and demand deposits in seven cities (Peiping, Tientsin, Shanghai, Wuhan, Canton, Sian, and Chungking) was 33 days in 1951, 112 in 1954, and 158 in the first eight months of 1955. See Wang and *Ta Kung Pao* cited below.

Sources: (1) For total deposits from 1949 through 1954, Wang Wei-ts'ai, "To Further Develop People's Deposits," *Jen-min jih-pao*, March 3, 1955. (2) For deposits of the rural areas in 1952 and 1956, T'an Chen-lin, "A Study of the Income and the Level of Living of the Chinese Peasants," *Hsin-hua pan-yueh-k'an*, 11: 105–111, June, 1957. (3) For deposits of cities in 1953 and 1954, *Jen-min jih-pao*, February 27, 1955. (4) For deposits of cities in 1955 and 1956, *Ta Kung Pao* (*Impartial Daily*), January 26, 1957.

are cleared through a transfer of account at the People's Bank.[85] The occasion for the enterprises to need cash is either the payment of wages, awards, and the like, or the purchase of consumption goods from the market and of agricultural raw materials not subject to state allocation. The control measure was further extended in May, 1951, to persons who were allowed to hold not more than 100 yuan in notes; and in June to private concerns, which were required to deposit daily with the People's Bank any amount of cash in excess of 200 yuan and to pay for their purchases in checks.

The objective of the measure is clearly to forestall speculative activities, to reduce the use of paper money to the minimum, and

---

[85] In fact, virtually all their output of producer goods is subject to state allocation and does not pass through marketing channels. See Hsieh Mu-ch'iao, "Discussing Again the Planned Economy and the Law of Value," *Hsin-hua pan-yueh-k'an*, 9: 135–137, May, 1957.

to enable the People's Bank to control the quantity of notes in circulation. The result has been a rapid growth of bank deposits of
the public—not including those of government agencies, armed
forces, public organizations, and state and private enterprises. (See
Table XXXVIII.) This is a new banking feature in the Chinese
scene. However, no evidence exists to indicate any extensive use
of bank checks among the public. The small amounts of their purchases and the inconvenience involved in writing checks (let alone
the difficulty of the illiterate in doing so) do not justify the practice. Nevertheless, workers, for example, are urged to deposit their
wages with the bank and withdraw only a little at a time, their
deposits being regarded as an important source of savings for economic development.[36]

Thus far, one important conclusion may be reached. For the
country as a whole, paper money is needed only for the purchase
of services and consumption goods by all consuming units, which
include the households and the "collective" units such as government agencies, armed forces, public organizations, and economic
enterprises. Moreover, the enterprises will need cash to pay for
agricultural raw materials that do not come under the scheme of
state allocation. The collective units using cash to buy services and
raw materials constitute the major source of cash income of the
households. Thus notes in circulation are largely accounted for
by cash balances in the hands of households.[37]

This introduces the statistical concept of "social purchasing
power" as used by Peiping. It is intended to be the measure of total
effective *monetary* demand for *consumption goods* of the country
as a whole. The exchange for consumption goods by barter among
the peasants is not included, nor would the monetary expenditures
for production or for trade. According to Peiping usage, the social
purchasing power is made up of that of the "residents" on the one
hand and that of the collective units (as defined above) on the
other.[38] The residents are both urban and rural. The urban resi-

---

[36] To the argument that the banking cost of handling all such small accounts must
be very high, the answer may well be that labor is relatively cheap and that even
if all deposits were payable on demand, the aggregate of the unspent balances could
be large enough to make the effort worthwhile. In fact, interest is paid on demand
deposits. The terms for the withdrawal of time deposits, as low as seven days in
1950, run from one month in the rural areas and from three months in the cities
to more than a year. For a revised list of interest rates on deposits and on various
types of loans, see *Jen-min jih-pao,* October 4, 1955.

[37] The term "cash" or "cash balance" is used in this discussion to refer to paper
money in hand, and does not include demand deposits.

[38] The major source of information for this concept is Wu Ting-ch'eng of the State

dents' purchasing power is chiefly made up of the total cash payments made to them by the collective units, but the money payments between residents for professional services or for the purchase of personal belongings (*e.g.*, used goods and jewelry) through commercial channels also contribute to the aggregate of their purchasing power. The payments of private enterprises and between residents are not a part of the state planning, whereas the payments of all other collective units are.

The purchasing power of the rural residents is derived from the sale of agricultural products to the collective units and to the urban households. It should logically be the total money income of the rural households alone, but, in fact, has also included that of the agricultural producer coöperatives.[39] It may be noted that an increase in the monetary purchasing power of the rural residents does not imply any improvement in their consumption, for, assuming unchanged output, the more farming activities are commercialized and the smaller the proportion of production that the farming household retains for self-consumption, the larger its monetary purchasing power will be. And the poor peasants may, and in some places do, have a larger money income than the better-off peasants, because the former's capacity for self-sufficiency is low.[40]

Thus, the aggregate purchasing power of the urban and rural residents so computed, with the deduction of the money income of the agricultural coöperatives, becomes the total monetary demand for consumption goods on the part of the households. As to the collective units, their purchasing power is partly directed to consumption goods, and partly to agricultural raw materials.

The magnitude of the social purchasing power has been stated to be 40,200 million yuan for 1955, 46,500 million for 1956, and 47,320 million (estimated) for 1957.[41] It has further been reported that about 84 per cent of the total is the residents' purchasing power, the other 16 per cent being that of the collective units.[42]

Statistical Bureau, "Explanation of Certain Problems Related to the Proposal for Computing the Social Purchasing Power," *Chi-hua ching-chi (Planned Economy)*, 9: 27–29, September, 1957.

[39] According to Wu Ting-ch'eng, *op. cit.*, the money income of these coöperatives and their bank deposits would be deducted under the new proposal of computation in the future.

[40] Ch'u Ch'ing and Chu Chung-chien, *op. cit.* For discussion of the relationship between commercialization and consumption, see chapter viii.

[41] Po I-po, chairman of the State Economic Commission, "Report on the Results of the 1956 Plan and on the Plan for 1957," *Jen-min jih-pao*, July 2, 1957.

[42] Wu Ting-ch'eng, *op. cit.*

With these and other sources of information, the following tabulation may be presented for the clarification of the concept.

As the magnitudes of social purchasing power for 1955 and 1956 are known, it is possible to estimate the aggregate *consumers' money income* for those two years. For any one year this aggregate must be smaller than the social purchasing power by two major items: (1) the cash expenditures of the collective units, expenditures which

TABLE XXXIX

Composition of Social Purchasing Power, 1956

Item	In millions of yuan	Per cent of total
1. Social purchasing power.	46,500	100.0
2. Residents..............	39,060	84.0
a. Rural.................	24,500	52.7
b. Urban...............	14,560	31.3
1) Within plan.........	12,910	27.8
2) Outside plan........	1,650	3.5
3. Collective units..........	7,440	16.0

Sources: (1) "Social purchasing power" and "Urban within plan," Po I-po, "Report on the Results of the 1956 Plan and on the Plan for 1957," *Jen-min jih-pao*, July 2, 1957. (2) "Residents" and "Collective units," Wu Ting-ch'eng, "Explanation of Certain Problems Related to the Proposal for Computing the Social Purchasing Power," *Chi-hua ching-chi (Planned Economy)*, 9: 27–29, September, 1957. (3) "Rural," T'an Chen-lin, "A Study of the Income and the Level of Living of the Chinese Peasants," *Hsin-hua pan-yueh-k'an*, 11: 105–111, June, 1957.

are actually a source of cash income for both the urban and the rural residents and therefore would have been recorded as such in the course of the year as a part of their purchasing power; and (2) the total money income and deposits of the agricultural producer coöperatives. As far as the two years under consideration are concerned, the allowance for the first item may be made by deducting 16 per cent from the social purchasing power.[43] No information is available regarding the second item, but since according to regulations the coöperatives are not allowed to hold any more than petty cash, their deposits must constitute the bulk of deposits of the rural areas. Data on the volume of their deposits and on the aggregate of their petty cash are completely lacking. We will assume

[43] The 16 per cent, it may be recalled, is given by Wu, *ibid.* In his original text, no time period is specified to which the percentage be applied. From the context, however, his statement implies that the ratio is rather stable during recent years. See also Liao Chih-lih, "Accelerating Agricultural Development—a Condition for Accelerating the Development of Heavy Industry," *Chi-hua ching-chi (Planned Economy)*, 8: 4–6, August, 1957.

that the total approximated the size of rural area deposits for each of the two years. Thus 510 million yuan would have to be further deducted from the social purchasing power of 1955, and 780 million from that of 1956 (see Table XXXVIII). The size of the second item to be deducted is much smaller than that of the first. With allowance for these two items, the consumers' money income for 1955 and 1956 may be estimated to be 33,260 million and 38,320 million yuan—an increase of 5,060 million between the two years.

The previous discussion has made it clear that the money income is received and spent in cash. While most money income is used for the purchase of consumption goods and services, a part of it may be either hoarded or kept at the bank as time deposits.[44] Any one of these operations will, of course, affect the income velocity of note circulation. The total money income during the year for the country as a whole may be taken as the product of the quantity of notes in circulation multiplied by the income velocity of circulation.

According to Minister of Finance Li Hsien-nien, the notes in circulation increased by 1,690 million yuan from the end of 1955 to the end of 1956.[45] At the same time, as we have estimated, the total cash income increased by 5,060 million. Thus it can be readily computed that the income velocity of note circulation for 1956 was 2.99, or 3; that is, the income period was four months.[46] If this velocity, calculated from the *increase* in both cash income and note circulation, is applied (as a rough approximation) to the total cash income of 38,320 million yuan for 1956, the quantity of note circulation in that year would be 12,770 million. This was the average volume of circulation for the year.

Generally, the volume fluctuates widely during the year, rising to the high points on the eve of the Chinese New Year (usually in February) and immediately after the autumn harvest (about October), and falling to a low point about the middle of the year.

---

[44] It may be repeated that if the money income is kept at the bank as demand deposits, they would be withdrawn from time to time in cash.

[45] "Report on the Final Accounting of the 1956 Budget and on the Planned Budget for 1957," *Jen-min jih-pao*, June 30, 1957.

[46] It may be a surprise to some that the velocity could be so slow. Perhaps the explanation is that the deposits, one-half of which may be taken to be time deposits, had increased most rapidly in 1956 among the years listed in Table XXXVIII, and, more importantly, that nation-wide collectivization of farms during the year resulted in a high degree of commercialization of farming and therefore in the peasants' holding a large quantity of notes. According to a report appearing in *Jen-min jih-pao*, February 27, 1957, about one-third of the notes circulating in the rural areas were estimated to have been hoarded by the peasants.

In fact, the volume did fall by 970 million yuan from the end of 1956 to the end of May, 1957, and by 130 million more one month later.[47] The important point is that in view of such seasonal variations, it is not unrealistic to assume that, barring war and other emergencies, the average volume of note circulation for the year may be close to that at the end of the year, when the volume is not so large as that at the peak points and not so small as that at the low point.

TABLE XL

ESTIMATED VOLUME OF NOTE CIRCULATION, 1949–1957
(In billions of yuan)

End of year	Notes in circulation
1949	1.0
1950	2.5[a]
1951	...
1952	7.4
1953	9.7
1954	...
1955	11.1
1956	12.8
1957–May	11.8
1957–June	11.7

[a] Average of the year.
Sources: See Text.

With this assumption, we will be able to see the development of notes in circulation since the end of 1949. In addition to the data already referred to, there is the information that the volume of circulation at the end of 1949 was equal to one-tenth of that at the end of 1953 and to one-twelfth of that at the end of June, 1957.[48] Moreover, the volume at the end of 1955 was about 50 per cent higher than that at the end of 1952, and the average volume in 1952 was about three times that in 1950.[49] All this information, plus the estimate for 1956, goes into the making of Table XL.

The reasonableness of the estimates above may be tested by com-

[47] For the figure for May, see Li Hsien-nien, *op. cit.* For the figure for June, see Tseng Ling, "Is There Inflation in China at the Present?" *Ching-chi yen-chiu (Economic Research),* 5: 36–49, October, 1957. The reduction by the middle of 1957 might not be entirely due to seasonal factors, for Li's budget message made it clear that the authorities were determined to stop the tide of inflation.

[48] Ho Wei, "The Real Nature of the Rightist Opposition to the Policy of State Monopoly in Purchases and Sales," *Hsueh-hsi (Study),* 14: 14–16, July, 1957.

[49] Tseng Ling, *op. cit.*

parison with the volume of note circulation at the end of June, 1937, when it was 1,400 million "yuan."[50] It will be observed that between that date and the end of June, 1957, the volume increased more than eight times. The important factors accounting for such an expansion of currency are several. (1) The 1937 unit had a foreign-exchange value—which was 0.295 American dollar—higher than the present yuan, and the official rate then was maintained rather effectively in the open market before the war with Japan broke out. (2) In terms of the present value of the monetary unit, the general price level had increased about three times from 1936 to 1956.[51] (3) The area of circulation is more extensive now than it was in the first half of 1937. The change from the silver exchange standard to managed paper money started only in November, 1935, and although by 1937 the paper money was widely accepted, it did not as yet penetrate into every village as the present currency has. Political control and unification of the country from the center is more effective now. (4) The degree of monetarization of the economy is much higher today than it was before, as a result of compulsory sale of agricultural products, agricultural productive coöperation, and collectivization. (5) In the middle of 1930's the government launched a program of industrial development (partly as preparation against Japanese aggression), which, however, could not be compared with the First Five Year Plan in the latter's all-inclusiveness in scope and full mobilization of resources. In other words, the high tempo of economic activity demands a larger volume of note circulation than that of the mid-1930's. (6) Finally while the annual natural rate of population increase is generally conceded to have been about 0.5 per cent before 1937, it has been officially estimated to be about 2.5 per cent at the present.[52] Do these six factors explain adequately the eightfold increase in note circulation?

Note Circulation and Internal Financing.—Since price stabilization was supposed to have been achieved by 1952, the first three factors mentioned above would go far to explain the difference in the volume of note circulation between then and 1937, if there had been no inflation resulting from the Korean war. How much

---

[50] *Ibid.* The unit of account bore the same name, but with a different meaning, to be made clear presently.

[51] Fan Jo-i, "The Pricing Policy of Products of Heavy Industry," *Ching-chi yen-chiu (Economic Research)*, 3: 54–67, June, 1957.

[52] See discussion on population growth in the concluding chapter. For demographic change before 1937, see Ch'iao Chi-ming, *Chung-kuo nung-ts'un she-hui ching-chi-hsueh (Chinese Rural Economics)*, Chungking, 1945, pp. 20 ff.

of the fivefold increase in circulation between 1937 and 1952 was due to war financing is difficult to estimate, especially as no budgetary message was published for 1951. Whatever that might be, the "five anti" movement in the first half of 1952 mopped up a good deal of purchasing power in the hands of the private industrial and commercial concerns, and the volume of note circulation must have been stabilized from wartime inflation, by the end of the year. If this was so, then the further increase in note circulation since 1952 must be due to the natural growth of the economy resulting from the operation of the last three factors or to monetary expansion as a means of internal financing of the development program.

It is impossible to determine the rate of increase in note circulation engendered by economic growth, because so many variables are included in the equation. However, it seems reasonable to assume in the first instance that an increase in circulation is closely related to credit expansion by the People's Bank and the state budgetary balance. If a positive budgetary balance existed and was used for retirement of notes in circulation, while there was no increase in credit extension to the economy, the note issue would, of course, be reduced. If an increase in the amount of credit extension took place and was equivalent to the positive budgetary balance, the note circulation would be more or less stabilized. If the net credit expanison was larger than the positive budgetary balance, an increase in note circulation would result. Finally, if for any year a net credit expansion should appear together with a budgetary deficit, the increase in note circulation would be unusually large. Are these propositions useful in analyzing the process by which the increase in note circulation had taken place on the Chinese mainland? The answer depends on the purpose for which the net credit expansion is intended.

The net annual increase in credit expansion is difficult to measure because no information has ever been released regarding the operation of the People's Bank. We know that during the period under study the working capital requirement of the economy depended on the bank's credit extension. While data on the requirements of the commercial agencies and the handicraft coöperatives are not available, the amount of agricultural credit each year is known and the annual requirements of industry have been estimated in the preceding chapter in this study. These latter two items doubtless represented a part of the bank's credit operations.

Could these operations provoke a significant if not proportional increase in note issue in the event that the budget had been balanced? The discussion above on the monetary control measure makes it clear that credit extension to industry and commerce *need not* increase the note circulation, and the earlier treatment of capital formation in agriculture has also brought out the fact that the use of agricultural credit is "supervised," only a small portion being directed to consumption. Thus, the note-issue effect of credit expansion for working capital requirements is much restricted. The net credit expansion that will result in an increase in note issue must have been used for purposes not explicitly provided for in the state budget, and must also *inevitably* induce an augmentation of the money income of the public. Credit extension to meet working capital requirements fulfills the first condition (not being provided for in the budget) but does not fulfill the second. Only credit expansion for investment meets both of these conditions. This leads to the rather surprising but significant proposition that the increase in note issue during the period of the First Five Year Plan was chiefly due to the financing of "basic construction investment," a large component of which, as brought out in the last chapter, was net fixed capital formation undertaken by the state.

The proposition is surprising because we have been led to believe, by the manner in which the annual budget is presented, that the investment funds for "basic construction" are entirely derived from the "current and developmental expenditures" for such items as economic construction, social and educational, and administration. In fact, the proportion between current expenses and basic investment for each item has never been indicated. The finance minister in his budget message used to mention merely a lump sum for "basic construction investment" without any explanation as to how it fits into the budget. It is not explicitly provided for, and may or may not be *entirely* covered by the regular "current and developmental expenditures." If it is not entirely covered by the latter, the basic investment would necessitate an expansion in credit, and therefore in note circulation, unless there is at the same time a budgetary surplus large enough to make up the difference. To test the validity of the proposition, we may examine the relationship among the following items: the budgetary balance, note circulation, basic construction investment, credit extension to industry and agriculture, and the gross agricultural and industrial product. (See Table XLI.)

TABLE XLI

BUDGETARY BALANCE, NOTE CIRCULATION, BASIC CONSTRUCTION INVESTMENT, INDUSTRIAL WORKING CAPITAL, AGRICULTURAL CREDIT, AND GROSS AGRICULTURAL AND INDUSTRIAL PRODUCT, 1950–1957

Item	1950	1951	1952	1953	1954	1955	1956	1957 planned
A. Budget balance (million yuan)	−289	1,065	773	274	1,605	476	−1,857	600
B. Note Circulation:								
1. Volume at year-end (million yuan)	2,500	...	7,400	9,700	...	11,100	12,800	...
2. Index (base year 1952)	34	...	100	131	...	150	173	...
C. Basic investment (million yuan)	...	...	3,711	6,506	7,498	8,632	13,986	11,100
1. Index (base year 1952)	...	...	100	175	202	233	377	299
2. As per cent of budget	...	...	22	30	30	32	44	38
D. Net increase in agricultural credit outstanding at end of year (million yuan)	...	218	140	132	189	241	2,030	270
E. Net increase in industrial working capital (million yuan)	463	871	962	1,211	842	454	1,968	373
F. Gross agricultural and industrial product: index (base year 1952)	68	...	100	114	125	136	156	161

Sources: (1) Line A from Table XXXIII. (2) Lines B and B.1 from Table XL. The volume for 1950 is an annual average. (3) Line C from Table XXVII; C.2 from Table XXXVII. (4) Line D from Table XXX. (5) Line E from Table XXIX. (6) Line F, see Statistical Appendix, Table 1, for absolute data.

From 1950 through 1952, note circulation increased threefold while a heavy budgetary surplus obtained in the last two years. If the budget figures were correctly reported, the increase in note circulation must have taken place largely in the latter part of 1950 shortly after the Korean war broke out when the monetary control measure was first applied. The volume of circulation at the end of 1952 might have been reduced from a previous peak volume because of the "five anti" movement taking place in that year.

The first year of the First Five Year Plan saw a tremendous expansion of the note issue—a 30 per cent increase over that of the previous year—when the budget showed a small surplus. Even if it were possible for the total increase in agricultural credit and industrial working capital to lead to an increase in note issue, the sum was far less than the increase of 2,300 million yuan in circulation. The reason must be found in the sharp increase of 2,800 million yuan in the basic investment which rose from the equivalent of 22 per cent of the budget in 1952 to that of 30 per cent in 1953. It will be further observed that the gross agricultural and industrial product increased only 14 per cent during the year. The situation was, indeed, "tense,"[53] and most likely accounted for the deferment to 1955 of the introduction of the new monetary unit originally scheduled for 1953.[54] This experience in the very first year of the Plan must have brought home to the authorities the lesson that the basic construction investment should be entirely included in the state budget. In any case, the monetary and fiscal factors were brought under control in the two ensuing years when the note circulation increased 14 per cent with an increase of 20 per cent in the gross value product.

The situation in 1956 was radically different. The bumper crop in the fall of 1955 and the successful drive for socialization of the economy early in 1956 furnished the basis for raising the amount of basic investment by more than 60 per cent, making it equal to 44 per cent of the budget expenditures. The result was the largest budgetary deficit on record (1,857 million yuan), slightly larger in amount than the increase in note circulation (1,700 million). This similarity in amount seems to indicate that basic investment had been entirely included in the regular budget by this time, so

---

[53] Wang Tzu-ying, "Experience and Lessons . . ."

[54] The new yuan notes bear the date of 1953. As explained by the governor of the People's Bank, "the new measure was scheduled to be put into effect in 1953, but, owing to technical reasons that required more preparatory time, it was postponed to 1955" (*Jen-min jih-pao*, March 1, 1955).

that a budget deficit did occur when the investment was too big to be financed out of current revenue.[55] Moreover, the fact that both agricultural credit and industrial working capital requirements had increased by about 4,000 million yuan while the increase in note circulation was far less, shows the restrictive nature of the monetary control measure. This is not to deny that credit expansion for working capital purposes might not be a contributing factor to the increase in note circulation, but such an effect did not seem significant.[56]

Thus, the proposition is established that the chief cause for the increase in note circulation during the First Five Year Plan had been the financing of basic investment and, therefore, of fixed capital formation, with economic growth and credit expansion for working capital requirements as contributory factors. As if to prove further the validity of this conclusion, the Peiping authorities adopted a policy of retrenchment in 1957, involving even a reduction, for the first time under the First Five Year Plan, of the absolute amount of basic investment from the level of the preceding year, and at the same time a contraction in note circulation.

This analysis also throws light on the subject of current prices.[57] In contrast to the showing of the official wholesale and retail price indices, there must have been severe inflationary pressure in 1953 and 1956. Both were years following a bumper crop, and each witnessed a tremendous increase in basic investment. This goes a long way to explain why the government had to institute the system of "planned purchase and planned supply" of food grains and edible vegetable oil in the latter part of 1953. Moreover, each severe inflationary year was followed by a period of recuperation, as it were. Thus, the decision on resource allocation cannot be taken by the state without giving due weight to internal financing which affects the market prices and the "social purchasing power."[58]

[55] See Wang, *op. cit.* Among the reasons he advanced for the "financial tension" in 1956, the large increase in basic construction investment was especially stressed. Collectivization of farms and a 13 per cent increase in wage rates since April of the year were also contributing factors to the deficit. It may be noted, too, that the gross value product increased by 15 per cent in 1956.

[56] It is also possible that the effect was found not so much in an increase in note circulation but in the velocity of note circulation. However, our previous computation shows that the income velocity was 3 during the year, not a particularly high figure.

[57] See chapter i, section 5.

[58] The basic factor—consumption—will be discussed in the concluding chapter.

3. SUMMARY

According to the official data, an annual budgetary surplus, calculated on the basis of current revenues net of carry-overs from preceding years, exisited from 1951 through 1955 and also in 1957 (planned). The surplus was used, not for retirement of note issue, but for financing through the People's Bank the working capital requirements of the economy, those of the state-operated enterprises and of agricultural coöperatives in particular. Both current revenues and expenditures were gross of Soviet loan proceeds. After allowance is made for these proceeds, it becomes clear that from two-thirds (1953) to more than 86 per cent (1957 planned) of the internal revenue came from the state-operated and joint enterprises and the marketing and handicraft coöperatives—in the form of tax payments and profits and depreciation reserves. The contribution of private industry and trade declined steadily from 17 per cent of the revenue in 1953 to about 1 per cent in 1957 (planned) because of growing socialization. Agricultural taxes also declined in relative importance from 13 per cent in 1953 to 10 per cent in 1957 (planned). However, the state depended for its revenue almost as much on profits and depreciation reserves as on tax collections. Since the prices of the products manufactured or handled by the state-operated and joint enterprises were set by the government, the profits were in fact a form of taxes, falling particularly heavily on the peasants as they were required to buy both consumer and producer goods and to sell their major crops at official prices. Government bonds, issued annually since 1954, played a very small part in the budget, and had operated as a device for forced saving and not as a form of taxation.

Current and developmental expenditures for economic and social enterprises grew fast in relative importance in the budget, accounting for 56 per cent of the total expenditures in 1953 and about two-thirds in 1956 and 1957, at the expense (relatively speaking) of national defense. But the basic investment called for in the First Five Year Plan had not been explicitly provided for in the budget, and was in fact partially financed by an increase in note issue during the first year of the Plan. However, that experience had apparently induced a change in budgetary practice, and the largest deficit on record appearing in 1956 resulted from a heavy increase in basic investment. Thus, for two years out of the five of the Plan, note issue played an important part in financing the fixed capital formation of the country. This, plus the factors of economic growth, accounted for the increase in note circulation from 7,400 million yuan at the end of 1952 to 12,800 million at the end of 1956—as compared to a threefold increase during the period of the Korean war. The credit expansion for financing the working capital requirements of the economy perhaps also accounted for a small increase in the note issue, but such an effect seems to have been much restricted by the monetary control measure introduced in 1950 and 1951, which had also produced the effect of increasing the public's bank deposits.

VII

External Financing and Export Drive

1. SOVIET ECONOMIC AID

How important to Chinese economic growth has been the aid received from abroad? According to what has been made public, no substantial grants have ever been received—only small "gifts" from some countries in Eastern Europe.[1] Among grants, certainly the most important—if it may be so classified—is the supply from Soviet Russia of whole sets of blueprints and related technical materials giving direction from the layout of a plant through construction to pilot manufacturing in such fields as machine making, coal mining, iron and steel, petroleum, electric power, transportation, and light industry.[2] Many Soviet engineers have been sent to China to help the Chinese edit and translate these materials. Except for the cost of duplication, no charge is made. Presumably the information embodies Soviet experience in industrialization, and making it available to China should have greatly facilitated the Chinese effort.[3]

---

[1] An example is Hungary's gift of an agricultural equipment and tractor station, established in Shantung Province. See *Jen-min jih-pao*, November 17, 1955, and January 7, 1956.

[2] Huang Chen Ming and Huang Jun-t'ing, *Ts'ung chung-su ching-chi ho-tso k'an chung-su jen-min wei-ta yu-i (Looking at the Great Sino-Soviet Friendship through Sino-Soviet Economic Coöperation)*, 1956, p. 29. Similar assistance was also extended by Poland, Czechoslovakia, East Germany, Hungary, Rumania, Bulgaria, and Albania. See *Jen-min jih-pao*, May 12, 1955.

[3] In return, Peiping has "for many years" furnished technical data to Russia on light industry (ink, tobacco leaf, soybean sauce), agriculture, heavy industry, medicine, and others. The only substantial grant from Russia that has been made public is the gift of a complete set of supplies for a wholly mechanized farm in October, 1954, with 98 tractors, repair shop, and transportation and communication equipment. The farm has been established in Heilungkiang Province in Manchuria. Russia has also promised to build a 6,500-kw. atomic reactor pile for Peiping and to

As far as foreign loans are concerned, the only source of long-term credit is Soviet Russia. Only two loans, both for basic construction purposes, have been made known. The first was the $300 million credit concluded in February, 1950, which was to run for five years from the beginning of that year and to be drawn 20 per cent a year against the Soviet supply of industrial equipment and supplies for rehabilitation and development. Interest, at 1 per cent per annum, was payable semiannually on the amount of credit actually used. The repayment of the principal was to be made in ten annual installments, each year with 10 per cent of the loan, from 1954 to 1963, in the form of raw materials, tea, gold, or American dollars.[4] No reason was given why the American dollar should have been adopted as the unit of account.[5] In later years the loan was officially referred to as one of 1,200 million rubles.[6] The second loan was made in October, 1954, amounting to 520 million rubles, also "for the supply of industrial equipment and supplies."[7] The terms have not been made public, except that it is a "long-term" credit.

In addition to these two economic loans, there is also a long-term credit established in 1955 representing the value of Soviet military supplies at the Port of Dairen and Soviet shares in the four Sino-Soviet joint-stock enterprises, both of which were transferred to Peiping.[8] Neither the amount nor the terms have been announced.

In a public speech, one of the deputy chairmen of the People's Republic stated, "The foreign loans that we need have been made to us by Soviet Russia at an interest rate of one or two per cent."[9] Probably both the second economic credit and the long-term loan

train Chinese personnel for nuclear power generation. See Huang Chen Ming and Huang Jun-t'ung, *op. cit.*, pp. 29–30, 32, and 15–16.

[4] *Jen-min jih-pao*, February 15, 1950.

[5] That Russia might have been considering at that time depreciation of the ruble is a possible explanation.

[6] See, for example, *Jen-min jih-pao*, April 21, 1956.

[7] *Ibid.*, October 12, 1954.

[8] The four enterprises were the Nonferrous and Rare Metals Company (started in January 1951) and the Petroleum Company (October 1950), both in Sinkiang Province; the Dairen Dockyard (1952); and the Civil Aviation Company (July 1950). By the time of the transfer, the Aviation Company had an airline of more than 9,000 km., with Peiping as the center of operations. See Huang and Huang, *op. cit.*, pp. 34–35. The credit representing the value of Soviet shares "is to be repaid within a few years." Military installations at Dairen were given to Peiping without charge.

[9] Madame Sun Yat-sen, "[Soviet Aid is] Practically a Gift," *Jen-min jih-pao*, February 14, 1955. It may be pointed out that the transfer of Soviet shares in the four joint-stock companies had been agreed upon in October, 1954.

on the transfer of military supplies and shares carry 2 per cent interest.

The two economic credits should not be confused with the Soviet-aid basic construction projects discussed in chapter i. From the 156 Soviet-aid projects that form the backbone of the industrialization program of the First Five Year Plan, 91 had started during the three years of rehabilitation and another 50 in 1953.[10] These 141 projects cost 5,200 million rubles in equipment and supplies. The 15 added in October, 1954, cost another 400 million. Thus the total value of the 156 projects is 5,600 million rubles, as compared to the total economic credit of 1,720 million.[11] In other words, foreign borrowing was sufficient to cover only 30.7 per cent of the necessary equipment and supplies of the 156 core projects, let alone other necessary imports under the First Five Year Plan.

Does the amount of 1,720 million rubles represent all economic loans that Peiping had received during the eight years from 1950 through 1957? Was there other Soviet credit that has not been made known? The answer has to be based on evidence which may be found in the state budget. It was brought out in the last chapter that the total amount of Soviet loan proceeds for the eight-year period came to 5,294 million yuan, including a large but unspecified sum for the transfer in 1955. If this were to be converted at the official rate of two rubles to a yuan, it would be equivalent to 10,588 million rubles—an amount almost twice the total cost of the 156 projects.[12] Does this mean that the amount of economic credit actually received was six times as much as was made known at the time? Or was a part of the actual foreign-loan proceeds military aid? This question is important enough to call for detailed analysis.

According to Peiping's finance minister, foreign-loan proceeds are recorded in the state budget only upon receipt of the supplies charged against the credit.[13] How are the supplies (chiefly machin-

[10] See Li Fu-ch'un's report in *Jen-min jih-pao*, September 15, 1953.

[11] The total cost of the 156 projects was given in an editorial, *Jen-min jih-pao*, April 9, 1956. The cost of the 15 projects added in 1954 was given in the official communiqué, *Jen-min jih-pao*, October 12, 1954. Twenty-one machine shops are attached to the 156 projects. In April, 1956, agreement was reached on another 55 projects (49 industrial and 6 others), primarily for the Second Five Year Plan, with a total cost of 2,500 million rubles in equipment and supplies. See editorial, *Jen-min jih-pao*, April 8, 1956.

[12] The conversion rate, "computed from relevant materials," is given in *Chi-hua ching-chi (Planned Economy)*, 12: 29, December, 1957. For a complete list of rates with different countries, see Statistical Appendix, Table 32.

[13] If the supplies arrive too late during the year to be recorded in the current budget, the amount will appear in the budget of the following year. See Li Hsien-nien's budget message for 1957, in *Jen-min jih-pao*, June 30, 1957.

ery and equipment) valued for budgetary purposes? It is known
that producer goods are priced relatively low in Russia and relatively high in China. Following perhaps Soviet practice, Peiping
has most likely valued the loan supplies at prices quite unrelated
to the foreign-exchange rate used in the Sino-Soviet trade account
or to any conversion rate used for other purposes.[14] This proposition can be tested. It was indicated in chapter v that a fixed capital
asset is officially defined as one with a value of more than 500 yuan
and a life of more than a year. In arriving at this standard, the
planning authorities "are guided mainly by the experience in
Soviet Russia where the rule is 200 rubles."[15] This clearly means
that as far as fixed capital assets are concerned, one ruble's worth
is equal to more than two yuan, though, because of rounding the
sum to 500, the exact conversion rate can be anywhere between
two to a little more than two and a half.

In the First Five Year Plan, it is stated that from the 156 Soviet-
aid projects 145 would be under construction during the five years
with an investment of 11,000 million yuan.[16] It is not clear whether
the amount includes the cost of local construction materials or
refers only to imported supplies. Since the Soviet aid includes,
among other things, both construction and installation, presumably much of the construction materials is also imported. In any
case, the total cost of the 145 projects is 5,300 million rubles.[17] If
the Chinese investment refers only to imported supplies, these
latter must have been valued at about two yuan per ruble.

More exact information on valuation of loan supplies can be
discovered from the state budget. Foreign-loan proceeds were
grouped together in one combined item with government bond
sales and "insurance and other receipts" in the state budget for
1954. When the *planned* budget for that year was presented in
June, 1954, the combined item amounted to 1,600 million yuan,
consisting very likely of 600 million for government bonds and
1,000 million for "insurance and other receipts."[18] None was budg-
eted for Soviet loan proceeds, which apparently had been ex-

[14] I am indebted to Professor Gregory Grossman for calling my attention to the probable Soviet budgetary practice regarding American lend-lease imports.
[15] Yen Ts'ui-yu, "The Standard of Fixed Assets and the Authority of the Enter-prise," *Chi-hua ching-chi (Planned Economy)*. 6: 23, June, 1957.
[16] The *First Five Year Plan*, pp. 30–31.
[17] That is, 5,200 million for the 141 projects and 107 million for the other four.
[18] All these figures, not given in the planned budget for 1954, are estimated accord-ing to information given in the realized budget for the same year. See the budget messages for 1954 and 1955, *Jen-min jih-pao*, June 17, 1954; and July 10, 1955.

hausted by this time. But in the *realized* budget for the year, the combined item was increased by 90.98 per cent over the planned receipt, "partly because government bond sales had exceeded the issue by 235.13 million yuan, but chiefly because Soviet loan proceeds were added to this combined item—a loan constituting another Soviet generous assistance to our construction."[19] The reference was clearly to the second Soviet credit of 520 million rubles, concluded in October, 1954.

From 1954 through 1957 the total foreign-loan proceeds as recorded in the state budget amounted to 2,681 million yuan (Table XXXIV), including 1,657 million of imported supplies and the transfer of materials and shares in 1955. By 1957, the economic credit was virtually exhausted, for the amount of 23 million yuan recorded in the planned budget for the year "represents the last balance of foreign credit concluded in the past."[20] Thus the total foreign-loan proceeds for those four years, minus the value of the transferred materials and shares in 1955, must be equal to 520 million rubles from the standpoint of the state budget. Assuming for the moment that the entire 1,657 million yuan in 1955 were military and share transfers, we would find that 1,024 million yuan's worth of imported supplies had been received against the economic credit, giving thereby a conversion rate of 1.97 yuan per ruble. But since some loan supplies must have been imported in 1955, the actual conversion rate was surely higher.

We are now in a position to determine precisely what the conversion rate was. The fact that no foreign-loan proceeds were expected in the planned budget for 1954 implies exhaustion of the first economic credit of 1,200 million rubles by the end of 1953. A total of 2,612 million yuan of supplies had been received from 1950 through 1953. One ruble of Soviet supply was therefore valued at 2.177 yuan. In the light of what has been said, this most probably was (and is) the valuation rate used in respect of loan supplies and it also implies that no military aid had been included in the total of 2,612 million yuan of loan proceeds. We can then understand why the 200-ruble standard for fixed capital assets in Russia becomes the 500-yuan standard. Furthermore, it may be readily estimated that the amount of Soviet transfers of military materials and joint-stock shares in 1955 was 1,550 million yuan, as the imported loan supplies during the year amounted to 110 million.

---

[19] Quotation from Finance Minister Li Hsien-nien's report on the realized budget for 1954, *ibid.*, July 10, 1955.

[20] Quotation from the budget message of 1957, *ibid.*, June 30, 1957.

This rather lengthy discussion of loan supply valuation is of vital importance to an appraisal of Sino-Soviet economic relations. It seems established, on the basis of all available evidence, that from 1950 through 1957 Communist China had received not more than two long-term economic credits from Soviet Russia amounting to 1,720 million rubles or 3,745 million yuan. This finding does not of course preclude the possibility of the existence of unannounced Soviet military credit, particularly during the Korean war period, although no suggestion of such assistance since 1954 (for which detailed budgetary information began to become available) has been found in budgetary and other related data. The earlier observation that from 1950 through 1957 Soviet credit had financed only 30.7 per cent of the necessary equipment and supplies for the 156 core projects is confirmed.

As far as the period of the First Five Year Plan is concerned, it should be realized that the first loan of 1,200 million rubles having been exhausted by the first year of the Plan, only 520 million rubles of credit was available for the remaining four years. The total cost of imported equipment and supplies for the Soviet-aid projects initiated during this five-year period came to 5,140 million yuan— that is, 4,060 million for the 50 out of the original 141 projects, 880 million for the 15 agreed on in 1954, and 200 million for two out of the 55 arranged in 1956.[21] At the same time, a total of 3,120 million yuan was received as long-term credit, from which 1,550 million was for transfer of military supplies and joint-stock shares. The amount remaining for financing the imported requirements of the Soviet-aid projects was therefore 1,570 million, an amount equivalent to 30.5 per cent of the project cost of 5,140 million.

Another way of appraising the size of Soviet economic aid during this period is to compare it with the total amount of net capital formation. As shown in Table XXXII in chapter v, the total net investment for the five years (at 1952 prices) has been estimated at 43,200 million yuan in fixed capital assets and 52,600 million in both fixed and working capital. Soviet credit accounted for 3.6 per cent of fixed capital formation and 3 per cent of total net investment.[22]

---

[21] Calculated on the basis of average cost per project. Of the 141 projects, the average cost per project is 81.2 million yuan. The average cost of the 55 projects agreed on in 1956 is 100 million yuan per project. The calculation is based on the fact that 91 of the original 141 projects had already been under construction before the beginning of the Plan, and that two of the 55 projects agreed on in 1956 were constructed before the end of 1957. See introductory discussion in chapter ii.

[22] If net capital formation is calculated at current prices, the percentage would be slightly smaller.

2. FOREIGN TRADE AND BALANCE OF INTERNATIONAL PAYMENTS

The foregoing discussion leads to a significant observation about the strategic importance of exports to Communist China's economic growth. During the First Five Year Plan, 70 per cent of the imported requirements for the Soviet-aid projects alone had to be paid for by commercial exports. This does not include imports of such supplies as petroleum, steel, cotton, heavy chemicals, rubber, fertilizers, and the like, all of which were necessary for the implementation of the Plan.

What was the total foreign-exchange cost of the Plan? The answer is simple: The total value of imports during the five years was the total foreign-exchange cost. This observation is based on two considerations. In the first place, private foreign-trade merchants had long ceased to operate except as agents for the state trading companies. While accounting for 31.65 per cent of the total foreign-trade volume in 1950, private merchants handled only 8.21 per cent in 1952, 7.88 per cent in 1953 and 1.83 per cent in 1954.[23] Since then, they have virtually disappeared altogether. Thus from the very beginning of the five-year period, no foreign trade had been conducted for the purpose of making commercial profit without any regard to the demand of the Plan.

In the second place, as far as the state is concerned, "the purpose of exporting is for importing, which in turn is for the sake of the country's industrialization."[24] That such a foreign-trade policy has been fully carried out is evidenced by the composition of imports. In the last few years, machinery, equipment, and supplies accounted for about 60 per cent of total imports, ferrous and non-ferrous metals 10 per cent, other industrial supplies and agricultural producer goods 22.2 per cent, and consumer goods 7.8 per cent.[25] The last-mentioned category included such items as pharmaceutical products, sugar, and kerosene, of which the country was in dire need. Imports had indeed been completely geared to

[23] Ma Nai-shu [sic], "Vneshniaia Torgovlia Kitaiskoi narodnoi respubliki" (Foreign Trade of the People's Republic of China), *Vneshniaia Torgovlia (Foreign Trade)*, Moscow, 5: 8–13, May, 1956; table on p. 12. In the publication, the author is identified as director of China's Institute of Foreign Trade. But the name of the director is actually Nan Han-shun. Either the name is printed wrong, or the author is not director of the Institute.

[24] Minister of Foreign Trade Yeh Chi-chuang, "Report on China's Foreign Trade for 1954," *Jen-min jih-pao*, July 30, 1955.

[25] Po I-po, "Report on the Results of the 1956 Plan and on the Plan for 1957," *Jen-min jih-pao*, July, 2, 1957; and Tien Lin, "Seven Years of Achievement—A Supplement," *Hsin-hua pan-yueh-k'an*, 15: 158–161, August, 1957.

the requirements of industrialization, and the total value of imports during the period represented the foreign-exchange cost of the Plan.

Total Value of Imports and Exports.—Determination of the total value of imports and exports during the five years of the Plan is not a simple matter. Foreign-trade returns have apparently been classified as economic secrets of the state.[20] Except for the last two years when import and export values were announced, the only absolute value figure available is the total trade volume for 1954. There are, of course, many percentage increases for different years in print. After a test of all available data for consistency, it is found that all such percentages and relatives concerning foreign trade as were published before July, 1955, are preliminary data and cannot be used together with those published thereafter. For example, in the State Statistical Bureau's communiqué (dated September 12, 1954) on the results of the 1953 Plan, it is stated that the total volume of foreign trade in 1953 had increased 36 per cent over the previous year, with 38 per cent increase in imports and 33 per cent increase in exports. But later, according to the July, 1955, report by the minister of foreign trade the increase in trade volume from 1952 to 1953 was 25 per cent instead of 36 per cent. And the minister's data were found completely consistent with those released later by other high government officials and by the bureau itself.

Another example concerns the only available data on the balance of international payments released by a responsible official of the People's Bank in February, 1955.[27] There it is said that the foreign-trade volume constituted 70.8 per cent of the total inpayments and outpayments of the international account in 1950 and 83.9 per cent in 1954, while the total value of the international account had increased by 121.5 per cent from 1950 to 1954. When the trade data for those two years, as given in Table XLII, are applied accordingly, the result is that the total turnover in the international account had increased by 75 per cent instead. Thus there is no question that all data published before July, 1955, differ radically from those released later.

A further observation on trade data may be made. From what has been said about valuation of loan imports, it is obvious that any attempt to convert Peiping's official trade data into foreign-

---

[20] See report on the results of a National Conference of Statistical Work on Foreign Trade, in *Ta Kung Pao (Impartial Daily)*, Tientsin, May 26, 1953.

[27] *Jen-min jih-pao*, February 20, 1955.

exchange equivalent, without investigating the basis of valuation, will lead to meaningless results. As a case in point, the volume of Chinese trade with the Soviet Union in 1956 was reported to be 5,800 million yuan. What conversion rate is to be used so that the result in, say, rubles would be meaningful for comparison with Russian statistics? Would it be the rate of two rubles to one yuan as given by the official publication of the State Economic and Planning Commissions? Or the rate of 2.177 yuan to a ruble as used for loan supplies in the state budget? As a matter of fact, the Tass News Agency has reported that in 1956 the largest single trade partner with the Soviet Union was Communist China with a total trade turnover of 5,989 million rubles.[28] After allowance is made for the usual differences between national trade returns concerning freight and insurance charges, timing and the like, it remains true that none of the rates suggested should be applied for conversion. The problem really lies in the pricing of different types of imports and exports. For this reason, Peiping's official trade returns have to be used as they stand.

Table XLII shows the value of total imports and exports from 1950 through 1957, computed from official data released since July, 1955. It will be observed that the total value of imports during the five-year period of the Plan was 25,170 million yuan. This may be compared with the amount of Soviet economic credit of 1,570 million yuan for the same period. On the assumption that Soviet loan supplies were valued on the same basis in trade returns as for budgetary purposes, Soviet credit accounted for 6.2 per cent of total imports.[29] In other words, about 94 per cent of the total foreign-exchange cost of the First Five Year Plan had to be met by commercial exports. The importance of exporting to the success of the Plan is beyond question.

It is also shown in the table that for the five-year period the realized trade deficit (except for 1957, which is planned) exceeds what was conceived in the First Five Year Plan by three-quarters of a billion yuan. This unplanned development implies not only that the export policy during this period was for the purpose of

---

[28] *New York Times,* December 30, 1957, p. 2. See also the Russian-language sources cited in the Addendum, n. 15.

[29] In the absence of any other information this assumption is the only one possible. In his report on foreign trade for 1956, Yeh stated that some imports like machinery and equipment were priced at cost in foreign exchange plus 2 or 3 per cent handling charges. It is not clear whether this pricing practice applies also to loan imports, and whether it applies also to trade statistics. Should loan supplies be valued in the way stated, Soviet credit would have financed a smaller portion of Chinese imports.

TABLE XLII
TOTAL TRADE, IMPORTS, AND EXPORTS, 1950–1957
(In millions of yuan)

Year	Total trade	Exports	Imports	Trade balance
1950	4,160	2,035	2,125	− 90
1951	5,950	2,440	3,505	−1,065
1952	6,490	2,750	3,740	− 990
1953	8,120	3,525	4,595	−1,070
1954	8,490	4,050	4,440	− 390
1955	11,020	4,935	6,085	−1,150
1956	10,865	5,568	5,297	+ 271
1957 (planned)	9,955	5,200	4,755	+ 445
1953–1957 actual (except 1957 planned)	48,450	23,280	25,170	−1,890
1953–1957 target in Plan	45,530	22,210	23,320	−1,110

Sources and bases for computation:
1) On total trade:
(a) From 1950 through 1955, computation is based on (i) a series of indices given in a dispatch on Chinese foreign trade development in *Jen-min jih-pao*, October 2, 1956. With 1950 as 100, the indices are as follows: 143 for 1951, 156 for 1952, 195 for 1953, 204 for 1954, and 265 for 1955. (ii) The increase of trade in 1954 over 1953 was 4.5 per cent, as given by the State Statistical Bureau's communiqué on the results of the 1954 plan, in *Jen-min jih-pao*, September 23, 1955. (iii) The value of total trade for 1954 was 8,486.73 million yuan, according to Yeh Chi-chuang, "Report on China's Foreign Trade for 1954," *Jen-min jih-pao*, July 30, 1955.
(b) For 1956 and 1957 (planned), absolute figures are given by Yeh Chi-chuang, "Report on China's Foreign Trade for 1956," *Hsin-hua pan-yueh-k'an*, 16: 90–94, August, 1957.
(c) For the 1953–1957 target, computed according to Yeh's report for 1956 that the actual volume from 1953 through 1957 (planned) would be 6.4 per cent higher than the five-year target in the Plan.
2) On exports and imports:
(a) The absolute figures for 1956 and 1957 (planned) are taken from Yeh's report for 1956.
(b) From 1950 through 1955, computed from indices officially released at the China Export-Commodity Fair, Canton, and which are reported in *Ajia Keizai Jumpo (Asia Economic Bulletin)*, 316: 6–13, March, 1957. This bulletin is published in Japanese every ten days by the China Research Institute, Tokyo. As given in the report, the indices for total trade are identical with those cited in source (1)(a)(i) above, while the export and import indices, based on 1950, are as follows:

	1951	1952	1953	1954	1955
Exports	120	135	173	199	242
Imports	165	176	216	209	286

These three indices, together with the total trade figure of 8,486.73 million yuan for 1954, furnish the basis for estimating the export and import values of these years. The results (in millions) are rounded to five if the last digits are between 3 and 7, and to ten if they are more than 7 or less than 3.
(c) The First Five Year Plan targets are computed according to Yeh's report for 1956 that the actual totals of exports and imports from 1953 through 1957 (planned) would exceed the five-year targets by 4.8 per cent and 8 per cent, respectively.

importing, as the foreign trade minister states, but also that the export volume must have been carried to the limit of the country's export capacity at the time. The largest annual gain in trade volume took place in the first and third year of the Plan, with an increase of 25 per cent and 30 per cent. The first year was one after a good harvest, and the third year reaped a record crop. And it was during the first three years that 2,610 million yuan of import surplus occurred. The trade volume for the last two years declined because of poor harvests. But when it fell by 8.4 per cent in 1957 (planned), exports dropped only 6.6 per cent as against 10.2 per cent in imports. All this seems to indicate that in an upward swing of the trade volume exports may gain less than imports, as in 1955, whereas in a downward movement exports tend to be maintained at a higher level and to fluctuate much less.

Balance of International Payments.—The fact that exports fell short of the foreign-exchange cost of the development program certainly constitutes a reasonable explanation of Peiping's continuous drive for exports. But the trade balance is only a part of the picture. What had been the changes in the international account during the period? Although we do not propose to discuss at length the balance of international payments, it is necessary to bring out certain underlying trends. Unfortunately, as was explained earlier, the only available data on the balance have been found not to be useful, and we will therefore not be able to present a complete statement of the account. What is proposed here is to estimate the major items in both the current and the transfer account so that the trend of the over-all balance may be traced.

The major items are, in the current account, imports and exports, interest payments on Soviet credits, and overseas-Chinese remittances; and, in the transfer account, Soviet credits, repayment of Soviet loans, and Chinese grants to foreign countries. Export and import values have already been computed. Foreign trade is carried either overland by rail or overseas by ocean-going vessels. With no merchant marine engaging in foreign trade, Peiping's annual payment of freight, insurance, and related charges on imports must be substantial. However, irrespective of the method of pricing imports, presumably they are valued at c.i.f., point of entry. Thus import values as recorded in the trade returns include those charges payable in foreign exchange, and there is no need to estimate them separately. By the same token, exports are probably valued at f.o.b., point of exit, so that similar charges will be paid by foreign buyers and do not concern the Chinese international account.[80]

---

[80] A suggestion has been put forth for the country to build ocean-going vessels with which to carry a part of the export trade. On the assumption that annually imports and exports amount to 10 million tons of goods traveling on the average over a distance of 10,000 nautical miles at £8 per ton, the annual freight bill on total trade amounts to £80 million. If about one-half of this amount pertains to exports, the freight would amount to "over 300 million yuan." The potential of a Chinese merchant fleet to earn foreign exchange is great. See the joint statement by Yang

Soviet loan proceeds have been estimated, but not amortization payments. It will be recalled that the first Soviet economic credit was to be repaid at the rate of 10 per cent of the principal per year beginning 1954. The foreign-debt services for 1952 and 1953 consisted only of interest payments, which may be estimated according to the terms to be 1 per cent of the loan supplies received cumulatively at the end of each year. The amount of interest may be overstated in this way, because while loan supplies are valued at two yuan to one ruble, it is probably not so with interest payments. However, the amount was very small in these two years and would not affect the international balance one way or another. The estimate for the next four years requires a different procedure. Until 1955, the servicing payments on both the (domestic) national debt and foreign loans were lumped together in the state budget under "Other expenditures" or "Credit, insurance and other outpayments." Since then, they have been singled out as one item, though the payments on the national debt are not differentiated from those on foreign loans. With information given in the annual budget messages, the total debt services may be computed for 1954 through 1957 (planned). And payments on foreign loans may be separated by estimating the annual services on the national debt according to the terms of government bonds given in Table XXXVI in chapter vi. The results are summarized in Table XLIII. Primarily because the precise terms are not known for the Soviet credits on the transfer of joint-stock shares and military supplies in 1955, it is impossible to separate interest payments from repayment of capital.

Although the terms of the first Soviet loan call for first repayment "before the end of 1954," the amount was apparently not fully entered into the state budget until the following year. The important point shown in the table is that amortization payments on foreign borrowing have been rapidly mounting since 1954. By 1956 and 1957, they had already exceeded the balance of the economic credit by 500 million and 600 million yuan—amounts equal to 9 per cent of total exports in 1956 and 11.5 per cent in 1957.

A major item on the current account is the remittances of overseas Chinese. Chinese emigrants live mostly in Southeast Asia.[31]

Chun-sheng and Sa Pen-hsin at the National Congress of People's Representatives, in *Hsin-hua pan-yueh-k'an*, 17: 87–88, September, 1957. According to this estimate the Chinese annual payments on incoming freight must be about £40 million, or more than 300 million yuan. The total tonnage seems a realistic figure.

[31] Peiping's estimate of the number of overseas Chinese, including students abroad, is 11,743,000 for 1953. See *Jen-min jih-pao*, November 1, 1954.

While a certain amount of remittances may have found its way to Communist China through other channels, the bulk must have gone through Hong Kong. According to information released by the exchange banks there, the amount of remittances back to the mainland was Hk.\$300 million in 1952, Hk.\$180 million in 1953,

TABLE XLIII

ESTIMATE OF SERVICING PAYMENTS ON NATIONAL DEBT AND
FOREIGN BORROWING, 1952–1957

(In millions of yuan)

Item	1952	1953	1954	1955	1956	1957 planned
A. National debt services........	59	71	83	158	129	222
B. Foreign loan services..........	22	26	127	508	604	621
C. Total payments (A + B)....	81	97	210	666	733	843
D. Soviet loan proceeds..........	520	438	884	1,657	117	23

Note: The estimates for 1955 through 1957 are at 1955 prices. See discussion of Table XXXIV in chapter vi.

Sources: (1) Total servicing payments for both national debt and foreign loans from 1954 through 1957 (planned) are computed from data given in the budget messages of 1955, 1956, and 1957. For sources, see notes appended to Table XXXIV. For 1952 and 1953, the payments are the sum of lines A and B. (2) National debt services are estimated according to the actual government bond sales and terms given in Table XXXVI. (3) Foreign debt services for 1952 and 1953 are estimated on the basis of 1 per cent interest payments on debt outstanding at the end of each year. For 1954 through 1957 (planned), they are the difference between lines C and A. (4) For Soviet loan proceeds, see Table XXXIV.

and Hk.\$390 million in 1954. In the light of what has been said about exchange rates, conversion of these sums into yuan is a problem. If converted at free-market rates (0.625 yuan per Hk.\$ up to the end of 1953 and 0.8547 yuan in 1954), the amount would be 188 million yuan for 1952, 113 million for 1953, and 333 million for 1954. If converted at official rates prevailing at Hong Kong (0.427 yuan per Hk.\$), it would be 128 million yuan in 1952, 77 million in 1953, and 167 million in 1954.[32] The latter set of figures will be adopted for two reasons. A good part of the remittances from Hong Kong to inland is probably handled through the Communist Chinese banks there, in which case the official rate applies. Then, for the sake of consistency with the valuation of trade and other items in the balance of international payments, the official rate is perhaps a better choice.

Overseas remittances dropped heavily in 1953 as a result of an allied effort by many non-Communist countries to stop the foreign-

[32] The sources of information are the financial market reports of Hong Kong given in *Far Eastern Economic Review*, August 26, 1954. p. 262; May 6, 1954, p. 567; May 27, 1954, p 676; and June 3, 1954, p. 703. The amounts cited in the text do not include those remittances retained in Hong Kong.

exchange leakage to Peiping. Despite this control, however, there was a sharp recovery the following year. This seems to signify that the amount of remittances for 1954 is a resasonable total for maintaining, on the part of the emigrants, their family folks in the home country. For lack of any better information, that amount (rounded to 170 million yuan) is adopted as the annual remittances for the three subsequent years as well.[33]

From the standpoint of Peiping's national income account, these remittances probably represent the most important source of current earnings by Chinese citizens abroad. There are two important sources of currently earned income by foreign citizens living in Communist China. One source consists of foreign business firms and personnel. Foreign businesses have been under strict government control since the Communists came to power, and the permission to remit interest or dividend payments abroad has apparently been very rarely given.[34] Soviet technicians and advisors have most probably formed the largest group of foreign citizens in the country. Their local expenditures are likely paid in yuan, while their home pay (in rubles) comes either out of the Soviet credits or out of Peiping's ruble account at Moscow. Even assuming that the last-mentioned possibility is the case, the amount of earnings would be far less than the overseas-Chinese remittances. The other source is the earnings from Soviet loans, that is, the annual interest payments. Since the terms for the second Soviet credit and for the transfer of joint stock shares and military supplies are not known, there is no way to separate interest charges from repayment of principal from 1954 through 1957. But working with the estimated figures at hand, we may surmise that the excess of overseas-Chinese remittances over foreign earnings in Communist China had continued to narrow during those four years. This is the basis for the assumption made in chapter iv that the net balance had been too small to be taken into account in estimating the net national product.[35]

---

[33] These estimates are necessarily tentative. One may argue that the amount is too small. But in many countries in Southeast Asia where most overseas Chinese reside, there are regulations restricting the amount of monthly remittances that an immigrant may send to his home country. An accurate estimate of the amount of Chinese remittances would require an extensive inquiry.

[34] See chapter i, section 3. The four Sino-Soviet joint-stock enterprises, all started in 1950 or 1951, were not likely to have produced any sizable earnings for remittances to Moscow.

[35] A more comprehensive definition of net national product may be employed so as to include the balance of the entire current account in the balance of international payments. But in view of the limitation of data, the narrow definition has been

A novel feature in the international account of the country is the economic grants given to foreign countries. How the obligation was incurred is not known. The receiving countries with the terms of the grants are as follows: 800 million yuan to North Korea from 1954 through 1957; 800 million yuan to North Vietnam beginning in 1955; £8 million to Cambodia in 1956 and 1957; 160 million rubles to Outer Mongolia from 1956 through 1959; 60 million Indian rupees to Nepal from 1956 through 1959; and, finally, 30 million rubles to Hungary and 20 million Swiss francs to Egypt in 1956. All the grants are given in the form of industrial supplies and equipment, except that a part of the grant to North Korea is in such consumer goods as cotton cloth and foodstuffs, one-third of the grant to Nepal in Indian rupees, a part of the grant to Hungary in rubles, and the entire grant to Egypt in Swiss francs.[36] Thus grants to foreign countries started in 1954 and reached the peak in 1957. The annual total of these grants for 1955 through 1957 (planned) may be readily computed from the data given in the budget messages for 1956 and 1957. The first grant given to North Korea in 1954 was also reported in another official source.[37]

The estimates of the major items in the balance of international payments are summarized in Table XLIV. It should be pointed out that for 1955, from the total loan proceeds of 1,657 million yuan, 1,550 million yuan was for the value of the transfer of Soviet joint-stock shares and military supplies. Being an international transaction during the year, this transfer should be entered in the balance, as is shown in the table, both as Soviet loan receipts (inpayments) and as additional imports (outpayments). As far as Soviet loan supplies are concerned, it is not clear whether they were included in the official import statistics. Perhaps they were. But if

purposely chosen for this study. For the sake of consistency, the net factor income received from abroad (positive or negative) should be valued gross of taxes and consumption expenditure incurred abroad by the recipient. Available data do not permit of such refinement.

[36] In June, 1957, a deputy minister of foreign affairs reported to the Standing Committee of the People's Congress at Peiping about an arrangement for making a loan to Hungary; no details, however, were given. For sources of information, see *Jen-min jih-pao*, November 24, 1953, for grant to North Korea; July 9, 1955, for grant to North Vietnam; June 23, 1956, for grant to Cambodia; August 30, 1956, for grant to Outer Mongolia; and November 13, 1956, for grant to Egypt. For grants to Nepal and Hungary, see *1957 Jen-min shou-tse (People's Handbook for 1957)*, pp. 387 and 371. For lending to Hungary, see *Hsin-hua pan-yueh-k'an* 14: 151–152, July, 1957. A five-year grant to Ceylon of 75 million rupees in goods is scheduled to begin in 1958.

[37] *Jen-min jih-pao*, November 21, 1954.

not, the deficit in the international account would have been larger each year than what the table shows by the value of loan supplies received.

During the whole period of the Plan, while the negative trade balance amounted to 1,890 million yuan, the balance in the international account was against Peiping to the extent of over 3,000 million. Moreover, the international deficit has taken on an upward

TABLE XLIV

Estimate of Major Items in the Balance of International Payments, 1953–1957
(In millions of yuan)

Item	1953	1954	1955	1956	1957 planned
I. Inpayments:					
A. Exports................	3,525	4,050	4,935	5,568	5,200
B. Overseas remittances....	80	160	170	170	170
C. Soviet credits..........	438	884	1,657	117	23
Total...................	4,045	5,095	6,760	5,855	5,395
II. Outpayments:					
A. Imports................	4,595	4,440	7,635	5,297	4,755
B. Foreign loan services....	26	127	508	604	621
C. Grants.................	0	300	393	404	508
Total...................	4,620	4,865	8,535	6,305	5,885
III. Balance.................	−575	+230	−1,775	−450	−490

Note: For sources and explanations, see text and Tables XLII and XLIII. The totals are rounded to five or ten.

trend since 1956. According to the existing commitments, grants to foreign countries should have reached the peak in 1957, to be followed by a decline. But amortization payments on Soviet loans should be growing, if the original terms are not going to be modified.

This underlying trend furnishes at least a part of the answer to the question raised earlier as to why Peiping should have been engaging in an export drive. Maximization of exports was needed as much for the payment of necessary imports as for meeting other international obligations. During the five-year period, the over-all international deficit was about 62 per cent more than the trade deficit. And in the last two years, the over-all deficit was growing in amount in spite of the trade account changing from an import balance to an export balance. This trend is likely to continue in the future. Export expansion has therefore become urgent, and the urgency must have been first felt in the middle of the five-year period when imported loan supplies together with overseas remittances dropped far below the outpayments for amortization and economic grants.[38]

Export Drive.—Export expansion requires an increasing volume of exportable commodities on the one hand and a growing demand in foreign markets on the other. Exports are heavily composed of agricultural products. "In the past few years," remarks the minister of foreign trade, "75 per cent of exports have been crude or processed agricultural products, and the other 25 per cent mining products and industrial equipment."[39] The chief agricultural exports are foodstuffs (especially rice and soybeans), oils and fats, subsidiary food (such as eggs and pork), tea, tung oil, bristles, skins and hides.[40] However, as a result of industrialization, manufactured goods (including processed agricultural products such as cloth) have figured increasingly in the composition. For example, they accounted for 40.4 per cent of exports in 1955 as compared to 15.4 per cent in 1950.[41] Although this comparison exaggerates the increase because of the low level of industrial activity in 1950, there is no doubt in the light of the discussion in chapter ii that a sizable increase in manufactured exports has taken place. For the future, the export policy is "to increase the relative importance of mining

---

[38] Since the international balance was in deficit, the loss in foreign-exchange reserves should logically be considered as foreign disinvestment, to be subtracted from domestic investment in order to arrive at total net investment during the period. In that event, the deficit of the international *current* account—not including, of course, grants to foreign countries which should be regarded as a part of national consumption—should also be deducted from the net national product. Then the rate of capital formation would have been lower than we have estimated. This procedure, however, has not been adopted in this study, because, in line with our interest in industrialization, capital formation is purposely so defined as to exclude any change in cash balances either on the part of enterprises or of the country as a whole. After all, a change in foreign-exchange reserves will not help increase capital assets of the country unless they are used to acquire capital imports, which will then be reflected in an increase in basic construction investment. Witness the case of an oil-exporting country which nets a heavy increase in foreign-exchange reserves every year, to be used mainly for consumption. Either the depletion of foreign-exchange reserves as a result of consumption is considered as disinvestment, just as the increase in reserves is recorded as a form of capital formation, or, at the first instance, the increase in reserves is treated just as an increase in stockpiles or commodity reserves. Obviously, the choice of method of treatment depends on the purpose.

[39] Yeh Chi-chuang, "Report on China's Foreign Trade for 1956."

[40] Deputy Minister of Foreign Trade Li Che-jen, "Consolidate the Economic Coöperation between China and Soviet Union and Other People's Democracies," *Jen-min jih-pao*, May 12, 1955.

[41] *Ibid.*, November 9, 1956, p. 6.

TABLE XLV

GEOGRAPHICAL DISTRIBUTION OF TOTAL FOREIGN TRADE, 1950–1956

Distribution	1950	1951	1952	1953	1954	1955	1956
	(Millions of yuan)						
I. Total Volume:........	4,160	5,950	6,490	8,120	8,487	11,024	10,865
A. Communist Bloc:....	1,393	3,765	5,068	6,130	6,789	9,019	8,149
1. Soviet Union.......	1,285	2,899	3,722	4,579	.....	6,810	5,800
2. Eastern Europe....	83	788	1,234	1,346	.....⎫	2,010	2,349
3. Other Asia.........	25	78	112	205	.....⎭		
B. Free World.........	2,767	2,185	1,422	1,990	1,698	2,005	2,716
1. Africa and Asia....	.....	.....	.....	.....	1,053	1,247	1,738
2. The West..........	.....	.....	.....	.....	645	758	978
II. Geographical Composition:	(Per cent of total)						
A. Communist Bloc:.....	33.47	63.28	78.08	75.49	80.00	81.80	75.00
1. Soviet Union.......	30.89	48.72	57.34	56.39	.....	61.78	53.40
2. Eastern Europe....	1.99	13.24	19.02	16.58	.....⎫	20.02	21.60
3. Other Asia.........	0.60	1.32	1.72	2.52	.....⎭		
B. Free World:.........	66.52	36.72	21.92	24.51	20.00	18.20	25.00
1. Africa and Asia....	.....	.....	.....	.....	12.40	11.30	16.00
2. The West..........	.....	.....	.....	.....	7.60	6.90	9.00

Sources and Bases for Computation:
  1) Total volume of trade is taken from Table XLII.
  2) The absolute volume of trade by areas is computed by applying the percentages given in Part II of the table to the total volume of trade, with the exception of the volume of trade with Soviet Union in 1955, which is computed according to Finance Minister Li Hsien-nien's statement (*Jen-min jih-pao*, February 14, 1956) that the volume of Sino-Soviet trade increased 5.3 times from 1950 through 1955.
  3) For geographical composition: (a) From 1950 through 1953, given by Ma Nai-shu [*sic*], "*Vneshniaia Torgovlia Kitaiskoi narodnoi respubliki*" (Foreign Trade of the People's Republic of China), *Vneshniaia Torgovlia (Foreign Trade)*, Moscow, 5: 12, May, 1956. (b) For 1954, the share of trade with the Soviet bloc is given by Deputy Minister of Foreign Trade Li Che-jen in *Jen-min jih-pao*, May 12, 1955. (c) For 1956, the share of trade with the Soviet bloc is given by Yeh Chi-chuang, "Report on China's Foreign Trade for 1956," *Hsin-hua pan-yueh-k'an*, 16: 90–94, August, 1957. (d) For the share of trade with the Soviet bloc in 1955 and for the trade volume with African-Asian countries and the West from 1954 through 1956, computation is based on the information given in *1957 Jen-min shou-t'se (People's Handbook for 1957)*, p. 522: (i) in 1956, trade with the African-Asian countries in the non-Communist world increased by 39.4 per cent over 1955 and represented 64 per cent of Communist China's trade with the free world; (ii) trade with these African-Asian countries had increased 18.4 per cent from 1954 to 1955; and (iii) trade with the West increased 29 per cent from 1955 to 1956.

and industrial products and to lower that of major agricultural products."[42] Thus, quite apart from the problem of swelling the volume of exports, the very change in composition of exportable commodities demands new markets. If the economic policy of each of the countries in the Communist bloc is to attain a reasonable degree of industrial self-sufficiency, new markets for Chinese exports must be found in the free world. This constitutes another part of the *raison d'être* of the export drive.

[42] Yeh, *op. cit.*

The geographical distribution of Communist China's total foreign trade is given in Table XLV. From 1950 through 1956 her trade with other countries in the Communist bloc had increased nearly six times while trade with the free world had not recovered to the 1950 level. Significantly, however, the free world's share increased from 18 per cent in 1955 to 25 per cent in 1956, when the volume of total trade with all countries declined. This seems to support the proposition that what Communist China prefers to offer to the export market—mining and industrial products—has to find its outlet, not in the Communist bloc, but in the free world, especially countries in Southeast Asia and Africa. As a matter of fact, that is exactly the area to which intense export promotion effort has been directed.

The drive began in 1954, when barter and payments agreements were entered into with Burma, Indonesia, Ceylon, India, and Pakistan.[43] Ever since then, trade with the free world has steadily increased. With 1954 as the base year, the trade volume was 118 in 1955 and 160 in 1956 with the free world, when it was 133 and 120 with the Communist bloc. By 1956 the drive had gathered momentum. As dictated by the changing composition of exports, trade with the African-Asian countries had been developing much faster than trade with the West. It is, therefore, no accident that in 1954 when the drive started, Communist China *"began* to export products of light industry," such as galvanized wire, nails, thermos bottles, and fountain pens, amounting to as much as 150 million yuan."[44] The first Chinese export to the free world of a complete set of machinery and equipment for a whole factory took place in 1955 when the equipment for a 20,000-spindle cotton spinning and weaving mill was sent to Burma.[45]

The importance of this trade with the free world would be better understood if the total trade with the Commnuist bloc on the one hand and with the free world on the other could be broken down into imports and exports. Unfortunately, the official data released by Peiping do not permit such an operation. There are, however, data available from the trade returns of free-world countries that have been trading with Communist China. The International Cooperation Administration of the United States government publishes such data in its reports to Congress as required by the Mutual

[43] Yeh Chi-chuang, "Report on China's Foreign Trade for 1954."
[44] Yeh, *ibid.,* Italics mine.
[45] Wang Pao-jen, "The Development of China's Economic and Commercial Relations with Asian and African Countries," *Jen-min jih-pao,* October 11, 1956.

Defense Assistance Control Act of 1951. The report of June, 1957, does not take into account—because of its early publication—the actual trade returns for 1956. The annual issue of the *Direction of International Trade,* published jointly by the United Nations, the International Monetary Fund, and the World Bank, is another source, and gives the complete trade returns for 1956. For this reason, the figures compiled by the United Nations will be used. It should be mentioned that many trade partners designate their trade with both Communist China and Nationalist China (Taiwan) under "China" without differentiation. The trade with "China" of a country like the Philippines is most probably meant to be with Nationalist China alone;[46] but no allowance along this line can be made in respect to the trade of many other countries with "China." By adding free world's trade with "China" to its trade with "China, Mainland," the trade volume with Communist China is overstated. But the overstatement is not serious, as a comparison of the trade of "China" with the trade of Nationalist China (Taiwan) will show. Table XLVI presents the results of such a compilation. Interestingly enough, the export values thus gathered are higher, and the import values are lower, than the United States ICA figures by a few million dollars.[47]

Table XLVI provides an approximate indication of the magnitude and direction of Communist China's trade with the free world. The import and export values given in American dollars cannot be directly compared with those given in Chinese currency in Table XLV because of differences in c.i.f. and f.o.b. valuations, in pricing, and in the timing of arrivals and departures.[48] Nevertheless, it is interesting to observe that with 1954 as the base Communist China's total trade with the free world was 123 in 1955 and 162 in 1956 as recorded by her trade partners, which may be compared to 118 and 160 as shown in her own trade returns.[49]

[46] Otherwise, trade with Communist China would be recorded in the trade returns of the Philippines as trade with Hong Kong.

[47] See United States Government, International Cooperation Administration, *Survey of East-West Trade in 1955,* Washington, D.C., October 10, 1956, and *The Strategic Trade Control System, 1948–1956,* June 28, 1957. The United Nations publication referred to is *Direction of International Trade,* Statistical Papers Series T, viii, no. 7, October, 1957.

[48] Communist China's exports as recorded by her trade partners also include Hong Kong imports, much of which is reëxported and recorded a second time as imports from Communist China. Thus her export values compiled from the trade returns of trade partners are overstated. See ICA, *Survey of East-West Trade,* p. 5n.

[49] According to ICA, industrial goods were the major items imported by Communist China from Western Europe and Japan. Chemical products, including fertilizers, dyes, drugs, and industrial chemicals accounted for the largest proportion of

TABLE XLVI

COMMUNIST CHINA'S EXPORT AND IMPORT TRADE WITH THE
FREE WORLD, BY AREAS, 1953–1956
(In millions of U. S. dollars)

Trade	1953	1954	1955	1956
A. China's exports to:				
1. Asia (except Middle East)	274.1	242.9	321.7	413.3
2. Middle East	4.0	13.3	13.8	31.1
3. Other Africa	8.7	14.0	23.5	24.1
4. Western Europe	129.1	100.5	132.6	165.3
5. United States and Canada	10.7	1.9	3.4	6.0
6. Latin America	2.2	2.9	1.9	2.9
7. Oceania	4.8	4.7	5.3	5.5
8. Total	433.6	380.2	502.2	648.2
B. China's imports from:				
1. Asia (except Middle East)	162.6	173.1	159.8	188.4
2. Middle East	10.9	12.7	26.0	28.3
3. Other Africa	0.1	0.7	0.2	– – –
4. Western Europe	100.5	89.4	111.5	194.2
5. United States and Canada	– – –	0.1	1.0	2.5
6. Latin America	1.0	3.8	5.9	3.5
7. Oceania	4.9	3.2	6.3	10.1
8. Total	280.0	283.0	310.7	427.0
C. Export Balance	153.6	97.2	191.5	221.2

Note: All data are derived from the trade returns of partner countries. Trade with "China" is added to trade with "China, Mainland," except that the trade of the Philippines and of unspecified countries is omitted.

Source: United Nations, *Direction of International Trade,* Statistical Papers Series T, vol. viii, no. 7, New York, October 16, 1957, pp. 236–237 and 240–241.

What is important, however, about the picture presented by Table XLVI is not so much the growth of total trade as the increasing export surplus in favor of Communist China since 1954. No doubt, the export surplus is exaggerated, because, as given in the table, her exports are actually valued at c.i.f., country of import (instead of at f.o.b., Chinese port of export, as would have appeared

shipments in 1955. Communist China's imports from Asia (excluding Japan and Hong Kong), Oceania, and the Near East consisted largely of agricultural products: such as raw cotton from Pakistan and Egypt, crude rubber from Ceylon, rice from Burma, copra and coconut oil from Indonesia and Malaya, wool and wool tops from Australia, and gunny bags and raw cotton from India. Communist China's exports to the free world, in the order of percentage of total, were foodstuffs (including rice, other cereals, vegetable oils for food use, eggs, fruits, vegetables, pulses, and tea); oilseeds and other agricultural raw materials (textile fibres, essential oils, skins and pelts, tung oil, and miscellaneous crude materials); and a variety of miscellaneous goods (mainly ores, minerals, and products of light industry). See ICA, *op. cit.,* p. 5. For 1956, the same order prevailed, except that manufactured exports almost doubled.

in her own trade returns), and her imports at f.o.b., country of export (instead of at c.i.f., Chinese port of entry). In other words, when compared with her own trade returns, the export values are overstated by the amount of freight, insurance, and related charges, and the import values are understated in the same manner. According to the trade figures compiled by Dr. Hans Staehle, director of research for GATT, we may judge that the export values are thus exaggerated by about 8 to 10 per cent.[50] If proper allowance is made for these charges in the import and export values, the export surplus will be considerably reduced. Even so, the fact remains that trade with the free world netted a surplus for Communist China and that the surplus had been growing since 1954. This was particularly true of the trade with the African-Asian area, and to a lesser extent, of the trade with Western Europe.

Thus the possibility of netting a heavy export surplus as well as the changing composition of exports goes a long way to explain Communist China's export drive in her trade with the free world. In this connection, it should be recalled that a trade deficit of 2,610 million yuan, as given in Table XLII above, was accumulated during the first three years of the Plan. If the data compiled from the trade partners in the free world are any guide, that deficit must have been derived, not from trading with the free world, but from trading with the Communist bloc. Thus the observation that Peiping depends in an important measure on the favorable trade balance with the free world for meeting trade deficits with the Communist bloc is warranted. In any case, it is true that beginning with the over-all deficit in the international account since 1955, Peiping seriously needs trade with those countries that will result in a substantial increase in the country's foreign-exchange reserves. Trade expansion with the free world serves this vital need.[51]

The Terms of Trade.—In her drive for trade with the free world, Communist China has even been willing to sell at prices below

---

[50] Dr. Staehle's compilation appears in M. L. Hoffman, "Problems of East-West Trade," *International Conciliation*, 511: 257–308, January, 1957; table on p. 261. The trade figures are compiled from the trade returns of free-world partners, with both exports and imports on an f.o.b. basis. GATT is the name for General Agreement on Tariffs and Trade. Staehle's figures for Communist China's imports from 1952 through 1955 are strikingly similar to the ICA figures, but those for exports differ because of different bases of valuation. The statement in the text is derived from a comparison of Staehle's export figures with those compiled by ICA.

[51] With such large international deficits China has had to rely heavily on short-term trade credits in her trade with other countries in the Soviet bloc. For a report on how these credits were arranged in 1955–1956, see Max Biehl, "The West and Trade with China," *Far Eastern Economic Review*, XXII: 208–211, February 14, 1957.

domestic cost in order to gain acceptance. "In our trade with the capitalist countries," admits the minister of foreign trade, "it is generally true that when prices for our exports and imports in the foreign markets, after having been converted into Chinese currency according to official exchange rates, are compared with domestic prices, we have been suffering a loss in the export trade and netting a profit in the import trade."[52] In other words, foreign prices for Chinese exports have been lower than the government-purchase prices for exports at home, while foreign prices of Chinese imports are lower than the prices at which they are resold in the Chinese market. Profits thus derived from imports are partly used to compensate for export losses, with the remainder going into the national treasury as foreign trade's contribution to the state's current revenue.

This raises the whole problem of the terms of trade. A discussion of this topic must be made from the standpoint of the planning authorities at Peiping, rather than from the interests of consumers. It will be observed, first of all, that the so-called losses and gains are all in terms of domestic currency. As long as the marginal utility of foreign exchange derived from a unit of export is higher than the marginal disutility of payment in domestic currency for a unit of export, exports will be a gain irrespective of the domestic-foreign price differential.

In the second place, the fact that exports have been sold below domestic purchase price does not necessarily mean that Communist China has suffered from adverse terms of trade in her transactions with the free world. It is true that if the free-world prices for Chinese exports should be higher than what they have been, the commodity terms of trade would doubtless become more favorable to Peiping. But taking the foreign-domestic price differentials as they exist for both imports and exports, we should realize that the high prices of imports (92 per cent of which are producer goods) in yuan do reflect relative market scarcities and high factor costs at home. Thus, even though exports are sold below domestic cost, the *factoral* terms of trade may well be in Communist China's favor, since imports are so much cheaper that they can be resold in the Chinese market at a profit high enough to cover export losses and at the same time to net the national treasury an annual surplus.[53]

---

[52] Yeh Chi-chuang, "Report on China's Foreign Trade for 1956." The report was delivered at the National Congress of People's Representatives on July 11, 1957.

[53] We are concerned here only with the unilateral factoral terms of trade from the standpoint of Peiping, and not with bilateral factoral terms of trade.

In the third place, comparison should also be made between the terms of trade with the free world and those with the Communist bloc. Unfortunately, data are lacking for this purpose. The minister of foreign trade has publicly stated that import and export pricing in trade with the Soviet Union has not changed, with a few exceptions, since the Commercial Agreement of April, 1950, and that in view of the wide fluctuation of prices in free-world markets during these several years, "the prices governing the Sino-Soviet trade are fair and just and we have not suffered any loss."[54] This cautious denial of any loss may be construed as to imply that the prevailing arrangement might not be the most desirable. Some interesting information is given in his statement. Between 1950 and 1956, among the Chinese exports to the Soviet Union, the prices of wool, rice, tung oil, and hemp had dropped 10–30 per cent in free-world markets, and the prices of soybeans, tea, silk, tin, and wolfram had increased 10–160 per cent.[55] At the same time, among the imports from the Soviet Union, the prices of diesel oil and gasoline had remained stable in free-world markets, and those of machinery, equipment, and heavy steel had increased 30–140 per cent. According to Yeh, since the prices for all these products were kept virtually unchanged in the Sino-Soviet trade during the whole period, any potential gain obtaining from trade with the free world would have been offset by potential loss because of price fluctuations. If the facts are correctly stated, it follows that the terms of trade would not have been any different between trading with the Communist world (as represented by trade with the Soviet Union) and trading with the free world.

However, such a conclusion is valid only if the country were confronted with the alternative of either trading exclusively with one or with the other. If both world markets are accessible to her, the situation would be different. A definite gain in the commodity terms of trade would obtain if she could sell in the high-price market and buy in the low-price sources. It may well be true that the Soviet Union might not have been willing to supply the producer goods required at low prices unless the prices of imports from Communist China had been determined on a long-term basis. But what is there to prevent Peiping from apportioning her exports in such a way as to be in a position to take advantage of the best terms that the two world markets can offer—except for the free-world trade

---

[54] Yeh, *ibid.*

[55] The latter group constitutes the largest percentage of Chinese exports.

restrictions? Without going further into the subject, we may conclude that an expansion of trade with the free world will unquestionably improve Communist China's terms of trade and that this prospective gain must have also been a part of the reason for the export drive.

3. CONCLUDING REMARKS

During the First Five Year Plan, Soviet economic credit accounted for less than 4 per cent of the net fixed capital formation in the country. About 70 per cent of the imported requirements for the 156 Soviet-aid projects must be paid for by regular exports. In fact, since imports are so completely geared to the needs of the industrialization program, the imports may be properly regarded as representing the foreign-exchange cost of the national plan. During the period under discussion, Soviet credit covered only 6 per cent of the imports. Furthermore, by 1957 the Soviet credit that had been outstanding was exhausted, and the amortization payments already exceeded the balance of the credit by 600 million yuan, an amount equivalent to 11 per cent of exports during the year. While economic grants to other countries may decline, the loan services are likely to grow for some years to come. Perhaps new Soviet credit will be concluded in the future, but unless the amounts are exceptionally large, it is doubtful if the loan proceeds net of amortization payments would contribute to the net capital formation in the country as much as it did during the first five years.

Realizing the situation, Peiping relies on two courses of action. One is to raise the degree of domestic supply of machinery and equipment from 50 per cent during the period of the First Five Year Plan to 70 per cent under the Second.[56] By 1957, the degree of self-sufficiency had reportedly reached 60 per cent.[57] It has even been stated that the country is at the present able to produce about one-half of the machinery and equipment that had to be imported from Soviet Russia for the 156 projects.[58] Many arsenals and related factories are expected to help produce machinery for civilian use.[59] In the future as long as a piece of equipment can be produced at

---

[56] Chia Fu, "The Rate of Economic Development under the Second Five Year Plan," *Hsin-hua pan-yueh-k'an*, 24: 40–42, December, 1956.

[57] Ching Lin, "The Proportionate Relationship between the Iron and Steel Industry and Machine-making Industry," *Chi-hua ching-chi (Planned Economy)*, 9: 11–15, September, 1957.

[58] See a news dispatch in *Jen-min jih-pao*, September 30, 1957, p. 5.

[59] Ching Lin, *op. cit.*

home, even at high cost and low quality, it will not be imported.[60]

However, as the country becomes more industrialized, the need for heavy equipment and precision machinery will grow, both of which must be largely imported. Manufacturing ability may well be accelerative in the course of economic development; in this way Soviet technical assistance will perhaps mean more to Peiping than economic credit. Nevertheless, as was indicated in the earlier discussion of industrial development, the declining dependence on foreign supply of capital equipment will likely be balanced by an increasing dependence in respect of industrial supplies and materials. Time is required to develop resources, and China is not as self-sufficient in natural endowment for rapid and large-scale industrialization as she expects to be.

The second course of action is the export drive, begun in 1954 and stepped up since 1956. It has been directed primarily at the free world. As a result of industrial development, the composition of Chinese exportables is fast changing in favor of machinery and equipment, manufactured consumer goods, and mining products. Agricultural produce will doubtless continue to be important for a long time to come, but its relative importance probably will decline. The change in composition demands new markets. Under the existing circumstances of trade restrictions by the free world and well-developed trade with countries of the Communist bloc, Peiping has found that the elasticity of demand for Chinese exports is much greater in the free world than in the Communist world. This is true particularly of the markets in Southeast Asia and Africa. Furthermore, trade with the free world has yielded to Communist China a substantial export surplus, which is needed for meeting a growing pressure from her international balance since 1955. For this reason alone, the free world has become the vital link in a system of triangular trade necessary for her economic development.

But trade with the free world entails other advantages. Even though Chinese exports have been selling below domestic cost in the free-world markets, the factoral terms of trade are likely to have been in Peiping's favor. More important, the access to free-world markets will enable Peiping to attain the best comodity terms of trade possible between the two world markets. Thus the aggressiveness with which Peiping has been pushing its trade with coun-

---

[60] Po I-po, "Problems of Setting the Planned Production Quotas for 1958," *Hsinhua pan-yueh-k'an*, 17: 206–208, September, 1957.

tries outside the Soviet bloc since 1956 should be understood not as a propaganda device as is generally interpreted, but as a manifestation of need and urgency, for the speed of industrialization of the country depends in no small measure on the success of the drive.

VIII

Prospects:
Some Strategic Factors of Growth

An evaluation of the industrialization prospects may best be made by discussing certain factors strategic to the rate of growth in the future. We are not concerned here with the social and cultural factors which have played an important part in arresting economic development of many other underdeveloped countries but which apparently have been effectively neutralized in Communist China through "socialist transformation" and political organization— witness the nation-wide collectivization of family farms within a few months after the autumn harvest of 1955. Nor are we concerned with the problem of labor supply. The shortage of technical skill, severe as it is, does not seem to have been insurmountable. It has been reported that engineering and technical personnel had increased from 170,000 in number in 1952 to 800,000 in 1957.[1] The potential supply of industrial labor is more than the state and joint enterprises can absorb for many years to come.[2] The discussion will be confined to population growth and per-capita consumption, and concluded with comments on the relation of agriculture to further economic growth.

1. POPULATION GROWTH

Population growth plays a crucial role in Chinese economic development. It affects not only per-capita consumption, but also labor supply, per-capita output, composition of output, and potential

[1] State Planning Commission, "Results and Achievements of the First Five Year Plan," *Jen-min jih-pao*, October 1, 1957. For the increase in student enrollment, college student enrollment in specialized fields, and polytechnical student enrollment, from 1949 to 1957, see Statistical Appendix, Tables 29–31.

[2] These remarks should not be construed to imply that the subjects mentioned are not important. They deserve separate study.

export volume; and there are other economic and social effects as well.[3] Although this is not the place to enter into details, it is necessary to bring out certain aspects.

Population Size.—The Peiping authorities, instead of relying on the reports of local police and village elders as formerly, undertook a national census, with June 30, 1953, as the critical date, of permanent population in the latter half of 1953 and the first quarter of 1954. The advice of Soviet census experts was sought, and some two and a half million workers were mobilized as census takers.[4] However, when the result of the census was announced, namely that the total population on the Chinese mainland was 582.6 million, the world was thrown into half-disbelief, for the previous official estimate given by the nationalist government for 1948 was 457 million.[5]

The doubt about the validity of the census lies not so much in the integrity of the statisticians as in the competence and dependability of the census takers in the field—a crucial factor in determining the soundness of any method used. It may be recalled that the census was taken not too long after the "five anti" campaign, when the Korean war was brought to a conclusion, and, above all, when the First Five Year Plan was launched. According to the propaganda line of Peiping at this time, the international status of the country was already established by at least the size of its population if not by military strength, and the country was due for a period of peace, construction, and prosperity. Historically, peace and prosperity have always been associated with a rapidly growing population. Inspired by this line of propaganda, and in order to exhort the people to work hard for construction by enhancing their confidence in the new regime, many census takers

---

[3] The best summary of all such effects is given in United Nations, Department of Social Affairs, Population Division, *The Determinants and Consequences of Population Trends,* New York, 1953, Part 3, pp. 181–315. See also H. Leibenstein, *Economic Backwardness and Economic Growth,* New York, 1957.

[4] For the methodology adopted, see S. Krotevich, "Vsekitaiskaia perepis' naseleniia 1953 g." (The All-China Population Census of 1953), *Vestnik Statistiki (Bulletin of Statistics)*, Moscow, 5: 31–50, September–October, 1955; especially pp. 36–49. Krotevich, probably the only Soviet expert participating actively in the planning, indicated that Peiping had originally intended to take a census of the *de jure* population. For a summary of Krotevich's article in English see T. Shabad, "Counting 600 Million Chinese," *Far Eastern Survey,* XXV: 58–62, April, 1956.

[5] For detailed figures of the census and sources, see Statistical Appendix, Table 28. For the 1948 estimate, see *China Handbook, 1950,* New York, 1950, p. 17, table 8. This is the last official figure released by the Ministry of Interior of the national government for the whole of China. The total given is 463.5 million, including 6.4 million for Taiwan.

might very well have overstated the results of their "survey and registration." Of questionable validity is the official claim that a sample check of about 9 per cent of the population actually "surveyed and registered" revealed only 0.139 per cent of duplication and 0.255 per cent of omission.[6] If the drive to exceed the annual production quotas has induced an upward "psychological bias" among the reporting agencies for agriculture, as was observed by the Delegation of India, how much more conceivable was it for the census workers to be subject to the same influence?[7]

It is significant that some prominent scholars, writing in Communist China about the population problem as late as 1957, made no reference to the size of the population in the course of their discussion.[8] In fact, Professor Ta Chen has criticized the method of the census as "unscientific" and the results as "dubious."[9] Another census is due to take place in 1958, and the results should be of great interest. But we should keep in mind that "the responsibility for population statistics has been assigned by the State Council to public security agencies."[10]

Rate of Population Growth.—For the purpose of this study, however, it is more important to know something about the rate of population increase than the exact size. Until about the late 1940's, the population change typical of an underdeveloped country manifested itself both in a high, stable fertility rate and in a high but widely fluctuating mortality rate due to frequent natural calamities, epidemics, and also wars and civil conflicts. While the curve of population change was discontinuous (zigzag), the slope of the

---

[6] State Statistical Bureau, "Communiqué on the Results of the National Population Census," *Jen-min jih-pao*, November 1, 1954.

[7] Evidence of overreporting is given in an editorial of *Jen-min jih-pao*, September 2, 1957, in which it is stated that as a result of the drive to curb unnecessary food consumption, the population of twenty towns in Kirin Province was found to be 27,000 less than reported. However, the size of the total population there was not given.

[8] Ta Chen, "Birth Control, Deferred Marriage and China's Population Problem," *Hsin chien-she (New Construction)*, 5: 1–15, May, 1957; and Chang P'ei-kang, Mao Kang, and Hu Chun-chieh, "The Socialist Law of Population and the Chinese Population Problem," *Ching-chi yen-chiu (Economic Research)*, 4: 30–63, August, 1957. The foremost demographer of the country, Chen is the author of *Population in Modern China*, Chicago, 1947. The article cited is his first publication since 1949. Chang is the author of *Agriculture and Industrialization*, Cambridge, Mass., 1949.

[9] This is revealed in an article, "Rightist Chen Ta Plots to Eliminate the Chinese Communist Party," *Hsin-hua pan-yueh-k'an*, 19: 87–88, October, 1957. Chen made the criticism at a meeting held at the office of the State Statistical Bureau.

[10] Director of the Statistical Bureau Hsieh Mu-ch'iao, "Our Experience in Statistical Work during the First Five Year Plan and Our Future Tasks," *T'ung-chi kung-tso (Statistical Work)*, 21: 1–21, November, 1957; quotation on p. 21.

underlying long-term trend might be either positive by varying degrees, or nearly neutral, or, in some rare cases, even negative. With respect to China's experience, the opinion of two well-informed scholars may be cited. One estimated the crude birth and death rates to be 38 and 34 for 1933, while the other maintained in 1945 that "on the basis of the changes in rural population during the recent sixty years as recorded by the Central Agricultural Research Bureau, the natural rate of increase in the Chinese population is around one-half of one per cent per year."[11]

If that describes the picture of prewar China, the situation has been vastly different since 1950, although we are not certain of the magnitude of the vital rates. The First Five Year Plan makes no reference to the subject of population. A national system of registration of vital statistics was not installed until the middle of 1955 when Peiping issued instructions for its establishment under local security agencies or as a part of them.[12]

Nevertheless, the results of two surveys have been made known. The first survey was conducted in 1952 and 1953, covering 29 cities, five counties, and three villages in 37 different areas in the country. It gave a birth rate of 38 and a death rate of 11 per thousand population, with therefore a natural increase of 2.7 per cent per annum.[13] The sample was broadened in the second survey to include the same number of cities, but 45 counties and 65 large and small villages. According to the result, the natural rate of increase was 2 per cent per year, derived from a birth rate of 37 and a death rate of 17.[14] Aside from the question of method and therefore reliability of the results, the substantial difference in the death rate between the two surveys must be due to the weight given to rural population in the samples. In other words, the

---

[11] The first estimate is given by Ta Chen, *Population in Modern China*, p. 29. The quotation comes from Ch'iao Chi-ming, *Chung-kuo nung-ts'un she-hui ching-chi-hsueh (Chinese Rural Economics)*, Chungking, 1945, p. 121. Ch'iao is perhaps the most outstanding rural sociologist in the country.

[12] The State Council issued the Regulations on Registration of Marriages and Divorces on June 1, 1955, and Regulations on Registration of Households and Population on June 22, 1955. In both regulations, the local machinery responsible for the work was designated. According to the second instruction, there would be regular registration of births, deaths, reasons of death, immigration, and emigration. See *1956 Jen-min shou-tse (People's Handbook for 1956)*, pp. 325–326, and 329–330.

[13] *Ta Kung Pao (Impartial Daily)*, Tientsin, March 11, 1954. The survey was made by the Ministry of Public Security, the Ministry of Interior, the Ministry of Civil Defense of the People's Revolutionary Military Council, and other agencies.

[14] Peh Chien-hua, "600 Million Population—a Great Strength for China's Socialist Construction," *Jen-min jih-pao*, November 1, 1954. It is stated that the sample consisted of 30 million people.

birth rate being about the same between urban and rural population, the larger the representation of rural population in the sample, the higher will be the national death rate.

The rapid decline of the death rate has been a common experience to most underdeveloped countries since the late 1940's. Perhaps the timing of the beginning of a substantial drop in the death rate was not very different in Communist China. War activities virtually ceased by 1949, and the national campaign to improve public sanitation started in earnest in the cities in 1952.[15] The number of hospital beds increased from 106,000 in 1950 to 180,000 in 1952 and 328,000 in 1956.[16] If the death rate did start to fall significantly in the late 1940's or the early 1950's, the natural rate of increase would have grown during the period under study—unless the birth rate was also declining as fast at the same time. While impossible to determine the precise behavior of the vital rates, it is important to obtain a general picture of the changing rate of population increase.

The change in population size from year to year has not been regularly released. The only consecutive series obtainable is given in Table XLVII, where population figures are computed from official data on the total output of food grains and on per-capita share. It will be observed that the population subject to food rationing is smaller than the total population on the mainland, the system having not been extended to certain minority areas such as Tibet. It is not clear whether the population figures given for a "food year" pertain to the beginning or to the middle of the period. Perhaps the latter is meant, since "planned supply" of food grains did not start until November, 1953. And the extension of rationing might have accounted for the 2.4 per cent increase in population in the following year. Since then, however, the rate of increase had stabilized at 2.2 per cent, and this perhaps furnishes the basis for the official estimate that "in recent years the Chinese population has been increasing at the rate of about 2.2 per cent each year."[17]

We have seen that the drive for economizing food consumption had resulted in reducing the overreporting of population in many areas. Under these circumstances, the 2.2 per cent increase for the

---

[15] See Minister of Public Health Li Teh-ch'uan's report to the National Congress of People's Representatives, *Jen-min jih-pao*, September 25, 1954.

[16] These are official figures released by the State Statistical Bureau in "Economic Statistical Bureau," *Hsin-hua pan-yueh-k'an*, 17: 50, September, 1956, and "Communiqué on the Results of the 1956 Plan," *Jen-min jih-pao*, August 2, 1957.

[17] Editorial, "The Need for Birth Control," *Jen-min jih-pao*, March 5, 1957.

last two years shown in the table might have covered up an increasing rate of population growth. In fact, as Professor 'Ta Chen observes, "the new demographic feature of China consists in a rising tendency of the birth rate, a sharp drop of the death rate (including the infant mortality rate), and therefore a growing rate

TABLE XLVII

RURAL AND URBAN POPULATION OF CENSUS, AND POPULATION
SUBJECT TO "PLANNED SUPPLY" OF FOOD GRAINS, 1953–1957

Population	Census, 1953 June 30	Population subject to "planned supply"			
		1953–54	1954–55	1955–56	1956–57
A. Total:					
1. In millions....................	582.6	575.2	589.0	601.9	615.1
2. Annual increase in per cent.....	———	———	2.40	2.19	2.19
B. Rural:					
1. In millions....................	505.3	499.1	509.1	520.7	527.6
2. Annual increase in per cent.....	———	———	2.00	2.28	1.33
C. Urban:					
1. In millions....................	77.3	76.1	79.9	81.2	87.5
2. Annual increase in per cent.....	———	———	5.00	1.63	7.76
D. Rural-Urban ratio:					
1. Rural (in per cent).............	86.74	86.77	86.43	86.51	85.77
2. Urban (in per cent).............	13.26	13.23	13.57	13.49	14.23

Sources and notes: (1) Census data from Statistical Appendix, Table 28. (2) "Planned supply" of food grains, started in November, 1953, is some form of rationing; see discussion in chapter i, section 4. Population figures are computed from data on food-grain sales and per-capita "food consumption," released by the State Statistical Bureau, "The Basic Situation of Planned Purchase and Planned Supply of Food Grains in China," *T'ung-chi kung-tso (Statistical Work)*, 19: 31–32 and 28, October, 1957. This is the same source as for Table XIV in chapter iii. The food year begins on July 1. Food grains include soybeans.

of natural increase.'"[18] This observation finds support in certain official estimates of total population. According to the State Statistical Bureau and the State Economic Commission, the total population was 626 million in 1956 and 640 million in 1957.[19] If these are taken as mid-year estimates, the average annual rate of increase from 1953 to 1957 was 2.38 per cent while the increase from 1956 to 1957 was 2.55 per cent.

[18] Ta Chen, "Birth Control ...," p. 1.

[19] These refer to total population on the mainland only. The 1956 figure is cited by T'an Chen-lin, "A Study of the Income and Level of Living of the Chinese Peasants," *Hsin-hua pan-yueh-k'an*, 11: 105–111, June, 1957; and the 1957 figure, by Sung Shao-wen, "The Principle of Diligence and Economy in Basic Economic Construction," *Hsueh-hsi (Study)*, 11: 22–24, June, 1957. Peiping uses different population estimates for different purposes. For example, in the calculation of general consumption per capita, an estimate of 624 million population for 1956 was used instead of 626 million. See Tien Lin, "Seven Years of Achievement—A Supplement," *Hsin-hua pan-yueh-k'an*, 15: 159, August, 1957.

An increasing rate of population growth requires an equal rate of increase in net national product in order to maintain the same net product per capita. It implies also that an increasing portion of net capital formation must be employed for this purpose alone. We have seen that calculated from official data, the marginal capital coefficient during the five-year period is 1.3 while the rate of net capital formation is 11 per cent. If population had been increasing at somewhere between 2.4 and 2.55 per cent a year, the rate of net capital investment required to maintain per-capita net product would have been between 3.1 to 3.3 per cent. But, as was brought out, the capital coefficient—even with the restrictive definition of net capital investment adopted in this study—must have been understated because of the exaggerated increase in net national product. If the coefficient should have been, say, two, then the rate of net capital investment required would be about 5 per cent. In any case, the effect of population growth on the rate of capital formation is clear.[20] The faster population grows, the lower will be the rate of capital formation available for raising per-capita net product.

Urban-rural Differential.—The national rate of population growth conceals a great disparity in the natural rate of increase between the rural and urban population. The 1953 census classifies the total population into 86.74 per cent rural and 13.26 per cent urban. The exact definition of "rural" and "urban" has not been given. According to the Peiping usage, "rural population" is probably not the same as, but larger than, "farming population." This stands to reason, for rural population should include all residents in rural areas, not all of whom are engaged in farming.[21] The natural rate of increase of rural population has been estimated to be 2 per cent and that of farming population 2.135 per cent.[22]

The natural rate of increase in urban population cannot be

---

[20] The effect on consumption will be discussed in the next section.

[21] According to Yueh Wei of the State Statistical Bureau, "The nonfarming population of the country has been estimated too low. . . . Upon investigation, it has been discovered that when statistics on farming population were reported from the village level upward through various agencies, somewhere along the way figures for both the farming and nonfarming population of the village areas were added together, with the result that the farming population became disproportionately large for the country as a whole." See his "On the Methods of Estimation and Interpolation," *T'ung-chi kung-tso t'ung-hsin (Statistical Bulletin)*, 18: 25–27, September, 1956; quotation on p. 26. Note that this contradicts the official claim concerning duplication.

[22] Computed from data given in Chang Hao-yen, "The Load on the Shoulders of the Peasants," *Hsueh-hsi (Study)* 16: 16–17, August, 1957; and Ma Yin-ch'u, "A New

computed directly from the changes in the number of urban residents because of the irregular influx of people from the rural areas. This is clearly shown in Table XLVII, Parts B and C. It has been estimated that a total of eight million people had permanently migrated into cities and towns during the five-year period of the Plan.[23] But if the rural population with the 2 per cent annual increase is taken to be the same as that defined in the census, and if the natural rate of increase for the country as a whole is 2.4 per cent, mathematically the *natural* rate of increase of urban population would be 4.9 per cent, or about two and a half times that of rural population. This finding is supported by some fragmentary data; for instance, the natural rate of increase in Shanghai, the largest city in the country, is reported to have been 3.9 per cent in 1953, and that of Anshan, the iron and steel center, 5.57 per cent in 1956.[24]

Such a wide divergence in the population growth rate between the two sectors of the economy is due to the difference in the death rate rather than in the birth rate, and explainable by the disparity in the advancement of public health, the increase in industrial employment, and the provision of medical insurance and other social benefits by the state and the employers in the urban areas. The influx of the able-bodied from villages must have also been an important factor contributing to a high birth rate and a low death rate in the industrial and mining cities.

Some Consequences on Economic Growth.—These rapid rates of population growth pose serious problems to further economic progress. In the urban areas, the shortage of work opportunities becomes more and more pressing. Despite the increase in employment in factories, mines, and construction, new opportunities available each year lag further and further behind the number of new entrants into the labor force. It has been estimated that during the Second Five Year Plan about five million persons will come to working age every year, consisting of 1.3 million from cities and towns and 3.7 million from villages, whereas all the state enterprises (chiefly industrial and commercial) will be able to absorb

---

Theory of Population," *Hsin-hua pan-yueh-k'an*, 15: 34–41, August, 1957. The data given in both these sources are "based on materials furnished by the State Statistical Bureau."

[23] Wang Kuang-wei, "A Suggestion on the Allocation of the Agricultural Labor Force [for the Second Five Year Plan]," *Chi-hua ching-chi (Planned Economy)* 8: 6–9, August, 1957.

[24] For Shanghai, see Ma Yin-ch'u, *op. cit.;* for Anshan, see "The Problem of Shortage of Factory Dormitories," *Jen-min jih-pao*, May 7, 1957.

annually about one million, a number less than the new entrants coming from the urban population itself.[25] It may be argued that more capital investment will create more jobs. But the rate of capital formation has probably been raised as far as the public can endure, as the frequent reference to "internal contradiction" between savings and investment demonstrates. Although the amount of investment will increase as the net national product grows, the potential working force swells even faster.

What is to be done about the situation? State policy, as enunciated in the middle of 1957, is that since industry can absorb only a limited number of the new entrants as it expands, "the major direction of their employment *for a long time to come* must lie in agriculture, with handicrafts and service trades as subsidiary outlets."[26] A great majority of primary and high-school graduates have already been required to seek work in farming activities.[27] Thus whereas during the First Five Year Plan peasants had intermittently migrated into cities in large numbers, the direction may well be reversed during the second five years. This means also that unlike the experience of Japan, rapid urbanization in Communist China has not significantly changed the urban-rural composition of population and is not likely to do so in the foreseeable future.

The shuttling of the surplus working force from urban to rural areas can only aggravate the problem of agriculture. The rural sector has been witnessing a decline in per-capita cultivated acreage, caused by the 2 per cent annual natural increase in population and less than 1 per cent increase in cultivated area. Collectivization has induced a great number of women to work on the farm. Under these circumstances, the influx of urban workers also serves to swell further the number of farm hands per unit area and accelerate the fall in per-capita cultivated area. The operation of the law of diminishing returns can only be counteracted by massive investment in agriculture that has not been forthcoming. Moreover, the incoming urban workers will probably bring in their train an improvement in public sanitation into the rural areas and a spread of the knowledge of personal hygiene among the rural population. If the death rate in the countryside should drop fast enough to approach that of the urban areas in the near future,

[25] Cheng Kang-ling, "Summarizing the Experience of Labor-Force and Wage Planning for 1956," *Chi-hua ching-chi (Planned Economy),* 8: 9–13, August, 1957.
[26] Premier Chou En-lai, "Report on the Work of the Government," *Jen-min jih-pao,* June 27, 1957. Italics mine.
[27] Editorial, *Jen-min jih-pao,* April 8, 1957.

the difficulty of raising the rate of capital formation and solving the problem of employment will multiply many times.

2. CONSUMPTION

In the face of a high rate of capital formation and a growing rate of population increase, what have been the changes in the level of consumption during these years of rapid industrialization? Despite the limitation of data, the subject requires careful consideration, for in the short run consumption is antithetical to net investment.

It is now clear that one of the important reasons for Peiping adopting a policy of encouraging "free criticism" from March to May in 1957 was the public's complaint about the deterioration of the level of living, as well as disparity of consumption between industrial workers and peasants. Not only did Mao himself take pains in his speech in February, that set off the theme of rectifying internal contradictions, to "prove" the improvement in the living conditions of the peasants, but numerous statements by high government authorities and articles written in newspapers and periodicals have since appeared, all trying to demonstrate with statistics that per-capita consumption of both urban and rural population has improved considerably. The most widely used statistics for this purpose show that at constant prices per-capita consumption of the agricultural population had increased from 72 yuan in 1952 to 81 in 1956 (12 per cent rise) against an increase from 151 yuan to 180 (19 per cent rise) in that of urban workers.[28] Apparently these calculations are based on the size of population on the one hand and the domestic material product minus accumulation on the other. Equally stressed as evidences of improvement in consumption are the increasing amounts of staple food, cloth, and rubber shoes supplied by the market to the public.[29]

Per-Capita Net National Product and Per-Capita Consumption.—We have seen that calculated from official data the net national product had increased at an average annual rate of 8.9 per cent from 1952 through 1957 (planned). If population had been increasing 2.4 per cent per year during this period, net product

---

[28] See, for example, Po I-po, "Report to the National Conference of Model Agricultural Workers," *Jen-min jih-pao*, February 24, 1957. All such official data on per-capita consumption stop short at 1956, when the net national product was highest on record.

[29] See, for example, Chou En-lai, as cited in n. 26.

per capita should have been growing at the rate of 6.3 per cent.[30]
We have established that a good part of the increase in net national product was statistical and not real. However, if proper
allowance could be made for the statistical and psychological factors that had inflated the rate of increase, the net national product
had doubtless been increasing at a rate faster than population
growth. In other words, net product per capita had also been improving. Does that imply necessarily an increase in per-capita consumption as well?

First, a part of the increase in net national product has gone
into augmentation of stockpiles and commodity reserves. The rate
of accumulation at constant prices had risen from 18.2 per cent
in 1952 to 25.3 per cent in 1956, as compared to our estimate of
the increase in net capital formation from 7 per cent to 14 per
cent. The difference between these two sets of rates is partly due
to the restrictive definition for capital formation adopted in this
study. The implication is that the rate of net savings was higher
than the rate of net capital formation.[31] The amount available for
consumption each year was less than what the rate of capital formation suggests.

Second, an increase in per-capita net national product means an
improvement in per-capita consumption only if the increase in
the output of consumer goods is substantial enough to warrant
such a result.[32] The point will be clearly brought out if we assume,
for the sake of argument, that all the net investment during the
period was put into producer-goods industries. In that event, even
if the net national product increased much more rapidly than
population so that per-capita net product also grew, per-capita consumption would have to fall. The availability of consumer goods
is therefore the crucial factor in determining whether an increase
in per-capita net national product will result in an increase in
per-capita consumption. Unfortunately, the basic official data are
not satisfactory enough to permit an estimate along this line. It
is reported that the total output of consumer goods had increased
on the average by about 3,000 million yuan a year from 1952
through 1956, and that after allowing for reserves and for the increase in population, "the amount available for improving the

[30] That is, $(1.089 \div 1.024) - 1$.

[31] More accurately, the rate of net savings and hoarding.

[32] The possibility of reducing commodity reserves can only be regarded as a temporary and makeshift measure.

per-person consumption was about four yuan per year."[33] There is no way to check the calculation. But, taking the statement as it stands, it is not clear whether exports of consumer goods had been deducted or not. Furthermore, the average of 1952 through 1956 inevitably exaggerates the increase; if 1957 should be chosen as the terminal year, the amount would be much less.

Third, for a country undergoing rapid industrialization, special attention must be paid to the effects of changing economic structure, and effects of urbanization and commercialization in particular. Urbanization has been developing rapidly. Urban population—residents of cities and towns, including immigrants from rural areas—increased from 71.6 million in 1952 to 92 million in 1957.[34] During the five-year period of the Plan, 26 cities had been newly built, 20 others extensively reconstructed, and another 74 remodeled.[35] There are now 13 cities of more than one million population each against only eight in 1950, and 18 cities of between half a million and one million each, most of which have been developed since 1951.[36] This growth is due to industrialization. In 12 cities were established from 11 to 20 big basic construction projects each, and in six others, more than 21 such projects each.[37]

Urbanization and industrialization have brought with them many services beneficial to consumers. Such municipal utilities as electric power and water supply, sewage, modern roads and transport are introduced to a large number of people for the first time. It is said that a total of 1,633 million yuan had been invested in these utilities during the five-year period, and, as a result, the number of people having the use of tap water, for example, had increased by 15 million.[38]

It would be idle to argue whether these services represent an improvement in the people's level of living, for the answer de-

[33] Yang Po, "An Understanding of the Proportion between Consumption and Accumulation in the Disposal of China's National Income," *Hsueh-hsi (Study)*, 20: 24–26, October, 1957; quotation on p. 25.

[34] Ts'ao Yen-hsing, "Municipal Construction in Accordance with the Principle of Diligence and Economy," *Chi-hua ching-chi (Planned Economy)*, 12: 4–9, December, 1957. See also Table XLVII.

[35] *Ibid.*

[36] Sung Shao-wen, "The Principle of Diligence and Economy in Basic Economic Construction," *Hsueh-hsi (Study)*, 11: 22–24, June, 1957.

[37] Ts'ao, *op. cit.*

[38] *Ibid.* For definition of municipal utilities, see Ku To-ching, "Tabulation Forms for Municipal Utilities," *Chi-hua ching-chi (Planned Economy)*, 7: 31–33, July, 1957.

pends a good deal on personal value judgment. Undoubtedly, living in the cities is quite a different mode of life from living in the villages, and requires a minimum set of services for mere existence. Moreover, urbanization does institutionalize a number of services, such as education, amusement, and even medical care, which would otherwise have been done at home or among relatives and neighbors, and which would not therefore have entered into national income accounting. The congregation of a large number of people in a small area demands an adequate supply of food from long distances, and even if per-capita consumption of food remains the same, the transport and commercial services required would have been reflected in a larger net national product and a larger per-capita product. Hence, it is safe to say that not all services made available in the cities represent an improvement in consumption.

However, there is another group of benefits for urban workers that has been brought into being not as a direct consequence of urbanization but as a result of state policy. It comprises the various social services provided by government agencies and enterprises for their workers, including insurance against sickness, disability, and old age, benefits for birth and death, direct welfare subsidies (medical, education, rent, utilities, and the like), and contribution to labor unions for operating nurseries, sanitaria, schools, and clubs. A total of 11,000 million yuan had been paid out for these benefits during the five-year period of the Plan, equivalent to about one-quarter of the total wage bill of 43,300 million.[39] Thus one-fifth of the total consumption of urban workers is provided for collectively. While this collective consumption, as it may be called, adds to private consumption, it is not necessarily true that to the urban worker the marginal utility of one yuan's worth of private consumption is equal to that of collective consumption. In fact, the suggestion of reducing the collective consumption fund in order to increase the wage bill has already appeared in print.[40] Without going into the treacherous ground of value and welfare, we may observe that collective consumption does constitute an important addition to private consumption for urban workers.

[39] Li Yueh, "The Need for Readjusting the Unreasonable Welfare Subsidies," *Chi-hua ching-chi (Planned Economy)*, 12: 15–17 and 3, December, 1957.

[40] Sung Ping, "The Principle of Income Distribution according to Labor Spent," *Chi-hua ching-chi (Planned Economy)*, 5: 1–4, May, 1957.

In sum, urbanization produces a large number of services contributing to the increase in net national product. While some of them do represent an improvement in the public's level of consumption, some others do not, although it is nearly impossible to make due allowance for the latter. On the other hand, urbanization has also brought forth, as a result of state policy, a group of welfare services to the workers, amounting to about one-fifth of their personal consumption of goods and services. The value of these services enters into the net national product and represents an addition to private consumption.

Commercialization affects the rural sector the most. It comes about through the reduction of the self-retained portion of farm or household production, so that peasants have to depend increasingly on the market for supply. The collection of agricultural taxes in kind and compulsory delivery at government prices helped step up the pace of commercialization of food crops from 23.4 per cent in 1952 to 30.8 per cent in 1954 and 26.7 per cent in 1955.[41] Collectivization might have brought the percentage up to 45 for 1956.[42] During the last two years of the period of the Plan, rapid commercialization was inseparable from collectivization.

The process of commercialization draws out certain parts of farm and household production that would otherwise have been omitted in the national income account. Furthermore, by taking away the usual food reserves kept in the household and then selling a part of them back when necessary, the volume of trade and in some cases the volume of transport would increase, thus swelling the national product; yet such an increase in consumption of services on the part of the peasant is not his preference and does not improve his real consumption. Such an observation should not be construed as taking a position against commercialization, for after all it is a necessary concomitant of economic development. What is said means simply that a part of the increase in national product resulting from commercialization represents nothing but institutionalization of the supply of a large variety of goods and services that do not add to real consumption.[43] Interestingly enough,

[41] Ch'u Ch'ing and Chu Chung-chien, "Variations in the Commodity Turnover in China's Rural Markets," *Ching-chi yen-chiu (Economic Research)*, 3: 100–126, June, 1957. The drop in 1955 was due to a reduction in the compulsory delivery quota which had been set too high in 1954, causing much discontent among the peasants.

[42] "A Survey of the Income of Agricultural Producer Coöperatives in 1955 and its Distribution," *Hsin-hua pan-yueh-k'an*, 24: 63–65, December, 1956.

[43] See the interesting remarks on this point by Simon Kuznets, "National Income and Industrial Structure," *Econometrica*, XVII: supplement, 205–241, July, 1949.

it is precisely in 1956 when commercialization attained the high degree of 45 per cent that the national product made the biggest gain in all these years.

But commercialization together with collectivization has other important effects on consumption. Unlike urban workers, no collective consumption has been provided for peasants, except that in an agricultural collective every one is paid according to the number of labor days he has put into the work during the year and that the sick and disabled will be taken care of from the welfare reserve equal to 1 or 2 per cent of the gross product of the collective.[44] There has also been an equalizing effect on staple food consumption in that the poor peasants who could afford to have only coarse grains before are now able to share the same kind of food as the rest in the same collective. Whether in the aggregate this means more consumption of superior food (like rice and wheat flour) or of inferior food (like sweet potatoes and millet) for the members is not known.

A more important effect is found in the attempt of everyone of working age in the farming household to work as many days as possible in the collective in order to augment family income. Women, in particular, have joined the collectives in large numbers, thereby foregoing such regular domestic production as shoemaking, tailoring, spinning and weaving, food processing, and the like.[45] Products that used to be made at home have to be bought from the market—at prices that include various kinds of taxes. The money income of the household has indeed increased, but this does not mean a net gain in real income until all money expenditures for the same amount of household consumption as before have been allowed for. In the meantime, an increasing market supply of cloth, shoes, processed food, and other daily necessities is required by the very process and does not signify any improvement in per-capita consumption. Thus the official data on increasing sales of daily necessities in the rural area have to be interpreted with this in mind. "To raise the degree of commercialization in respect of food grains and cotton is the most pressing task at the present," states the chairman of the State Economic Commission.[46]

---

[44] This is in accordance with the regulations and apparently has not materialized thus far. See Li Po-kuan, "Income Distribution among Members of Agricultural Collectives," *Hsin chien-she (New Construction)*, 7: 1–5, July, 1957.

[45] Ch'u Ch'ing and Chu Chung-chien, *op. cit.*

[46] Po I-po, "Problems of Setting the Planned Production Quotas for 1958," *Hsin-hua pan-yueh-k'an*, 17: 206–208, September, 1957.

We may confidently anticipate a growing demand for consumer goods in the rural areas to make up for what used to be produced at home.

How much money income of a farming household has to be increased in order to maintain the same level of consumption may be gauged from the following report. An investigation was made of a family of six, located in a village in Hunan Province. During 1955, the total consumption of the family, of which 60 per cent was produced either at home or on their own farm, was priced at 301 yuan locally, but the same basket of consumption goods would have cost 729 yuan at Peiping or 744 yuan at Shanghai.[47] The close similarity between the Peiping and Shanghai valuation implies that most of the products were controlled by the state and sold at official prices, which do not vary widely from one area to another. If the family now has to buy 70 per cent (instead of 40) of the consumer goods from the market, one can visualize that the family's money income has to increase several times in order to maintain the same consumption level, especially when most of the daily necessities besides food must come from the cities. An annual increase of four yuan per capita in consumption goods—assuming for the moment that the estimate is reasonably accurate—would be far from sufficient to compensate for the effect of commercialization.

According to official statistics, one-half of the market supply of coal had been for the rural areas in 1956 and 1957 and the sales of kerosene to the rural population had increased from 25,000 tons in 1950 to 334,000 tons in 1956.[48] These are not products that could be made in the farming household. Does the increase of their sales reflect an improvement in the level of consumption? As for coal, the increased supply is necessitated by the shortage of animal feed and fertilizers, for which stalks and straw are substitutes. The latter products are generally used as fuel for the farming household. If coal is not supplied, stalks and straw would be withdrawn from productive use and the shortage of animal feed and fertilizers would hamper agricultural output. An analogous situation exists for kerosene. We have seen that the shortage of edible vegetable oil has been nation-wide for several years. The

---

[47] Editorial, *Jen-min jih-pao*, April 1, 1957.

[48] For the supply of coal, see "Industrial Development Requires Simultaneous Development of Agriculture," *Chi-hua ching-chi (Planned Economy)*, 10: 1–2, October, 1957. For the supply of kerosene, see Chi Ch'ung-wei, "Industry Should Assist Agricultural Development," *ibid.*, 10: 7–10, October, 1957.

supply of kerosene merely serves to preserve the supply of vegetable oil for food use. The fact that the authorities find it necessary to import as much as 265,000 tons of kerosene a year shows the severe shortage of oils and fats.[49] Thus the increase in sales of such products as coal and kerosene has nothing to do with improvement in personal consumption.

The discussion thus far may be briefly summarized. An increase in per-capita net national product does not necessarily mean an increase in per-capita consumption, because, as demonstrated for China, (1) a part of the national output is withheld to increase stockpiles and commercial reserves. (2) the output of consumer goods may not be increasing fast enough, and (3) a part of the increase in national product is the result of urbanization and commercialization and hardly increases per-capita consumption. However, city life does offer certain amenities not available in the villages, although they are difficult to measure. Furthermore, apart from personal or private consumption, urban workers have been provided with certain collective welfare services amounting to about one-fourth of the total wage bill. These have to be taken into account in evaluating the changing consumption level of those working in cities and towns. The farming population fares differently. Collective welfare services have not been extended to them. Commercialization, stepped up by collectivization, has the effect of inducing women as well as men to give up subsidiary work that used to produce goods for the family's own household consumption. In the aggregate these goods must have constituted a sizable proportion of the annual national output of consumables. Now the loss in the domestic output must be made up by an increase in market supply. Thus the second point mentioned above is strengthened. In order to maintain, let alone increase, per-capita consumption, the output of consumer goods not only has to keep apace with population growth, but must be much higher than that, depending on the speed of commercialization. As far as private consumption is concerned, the commercial supply of consumer goods is the crucial factor.

Per-Capita Consumption.—The shortage of consumption goods has been freely admitted by the Peiping authorities. Interestingly, the admission is always coupled with the explanation that the

---

[49] See Chi Ch'ung-wei, *op. cit.* In 1956, the total sales of kerosene in both rural and urban areas amounted to 465,000 tons, of which less than 200,000 tons were produced at home; the rest had to be imported. The explanation of increasing supply of coal to the rural areas is given by Chi.

shortage is caused, not by any lack of improvement in per-capita consumption, but "by the people's desire to improve their level of living at too fast a rate."[50] Of course, the mere desire does not result in market scarcity unless the desire is translated into effective demand. Thus the official explanation is tantamount to saying that aggregate monetary demand has outstripped market supply. And this is the truth. As was discussed in chapter vi, severe inflation did take place during the first and the fourth year of the Plan. The shortage of goods under inflationary conditions gives no clue to the underlying change in per-capita consumption. For the present purpose, it is necessary to find out, with whatever data available, the change in per-capita consumption of such essential commodities and services as food grains, other food, cloth, and housing.

In chapter iii, data were presented concerning per-capita consumption of food grains (including soybeans) among both the urban and the rural population.[51] It was found that per-capita consumption declined from 1953 to 1957 among the urban residents but increased among the rural people. There is no need to repeat the discussion given there.[52] In the light of what has been said about commercialization, however, it may be further noted that the increase in the number of women as well as men working on the farm instead of in the household requires a larger per-capita consumption of food grains for sustenance.[53] Moreover, because of the curtailment of subsidiary work and therefore subsidiary income, the retained food grains (or those distributed by the agricultural collective for household consumption and for seeds) were used in part for raising animals, operating restaurants, or selling in the black market.[54] If the supply through black markets was taken into account, per-capita consumption among the urban population might have been higher than the official figures indicate. All in all, perhaps per-capita consumption of food grains

---

[50] See, for example, editorial, "People's Livelihood Can Only Be Improved Gradually," *Jen-min jih-pao*, November 27, 1956.

[51] See Table XIV. The per-capita share shown in the table includes the amount needed for animal feed and seeds. Changes in the per-capita share of the annual output reflects changes in per-capita consumption only if the amount for animal feed and seeds bears a constant relationship to the annual output.

[52] See concluding section of chapter iii.

[53] Wu Shih, "An Exploration of the Food Problem during the Period of Transition," *Hsin-hua pan-yueh-k'an*, 10: 104–109, May, 1957.

[54] These practices are explicitly or implicitly mentioned in the instruction issued by the State Council concerning the work of food control, in *Jen-min jih-pao*, November 22, 1956.

had remained unchanged for both urban and rural population, except that the poor peasants might have increased their consumption because of the leveling process under collectivization.[55] An observation of a Chinese writer in Peiping seems quite realistic: "During the present period, although China's food grains are sufficient to meet the basic needs of livelihood and production, the supply is clearly tight when distributed into hundreds of different uses such as staple food for the people, seeds, animal feed, and requirements in agricultural subsidiary work and in industry."[56]

Of other foodstuffs for daily consumption, vegetable oil, salt, and meat have been among the most scarce items. An inspection of the production data given in the relevant tables will tell the story.[57] The decline in per-capita consumption of these foodstuffs must have started in 1953 or 1954. The curtailment of farm subsidiary work beginning in 1956 has greatly reduced the supply of green vegetables, bean curds, and eggs.[58] It is certain that per-capita consumption of "other foodstuffs" has decreased in absolute terms.

The annual output of cotton cloth is far from being entirely used for civilian consumption; the needs of the armed forces, certain industries, government agencies, exports, and stockpiles must also be satisfied. According to the Ministry of Trade, the market supply of cloth for civilian use had been as follows: 114.8 million bolts in 1953, 112.2 million in 1954, 112.3 million in 1955, 149.5 million in 1956, and about 110 million in 1957.[59] Keeping the rate of population increase in mind, we can readily see that per-capita consumption of cloth had steadily declined throughout the period, with the exception only of 1956 when commercialization required a larger supply to the rural areas than before. Short as the supply of cloth had been, the cotton-growing area was reduced from 6.2 million hectares in 1956 to 5.8 million in 1957 in favor of foodgrain production. As a result, the per-capita ration of cloth for

[55] As has been said, the leveling process might have resulted in reducing per-capita consumption of superior food grains (rice or wheat) for the population as a whole.

[56] Chin Ch'ao, "Proper Rectification of the Contradiction between the Supply and Demand of Food Grains," *Hsueh-hsi (Study)*, 19: 16–17, October, 1957. Another important use not explicitly mentioned in the quotation is exports.

[57] See Tables VIII and XII. It should also be remembered that salt has been increasingly used for industrial purposes and that both salt and pork are on the regular export list.

[58] See chapter i, section 5.

[59] Ministry of Trade, "Report on the Problem of Cotton Cloth Supply in 1957," *Hsin-hua pan-yueh-k'an*, 10: 112–113, May, 1957; and "Report on the Supply of Cotton Cloth for Civilian Use during the Fourth Year of 'Planned Supply,'" *Jen-min jih-pao*, August 20, 1957. For definition of a bolt, see note to Table VIII.

1957–58 was less than six meters as compared to nearly seven meters in the previous year.[60]

The discussion of capital formation in chapter v shows that not only was there no net private investment in residential construction during the five-year period, but a general disinvestment in private housing had probably taken place in the urban areas. The situation was aggravated by the rapid growth of urban population. Between 1949 and 1956, per-capita housing space had declined from 6.6 square meters to 5.1 in Peiping, from 4.06 to 3.06 in Wuhan, and from 5.7 to 2.97 in Shanghai.[61] For 1957, the average housing space per capita in 175 cities was 3.5 square meters, varying from 4.9 in small cities to 3.2 in big cities.[62]

This brief review establishes the fact that during the five-year period under study per-capita consumption of food, cloth, and housing services had declined in absolute terms, with the exception of staple food grains, the total consumption of which probably had increased a little for the country as a whole, owing primarily to the growing need for energy food by those not used to work on the farm and to the leveling process of collectivization. The shortage was real, and was intensified by the increase in aggregate monetary demand. Thus black-market activities became rampant. And clandestine factories came into existence "in many parts of the country, ranging from Chungking to Shenyang (Mukden," operated by staff workers of state-operated and joint enterprises, who took advantage of their position to obtain raw materials for the lucrative production of consumer goods.[63]

This finding throws a different light on the situation prevailing in the last two years of the five-year period already referred to in the earlier discussion of internal financing. In 1956 when basic construction investment was raised more than 60 per cent from 8,600 million yuan in 1955 to 14,000 million, the government increased the note issue by 1,690 million—that is, by about 15 per cent in currency in circulation. As a result, the total monetary purchasing power of the public increased nearly 16 per cent within

[60] Ministry of Trade, "Report on the Supply . . ." A campaign was started in August, 1957, to urge women to return to wearing the traditional long gowns instead of the Communist party uniforms, on the ground that the change would save half as much cloth. See editorial, *Jen-min jih-pao*, August 20, 1957.

[61] Sun Kuang, "The Pressing Need to Control Urban Population Growth," *Jen-min jih-pao*, November 27, 1957.

[62] Ts'ao Yen-hsing, as cited in n. 34.

[63] See news dispatch on "self-developed factories" in *Ta Kung Pao (Impartial Daily)*, September 5, 1957, p. 1. For black-market activities, see chapter i, section 4 above.

one year to 46,500 million yuan, against which only 38,500 million yuan's worth of consumption goods was available. Tight rationing of strategic consumer goods and a reduction of government commodity reserves by 2,000 million yuan neither helped ease the lining up of the public in front of the state-operated stores nor prevented the widespread activities of black markets and clandestine factories. The state was soon compelled to raise retail prices, to increase the import of consumption goods, and to reopen "free" markets to the peasants in order to encourage them to increase production for the public on their retained lots. Significantly the planned budget for 1957 called for an investment 20 per cent less than in 1956, despite the fact that the national product had made the biggest gain in 1956.

What this development signifies is clear. Behind the money veil we find that the state had attempted to reduce further the level of consumption in favor of net investment and, despite its political and organizational apparatus, had to retreat. In view of the absolute decline in per-capita consumption during the five-year period, it is doubtful if the state will again try in the future to raise net investment by such a large margin in any one year. It is even more doubtful that consumption will be allowed to improve appreciably, given the objectives of "socialist industrialization" and the rate of population growth.

Indeed, the public has been prepared for this eventuality. An editorial in the Chinese Communist party paper calls for less discussion of improving the level of consumption and more explanation of the necessary hardships entailed in the process of economic development.[64] Following this instruction, another newspaper of national circulation editorializes, "The shortage of supply of commodities has been developing from year to year, becoming especially severe in 1956. Inconvenience is being felt by the public in every phase of their daily life. This is going to be the basic situation for many years to come—and not a temporary accidental phenomenon."[65]

3. CONCLUSION

The prospect for further growth of the Chinese economy has to

---

[64] "People's Livelihood Can Only Be Improved Gradually," *Jen-min jih-pao*, November 27, 1956.

[65] "The Proper Understanding of the Present Problems and Difficulties of People's Livelihood," *Ta Kung Pao (Impartial Daily)*, December 14, 1956. The editorial goes on to indicate that the commodities in shortest supply are food grains and edible oil, followed by cotton cloth and other daily necessaries.

be appraised in terms of the basic industrialization objective of the Peiping regime, which is to build up within about fifteen years a complete heavy-industry complex capable of producing virtually all machinery and equipment needed by industry and national defense. The examination of other possible objectives falls beyond the purview of this study.

Given the basic objective, the prospect depends on the state's ability to keep the people reasonably satisfied with a low level of consumption. The system of collective welfare services may be interpreted as an important measure designed for this purpose. But during the First Five Year Plan, private consumption per capita had been declining (except for staple food grains). This was caused, not by the lack of a substantial increase in national product, but by the shortage of consumer goods and certain services. In 1956 the state overstepped the limit of the consumers' tolerance by raising the rate of capital formation unduly, with serious consequences to the economy, which forced the authorities to beat a retreat in the following year. Thus in the future the rate of investment will not likely be appreciably raised unless the decline in per-capita consumption can be arrested and, if possible, reversed to some extent.

Critical Role of Population Control.—The increase in demand for consumer goods has three sources. Commercialization and urbanization requires an increased market supply to make up for the loss of handicraft products formerly produced at home. This demand will grow as the drive for a high degree of commercialization proceeds. However, when the demand is fully met, per-capita consumption will be restored only to its former level.

The second source is exports, which constitute a form of capital formation. About 7 per cent of the annual output of consumer goods had been exported from 1953 through 1956.[66] The need for exports has become increasingly pressing. Soviet economic credits, accounting for 7 per cent of imports during the five-year period, have been exhausted, and amortization payments are mounting. It is not likely that any further Soviet loans would give Peiping a *net* amount comparable to the proceeds of the first five years. Although the export policy is to develop the sale of machinery and equipment, the vigorous drive for markets, especially in the

[66] Liao Chi-lih, "Accelerating Agricultural Development—a Condition for Accelerating the Development of Heavy Industry," *Chi-hua ching-chi (Planned Economy)*, 8: 4–6, August, 1957.

African-Asian area, implies that large quantities of consumer goods will be exported if necessary.

The third source of demand is population growth, estimated to be at the rate of 2.4 per cent per annum. That means an additional 14 million people have to be fed, clad, and housed every year. The rate of increase seems to have been rising. It is not merely a question of increasing *pari passu* the supply of consumer goods and services, but resource allocation of the whole economy has to be adjusted to the demands of a young population.[67] If the rate of natural increase can be stabilized and reduced by lowering the fertility rate, the problem of per-capita consumption, and therefore of capital formation for development of heavy industry will be less difficult to manage. Thus on the demand side for consumer goods and services, population control becomes the crucial factor in determining the future speed of industrialization.

It is not surprising, therefore, that the Peiping authorities should have put into effect a policy of population control as early as August, 1953, spreading information on the methods of birth control and legalizing abortion and surgical contraception. Realizing that this policy is at variance with the orthodox Marxian views and is too much like neo-Malthusianism, some Chinese scholars have been induced to expound what they call a "new theory of population." Appropriately, the theory explains and justifies the need for reducing the birth rate on the ground that population growth cuts down, through increasing total consumption, the maximum possible amount of capital formation needed for raising labor productivity and therefore the level of living of the people.[68] It will be observed that the incompatibility of maximum capital formation and improving the living conditions of the people is conveniently overlooked. The theory, however, has been later criticized by other Chinese writers on the ground that it is against the "basic economic law of socialism" which requires a growing labor force as well as improved labor productivity to increase total product; but the critics are also in strong favor of population control as necessary to promote the health and welfare of the people.[69]

---

[67] For details see United Nations, *The Determinants and Consequences . . .*, Part 3.

[68] The theory was apparently first worked out by Wu Ching-ch'ao, "A New Approach to the Chinese Population Problem," *Hsin chien-she (New Construction)*, 102: 1–9, March, 1957. He was followed by Ma Yin-ch'u, "A New Theory of Population," *Hsin-hua pan-yueh-k'an*, 15: 34–41, August, 1957.

[69] See Chang P'ei-kang, *et al.*, "The Socialist Law of Population and the Chinese Population Problem," *Ching-chi yen-chiu (Economic Research)*, 4: 30–63, August, 1957.

Theory merely serves to justify state policy which has been pushed with increasing vigor. It is significant that in the revised draft of the agricultural development plan from 1956 to 1967, one of the new items introduced is the call for birth control and family planning in villages (except minority areas).[70] We can be reasonably sure that during the Second Five Year Plan, population control will become a major effort of the state. Some Chinese planners are already confident that the natural rate of increase will be lower in the second five-year period than in the first.[71]

Critical Role of Agriculture.—Population control is at best a slow process. An immediate solution for arresting the decline of per-capita consumption and sustaining a high rate of capital formation must be found on the supply side. Here agriculture predominates: From 1953 through 1956, the total supply of consumer goods consisted of 65 per cent in food, 13 per cent in clothing, and 22 per cent in articles for daily use; and agriculture directly or indirectly accounted for 85 per cent of it.[72] The rural sector provides 90 per cent of the raw materials for consumer-goods industries and at the same time buys 70 per cent of their output. Moreover, three-quarters of exports are either farming products or finished manufactures made of agricultural raw materials.[73]

The importance of agriculture does not simply lie in the supply of consumer goods and exports. Its influence is so pervasive that the whole economy fluctuates with it. In the earlier discussion of net investment, it was pointed out that there had been a one-year lag between a good harvest and a substantial increase in the rate of capital formation. In fact, the correlation between agriculture and all other economic activities has been much closer than that observation suggests. As shown in Table XLVIII, the whole economy—as represented by the output of consumer and producer goods, retail trade, state budgetary revenue, net investment, foreign trade, and net national product—fluctuates cyclically. It stands on a peak one year after a good harvest, and then takes a downturn until one year after the next good (or normal) harvest when it abruptly climbs to a new peak.

---

[70] *Jen-min jih-pao*, October 26, 1957.

[71] Wang Nai-kuang and Shan Tung, "The Method of Estimating Population Increase in Long-term Planning," *Chi-hua ching-chi (Planned Economy)*, 5: 22–23, May, 1957.

[72] Liao Chi-lih, *op. cit.*

[73] See Deputy Premier Teng Tzu-hui's report in *Jen-min jih-pao*, February 22, 1957, and Minister of Agriculture Liao Lu-yen's report in the same newspaper, February 19, 1957.

No exception to this conclusion is shown in the table except in foreign trade, which gained 30 per cent in 1955 instead of in 1956. That must be due to the start of the collectivization drive immediately after the autumn harvest in 1955, enabling the state commercial apparatus to overfulfill its "planned purchase" plan, and therefore its export and import plan ahead of schedule. The

TABLE XLVIII

Effect of Agricultural Year on the National Economy, 1952–1957

(In percentage change over preceding year)

Item	1952	1953	1954	1955	1956	1957 est.
1. Agricultural year (XI)...	Good	Normal	Poor	Good	Poor	Poor
2. Factory industry:						
a. Consumer goods (VII).	——	28	15	1	22	−1
b. Producer goods (VII) .	——	37	20	17	42	7
3. Institutionalized retail trade volume (Stat. App. 13).....................	——	33	13	2	19	..
4. Budget revenue (XXXIV)	——	25	19	1	16	2
5. Basic construction investment (XXVII)......	——	67	16	13	62	−21
6. Total net investment (XXXII)..............	——	64	7	7	63	−22
7. Net national product (XXV).................	——	10	8	8	14	4
8. Total foreign trade (XLII).................	——	25	5	30	−1	−8

Note: Source tables are given in parentheses. Factory production, basic construction investment, net investment, and net national product are all at 1952 prices. Budget revenue is given at current prices except for the last two years, the revenue of which is at 1955 prices. Foreign trade is valued at current prices.

fact that foreign trade did behave very much like the other items in 1953 lends support to the explanation. Moreover, the 8 per cent decline in 1957 was "a result of poor harvest in 1956."[74]

Such tremendous influence of the agricultural year upon the economy must be exercised through fluctuations in agricultural output. Yet, as we have seen in chapter iii, the official data on the gross agricultural value product show a yearly increase of 3 per cent each in 1953 and 1954, an 8 per cent increase in 1955, and a 5 per cent increase each in the two following years. If that were true, the behavior of the economy in 1957, for example, would have been much better than it actually was. Thus further support is found for the observation that agricultural growth had been

[74] Ma Yin-ch'u, *op. cit.,* p. 38.

greatly overstated by dint of statistical and "psychological" factors. It has also been found that the growth rate of net national product had been exaggerated by the nature of agricultural as well as industrial data. This accounts for the showing in Table XLVIII that the net national product had not fluctuated as strikingly as the other items.

The lesson should have been brought home to the Peiping authorities that the short-run solution of the "contradiction" between a high rate of capital formation and the level of per-capita consumption must be found in agricultural development. However, it was not fully appreciated until the experience in 1956 established its basic importance. For a much greater amount of investment in agriculture was needed than the planning authorities were willing to allocate. Thus in the Second Five Year Plan proposed by the Chinese Communist party in September, 1956, investment in agriculture, forestry, and water conservation was to be about 10 per cent of the total basic construction investment— a percentage not much more than the actual share during the first five years. Moreover, the draft plan for agricultural development from 1956 through 1967, proposed by Mao Tse-tung in January, 1956, required that during the twelve-year period more than 90 per cent of the fertilizers needed for increasing agricultural output to the planned quota be supplied locally. The production target for chemical fertilizers was only between 3 and 3.2 million tons for the end of 1962.

But the thinking took a significant turn in the latter half of 1957. It is succinctly summarized in the title of an editorial appearing in the official publication of the State Economic and Planning Commissions, namely, "Industrial Development Requires Simultaneous Development of Agriculture."[75] The revised plan of agricultural development up to 1967, published in October, 1957, calls for an output of about six million tons of chemical fertilizers by 1962 and 15 million tons by 1967. We may anticipate that the state investment program in the proposed Second Five Year Plan will be amended in the direction of a more substantial increase of funds for agricultural development. The increase of investment in agriculture will be facilitated by the fact that the annual reserves required of each collective to set aside for net expansion, amounting to about 4 or 5 per cent of its gross product at the present, will be amenable to direct state planning.

---

[75] *Chi-hua ching-chi (Planned Economy)*, 10: 1–2, October, 1957.

It must be remembered that such a modification of the invest‑ ment program in favor of agriculture is for the sake of promoting the development of heavy industry and will not represent any change in basic objectives. As the chairman of the State Economic Commission has stated, "from now on, *since* our production of consumer goods is slow to increase, thus restricting the rise in the people's consumption, the bulk of the annual increase in national income and budgetary revenue can be used only for accumulation."[70] It is therefore quite clear that the present invest‑ ment policy which has been responsible for the slow growth in the output of consumer goods will not be altered significantly. As long as the decline in per-capita consumption can be checked and main‑ tained at a level tolerable to the people, the entire net increase in agricultural output will be devoted to the capital formation proc‑ ess. The speed of industrialization in the future will depend, from the economic standpoint, on the availability of export markets, the rate of population growth, the level of domestic consumption, and above all, the increase of agricultural output.

---

[70] Po I-po, "Problems of Setting the Planned Production Quotas for 1958," *Hsin-hua pan-yueh-k'an*, 17: 206–208, September, 1957; quotation on p. 208. Italics mine.

Statistical Appendix

Introduction

This statistical appendix is compiled for several purposes: First, not to overburden the text with tables which cannot be properly presented without the sources of information and explanatory notes when necessary. The sources are so scattered and the explanations sometimes so lengthy that it is best to relegate them to this appendix. The text makes direct references to these tables. Second, in order to show the rate of growth in discussion, it is clearer to present the indices than the absolute data. Yet, the indices do not mean much if the absolutes are not given. This appendix makes it possible to omit from the text the real data whenever that is convenient. Apart from a few unavoidable exceptions no indices are used in the text when the absolutes are not known and presented. On the other hand, no relative data are given in this appendix. The third purpose is to make the materials available to those interested in following up the development in Communist China, since they are not easily accessible. Even for those who read Chinese, this collection may prove useful, as the search for data, the test of their consistency, and the checking on their meaning are time-consuming.

Despite the remarks in the text concerning the data for the three years before 1952, they are given in this appendix if they satisfy the rule followed in the preparation of this appendix—and, for that matter, in the use of Peiping data generally: no data are accepted for *any* date that were published before the appearance of the First Five Year Plan (July, 1955) unless they have been tested for consistency with those released since. Moreover, in regard to the data published after that date, if two different figures are available for the same item, the one more recently published is always preferred unless there is a compelling reason to reject it. The data given as "estimated for 1957" were all released in the latter half of the year, those published earlier being generally considered as not comparable with the later estimates and therefore not usable. Needless to say, strict adherence to the rule means only the use of the most recently revised data and certainly does not insure their accuracy.

It is worth repeating that with the establishment of the State Statistical Bureau late in 1952 the semblance of a national statistical system started to operate only in 1954 and that the quality, coverage, and quantity of statistical data have since been improving, thus rendering the data for the early years less and less comparable. Although some effort has been made by the bureau to bring the early data in line, it is questionable if this can be done satisfactorily. The data for 1949–1951 are presented here entirely as a matter of general interest.

The 1957 and 1962 targets (the latter, if not found in the text) are given, but the dates indicated in the title of a table end with the year in which the actual or "estimated" data are available. In official statistics Peiping uses both the Chinese "market" and the metric systems of weights and measures; for uniformity the latter is adopted for this study. The following signs are used:

> .... not available
> – – – negligible
> —— not applicable
> [   ] my estimate

TABLE 1
GROSS AGRICULTURAL AND INDUSTRIAL PRODUCT AT 1952 PRICES, 1949–1957
(In millions of yuan)

Year	Agricultural product	Industrial product	Total
1949	32,595	14,018	46,613
1950	37,230	19,110	56,340
1951	......	26,350	......
1952	48,392	34,326	82,718
1953	49,915	44,696	94,611
1954	51,566	52,099	103,665
1955	55,544	54,876	110,420
1956	58,290	70,360	128,650
1957 estimated	61,150	72,040	133,190
1957 target	59,660	65,330	124,990
1962 target	81,000	131,000	212,000

Note: For discussion of grossness, see text.
Sources:
1) For 1949, 1952, and 1953. State Statistical Bureau, "Economic Statistical Abstract," *Hsin-hua pan-yueh-k'an,* 17:39–50, September, 1956.
2) For 1950, 1951, 1954, and 1955: (a) "A General Survey of Socialist Industrialization in China," *ibid.,* 2:54–62, January, 1957. (b) Chao I-wen, "The Process for Socialist Transformation of China's Capitalistic Industry," *ibid..* 2:62–66, January, 1957. (c) Nan Ping, "Breaking the Two Poisoned Darts of Rightists," *Hsueh-hsi (Study),* 19:18–19, October, 1957.
3) For 1956 and 1957 (estimated); (a) State Statistical Bureau, "Communiqué on the Results of the 1956 Plan," *Jen-min jih-pao,* August 2, 1957. (b) Po I-po, "Report on the Results of the 1956 Plan and on the Plan for 1957," *Jen-min jih-pao,* July 2, 1957.
4) For targets, the *First Five Year Plan,* and the Chinese Communist Party's proposal of the Second Five Year Plan, *Jen-min jih-pao,* September 29, 1956.

TABLE 2

INDUSTRIAL PRODUCTION AT 1952 PRICES BY SECTORS, 1949–1957

(In millions of yuan)

Sector	1949	1950	1951	1952	1953
1. Gross industrial product	14,018	19,110	26,350	34,326	44,696
2. Factory product	10,781	14,050	20,210	27,014	35,577
a. Modern factory	7,913	......	......	22,049	28,809
b. Handicraft factory	2,868	......	......	4,965	6,768
3. Handicraft product	3,237	5,060	6,140	7,312	9,119
a. Individual operators	3,222	5,020	6,006	7,066	8,633
b. Coöperatives	15	40	134	246	486
	1954	1955	1956	1957 est.	1957 target
1. Gross industrial product	52,099	54,876	70,360	72,040	65,330
2. Factory product	41,533	44,748	58,660	60,340	53,560
a. Modern factory	33,986	37,082	......	51,944	44,900
b. Handicraft factory	7,547	7,666	......	8,396	8,660
3. Handicraft product	10,566	10,128	11,700	11,700	11,770
a. Individual operators	9,606	8,822	......	......	7,220
b. Coöperatives	960	1,306	......	......	4,550

Sources for Tables 2, 3, 4, 5, and 6: (1) Kuan Ta-t'ung, "Changes in Class Relationships during the Transitional Period in China," *Hsin-hua pan-yueh-k'an,* 2:119–122, January, 1957. (2) "A General Survey of Socialist Industrialization in China," *ibid.,* 2:54–62, January, 1957. (3) "A Survey of the Development of State Capitalism in Industry in China," *ibid.,* 2:66–70, January, 1957. (4) Chao I-wen, "The Process of Socialist Transformation of China's Capitalistic Industry," *ibid.,* 2:62–66, January, 1957. (5) "Several Problems of China's Socialist Industrialization," *ibid.,* 1:67–71, January, 1957. (6) State Statistical Bureau "Economic Statistical Abstract," *ibid.,* 17:39–50, September, 1956. (7) State Statistical Bureau, "Communiqué on the Results of the 1954 Plan," *Jen-min jih-pao,* September 23, 1955. (8) State Statistical Bureau, "Communiqué on the Results of the 1955 Plan," *ibid.,* June 14, 1956. (9) State Statistical Bureau, "Communiqué on the Results of the 1956 Plan," *ibid.,* August 2, 1957. (10) Po I-po, "Report on the Results of the 1956 Plan, and on the Plan for 1957," *ibid.,* July 2, 1957. (11) the *First Five Year Plan.* (12) Chinese Communist Party's Proposal of the Second Five Year Plan, *Jen-min jih-pao,* September 29, 1956. (13) Chang Hsing-fu, "The Road and Method China's Industrialization," *Kung-jen jih-pao (Workers' Daily),* May 23, 1957.

TABLE 3

Industrial Production at 1952 Prices: Producer and Consumer Goods, 1949–1957
(In millions of yuan)

Category	1949	1950	1951	1952	1953	1954	1955	1956	1957 est.	1957 target	1962 target
1. Gross industrial product	14,018	19,110	26,350	34,326	44,696	52,099	54,876	70,360	72,040	65,330	131,000
a. Producer goods	3,729	......	......	12,220	......	......	23,322	......	......	24,825	65,000
b. Consumer goods	10,289	......	......	22,106	......	......	31,554	......	......	40,505	65,000
2. Factory product	10,781	14,050	20,210	27,014	35,577	41,533	44,748	58,660	60,340	53,560	......
a. Producer goods	3,100	......	......	10,730	14,670	17,598	20,578	29,170	31,130	24,315	......
1) Machine-making	188	......	......	1,401	2,157	2,643	3,030	5,760	5,490	3,460	......
b. Consumer goods	7,681	......	......	16,284	20,907	23,935	24,170	29,490	29,210	29,245	......
3. Individual handicrafts and coöp.	3,237	5,060	6,140	7,312	9,119	10,566	10,128	11,700	11,700	11,770	......
a. Producer goods	629	......	......	1,490	......	......	2,744	......	......	510	......
b. Consumer goods	2,608	......	......	5,822	......	......	7,384	......	......	11,260	......

Note: For definition of factory production, see Table 2.
Sources: See Table 2.

TABLE 4

Socialization of Industry, by Sectoral Value Product at 1952 Prices, 1949–1957

(In millions of yuan)

Category	1949	1950	1951	1952	1953	1954	1955	1956	1957 est.	1957 target
I. Gross industrial product.	14,018	19,110	26,350	34,326	44,696	52,099	54,876	70,360	72,040	65,330
1. State-operated.	3,683	6,238	9,083	14,258	19,239	24,488	28,142	38,346	......	32,820
2. Joint.	220	414	806	1,367	2,013	5,110	7,188	19,068	......	11,830
3. Coöperatives.	65	152	336	1,109	1,702	2,558	3,458	12,031	......	6,910
a. Factory.	50	112	202	863	1,216	1,598	2,152	......	......	2,360
b. Handicraft.	15	40	134	246	486	960	1,306	......	......	4,550
4. Private.	6,828	7,286	10,119	10,526	13,109	10,337	7,266	} 915	......	6,550
5. Individual handicrafts.	3,222	5,020	6,006	7,066	8,633	9,606	8,822	}	......	7,220
II. Factory product.	10,781	14,050	20,210	27,014	35,577	41,533	44,748	58,660	60,340	53,560
1. State-operated.	3,683	6,238	9,083	14,258	19,239	24,488	28,142	38,346	......	32,820
2. Joint.	220	414	806	1,367	2,013	5,110	7,188	19,068	......	11,830
3. Coöperative.	50	112	202	863	1,216	1,598	2,152	......	......	2,360
4. Private.	6,828	7,286	10,119	10,526	13,109	10,337	7,266	......	......	6,550

Sources: See Table 2.

TABLE 5

Operation of Private Factory Industry by Value of Production at 1952 Prices, 1949–1955

Item	1949	1950	1951	1952	1953	1954	1955
	(In millions of yuan)						
1. Gross value product.............	6,828	7,286	10,119	10,526	13,109	10,337	7,266
2. Output for state under contract...........	811	2,098	4,321	5,898	8,107	8,121	5,935
3. Output for market............	6,017	5,188	5,798	4,628	5,002	2,216	1,331
	(In per cent)						
4. Share of gross output:							
a. For state...........	11.9	28.8	42.7	56.0	61.8	78.5	81.7
b. For market...........	88.1	71.2	57.3	44.0	38.2	21.5	18.3

Note: In 1956 private factory industry virtually disappeared.
Sources: See Table 2.

TABLE 6

STRUCTURE OF INDUSTRY BY NUMBER AND SIZE OF ESTABLISHMENTS, 1949–1955

Establishment	1949	1950	1951	1952	1953	1954	1955
Grand Total	...	...	...	167,403	176,405	167,626	125,474
a. Large	...	...	...	27,527	31,379	31,187	......
b. Small	...	...	...	139,876	145,026	136,439	......
1. State-operated	2,720	...	...	10,671	12,295	13,666	15,190
a. Central and local government:							
1) Central	...	...	...	2,409	2,722	3,392	4,077
2) Local	...	...	...	8,262	9,573	10,274	11,113
b. By size:							
1) Large	...	...:	...	8,609	9,351	10,273	......
a) Central	...	...	...	2,035	2,338	2,658	......
b) Local	...	...	...	6,574	7,013	7,615	......
2) Small	...	...	...	2,062	2,944	3,393	......
a) Central	...	...	...	374	384	734	......
b) Local	...	...	...	1,688	2,560	2,659	......
2. Coöperative-operated	...	...	...	6,164	12,799	17,938	18,282
a. Large	...	...	...	1,025	1,988	2,173	......
b. Small	...	...	...	5,139	10,811	15,765	......
3. State-private joint	193	294	706	997	1,036	1,744	3,193
a. Large	...	...	...	820	878	1,603	......
1) Central-private	...	...	...	88	101	129	......
2) Local-private	...	...	...	732	777	1,474	......
b. Small	...	...	...	177	158	141	......
1) Central-private	...	...	...	0	0	1	......
2) Local-private	...	...	...	177	158	140	......
4. Private	123,165	133,018	...	149,571	150,275	134,278	88,809
a. Large	...	...	...	17,073	19,162	17,138	......
b. Small	...	...	...	132,498	131,113	117,140	......

Note: (a) In 1956 about 70,000 private establishments became state-private joint enterprises. They had accounted for 99.6 per cent of the value of production and 99 per cent of the labor force in the private industry in 1955. See State Statistical Bureau, "Communiqué on the Results of the 1956 Plan," *Jen-min jih-pao*, August 2, 1957. (b) The distinction between central government-operated and local government-operated enterprises lies in the immediate source of investment funds and in the agency responsible for the operation. (c) Large and small establishments are distinguished by either one of these criteria: By motive-power—all independent electric power plants with a capacity of over 15 kw. are regarded as of large size, regardless of the number of workers employed; by motive power and number of staff and workers—any establishment with mechanical power and a work force of over 15 men, or any establishment with no mechanical power but a work force of over 30 men, is considered large; otherwise it is small. See Yu Chien-t'ing, "The Question of the Rate of Industrial Growth under the First Five Year Plan," *Jen-min jih-pao*, August 17, 1955.
Source: See Table 2.

TABLE 7
STRUCTURE OF INDUSTRY BY EMPLOYMENT, 1949–1955
(In thousands)

Employment at end of year	1949	1950	1951	1952	1953	1954	1955
1. State and coöperative-operated factories	1,390	.....	2,480	2,960	3,620	3,960	3,895
2. State-private factories[a]	105.4	130.9	166.3	247.8	270.1	533.3	784.9
3. Private factories	1,643.8	1,815.9	.....	1,980	2,140	1,800	1,330
Total factory employment[b]	3,140	.....	.....	5,190	6,030	6,290	6,010
4. Handicraft coöperatives	.....	.....	.....	90	.....	.....	1,000
5. Individual handicrafts	5,840	.....	.....	6,870	.....	.....	7,260
Total industrial employment	8,980	.....	.....	12,150	.....	.....	14,270

[a] Figures with decimals are actually given data.
[b] Rounded to the nearest ten.

Note: (a) Employment at the end of the year has consistently been larger than the average employment of the year, the latter being the aggregate of the employment each work day throughout the year divided by 365 days. The drive for meeting or exceeding the production quota toward the end of the year as well as the number of Sundays and holidays accounts largely for the difference. (b) According to the State Economic Commission, the estimated average employment in the factory industry in 1956 was 6,467,880 and, the average employment of state-operated and joint factories (net of the employment in their subsidiary enterprises) and the year-end employment of coöperative-operated and private factories totaled 5,052,800 in

1953. Ma Yin-ch'u, "A New Theory of Population," *Hsin-hua pan-yueh-k'an*, 15: 34–41, August, 1957.

Sources: This table is computed from data found in: (1) "A General Survey of Socialist Industrialisation in China," *Hsin-hua pan-yueh-k'an*, 2:54–62, January, 1957; (2) "A Survey of Development of State Capitalism in China's Industry," *ibid.,* 2:66–70, January, 1957; (3) State Statistical Bureau, "Communiqué on the Results of the 1954 Plan," *Jen-min jih-pao*, September 23, 1955; (4) Chao-I-wen, "The Process of Socialist Transformation of China's Capitalist Industry," *Hsin-hua pan-yueh-k'an*, 2:62–66, January, 1957; (5) Wu Tsiang, "The Transition from Capitalist Economy to State-Capitalist Economy," *Ching-chi yen-chiu (Economic Research)*, 2:54–99, April, 1956.

TABLE 8

DISTRIBUTION OF FACTORY INDUSTRY BETWEEN INLAND AND
COASTAL AREAS, BY VALUE OF PRODUCTION 1949–1956
(In billions of yuan)

Location	1949	1952	1953	1954	1955	1956
1. Inland.................	2.4	7.3	9.9	12.5	14.3	18.83
2. Coastal................	8.4	19.7	25.7	29.1	30.5	39.83
Shanghai...............	*3.6*	*6.6*	*8.8*	*9.5*	*9.1*	.....
Tientsin...............	*0.7*	*1.8*	*2.5*	*2.8*	*2.9*	.....
Peiping................	*0.2*	*0.8*	*1.1*	*1.2*	*1.4*	.....
Seven provinces[a].......	*3.9*	*10.5*	*13.3*	*15.6*	*17.1*	.....
Total factory product....	10.8	27.0	35.6	41.5[b]	44.8	58.66

[a] The seven coastal provinces are Liaoning, Hopei, Shantung, Kiangsu, Chekiang, Fukien, and Kwangtung.
[b] The figures for 1954 do not add up exactly to the total factory product because of an apparent inaccuracy in the index numbers for that year.
Sources: This table is computed from relative weights and index numbers given in: (1) "Several Problems of China's Socialist Industrialization," *Hsin-hua pan-yueh-k'an,* 1:67–71, January, 1957. (2) Yang Ch'ing-wen, "Two Problems of Industrial Location," *Chi-hua ching-chi (Planned Economy);* 8:13–15, August, 1957.

TABLE 9

MECHANIZATION OF INDUSTRIAL PRODUCTION:
FIXED CAPITAL ASSETS PER WORKER IN STATE-OPERATED AND STATE-PRIVATE
JOINTLY-OPERATED ESTABLISHMENTS OF VARIOUS INDUSTRIES, 1952–1955
(In yuan, except II)

Classification	1952	1953	1954	1955
I. Over-all average per worker.......	5,656	5,273	6,072	6,835
1. Electric power................	......	51,197	58,828	58,196
2. Mining of fuels................	......	5,021	5,574	6,020
a. Coal mining................	5,029	......	......	5,417
b. Crude oil...................	24,945	......	......	27,785
3. Iron and manganese mining....	......	1,887	4,407	4,057
4. Mining of chemicals............	......	828	939	949
5. Other nonmetallic mining......	......	952	1,128	3,599
6. Lumber: logging...............	......	497	1,443	2,931
7. Processing of fuels.............	......	18,307	18,643	16,248
8. Iron and Steel................	9,251	19,151	12,385	14,411
9. Mining and smelting of non-ferrous metals..............	3,192	3,362	5,684	6,480
10. Metal fabrication..............	4,750	5,029	5,528	6,035
11. Chemical.....................	8,120	9,066	9,867	11,114
12. Construction materials.........	2,431	2,291	2,531	3,641
13. Glass........................	......	4,273	3,431	3,502
14. Ceramics.....................	......	2,456	1,925	1,482
15. Rubber goods.................	4,725	4,714	4,372	10,688
16. Lumber manufacturing.........	......	1,210	1,480	1,945
17. Matches......................	......	466	440	449
18. Paper........................	9,528	8,923	9,856	10,307
19. Textiles......................	4,806	4,943	5,125	5,107
20. Tailoring.....................	......	943	1,124	1,292
21. Leather and furs..............	......	1,750	2,080	2,471
22. Oils and fats, soap, spices, and cosmetics...................	......	6,000	6,090	6,107
23. Food.........................	......	3,373	3,312	3,566
24. Salt.........................	......	3,653	3,431	3,307
25. Printing......................	......	3,072	3,240	3,256
26. Educational supplies...........	......	1,558	1,755	6,292
27. Water supply.................	......	49,129	54,743	59,557
28. Other industries..............	......	4,530	7,087	8,973
II. Mechanical power per worker (in kw.).....................	2.1	2.2	2.4	3.0

Sources: (1) For 1952, "The Technological Level of Industrial Production in China," *T'ung-chi kung-tso t'ung-hsin,* No. 8, April, 1957, reprinted in *Hsin-hua pan-yueh-k'an,* 12:115–118, June, 1957. (2) For 1953 through 1955, Ma Yin-ch'u, "A New Theory of Population," *Hsin-hua pan-yueh-k'an,* 15: 34–41, August 1957. The data were prepared for him by the State Economic Commission. The first source also gives some figures for 1955 which are the same as those given by Ma, except for thᵉ iron and steel industry, for which the figure given is 13,302.

TABLE 10

DEVELOPMENT OF RAILWAY, HIGHWAY, AIR TRANSPORTATION, AND POST AND TELECOMMUNICATIONS, 1950-1957

Item	1950	1951	1952	1953	1954	1955	1956	1957 est.	1957 target
1. Railway lines (thousand km.)	22.2	23.1	24.2	24.7	25.4	26.9	29.1	30.0	.....
a. New construction (km.):									
1) Annual	.....	771	480	589	831	1,222	1,747	535	4,084
2) Cumulative from 1953				589	1,420	2,642	4,389	4,924	
b. Freight:									
1) In million tons	.....	.....	132.1	160.4	192.6	193.4	246.1	256	245.5
2) In billion ton-km.	.....	.....	60.2	78.1	93.2	98.1	120.4	126.5	121.0
2. Highways (thousand km.)	104.1	111.6	129.6	138.6	142.4	162.5	227.0	228.1	.....
Freight by motor vehicles:									
1) In million tons	7.4	.....	20.7	30.4	43.5	50.1	79.1	.....	67.5
2) In billion ton-km.	.....	.....	0.7	1.2	1.9	2.5	3.5	.....	3.2
3. Civil aviation:									
a. Airlines (thousand km.)	0.8	.....	13.0	15.9	.....	15	19	.....	30.2
b. Freight (incl. mail):									
1) Thousand tons	.....	.....	2.0	3.6	4.7	4.7	.....	.....	5.6
2) Million ton-km.	.....	.....	2.4	4.5	5.6	5.1	.....	.....	8.1
4. Post and Telecommunications: Volume of business at 1952 prices (in million yuan)	149	.....	218	272	297	337	397	.....	.....

Note: (a) Railway lines refer to the operating trunk and branch lines. The double-tracked lines are included at one-half of their length. Special lines for industrial uses are not included. (b) Newly constructed railway trunk and branch lines do not include the rehabilitated lines, or the newly constructed double-tracked lines. The cumulative total from 1953 through 1956 (4,389 km.) is 2 km. more than the total given by Po I-po, Jen-min jih-pao, July 2, 1957.

Sources:
1) State Statistical Bureau: (a) Annual communiqués on the results of the previous year's plan, Jen-min jih-pao, September 28, 1954, September 16, 1954, September 23, 1955, June 15, 1956, and August 2, 1957. (b) "Statistical Abstract for 1949 to 1954," Hsin-hua yüeh-pao, 11:181-189, November, 1955. (c) "Economic Statistical Abstract," Hsin-hua pan-yüeh-k'an, 17:39-50, September, 1956.
2) Po I-po, "Report on the Results of the 1956 Plan," Jen-min jih-pao, July 2, 1957.
3) News dispatch, ibid., June 30, 1952.
4) 1957 Jen-min shou-ts'e (People's Handbook for 1957), 1957, p. 534.
5) State Planning Commission, "Results and Achievements of the First Five Year Plan," Jen-min jih-pao, October 1, 1957.

TABLE 11

DEVELOPMENT OF WATER TRANSPORTATION (STEAM BARGES AND SHIPS) 1950-1956

Classification	1950	1952	1953	1954	1955	1956
1. Coastal: freight						
a. In million tons........	...	5.8	5.9	9.9	10.5	10.9
b. In billion ton-km......	...	5.0	4.7	8.0	8.4	8.6
2. Inland river: freight						
a. In million tons........	4.5	9.4	15.3	20.5	26.3	35.4
1) Yangtze and Sungari	2.2	4.9	6.6	8.6	....	....
2) Other rivers.........	2.3	4.5	8.7	11.9	....	....
b. In billion ton-km......	1.7	3.6	5.6	7.9	10.4	12.9
1) Yangtze and Sungari	1.1	2.7	4.0	5.5	....	....
2) Other rivers.........	0.6	0.9	1.6	2.4	....	....

Note: (a) The 1956 figures were released by the State Statistical Bureau on August 1, 1957, with percentage increases over 1955. When so calculated, the 1955 figures are greatly different from those given above which were released by the Bureau in September 1956. Thus, this table *should not be used without further checking* with data to be released. (b) l.b. is originally given in terms of ton-nautical miles, and has been converted at the rate of 1.852 km. per international nautical mile. (c) Freight carried by junks is not included. According to Ch'i Hua, there are 2,920,000 tons of junks specialized in transport. See his "To Develop Transport According to the Needs of Agricultural Production," *Chi-hua ching-chi (Planned Economy)*, 10:17-20, October, 1957.

Sources: State Statistical Bureau: (1) "Economic Statistical Abstract," *Hsin-hua pan-yueh-k'an,* 17:45, September, 1957; (2) "Statistical Abstract," *Hsin-hua yueh-pao,* 11:135, November, 1955; (3) "Communiqué on the Results of the 1956 Plan," *Jen-min jih-pao,* August 2, 1957.

TABLE 12
Socialization of Transportation by Freight Carried, 1952–1956
(In million ton-km.)

Classification	1952	1953	1954	1955	1956
I. Coastal and inland-river steam barges and ships	8,642	10,286	15,936	18,823	21,500
1. State-operated	5,392	6,636	10,991	12,730	......
2. State-private	555	1,261	3,540	5,765	......
3. Private	2,695	2,389	1,405	328	......
II. Highway motor vehicles	678	1,182	1,867	2,517	3,500
1. State-operated: Local government	339	647	1,307	1,958	......
2. State-private	4	11	37	101	......
3. Transportation coöperatives	– –	– –	– –	6	......
4. Private	335	524	523	452	......
III. Total (I and II)	9,320	11,468	17,803	21,340	25,000
1. State- and joint-operated	6,290	8,555	15,875	20,554	19,500
2. Transportation coöperatives	– –	– –	– –	6	4,250
3. Private	3,030	2,913	1,928	780	1,250

Note: (a) On water traffic, see Table 11, notes. (b) The relative rise in the private share in 1956 was made possible by an over-all shortage of transportation facilities and severe congestion of railway traffic in particular. In 1957 the private carriers continued to be organized into transportation coöperatives. (c) Railways and air transportation have been state-owned and state-operated from the start. (d) Ninety-five per cent of the private junks had either become state-private joint enterprises or been organized into transportation coöperatives by the end of 1956. (e) There were 140,000 animal-pulled carts operating in urban areas and five million in rural areas in 1957. At the end of 1956, 77 per cent of the privately operated carts (number not revealed) was organized into transportation coöperatives.

Source: See Table 11.

TABLE 13

WHOLESALE AND RETAIL TRADE (SALES VOLUME), 1950–1956

(In millions of yuan)

Classification	1950	1951	1952	1953	1954	1955	1956	1957 target
I. Institutionalized wholesale volume	10,544	16,420	18,969	26,449	27,842	27,847	.....	.....
1. State-operated stores	2,448	.....	11,469	17,543	23,347	22,884	.....	.....
2. "Marketing" coöperatives	58	} 5,650	516	772	1,528	3,521	.....	.....
3. State-private, and coöperative shops	12	.....	102	119	134	226	.....	.....
4. Private shops	8,026	10,770	6,882	8,015	2,833	1,216	.....	.....
II. Institutionalized retail volume	12,083	17,750	21,027	27,981	31,586	32,321	38,500	.....
1. State-operated stores	1,172	.....	3,841	5,453	7,017	10,204	} 26,180	.....
2. "Marketing" coöperatives	810	} 4,490	4,999	8,368	14,444	11,548	.....	.....
3. State-private stores	} 12	.....	} 38	} 79	} 1,770	} 4,919	6,545	.....
4. Coöperative shops	.....	.....	.....	.....	.....	.....	4,620	.....
5. Private shops	10,089	13,260	12,149	14,081	8,355	5,650	1,155	.....
III. Institutionalized and non-institutionalized retail volume	16,794	.....	27,665	35,041	38,962	40,002	.....	49,800
1. State-operated channels	1,331	.....	4,384	5,941	7,611	10,785	.....	10,220
2. "Marketing" coöperatives	819	.....	5,051	8,519	14,901	12,211	.....	17,150
3. State-private and coöperative shops	31	.....	77	152	1,827	5,065	.....	11,950
4. Private, including peasants	14,613	.....	18,153	20,429	14,623	11,941	.....	10,510

Note: (a) The volume is recorded presumably at current prices. (b) "Marketing" coöperatives refer to the "supply and selling coöperatives" operating in rural areas and "consumers' coöperatives" operating in urban and industrial and mining areas. (c) State-private are the "joint" enterprises. Coöperative shops are organized by private shops under the sponsorship of the state. (d) Noninstitutionalized retail trade is carried on, especially by peasants, outside the regular commercial organizations.

Sources: (1) For 1950 and 1952 through 1955, State Statistical Bureau, "Economic Statistical Abstract," *Hsin-hua pan-yüeh-k'an*, 17:46, September, 1956. (2) For 1951, computed from indices given by Yang Po, "A Preliminary Analysis of the Process of Socialist Transformation of Private Trade in China," *T'ung-chi kung-tao t'ung-hsin* (*Statistical Bulletin*), 15:7-10, August, 1956. (3) For 1956. State Statistical Bureau, "Communiqué on the Results of the 1956 Plan," *Jen-min jih-pao*, August 2, 1957. (4) *The First Five Year Plan.*

TABLE 14

DEVELOPMENT OF "SUPPLY AND SELLING" COÖPERATIVES AND CONSUMER'S COÖPERATIVES, 1949–1954

Item	1949	1950	1951	1952	1953	1954
1. "Supply and Selling" coöperatives, rural:						
a. Number of coöperatives	20,133	39,436	......	32,788	30,445	30,576
b. Number of members (in thousands)	10,640	25,690	79,630	138,210	146,980	161,100
c. Share capital (thousand yuan)	11,580	27,360	......	224,331	261,170	317,235
2. Consumers' coöperatives, urban:						
a. Number of coöperatives	......	4,065	......	2,308	1,868	1,486
b. Number of members (in thousands)	......	4,780	8,770	9,750	10,770	9,380
c. Share capital (thousand yuan)	......	5,530	......	19,346	25,158	24,231
3. Capital funds:						
a. Total share capital (1.c. + 2.c.)	......	32,890	105,580	243,677	286,328	341,466
b. Share capital as per cent of total capital funds	......	55.4	40.5	38.2	26.4	......
4. Total retail volume:						
a. Institutionalized and noninstitutionalized retail (thousand yuan)	......	819	5,051	8,519	14,901	12,211
b. As per cent of national total	......	4.9	......	18.3	24.3	30.5

Sources: (1) Ch'u Ch'ing and Chu Chung-chien, "Variations in the Commodity Turnover of China's Rural Markets," *Ching-chi yen-chiu* (*Economic Research*), 3: 100–126, June, 1957. (2) "The Development of Marketing Coöperatives," *Ta Kung Pao*, July 28, 1954. (3) State Statistical Bureau: (a) "Communiqué on the Economic Rehabilitation and Development in 1952 (Revised)," *Jen-min jih-pao*, September 28, 1954. This early source is used because the data on this subject given there tally with those released later; (b) "Statistical Abstract of the National Economic, Cultural and Educational Achievements," *Hsin-hua yueh-pao* 11:181–189, November, 1955.

TABLE 15

DEVELOPMENT OF INSTITUTIONALIZED INTERNAL TRADE BY NUMBER OF AGENCIES, OPERATING PERSONNEL, AND TRADE VOLUME, 1950–1955

Trade	Commercial agencies (in thousands)			Operating personnel (in thousands)			Wholesale and retail volume (in million yuan)
	1950	1952	1955	1950	1952	1955	1955
1. Socialized...............	52	144	515	382	1,246	2,490	49,570
a. State operated............	8	91	97	216	635	1,122	33,410
b. "Marketing" coöperative-operated...........	44	113	236	166	711	1,101	15,090
2. Private.................	4,020	4,300	2,772	6,620	6,768	3,642	10,940
Total..............	4,072	4,444	3,287	7,002	8,014	6,132	60,510

Note: (a) "Marketing" coöperatives refer to the "supply and selling coöperatives" in the rural areas and the consumers' coöperatives in urban areas. (b) Private agencies include small merchants and peddlers operating in rural areas. (c) For 1955, 1.a. and 1.b. do not add up to the figures in row 1: no explanation is given in the source.

Source: "A Survey of the Development of China's Commercial Network and of the Situation in 1955," prepared by the research department of *T'ung-chi kung-tso t'ung-hsin (Statistical Bulletin)*, reprinted in *Hsin-hua pan-yueh-k'an*, 24:80–83, December, 1956. According to this survey the trade volume, compiled from materials supplied by the operations departments of the commercial agencies, differs somewhat from the figures released by the State Statistical Bureau.

TABLE 16

GEOGRAPHICAL DISTRIBUTION OF INTERNAL TRADE, 1955

Location	Commercial agencies		Operating personnel		Retail volume	
	Thousands	Per cent	Thousands	Per cent	Million yuan	Per cent
1. Urban areas.......	1,860	56.6	3,708	60.5	14,800	46.9
a. Eight big cities .	*482*	*14.7*	*920*	*15.0*	*4,810*	*15.2*
b. Others..........	*1,378*	*41.9*	*2,788*	*45.5*	*9,990*	*31.7*
2. Rural areas.......	1,427	43.4	2,424	39.5	16,740	53.1
Total...........	3,287	100.0	6,132	100.0	31,540	100.0

Note: The eight big cities are Peiping, Tientsin, Shanghai, Wuhan, Canton, Chungking, Sian, and Shenyang (Mukden).
Source: See Table 15.

TABLE 17

COMPOSITION OF THE GROSS AGRICULTURAL VALUE PRODUCT
AT 1952 PRICES, 1952–1956
(In billions of yuan)

Item	1952	1953	1954	1955	1956
1. Gross agricultural value product..	48.4	49.9	51.5	55.5	58.3
2. Crop and animal raising..........	38.5	39.2	40.6	43.7	46.2
a. Crops........................	....	....	....	....	39.8
b. Animal raising................	....	....	....	....	6.4
3. Subsidiary work.................	9.9	10.7	10.9	11.8	12.1
a. Processing for own use.........	7.6	8.3	8.4	8.8	....
b. Work for others..............	2.3	2.4	2.5	3.0	....

Sources: (1) For 1952 to 1955, Chao Ch'ing-hsin, "Seasonal Variations of the Market after Agricultural Coöperation," *Ching-chi yen-chiu (Economic Research)*, 5:19–38, October, 1956. (2) For 1956, Teng Shuang, "Introducing the National Agricultural Exhibition," *Hsin-hua pan-yueh-k'an*, 8:91–98, April. 1957.

TABLE 18

SOCIALIZATION OF AGRICULTURE BY FARMING HOUSEHOLDS, 1950-1956

(In thousands)

Farming households	\multicolumn{6}{c}{At the end of autumn harvest}	End of 1956
	1950	1952	1953	1954	1955	1956	End of 1956
1. National total	105,536	113,683	116,324	117,331	119,201	120,000	121,480
2. Those joining agricultural producers' coöperatives	– – –ᵃ	59	275	2,297	16,921	110,000	116,980
a. Collectives	– – –ᵃ	2	2	12	40	100,000	106,660
b. Less-developed type	– – –ᵃ	57	273	2,285	16,881	10,000	10,320
3. Those joining mutual-aid teams	11,313	45,364	45,637	68,478	60,389	......	......
a. Full year	......	11,448	13,329	30,713	32,843	......	......
b. Seasonal	......	33,916	32,308	37,765	27,546	......	......
4. Total joining coöperatives and teams (2 + 3)	11,313	45,423	45,912	70,775	77,310	......	......
5. (4) As per cent of (1)	10.7	40.0	39.5	60.3	64.9	......	......
6. (2) As per cent of (1)	– – –	0.1	0.2	2.0	14.2	92.0	96.3

ᵃ32 households joined collectives and 187 joined the other coöperatives.

Note: (a) Except for the last column, the households joining coöperatives and teams are only those that have participated in the autumn harvest of the year and in the sharing of the harvest product according to regulations. The number is therefore less than that at the end of the year. (b) For definition of the less-developed type

of producer's coöperatives, see text.

Sources: (1) State Statistical Bureau, "Economic Statistical Abstract," Hsin-hua pan-yueh-k'an, 17:39–50, September, 1956. (2) For 1956: (a) State Statistical Bureau, "Communiqué on the Results of the 1956 Plan," Jen-min jih-pao, August 2, 1957; (b) ibid., May 16, 1957; (c) Po I-po, "Report on the 1956 Plan," ibid., July 2, 1957.

TABLE 19

DEVELOPMENT OF AGRICULTURAL PRODUCERS' COÖPERATIVES, 1950–1956

(In number of coöperatives)

Type	At the end of autumn harvest					End of 1956
	1950	1952	1953	1954	1955	
1. Highly developed: collectives.......	1	10	15	201	529	746,000
2. Less-developed....	18	3,634	15,053	114,165	633,213	14,000
Total.............	19	3,644	15,068	114,366	633,742	760,000

Note: See Table 18.
Sources: (1) For 1950 to 1955, State Statistical Bureau, "Economic Statistical Abstract," *Hsin-hua pan-yueh-k'an*, 17:39–50, September 1956. (2) For 1956: (a) Teng Tzu-hui's report at the National Conference of Model Agricultural Workers, *Jen-min jih-pao*, February 22, 1957; (b) Chen Cheng-jen, "The Problems of Agricultural Coöperation and Production," *Hsin-hua pan-yueh-k'an*, 7:20–26, April 1957. He gave the number of collectives that may pertain to the end of February, 1957.

TABLE 20

CULTIVATED LAND AND CROP AREA, 1949–1957

(In thousands of hectares)

Item	1949	1952	1953	1954	1955	1956	1957 estimated	1957 target
1. Cultivated land	97,881	107,919	108,529	109,355	110,156	111,850	113,200	110,496
a. Wet fields	22,818	25,853	25,955	26,268	26,540	……	……	……
b. Dry fields	75,063	82,066	82,574	83,087	83,616	……	……	……
1) Irrigated	3,229	4,890	5,019	5,324	5,516	……	……	……
2. Crop area	……	141,256	144,035	147,926	151,082	159,300	160,000	151,585
a. Grains	101,640	112,300	114,275	116,341	118,397	124,000	123,300	114,971
1) Rice	25,708	28,382	28,321	28,722	29,173	33,330	……	29,658
2) Wheat	21,516	24,780	25,636	26,967	26,739	27,330	……	26,684
3) Coarse	47,405	50,450	51,302	50,871	52,431	52,670	……	48,816
4) Potatoes	7,011	8,688	9,016	9,781	10,054	10,670	……	9,813
b. Soybeans	8,319	11,679	12,362	12,654	11,442	……	……	12,682
c. Cotton	2,770	5,576	5,180	5,462	5,773	6,253	5,800	6,333
d. Jute and hemp	28	158	79	72	116	……	……	139
e. Tobacco	61	186	191	218	252	……	……	279
f. Sugar cane	108	182	192	219	204	……	255	270
g. Sugar beets	16	35	49	73	115	……	143	142
h. Groundnuts	1,254	1,804	1,775	2,097	2,268	……	……	……
i. Rapeseed	1,515	1,863	1,667	1,706	2,338	……	……	……

Note: For definitions, see text.

Sources: (1) State Statistical Bureau, "Economic Statistical Abstract," *Hsin-hua pan-yüeh-k'an,* 17:39–50, September, 1956. (2) State Statistical Bureau, "Communiqué on the Results of the 1956 Plan," *Jen-min jih-pao,* August 2, 1957. (3) Po I-po, "Report on the Results of the 1956 Plan," *ibid.,* July 2, 1957. (4) Teng Tzu-hui's report, *ibid.,* February 22, 1957. (5) Teng Shuang, "Introducing the National Agricultural Exhibition," *Hsin-hua pan-yüeh-k'an,* 8:91–98, April, 1957. (6) Editorial, *Jen-min jih-pao,* July 24, 1957. (7) The *First Five Year Plan.* (8) State Planning Commission, "Results and Achievements of the First Five Year Plan," *Jen-min jih-pao,* October 1, 1957. (9) Teng Ling, "The Economic Significance of Potato Production under Different Social Systems," *Ching-chi yen-chiu (Economic Research),* 5:39–44, May, 1958. (10) Ti Ching-hsiang, "Increase Sugar Output for the People," *Ta Kung Pao (Impartial Daily),* January 5, 1958.

TABLE 21

AGRICULTURAL PRODUCTION, 1949-1957
(In thousands of metric tons)

Product	1949	1952	1953	1954	1955	1956	1957 estimated	1957 target
1. Grains	108,095	154,394	156,901	160,433	174,812	182,500	191,000	181,590
a. Rice	48,645	68,426	71,272	70,851	78,024	82,450	......	81,770
b. Wheat	13,808	18,123	18,281	23,332	22,965	24,800	......	23,725
c. "Coarse": millet, corn, etc.	35,799	51,519	50,695	49,269	54,926	53,350	......	54,795
d. Potatoes	9,843	16,326	16,653	16,981	18,897	21,900	......	21,300
2. Soybeans	5,086	9,519	9,931	9,080	9,121	10,250	......	11,220
3. Raw cotton	444	1,304	1,175	1,065	1,518	1,445	1,500	1,635
4. Jute and hemp	37	305	138	137	257	257	......	365
5. Cured tobacco	43	222	213	232	298	399	......	390
6. Sugar cane	2,642	7,116	7,209	8,592	8,110	8,678	......	13,175
7. Sugar beets	191	479	505	989	1,596	1,654	......	2,135
8. Groundnuts	1,268	2,316	2,127	2,767	2,926	3,336	......	......
9. Rapeseed	734	932	879	878	969	920	......	......
10. Tea leaves	41.1	82.4	84.7	92.1	108.0	120.5	126.3	112
12. Silk cocoons:								
a. Domestic	30.9	62.2	59.3	65.1	67.0	72.5	81.3	93.4
b. Wild	11.9	61.1	12.3	25.7	63.8	62.0	73.8	61.8
13. Aquatic products	447.9	1,666.3	1,899.7	2,293.5	2,517.9	2,640.0	2,816.0	2,807.0

Note: Potatoes have been converted into grain equivalents by taking 4 kg. of potatoes as 1 kg. of grain.

Sources: (1) State Statistical Bureau, "Economic Statistical Abstract," *Hsin-hua pan-yueh-k'an*, 17:39-50, September, 1957. (2) Po I-po, "Report on the Results of the 1956 Plan," *Jen-min jih-pao*, July 2, 1957. (3) State Statistical Bureau, "Communiqué on the Results of the 1956 Plan," *ibid.*, August 2, 1957. (4) The rice produc- tion figure for 1956 is a preliminary estimate given by Teng Tzu-hui, *ibid.*, February 22, 1957. (5) The *First Five Year Plan*. (6) Wang Kuang-wei, "A Suggestion on the Allocation of the Agricultural Labor Force," *Chi-hua ching-chi* (*Planned Economy*), 8:6-9, August, 1957. (7) Hsu Teh-yen's statement at the National Congress of People's Representatives, in *Hsin-hua pan-yueh-k'an*, 15:84-87, August, 1957. (8) Tseng Ling, as cited in Table 20, source (9).

TABLE 22
YIELD PER UNIT OF CROP AREA FOR SELECTED CROPS, 1949–1957
(In kilograms per hectare)

Product	1949	1950	1951	1952	1953	1954	1955	1956	1957 estimated	1957 target
1. Grains	1,064	.....	.....	1,375	1,373	1,379	1,477	1,472	1,549	1,579
a. Rice	1,892	2,109	2,249	2,411	2,516	2,467	2,675	2,474	.....	2,762
b. Wheat	642	636	748	731	713	866	859	907	.....	889
c. Coarse	755	.....	.....	1,021	988	969	1,048	1,013	.....	1,123
d. Potatoes	1,404	1,610	1,690	1,880	1,847	1,736	1,880	2,052	.....	2,171
2. Soybeans	611	.....	.....	815	803	718	797	.....	.....	885
3. Raw cotton	159	185	187	234	227	195	263	231	259	276
4. Rapeseed	485	.....	.....	500	527	515	414	.....	.....	.....

Note: Potatoes have been converted into grain equivalents by taking 4 kg. of potatoes as 1 kg. of grain.
Sources: (1) See Tables 20 and 21. (2) For 1950 and 1951: (a) Sun Ching-chih, "Food Resources and Population Growth," *Peoples' China*, 5:4-10, May, 1956; (b) Ho Wei, "The Meaning and Method of Comparing the Current Agricultural Prices with those of the 1930's," *Hsueh-hsi (Study),* 7:15-17 and 21, April, 1957.

TABLE 23

LIVESTOCK ON FARMS AND RANCHES, 1949-1957

(In thousands)

Animal	1949	1952	1953	1954	1955	1956	1957 target	1962 target
1. Oxen and buffaloes	43,936	56,600	60,083	63,623	65,951	66,748	73,610	90,000
a. Oxen	......	......	......	......	53,481	54,357	......	......
b. Buffaloes	......	......	......	......	12,470	12,391	......	......
2. Horses	4,875	6,130	6,512	6,939	7,312	7,411	8,340	11,000
3. Asses	9,494	11,806	12,215	12,700	12,402	11,796	13,950	......
4. Mules	1,471	1,637	1,645	1,717	1,723	1,708	1,970	......
5. Camels	......	285	300	320	357	374	......	......
6. Sheep and goats	42,347	61,779	72,023	81,304	84,218	92,130	113,040	170,000
a. Sheep	......	36,890	42,830	48,150	50,213	53,489	68,720	......
b. Goats	......	24,890	29,190	33,150	34,005	38,641	44,320	......
7. Pigs	57,752	89,765	96,131	101,718	87,920	84,414	138,340	250,000

Note: (a) The animal census covers the whole country as of July 1 each year. However, for 1956, the numbers of farm animals in Chinghai province and the numbers of horses, asses, mules, and goats in Hunan province are those of 1955. (b) The numbers of camels, sheep, and goats for 1952, 1953 and 1954 are computed from index numbers and have been rounded to tens of million head. But the totals of "sheep and goats" are originally given. (c) According to Po I-po, "Results of the 1956 Plan,"

Jen-min jih-pao, July 2, 1957, the number of pigs at the end of 1956 was 97.8 million and the estimated number at the end of 1957 was 110 million.

Sources: (1) "A National Survey of Animals for 1956," *Hsin-hua pan-yueh-k' an* 1.88-90, January 1957. (2) State Statistical Bureau, "Economic Statistical Abstract," *ibid.*, 17:39-50, September, 1956. (3) The *Five Year Plan*. (4) The Chinese Communist Party's Proposal of the Second Five Year Plan, *Jen-min jih-pao,* September 29, 1956.

TABLE 24

OWNERSHIP OF LIVESTOCK, 1956

(In per cent)

Animal	Total	State owned	Collectively owned	Privately-owned by	
				Individual members of agric. coöperatives	Independent peasant-herders
1. Oxen	100.0	0.2	72.8	12.8	14.2
a. Yearlings	100.0	18.7	25.4	9.7	46.2
2. Buffaloes	100.0	0.5	79.3	9.8	10.4
3. Horses	100.0	1.7	68.9	11.2	18.2
4. Asses	100.0	0.1	69.9	24.8	5.2
5. Mules	100.0	1.2	75.0	10.6	13.2
6. Camels	100.0	0.3	7.6	14.9	77.2
7. Sheep	100.0	1.2	30.8	41.5	26.5
8. Goats	100.0	0.4	39.2	43.4	17.0
9. Pigs	100.0	0.6	16.3	73.1	10.0

Note: (a) The total covers the whole country, except the provinces of Chinghai, Sinkiang, and Hunan, as of July 1, 1956. (b) State-owned are those found in state-operated farms and ranches. Collectively owned refer to those owned by agricultural collectives and producers' coöperatives. (c) The number of ox yearlings in 1956 was 233,250.

Source: ' A National Survey of Animals for 1956," *Hsin-hua pan-yueh-k'an*, 1:88-90, January, 1957

TABLE 25

DEVELOPMENT OF STATE-OPERATED FARMS (MECHANIZED AND NONMECHANIZED), 1950-1955

Item	1950	1952	1953	1954	1955	1957 target
1. Number of farms	1,215	2,336	2,376	2,415	2,242	3,038
2. Area cultivated (thousand ha.)	155	247	251	295	395	1,125
3. Labor force (thousand)	43	97	111	137	134	.....
a. Staff	19	28	33	34	29	.....
b. Workers	24	69	78	103	105	.....
4. Number of tractors	1,160	1,532	1,627	2,235	2,839	5,146
5. Number of harvesting combines	155	275	352	430	657	.....
6. Draft animals (thousand)	19	42	50	52	58	.....

Note: (a) The state-operated farms include both central-government and provincial government arms. (b) The number of tractors is given in terms of 15-horse-power per tractor. (c) The decline of the number of state-operated farms in 1955 was due to amalgamation of some farms and to conversion of some others into ranches.

Sources: (1) State Statistical Bureau, "Economic Statistical Abstract," *Hsin-hua pan-yueh-k'an*, 17:39-50, September 1956. (2) The *Five Year Plan*.

TABLE 26

Development of State-operated Mechanized Farms, 1950–1956

Item	1950	1952	1953	1954	1955	1956	1957 target
1. Farms	36	50	59	97	106	166	141
2. Area cultivated (in ha.)	89,300	135,800	141,300	185,500	269,300	448,000	505,000
3. Labor force	11,200	24,900	28,800	56,600	57,200	......	......
a. Staff	3,500	5,900	7,500	13,700	12,700	......	......
b. Workers	7,700	19,000	21,300	42,900	44,500	......	......
4. Tractors	1,160	1,532	1,627	2,235	2,839	4,422	5,146
5. Harvesting combines	155	275	352	430	657	950	......
6. Draft animals	4,100	8,300	7,900	13,300	13,100	......	......

Note: See Table 25.
Sources: (a) For 1950 to 1955, State Statistical Bureau, "Economic Statistical Abstract," *Hsin-hua pan-yueh-k'an,* 17: 39–50, September, 1956. (b) For 1956, State Statistical Bureau, "Communiqué on the Results of the 1956 Plan," *Jen-min jih-pao,* August 2, 1957.

TABLE 27

Development of State-operated Tractor Stations, 1953–1956

Item	1953	1954	1955	1956	1957 target
1. Number of stations	11	89	138	326	194
2. Number of tractors	113	778	1,896	9,862	2,897
3. Areas cultivated (thousand ha.)	..	80	330	1,915	236

Note: The number of tractors is given in terms of 15 horse-power each.
Sources: (1) For 1954 to 1956, State Statistical Bureau's annual communiqué on the results of the yearly plans, *Jen-min jih-pao,* September 23, 1955, September 15, 1956, and August 2, 1957. (2) For 1953, Li Fu-ch'un's report, *ibid.,* September 29, 1955. (3) The *Five Year Plan.*

TABLE 28

POPULATION CENSUS OF THE MAINLAND, JUNE 30, 1953

I. Geographical Distribution	*Population*
A. Special Cities:	
1. Shanghai	6,204,417
2. Peiping	2,768,149
3. Tientsin	2,693,831
B. Provinces:	
1. Szechuan	62,303,999
2. Shantung	48,876,548
3. Honan	44,214,594
4. Kiangsu	41,252,192
5. Hopei	35,984,644
6. Kwangtung	34,770,059
7. Hunan	33,226,954
8. Anhwei	30,343,637
9. Hupei	27,789,693
10. Chekiang	22,865,747
11. Kwangsi	19,560,822
12. Liaoning	18,545,147
13. Yunan	17,472,737
14. Kiangsi	16,772,865
15. Shensi	15,881,281
16. Kweichow	15,037,310
17. Shansi	14,314,485
18. Fukien	13,142,721
19. Kansu	12,928,102
20. Heilungkiang	11,897,309
21. Kirin	11,290,073
22. Jehol	5,160,822
23. Sinkiang	4,873,608
24. Sikang	3,381,064
25. Chinghai	1,676,534
C. Special Regions:	
1. Inner Mongolia	6,100,104
2. Tibet and Changtu Area	1,273,969
Total Population	582,603,417
II. Ethnic Composition	
1. Chinese	547,283,057
Per cent of total	93.94
2. Minorities	35,320,360
Per cent of total	6.06
III. Urban-Rural Distribution	
1. Urban	77,257,282
Per cent of total	13.25
2. Rural	505,346,135
Per cent of total	86.74

Note: (a) According to the official announcement, the number of people "directly surveyed and recorded" was 574,205,940, of whom 51.82 per cent were males and 48.18 per cent females. (b) The official announcement also gave an estimate of the population at Taiwan and of the Chinese population abroad. Since these are not residents of the mainland, they are omitted here. (c) No definition has been given of "urban" and "rural" population. (d) The following changes in the administrative divisions of the country have taken place since the census: the province of Jehol has been eliminated with its area distributed among Hopei, Liaoning, and Inner Mongolia Autonomous Region; and the province of Sikang, merged into that of Szechuan. Sinkiang Province has been made into Sinkiang Uigur Autonomous Region; Tibet Special Area, into Tibet Autonomous Region; and Kwangsi Province, into Kwangsi Chuang Autonomous Region. Kansu Province has been reduced in size by the establishment of Ninghsia Hui Autonomous Region. There have also been minor changes in boundaries among many of the administrative divisions. (It will be noticed that Uigur, Chuang, and Hui are names of big minority groups in the country.)

Source: State Statistical Bureau, "Communiqué on the Results of the National Population Census," *Jen-min jih-pao*, November 11, 1954.

TABLE 29

STUDENT ENROLLMENT, 1949–1957

(In thousands)

Level of education	1949–50	1950–51	1951–52	1952–53	1953–54
1. Higher................	117	139	156	194	216
a. Postgraduate........	*1*	*1*	*2*	*3*	*4*
b. College..............	*116*	*138*	*154*	*191*	*212*
2. Secondary.............	1,268	1,567	1,964	3,145	3,629
a. Polytechnic..........	*229*	*257*	*383*	*636*	*668*
b. High School.........	*1,039*	*1,305*	*1,568*	*2,490*	*2,933*
1) Senior High.......	*207*	*238*	*184*	*260*	*360*
2) Junior High........	*832*	*1,067*	*1,384*	*2,230*	*2,573*
c. Short courses........	– – –	*4*	*13*	*19*	*28*
3. Primary..............	24,391	28,924	43,154	51,100	51,664
Total..................	25,776	30,630	45,274	54,439	55,509

Level of education	1954–55	1955–56	1956–57	1957–58 estimated	1957–58 target
1. Higher................	258	292	408	......	......
a. Postgraduate........	*5*	*5*	......	......	......
b. College..............	*253*	*288*	......	*440*	*435*
2. Secondary.............	4,246	4,473	......	......	......
a. Polytechnic..........	*608*	*537*	*812*	......	*672*
b. High School.........	*3,587*	*3,900*	*5,165*	*5,567*	.....
1) Senior High.......	*478*	*580*	......	*822*	*724*
2) Junior High........	*3,109*	*3,320*	......	*4,745*	*3,984*
c. Short courses........	*51*	*36*	......	......	......
3. Primary..............	51,218	53,126	63,464	65,814	60,214
Total..................	55,721	57,892	......	......	......

Note: (a) Those for 1950–51 and 1951–52 are apparently not final figures. (b) Polytechnical schools include normal schools. (c) "Short courses" refers to special-course high schools for technical and agricultural subjects.

Sources: (1) For 1950–51 and 1951–52, *1955 Jen-min shou-ts'e (1955 People's Handbook)*, Tientsin, 1955, pp. 577–578. (2) For other years, State Statistical Bureau, "Economic Statistical Abstract," *Hsin-hua pan-yueh-k'an*, 17:39–50, September, 1957. (3) The *First Five Year Plan*. (4) Ko Chu-po and Liu Hsiang, "On the Planning of the Development of China's Secondary and Primary Education," *Chi-hua ching-chi (Planned Economy)*, 10:20–22 and 27, October, 1957. (5) Yeh Feng "How to Compile Properly the Educational, Cultural and Health Plan for 1958," *ibid.*, 9:18–19, September, 1957.

TABLE 30

COLLEGE STUDENT ENROLLMENT IN SPECIALIZED FIELDS, 1949–1957

(In thousands)

Field of study	1949–50	1952–53	1953–54	1954–55	1955–56	1956–57	1957–58 target
1. Engineering	30.3	66.6	80.0	95.0	109.6	150	177.6
2. Agriculture	9.8	13.3	12.8	12.8	17.3	...	37.2
3. Forestry	0.6	2.2	2.6	3.1	4.0	...	12.7
4. Finance and economics	19.4	22.0	13.5	11.2	11.4	...	9.3
5. Political science and law	7.3	3.8	3.9	4.0	4.8	...	54.8
6. Medical	15.2	24.7	29.0	33.9	36.5	...	3.6
7. Physical education	0.3	0.3	1.1	1.9	2.3	...	27.1
8. Sciences	7.0	9.6	12.4	17.1	20.0	25	20.4
9. Liberal arts	11.8	13.5	14.2	18.3	18.9	...	89.0
10. Education	12.0	31.5	40.0	53.1	60.7	99	2.9
11. Art	2.8	3.6	2.7	2.6	2.2	...	
Total	116.5	191.1	212.2	253.0	287.7	408	434.6

Note: Medical includes public health.
Sources: (1) See Table 27. (2) For 1956–57, reports of Tseng Chao-lun and of Chang Hsi-jo, in Jen-min jih-pao, March 18 and 19, 1957.

TABLE 31

POLYTECHNICAL STUDENT ENROLLMENT IN SPECIALIZED FIELDS, 1949–1956
(In thousands)

Field of study	1949–50	1952–53	1953–54	1954–55	1955–56	1957–58 target
1. Engineering.......	21.4	111.4	129.7	151.7	177.6	244.0
2. Agriculture and forestry........	21.7	66.6	68.7	58.7	53.3	98.8
3. Health...........	15.4	59.4	57.7	58.6	57.3	70.9
4. Finance and economics.......	14.8	52.3	42.3	28.8	26.0	33.3
5. Education........	151.7	345.2	369.0	308.0	219.0	218.5
6. Art and others.....	3.8	0.7	1.0	2.2	3.9	6.3
Total.............	228.8	635.6	668.4	608.0	537.1	671.8

Note: Students specialized in finance and economics are mostly trained to become accountants.
Source: See Table 29.

TABLE 32

CONVERSION RATES BETWEEN YUAN AND CERTAIN FORREIGN CURRENCIES, AS OF
DECEMBER, 1957

Countries	Currency unit	Yuan equivalent
1. Albania.......................	Lek	0.040
2. Bulgaria......................	Leva	0.294
3. Czechoslovakia.................	Koruna	0.277
4. East Germany..................	Deutsche Mark	0.899
5. Hungary......................	Forint	0.170
6. North Korea...................	Won	0.125
7. Poland........................	Zloty	0.500
8. Soviet Union..................	Ruble	0.500
9. Yugoslavia....................	Dinar	0.008
10. France.......................	Franc	0.007
11. India........................	Rupee	0.522*
12. Indonesia....................	Rupiah	0.1423*
13. Japan.......................	Yen	0.006
14. United Kingdom...............	Pound	6.630*
15. United States................	Dollar	2.617
16. West Germany................	Deutsche Mark	0.586

Original notes:
a) "This table is compiled at the request of readers. Because the conversion rates between yuan and most of the currencies listed in the table are computed from relevant [*sic*] materials, the table is meant for general reference only."
b) "Those with an asterisk are the current official (selling) rates of the People's Bank."
Note: What the "relevant materials" are is not explained in the source. For discussion of conversion rates, see chapter i, section 1, and chapter vii, section 1. Compare also with Table 33 below.
Source: Chi-hua ching-chi (Planned Economy), 12:29, December, 1957.

TABLE 33
FOREIGN-EXCHANGE RATES (TELEGRAPHIC TRANSFER) OF THE PEOPLE'S BANK FOR CERTAIN CURRENCIES AS OF MARCH, 1957

Countries	Currency units	Buying (in yuan)	Selling (in yuan)
1. Burma	Kyat 100	51.60	52.20
2. Ceylon	Rupees 100	51.60	52.20
3. Hongkong	Dollars 100	42.70	43.10
4. India	Rupees 100	51.60	52.20
5. Indonesia	Rupiah 100	14.09	14.23
6. Malayan Federation	Dollars 100	80.60	81.40
7. Pakistan	Rupees 100	51.60	52.20
8. Switzerland	Francs 100	58.20	58.80
9. United Kingdom	Pounds 100	685.90	692.70
10. Hong Kong	Notes Hk. $100	40.60	41.00
11. United States	Notes U. S. $100	234.30	236.70

Notes: (a) The People's Bank's quotations are uniform throughout the country. (b) The last two rates are for cash notes only. There is no official cable rate or sight rate for United States currency. (c) These official rates have not changed for several years. But see below.

Source: 1957 Jen-min shou-tse (People's Handbook for 1957), p. 631. The volume being published in April, 1957, the official rates were those prevailing up to March of the year. Compare the official selling rate for British pound sterling given above with that given on the preceding table. In terms of the official rate, the British pound had depreciated between March and December of 1957, although the Indian rupee, which has been tied to the British pound, maintained its yuan value in the meanwhile. For discussion of foreign-exchange and conversion rates, see chapter i, section 1, and chapter vii, section 1.

ADDENDUM

COMPARISON OF THE ESTIMATED AND REALIZED (PRELIMINARY) DATA FOR 1957

Throughout this study the 1957 data used for analysis are official estimates released in the latter part of 1957. The following tabulation compares the more important of these estimates with the realized (preliminary) data for the year as well as the planned quotas for 1958. To facilitate reference to the text, chapter numbers are indicated. Notes and sources are given at the end of Table 36.

TABLE 34

INDUSTRIAL DEVELOPMENT (CHAP. II)

Item	1957 est.	1957 prel.	1958 planned[1]
A. Gross industrial value product			
(in millions of yuan).................	72,040	75,120[2]	......
1. Factory product......................	60,340	62,810[3]	71,960
a. Producer goods.....................	31,130	32,780[2]	......
i. Machine-making...................	5,490	5,950[4]	......
b. Consumer goods....................	29,210	30,020[2]	......
2. Handicraft product....................	11,700	12,310[2]	......
B. Output of heavy industry:			
1. Pig iron (thousand tons)...............	5,554	5,857[3]	......
2. Steel (thousand tons)..................	4,987	5,245[3]	6,248
3. Rolled steel (thousand tons)...........	4,478	4,260[5]	4,820[5]
4. Coal (thousand tons)..................	117,270	123,230[6]	150,724
5. Crude oil (thousand tons).............	1,500	1,440[7]	......
6. Electric power (million kw-hr.)........	18,860	19,025[3]	22,450
7. Lathes (units)........................	22,640	29,100[7]	......
8. Chemical fertilizers (thousand tons)....	755	798[3]	1,102
9. Lumber (thousand cu. m.)..............	25,060	25,780[7]	28,200
10. Cement (thousand tons)...............	6,807	6,690[7]	7,650
C. Output of light industry:			
1. Paper and paper boards (thousand tons)	836[8]	906[7]	......
2. Cotton yarn (thousand bales)...........	4,635	4,617[2]	5,200
3. Sugar (thousand tons).................	874	850[9]	1,016
4. Salt (thousand tons)..................	7,000	8,260[9]	......
5. Edible vegetable oil (thousand tons)....	896[8]	1,196[2]	......
6. Cigarettes (thousand cases)...........	4,030[2]	4,320[3]	......

TABLE 35

AGRICULTURAL DEVELOPMENT (CHAP. III)

Item	1957 est.	1957 prel.	1958 planned[1]
A. Gross agricultural value product (in millions of yuan)	61,150	60,350[3]	64,250
B. Agricultural area (thousand ha.):			
1. Cultivated land	113,250	112,146[3]	112,830
2. Irrigated area	34,500	34,670[10]	......
3. Crop area	160,000	156,393[3]	160,987
a. Food grains	123,300	120,583[10]	122,617
1) Rice	......	32,185[10]	......
2) Potatoes	......	10,489[10]	......
b. Cotton	5,800	5,745[3]	6,020
C. Multiple dropping index (in per cent)	141	139	143
D. Production (thousand tons):			
1. Food grains	191,000	185,000[3]	196,000
a. Rice	......	86,533[10]	......
b. Wheat	......	23,622[10]	......
c. Coarse grains	......	53,490[10]	......
d. Potatoes	......	21,359[10]	......
2. Soybeans	......	9,950[16]	......
3. Raw cotton	1,500	1,640[3]	1,750
4. Cured tobacco	......	293[2]	434[2]
5. Sugarcanes	......	10,220[3]	13,033
6. Sugar beets	......	1,849[3]	2,394
7. Rapeseed	......	910[3]	1,180
8. Groundnuts	......	2,870[2]	3,445
9. Tea leaves	126	114[11]	......
10. Aquatic products	......	2,950[12]	3,520[12]
E. Yield per ha. (in kg.):			
1. Food grains	1,549	1,533	1,599
a. Rice	......	2,689	......
b. Potatoes	......	2,036	......
2. Raw cotton	259	285	291
F. Livestock (thousand head):			
1. Pigs	110,000	127,800[13]	150,000
2. Oxen, buffaloes, horses, asses and mules.	......	84,390[3]	88,270
G. Tractor stations:			
1. Number of stations	......	352[10]	......
2. Number of tractors (15 H.P. each)	......	10,933[10]	13,493
3. Land cultivated (thousand ha.)	......	1,733[10]	......

TABLE 36

FINANCING

(In millions of yuan)

Item	1957 est.	1957 prel.	1958 planned[1]
A. Internal (chap. vi):			
1. State budget:			
a. Receipts............................	29,393	30,702[13]	33,198[13]
b. Expenditures........................	28,793	28,923[13]	32,396[13]
2. Government bonds issued..............	600	650[13]	630[13]
3. Basic investment......................	11,100	12,370[3]	14,577
4. Social purchasing power................	47,320	47,000[3]	49,400
5. Currency in circulation.................	......	[12,300][14]	......
B. External (chap. vii):			
1. Soviet loan proceeds...................	23	23[13]	0[13]
2. China's foreign trade:[17]			
a. Exports............................	5,200	5,230[15]	......
b. Imports............................	4,755	5,120	......
c. Total..............................	9,955	10,350[3]	11,000
d. Trade balance......................	+445	+110	......

Notes and sources for Tables 34, 35 and 36:

[1] Unless otherwise stated, all data for 1958 are from source (3) below. The 1958 targets have since been substantially raised.

[2] Chi Ch'ung-wei, "Industry must Assist and Promote Agricultural Development," *Ching-chi yen-chiu (Economic Research)*, 2:1–11, February, 1958.

[3] Po I-po, "Report on the Draft Plan for 1958," *Hsin-hua pan-yueh-k'an*, 5:12–23 and 31–32, March, 1958.

[4] Ch'eng Chen-chia, "The Anti-waste and Anti-conservatism Movement will Help the Planning Work Take a Big Leap Forward," *Chi-hua ching-chi (Planned Economy)*, 4:5–6, April, 1958.

[5] Li Chi-chung, "The Plan for 1958," *Ts'ai-ching yen-chiu (Financial and Economic Research)* Shanghai, 2:21–26 and 44, April, 1958.

[6] State Statitsical Bureau, "The Basic Situation of China's Coal Industry," *T'ung-chi yen-chiu (Statistical Research)*, 4:18–23, April, 1958.

[7] "The Gross Industrial Value Product of 1957," *Hsin-hua pan-yueh-k'an*, 2:56, January, 1958.

[8] State Statistical Bureau, "The Situation of China's Light Industry," *T'ung-chi yen-chiu (Statistical Research)*, 2:12–15, February, 1958.

[9] Li Chu-ch'en, "Report on the Food Processing Industry," *Hsin-hua pan-yueh-k'an*, 7:51–53, April, 1958.

[10] Ministry of Agriculture, Bureau of Food Grains Production, "Food Grains Production during the First Five Year Plan," *ibid.*, 9:80–83, May, 1958.

[11] Editorial, "The Urgent Need for Developing Tea Production," *Jen-min- jih-pao*, February 17, 1958.

[12] Hsu Teh-yen, "Strive to Lead the World Output of Aquatic Products in Five Years," *Hsin-hua pan-yueh-k'an*, 6:97–99, March, 1958.

[13] Li Hsien-nien, "Report on the Budget for 1958," *ibid.*, 5:3–12, March, 1958. The budget figures, all at current prices, are those approved by the National Congress of People's Representatives.

[14] The figure on note circulation is derived from my estimate in the text together with Finance Minister Li's statement (see source 13, above) that the volume of note circulation at the end of 1957 had been reduced by 450 million yuan from that at the end of 1956.

[15] Li Po-fong, "The Need for Organizing the Sources of Export Commodities," *Chi-hua ching-chi (Planned Economy)*, 2:28–31, February, 1958. For the value (in rubles) of imports and exports between the Soviet Union and China from 1950 to 1956, see Ministry of Foreign Trade of the USSR, Business Research Institute, *Vneshniaia torgovlia SSSR s sotsialisticheskimi stranami (Foreign Trade of the USSR with Socialist Countries)*, Moscow: Foreign Trade Publishing House, 1957, pp. 39–62, and M. I. Sladkovakii, *Ocherki ekonomicheskikh otnoshenii SSSR s Kitaem (Essays on the Economic Relations of the USSR with China)*, Moscow: Foreign Trade Publishing House, 1957, especially Appendix, pp. 359–361. I am indebted to Gregory Grossman and Alexander Eckstein for calling my attention to these Russian sources.

[16] Wu Po, "Explanations for the Draft Regulations of Agricultural Tax of the People's Republic of China," *Jen-min jih-pao*, June 5, 1958.

[17] According to United States, Department of State, *Statistical Review of East-West Trade 1956–57*, (Washington: July, 1958), Communist China's trade with the free world in 1956 and 1957 (preliminary) may be summarized as follows (in millions of U. S. dollars):

Area	China's exports		China's imports	
	1956	1957	1956	1957
African-Asian	454.8	444.9	220.5	252.3
Western Europe	165.7	149.3	194.5	236.0
Other	20.9	22.1	19.2	35.9
Free-world	641.4	616.3	434.2	524.2

Bibliography

The listing is confined to the publications cited in the text and the Statistical Appendix. News dispatches and publications cited in the Addendum, however, are not included. Virtually all Chinese-language sources are published in Peiping—mostly by the People's Press, New China Press, the Science Press, and the Financial and Economic Press. It does not seem necessary to indicate the name of the publisher in every case.

In the Chinese-language sources, two groups of citations are not fully listed—government regulations and editorials. Reports and releases, originally published in the editorial section of the State Statistical Bureau's official journal, are listed under the bureau. The names of authors and publications are given only in romanized form. In the absence of Chinese characters, romanization of titles of reports and articles does not seem to serve any purpose and is therefore omitted.

I. CHINESE-LANGUAGE SOURCES

A. OFFICIAL DOCUMENTS:

Chinese Communist Party. "Proposal of the Second Five Year Plan," *Jen-min jih-pao*, September 29, 1956.
——— ———. Central Political Bureau. "Draft Outline of Agricultural Development from 1956 to 1967," *Jen-min jih-pao* January 26, 1956.
——— ———. "Revised Draft Outline of Agricultural Development from 1956 to 1967," *Jen-min jih-pao*, October 26, 1957.
Chung-hua-jen-min-kung-ho-kuo fa-chan kuo-min-ching-chi ti-i wu-nien-chi hua (*The First Five Year Plan for National Economic Development of the People's Republic of China*), (August, 1955), 238 pp.
State Council, Financial and Economic Commission. *Chung-yang ts'ai-ching cheng-ts'e fa-ling hui-pien* (*Collection of Laws, Regulations, and Statements concerning the Fiscal and Economic Policies of the Central Government*), Vol. 1 (August, 1950), 824 pp., Vol. 2 (June, 1951), 1149 pp.
T'ung-i kuo-chia ts'ai-cheng kung-tso (*National Unification of Financial and Economic Operations*), Hankow (May, 1950), 121 pp.

B. DIRECTIVES AND REGULATIONS ISSUED BY THE STATE COUNCIL:

Directive Concerning the High-handedness of Banks and Credit Coöperatives Operating in Rural Areas, in *1957 Jen-min shou-tse* (*People's Handbook for 1597*), pp. 538–539.
On Planned Purchase and Planned Supply of Cotton Cloth, *Jen-min jih-pao* September 15, 1954.
On Planned Purchase and Planned Supply of Food Grains, *Jen-min jih-pao* November 24, 1953.
On Planned Purchase and Planned Supply of Food Grains, *Jen-min jih-pao* October 13, 1957.

On Planned Purchase of Raw Cotton, *Jen-min jih-pao,* September 15, 1954.

On the Ban of Certain Commodities From Entering the Free Market, *Hsin-hua pan-yueh-k'an,* 18 (September, 1957), 207–208.

Provisional Measures for Planned Purchase and Planned Supply of Food Grains in Rural Areas, *Jen-min jih-pao,* August 25, 1955.

Provisional Measures for Rationing of Food Grains in Urban Areas, *Jen-min jih-pao,* August 25, 1955.

Provisional Regulations on State-private Joint Enterprises, *Jen-min jih-pao* September 6, 1954.

Regulations on Food Markets, *Jen-min jih-pao,* November 24, 1953.

Regulation on Unifying Fiscal Control for 1950, *Jen-min jih-pao,* April 2, 1950.

Revised Regulations on Agricultural Producers' Coöperatives, *Jen-min jih-pao,* July 1, 1956.

C. OFFICIAL REPORTS AND STATEMENTS:

Chang Tzu-liang. "Report on the Lumber Industry," *Jen-min jih-pao,* May 31, 1955.

Chen Wei-chi. "Report on the Progress and Condition of the Textile Industry," *Jen-min jih-pao,* March 9, 1954.

Chen Yun. "Problems of State-private Joint Enterprises," *Jen-min jih-pao,* June 19, 1956.

———. "Report on the Economic and Fiscal Work," in *San-nien-lai hsin-chung-kuo ching-chi ti cheng-chiu (New China's Economic Achievements during the Last Three Years),* (1951), pp. 74–82.

———. "Report on the Financial and Food Situation," *Jen-min jih pao,* April 15, 1950.

———. "Statement at the National Congress of People's Representatives [on food]," *Jen-min jih-pao,* September 24, 1954.

———. "The Problem of Government Monopoly in the Purchase and Sale of Food," *Jen-min jih-pao,* July 22, 1955.

———. "The Problem of Increasing Production and Economizing," *Hsin-hua pan-yueh-k'an,* 7 April, 1957), 15–18.

———. "The Problem of Internal Trade and Its Relationship with Industry," *Jen-min jih-pao,* July 1, 1956.

Chia To-fu. "Report on the Drafting of the 1957 Plan for the National Economy," *Chi-hua ching-chi (Planned Economy),* 4 (April, 1957), pp. 1–9.

———. "Summarizing the Discussion at the National Planning Conference," *Hsin-hua pan-yueh-k'an,* 18 September, 1957), pp. 306–307.

Ch'ien Ying. "Report to the National Congress of People's Representatives [on production waste and corruption]" in *1956 Jen-min shou-tse (People's Handbook for 1956),* pp. 228–229.

Chou En-lai. "Report on the Work of the Government," *Jen-min jih-pao,* June 27, 1957, September 24, 1954.

Chu Hsueh-fan. "Report to the National Congress of the People's Representatives [on the improvement of workers' welfare]," *Hsin-hua pan-yueh-k'an,* 16 (August, 1957), pp. 51–54.

Hsieh Chueh-tsai. "Statement at the National Congress of the People's Representatives [on damaged agricultural areas]," *Jen-min jih-pao,* September 28, 1954.

Hsieh Mu-ch'iao. "Our Experience in Statistical Work During the First Five Year Plan Period and Our Future Tasks," *T'ung-chi kung-tso (Statistical Work),* 21 (November, 1957), pp. 1–21.

Jui Mu. "The Development of Civil Legislation since 1949," in *1956 Jen-min shou-tse (People's Handbook for 1956),* pp. 334–339.

Jung Tzu-ho. "Report on the National Finances for 1950–51," *Hsin-hua yueh-pao*, 6 (April, 1951), pp. 1354–1355.

Li Che-jen, "Consolidate the Economic Cooperation between China and Soviet Union and Other People's Democracies," *Jen-min jih-pao*, May 12, 1955.

Li Fu-ch'un. "A Detailed Report on the First Five Year Plan," *Jen-min jih-pao*, July 8, 1955.

———. "Achievements during the First Three Years of the First Five Year Plan," *Jen-min jih-pao*, September 29, 1955.

———. "Economic Progress from 1953 to 1956," *Jen-min jih-pao*, June 19, 1956.

———. "On the First Five Year Plan," *Ta Kung Pao (Impartial Daily)*, September 16, 1953.

Li Hsien-nien. Annual report on the final accounting of the previous year's budget and on the planned budget for the current year: (1) The 1955 Budget Message, *Jen-min jih pao* July 10, 1955; (2) The 1956 Budget Message, *ibid.* June 16, 1956; (3) The 1957 Budget Message, *ibid.* June 30, 1957.

———. "Price as an Instrument to Promote Production," *Jen-min jih-pao*, September 23, 1956.

Li Teh-ch'uan. "Report to the Natioinal Congress of People's Representatives on the Work of National Health," *Jen-min jih-pao*, September 25, 1954.

Liao Lu-yen. "Opening Statement at the National Conference of Agricultural Model Workers," *Jin-min jih-pao*, February 19, 1957.

———. "Summarizing the Work on Agricultural Production for 1956 and Setting the Task for 1957," *Hsin-hua pan-yes-k'an*, 8 (April, 1957), pp. 81–88.

Liu Shao-ch'i, "Political Report to the National Congress of Representatives of the Chinese Community Party," *Jen-min jih-pao*, September 17, 1956.

Lo Shu-chang. "Report to the National Congress of People's Representatives on Agriculture," *Hsin-hua pan-yueh-k'an*, 16 (August, 1957), pp. 125–127.

Mao Tse-tung, "Concerning the Correct Disposal of the Problem of People's Internal Contradictions," *Jen-min jih-pao*, June 19, 1957.

———. "The Problem of Agricultural Coöperation," *Jen-min jih-pao*, October 17, 1955.

Ministry of Trade. "Report on the Problem of Cotton Cloth Supply in 1957," *Hsin-hua pan-yueh-k'an*, 10 (May, 1957), pp. 112–113.

———. "Report on the Supply of Cotton Cloth for Civilian Use during the Fourth Year of 'Planned Supply,'" *Jen-min jih-pao*, August 20, 1957.

Peh Chien-hua. "600 Million Population—A Great Strength for China's Socialist Construction," *Jen-min jih-pao*, November 1, 1954.

Po I-po. "The Correct Disposition of the Relationship between Accumulation and Consumption," *Jen-min jih-pao*, September 20, 1956.

———. "Problems of Setting the Planned Production Quotas for 1958," *Hsin-hua pan-yueh k'an*, 17 (September, 1957), 206–208.

———. "Report on the Results of the 1956 Plan and on the Plan for 1957," *Jen-min jih-pao*, July 2, 1957.

———. "Report to the National Conference of Model Agricultural Workers," *Jen-min jih-pao*, February 24, 1957.

———. Reports on the State Budget: (1) "The Planned Budget for 1950," *Jen-min jih-pao*, December 4, 1949; (2) "The Estimated Results of the 1951 Budget and the Planned Budget for 1952," *ibid.* (August 11, 1952); (3) "The Estimated Results of the 1952 Budget and the Planned Budget for 1953," *ibid.* (March 16, 1953).

State Economic Commission. "Major Changes in the Tabulation Forms for National Economic Planning for 1958," *Chi-hua ching-chi (Planned Economy)*, 8 (August, 1957), pp. 24–27.

State Planning Commission, "Results and Achievements of the First Five Year Plan," *Jen-min jih-pao*, October 1, 1957.

(Madame) Sun Yat-sen. "[Soviet Aid is] Practically a Gift," *Jen-min jih-pao*, February 14, 1955.

Teng Hsiao-ping. "Report on the Planned Budget for 1954," *Jen-min jih-pao*, June 17, 1954.

Teng Tzu-hui. "Report at the National Conference of Model Agricultural Workers on Agricultural Development," *Jen-min jih-pao*, February 22, 1957.

T'eng Tai-yuan. "Report on the Development of Railways," in *1956 Jen-min shou-tse (People's Handbook for 1956)*, pp. 206–208.

Yeh Chi-chuang. "Report on China's Foreign Trade for 1956," *Hsin-hua pan-yueh-k'an*, 16 (August, 1957), pp. 90–94.

———. "Report on China's Foreign Trade for 1954," *Jen-min jih-pao*, July 30, 1955.

D. State Statistical Bureau:

1. Annual Communiqués

Annual communiqués on the previous year's achievements or on the results of the previous year's plan: (1) For 1952 (revised), *Jen-min jih-pao*, September 28, 1954; (2) For 1953, *ibid.*, September 16, 1954; (3) For 1954, *ibid.*, September 23, 1955; (4) For 1955, *ibid.*, June 15, 1956; (5) For 1956, *ibid.*, August 2, 1957.

2. Special Releases

"Economic Statistical Abstract," *Hsin-hua pan-yueh-k'an*, 17 (September, 1956), pp. 39–50.

"Results of the National Population Census," *Jen-min jih-pao*, November 11, 1954.

"Statistical Abstract of the Economic, Cultural and Educational Achievements, 1949–1954," *Hsin-hua yueh-pao*, 11 (November, 1955), pp. 181–189.

3. Statistical Surveys

"A General Survey of Socialist Industrialization in China," *Hsin-hua pan-yueh-k'an*, 2 (January, 1957), pp. 54–62.

"A National Survey of the Composition and Distribution of the Labor Force in 1955," *Hsin-hua pan-yueh-k'an*, 2 (January, 1957), pp. 87–88.

"A National Survey of Farm Animals for 1956," *Hsin-hua pan-yueh-k'an*, 1 (January, 1957), pp. 88–90.

"A Survey of Market Prices in China for 1956," *Hsin-hua pan-yueh-k'an*, 10 (May, 1957), pp. 114–115.

"A Survey of the Development of China's Commercial Network and of the Situation in 1955," *Hsin-hua pan-yueh-k'an*, 24 (December, 1956), pp. 80–83.

"A Survey of the Development of State Capitalism in Industry in China," *Hsin-hua pan-yueh-k'an*, 2 (January, 1957), 66–70.

"A Survey of the Income of Agricultural Producers' Cooperatives in 1955 and its Distribution," *Hsin-hua pan-yueh-k'an*, 24 (December, 1956), 63–65.

"Achievements in Socialist Construction and Socialist Transformation in the First Half of 1956," *T'ung-chi kung-tso t'ung-hsin (Statistical Bulletin)*, 15 (August, 1956), 5–6 and 26.

"Several Problems of China's Socialist Industrialization," *Hsin-hua pan-yueh-k'an*, 1 (January, 1957), 67–71.

"The Basic Situation of China's Construction Enterprises," *T'ung-chi kung-tso t'ung-hsin (Statistical Bulletin)*, 24 (December, 1956), 31–33.

"The Basic Situation of Planned Purchase and Planned Supply of Food Grains in China," *T'ung-chi kung-tso (Statistical Work)*, 19 (October, 1957), 31–32, and 28.

"The Scope and Development of China's Basic Construction Investment,"

T'ung-chi kung-tso t'ung-hsin (Statistical Bulletin), 18 (September, 1956), 4–6.
"The Technological Level of Industrial Production in China," *Hsin-hua pan-yueh-k'an*, 12 (June, 1957), 115–118.
4. Work Papers:
"Diverse Opinions on the Methods of Computing the Gross Industrial Value Product," *T'ung-chi kung-tso t'ung-hsin (Statistical Bulletin)*, 24 (December, 1956), 5–10.
"Explanations of Certain Problems Arising from the Computation of 1957 Constant Prices for Industrial Products," *T'ung-chi kung-tso (Statistical Work)*, 10 (October, 1957), 11–13.
"Materials on Methods of Computing the Gross Industrial Value Product," *T'ung-chi kung tso t'ung-hsin (Statistical Bulletin)*, 17 (September, 1956), 2–5.
"Several Problems of Computing the Gross Industrial Value Product," *T'ung-chi kung-tso t'ung-hsin (Statistical Bulletin)*, 17 (September, 1956), 1–2.
E. NEWSPAPERS:
Jen-min jih-pao (People's Daily). The official newspaper of the Chinese Communist party, containing current government policy statements, economic reports, and statistical releases.
Kuang-ming jih-pao (Kuang Ming Daily), interested primarily in cultural and educational subjects.
Kung-jen jih-pao (Workers' Daily), the official newspaper of the All-China Federation of Labor.
Ta Kung Pao (Impartial Daily), Tientsin-Peiping. Formerly the most influential independent newspaper in the country; strong interest in economic subjects.
F. JOURNALS AND MAGAZINES:
Chi-hua ching-chi (Planned Economy), monthly. The official publication of the State Economic Commission and State Planning Commission.
Ching-chi yen-chiu (Economic Research), bimonthly. The journal of the Economic Research Institute of the Chinese Academy of Sciences. First issue, February, 1955.
Hsin chien-she (New Construction), monthly. Published by *Kuang-ming jih-pao*; interested in social sciences and cultural subjects.
Hsin-hua pan-yueh-k'an (New China Semimonthly), beginning in January, 1956, succeeding the *New China Monthly*. An official publication of the Chinese Communist party. Chiefly a repository of important government directives and selected articles on politics, economics, culture, and international relations, already published elsewhere in the periodical literature.
Hsin-hua yueh-pao (New China Monthly). See preceding item.
Hsueh-hsi (Study). Monthly up to the end of 1956, then semimonthly. Apparently a publication for Chinese Communist party members and government employees.
Jen-min shou-ts'e (People's Handbook), Tientsin-Peiping, 1950, 1951, 1952, 1953, 1955, 1956, and 1957. A yearbook published by *Ta Kung Pao*. A convenient collection of documents, official reports, and statistics.
T'ung-chi Kung-tso (Statistical Work), semimonthly, beginning January, 1957. Official publication of the State Statistical Bureau.
T'ung-chi kung-tso t'ung-hsin (Statistical Bulletin), semimonthly up to the end of 1956, and succeeded by *T'ung-chi kung-tso (Statistical Work)*.
G. BOOKS:
Academy of Sciences, Institute of Economic Research. *Kuo-min ching-chi*

hui-fu shih-ch'i nung-yeh sheng-ch'an-ho-tso tzu-liao hui-pien, 1949–1952 (Collection of Materials on Agricultural Producers' Coöperation during the Period of Rehabilitation of the National Economy, 1949–1952). Peiping: June, 1957. 2 vols.

Ch'iao Chi-ming. *Chung-kuo nung-ts'un she-hui ching-chi-hsueh (Chinese Rural-Economics)*. Chungking: 1945.

Fang Wei-chung. *Ti-i-ko wu-nien-chi-hua chieh-shuo (Explanations of the First Five Year Plan)*. Peiping: 1955.

Huang Chen Ming and Huang Jun-t'ing. *Ts'ung chung-su ching-chi ho-tso k'an chung-su jen-min wei-ta yu-i (Looking at the Great Sino-Soviet Friendship through Sino-Soviet Economic Coöperation)*. Peiping: October, 1956.

Ou Pao-san, et al. *Chung-kuo kuo-min-so-te (China's National Income)*. Shanghai: 1947. 2 vols.

Peh Tuan-hsi. *Kai-tsao tzu-pen chu-i kung-shang-yeh ti tao-lu (The Road to Transforming Capitalist Industry and Trade)*. Peiping: July, 1956.

San-nien-lai hsin-chung-kuo ching-chi ti cheng-chiu (New China's Economic Achievements in the Past Three Years). Peiping: October, 1952.

Ti-i wu-nien-chi-hua chiang-hua (Talks on the First Five Year Plan). Prepared by the Editorial Board of *Ta Kung Pao*, Peiping: 1955.

H. ARTICLES:

Chang Hao-yen. "The Load on the Shoulders of the Peasants," *Hsueh-hsi (Study)*, 16 (August, 1957), 16–17.

Chang Hsing-fu ."The Road and Method of China's Industrialization," *Kung-jen jih-pao (Workers' Daily)*, May 23, 1957.

Chang P'ei-kang, Mao Kang, and Hu Chun-chieh. "The Socialist Law of Population and the Chinese Population Problem," *Ching-chi yen-chiu (Economic Research)*, 4 (August, 1957), 30–63.

Chang Shih. "An Important Problem in the System of Rationalized Transport of Coal," *Chi-hua ching-chi (Planned Economy)*, 10 (October, 1957), 24–25.

Chang Shih-hung. "The Need for Self-governing Authority in Enterprises," *Jen-min jih-pao*, November 6, 1956.

Chang Wei-ta. "The Methods of Calculating the Depreciation Rate of Fixed Assets Employed in Production," *Ching-chi yen-chiu (Economic Research)*, 3 (June, 1956), 99–112.

Ch'and Sun and Wang En-yung. "A Brief Discussion about the Fixed Assets of Industrial Enterprises and Their Depreciation," *Ching-chi yen-chiu (Economic Research)*, 5 (October, 1956), 69–78.

Chao Ch'ing-hsin. "Seasonal Variations of the Market after Agricultural Coöperation," *Ching-chi yen-chiu (Economic Research)*, 5 (October, 1956), 19–38.

———. "A Preliminary Study of the Opening of the Free Market under State Direction," *ibid.*, 3 (June, 1957), 78–99.

Chao Hsueh. "Mechanization of Chinese Agriculture," *Chi-hua ching-chi (Planned Economy)*, 4 April, 1957), 16–18.

Chao I-wen. "The Process of Socialist Transformation of China's Capitalistic Industry," *Hsin-hua pan-yueh-k'an*, 2 (January, 1957), 62–66.

Chen Cheng-jen. "The Problems of Agricultural Coöperation and Production," *Hsin-hua pan-yueh-k'an*, 7 (April, 1957), 20–26.

Chen Ta. "Birth Control, Deferred Marriage, and China's Population Problem," *Hsin-chien-she (New Construction)*, 5 (May, 1957), 1–15.

Cheng Kang-ling. "Summarizing the Experience of Labor-Force and Wage Planning for 1956," *Chi-hua ching-chi (Planned Economy)*, 8 (August, 1957), 9–13.

Cheng Sung-shen and Lo Lai-yuen. "The Present Problem of Urban Housing in China," *Ta Kung Pao (Impartial Daily)*, March 3, 1957.

Ch'eng Tzu-hua. "The Development of Supply and Selling Coöperatives in the Past Five Years," *Ta Kung Pao (Impartial Daily)*, September 24, 1954.

Chi Ch'ung-wei. "How to Make China's Industry Develop Evenly," *Chi-hua ching-chi (Planned Economy)*, 7 (July, 1957), 4–8.

Chi Ch'ung-wei. "Industry Should Assist Agricultural Development," *Chi-hua ching-chi (Planned Economy)*, 10 (October, 1957, 7–10.

Ch'i Hua. "To Develop Transportation According to the Needs of Agricultural Production," *Chi-hua ching-chi (Planned Economy)*, 10 (October, 1957), 17–20.

Chia Fu. "The Rate of Economic Development under the Second Five Year Plan," *Hsin-hua pan-yueh-k'an*, 24 (December, 1956), 40–42.

Chin Ch'ao. "Proper Rectification of the Contradiction between the Supply and Demand of Food Grains," *Hsueh-hsi (Study)*, 19 (October, 1957), 16–17.

Chin Fu-hsiang. "Diverse Means to Solve the Problem of Insufficient Varieties in Rolled-Steel Production," *Chi-hua ching-chi (Planned Economy)*, 9 (September, 1957), 15–17.

Ching Lin. "The Proportionate Relationship between the Iron and Steel Industry and Machine-making Industry," *Chi-hua ching-chi (Planned Economy)*, 9 (September, 1957), 11–15.

Ching Wei. "The Problems of Textile Production in 1957," *Chi-hua ching-chi (Planned Economy)*, 5 (May, 1957), 5–7 and 19.

Chu Cheng-ping. "Production and Consumption under the First and Second Five Year Plans," *Hsin-chien-she (New Construction)*, 101 (February 1957), 1–6.

Ch'u Ch'ing and Chu Chung-chien. "Variations in the Commodity Turnover in China's Rural Markets," *Ching-chi yen-chiu (Economic Research)*, 3 (June, 1957), 100–126.

Fan Jo-i. "The Pricing Policy of Products of Heavy Industry," *Ching-chi yen-chiu (Economic Research)*, 3 (June, 1957), 54–67.

Ho Wei. "Discussion of the Economic Contradiction between the State and the Peasants," *Hsueh-hsi (Study)*, 12 (June, 1957), 22–26.

———. "The Meaning and Method of Comparing the Current Agricultural Prices with Those of the 1930's," *Hsueh-hsi (Study)*, 7 (April, 1957), 15–17 and 21.

———. "The Real Nature of the Rightist Opposition to the Policy of State Monopoly in Purchases and Sales," *Hsueh-hsi (Study)*, 14 (July, 1957), 14–16.

Hsiao Kung-yu. "The Principles of Wage Increases," *Hsueh-hsi (Study)*, 15 (August, 1957), 17–18.

Hsiao Yu. "Proper Allocation of Agricultural Investment," *Chi-hua ching-chi (Planned Economy)*, 9 (September, 1957), 5–8.

Hsieh Mu-ch'iao. "Discussing Again the Planned Economy and the Law of Value," *Hsin-hua pan-yueh-k'an*, 9 (May, 1957), 135–137.

———. "How to Strengthen and Improve Statistical Work on Basic Construction," *T'ung-chi kung-tso t'ung-hsin (Statistical Bulletin)*, 6 (March, 1956), 7–9.

Hsieh Shu-an. "An Opinion on the Question of Apportioning the Investment in Water Conservation," *Chi-hua ching-chi (Planned Economy)*, 10 (October, 1957), 23–24.

Hua Shu. "Has Agricultural Development in China been Rapid or Slow?," *Jen-min jih-pao*, January 8–9, 1957.

Huang Meng-fan. "Agricultural Production Statistics," *Tung-chi kung-tso t'ung-hsin (Statistical Bulletin)*, 12 (June, 1956), 30–33.

I Lin. "The Problem of Maximizing the Results of Industrial Investment,"
    Chi-hua ching-chi (Planned Economy), 6 (June, 1957), 5–7 and 15.

Kang Wei-chung. "Why must State-directed Food Markets be Established in
    Rural Areas?," *Jen-min jih-pao*, March 19, 1955.

Kao Kuang-chien. "The Recent Development of the Chemical Industry,"
    Kung-jen jih-pao (Workers' Daily), September 30, 1957.

Ko Chih-ta. "The Nature of China's National Budget and Its Role in the
    Transition Period," *Ching-chi yen-chiu (Economic Research)*, 3 (June,
    1956), 67–80.

Ko Chu-po and Liu Hsiang. "The Planning of the Development of China's
    Secondary and Primary Education," *Chi-hua ching-chi (Planned Economy)*,
    10 (October, 1957), 21–22 and 27.

Ku To-ching. "Tabulation Forms for Municipal Utilities," *Chi-hua ching-chi
    (Planned Economy)*, 7 (July, 1957), 31–33.

Kuan Ta-t'ung. "Changes in the Class Relationships During the Transitional
    Period in China," *Hsin-hua pan-yueh-k'an*, 2 (January, 1957), 119–122.
——. "The Problems of Peaceful Transformation of Capitalist Enterprises,"
    Ching-chi yen-chiu (Economic Research), 2 (April, 1956), 40–53.

Kung Chien-yao. "The Method of Computing the Harvest Rate," *T'ung-chi
    kung-tso t'ung-hsin (Statistical Bulletin)*, 6 (March, 1956), 16–18.

Lee, Franklin C. H. "A Comparison Between 1926 and 1956 of the Family
    Living Conditions in the Villages Around Peiping," *Hsin-hua pan-yueh-
    k'an*, 5 (March, 1957), 66–71.

Li Jui. "China's Water Power Potential and the Advantages of Building Hy-
    draulic Power Stations," *Jen-min jih-pao*, December 12, 1955.

Li Keng-hsin. "About the Different Ways of Distributing Producer Goods in
    China," *Chi-hua ching-chi (Planned Economy)*, 8 (August, 1957), 18–22.

Li Po-kuan. "Income Distribution Among Members of Agricultural Collec-
    tives," *Hsin chien-she (New Construction)*, 7 (July, 1957), 1–5.

Li Yueh. "The Need for Readjusting the Unreasonable Welfare Subsidies,"
    Chi-hua ching-chi (Planned Economy), 12 (December, 1957), 15–17 and 3.

Li Yung. "Tabulation Forms for the Planning of Construction and Installa-
    tion," *Chi-hua ching-chi (Planned Economy)*, 6 (June, 1957), 28–31.

Liang Ming and Ts'ao Yen. "A New Type of Food Market," *Jen-min jih-pao*,
    February 5, 1955.

Liao Chi-lih. "Accelerating Agricultural Development: A Condition for Ac-
    celerating the Development of Heavy Industry," *Chi-hua ching-chi (Planned
    Economy)*, 8 (August, 1957), 4–6.

Liao Hsien-hao. "Tabulation Forms for Agricultural Production Planning,"
    Chi-hua ching-chi (Planned Economy), 4 (April, 1957), 30–33.

Lin Chung-fan. "The State Assistance to the Peasants," *Kung-jen jih-pao
    (Workers' Daily)*, September 21, 1957.

Liu Ching-fan. "Natural Resources of China," *Hsin-hua pan-yueh-k'an*, 17
    (September, 1957), 49–51.

Liu Hsien-kao. "Tabulation Forms for the Planning of Agricultural Produc-
    tion," *Chi-hua ching-chi (Planned Economy)*, 4 (April, 1957), 30–33.

Liu Shui-hua. "An Exploration of the Problem of Delegating Authority to the
    Lower Levels Regarding the Government Supply of Centralized Controlled
    Commodities," *Chi-hua ching-chi (Planned Economy)*, 8 (August, 1957),
    22–23 and 29.

Liu Wen. "Drive for Overfulfillment of the Lumber Production Plan for
    1957," *Chi-hua ching-chi (Planned Economy)*, 5 (May, 1957), 8–9.

Lo Wen and Shang-kuan Chang-chun. "The Problem of Irrigation of Agri-
    cultural Fields," *Chi-hua ching-chi (Planned Economy)*, 10 (October, 1957),
    15–17.

Ma Chi-k'ung, Hsieh Cheng-siu, and Kuo Tzu-ch'eng. "Rectify the Capitalist Rightists' Contempt for Planned Economy," *Chi-hua ching-chi (Planned Economy)*, 10 (October, 1957), 3–6.

Ma Yin-ch'u. "A Realistic Interpretation of the Theory of General Equilibrium and the Law of Proportionate Development," *Jen-min jih-pao*, December 28–29, 1956.

———. "A New Theory of Population," *Hsin-hua pan-yueh-k'an*, 15 (August, 1957), 34–41.

Nan Ping. "Breaking the Two Poisoned Darts of the Rightists," *Hsueh-hsi (Study)*, 19 (October, 1957), 18–19.

Nan Ping and Soh Chen. "The Pricing Problem of Producers' Goods," *Ching-chi yen-chiu (Economic Research)*, 2 (April, 1957), 12–24.

Niu Chung-huang. "Accumulation and Consumption in China's National Income," *Hsueh-hsi (Study)*, 16 (August, 1957), 20–23.

———. "The Problem of Calculating Labor Productivity and Wage Levels," *Hsueh-hsi (Study)*, 9 (May, 1957), 5–6.

Peng Yung-ch'uan. "Tabulation Forms for Basic Construction Planning," *Chi-hua ching-chi (Planned Economy)*, 5 (May, 1957), 29–33.

Sha Ying. "The Relationship between Coastal and Inland Industries," *Jen-min jih-pao*, November 24, 1956.

Sun Chung-ta. "The Several Forms of State-Capitalist Trade," *Jen-min jih-pao*, May 15, 1955.

Sung Hai-wen. "The Problem of Retained Plots in Agricultural Producers' Coöperatives," *Ching-chi yen-chiu (Economic Research)*, 4 (August, 1957), 7–17.

Sung Ping. "The Principle of Income Distribution According to Labor Spent," *Chi-hua ching-chi (Planned Economy)*, 5 (May, 1957), 1–4.

———. "The Problem of Employment," *Hsueh-hsi (Study)*, 12 (June, 1957), 25–28.

Sung Shao-wen. "The Principle of Diligence and Economy in Basic Economic Construction," *Hsueh-hsi (Study)*, 11 (June, 1957), 22–24.

———. "Several Problems of the Movement for Increasing Industrial Production and Economizing," *Kung-jen jih-pao (Workers' Daily)*, February 26, 1957.

Ta Sun. "The Meaning and Method of Studying Comparative Prices for Agricultural Products," *Ta Kung Pao (Impartial Daily)*, August 18, 1957.

T'an Chen-lin. "A Study of the Income and Level of Living of the Chinese Peasants," *Hsin-hua pan-yueh-k'an*, 11 (June, 1957), 105–111.

Teng Shuang. "Introducing the National Agricultural Exhibition," *Hsin-hua pan-yueh-k'an*, 8 (April, 1957), 91–98.

Ti Ching-hsiang. "Increase Sugar Output for the People," *Ta Kung Pao (Impartial Daily)*, January 5, 1958.

Tien Lin. "Seven Years of Achievement: A Supplement," *Hsin-hua pan-yueh-k'an*, 15 (August, 1957), 158–161.

Ts'ao Yen-hsing. "Municipal Construction in Accordance with the Principle of Diligence and Economy," *Chi-hua ching-chi (Planned Economy)*, 12 (December, 1957), 4–9.

Tseng Ling. "Is There Inflation in China at the Present?," *Ching-chi yen-chiu (Economic Research)*, 5 (October, 1957), 36–49.

———. "The Rural Market in the Surging Tide of Agricultural Collectivization," *Ching-chi yen-chiu (Economic Research)*, 2 (April, 1956), 1–29.

———. "The Economic Meaning of Potato Production under Different Social Systems," *Ching-chi yen-chiu (Economic Research)*, 5 (May, 1958), 39–44.

Tzu Yao-hua and Mi Tsan-ch'en. "Promoting National Savings," *Jen-min jih-pao*, March 25, 1957.

Tung Chih-fu. "Why has Handicraft Paper Production Declined?," *Jen-min jih-pao*, November 11, 1956.

Tung Hsin. "China's Achievements in Industrial Production," *Kung-jen jih-pao (Workers' Daily)*, September 13–14, 1957.

Wang Cheng-yao. "The Incidence of China's Taxes During the Transition Period," *Ching-chi yen-chiu (Economic Research)*, 2 (April, 1957), 62–79.

Wang Chien-chen. "Evaluation of People's Living Conditions through Price Indices," *Ta Kung Pao (Impartial Daily)*, September 24, 1957.

Wang Ching-yu. "Six and Sixty Years: the Past and Present Development of the Textile Industry," *Jen-min jih-pao*, July 13, 1956.

Wang Hsing-fu and Nan Chien-chao. "Develop the Chemical Industry," *Chi-hua ching-chi (Planned Economy)*, 10 (October, 1957), 11–15.

Wang Hung-ting. "The Nature of Special Companies for Joint Operation," *Hsin Chien-she (New Construction)*, 2 (February, 1957), 12–16.

Wang Kuang-wei. "A Suggestion on the Allocation of the Agricultural Labor Force for the Second Five Year Plan," *Chi-hua ching-chi (Planned Economy)*, 8 (August, 1957), 6–9.

Wang Nai-kuang and Shan Tung. "The Method of Estimating Population Increase in Long-term Planning," *Chi-hua ching-chi (Planned Economy)*, 5 (May, 1957), 22–23.

Wang Pao-jen. "The Development of China's Economic and Commercial Relations with Asian and African Countries," *Jen-min jih-pao*, October 11, 1956.

Wang shu-ch'un. "The Question of Apportioning Investment in Water Conservation," *Chi-hua ching-chi (Planned Economy)*, 5 (May, 1957), 14–15.

Wang Si-hua. "The Rapid Development of China's Socialist Industrialization," *Ching-chi yen-chiu (Economic Research)*, 4 (August, 1956), 11–22.

———. "The Mutual Adjustment between Industrialization and Agricultural Coöperative Movement in the Transition Period," *ibid.*, 1 (February, 1956), 5–18.

Wang Tzu-ying. "China's National Finance," *Ta Kung Pao (Impartial Daily)*, January 27, 1955.

———. "The Experience and Lessons Gained from Compiling and Administering the 1956 National Budget," *Hsin-hua pan-yueh-k'an*, 5 (March, 1957), 91–93.

Wang Wei-ts'ai. "To Further Develop People's Deposits," *Jen-min jih-pao*, March 3, 1955.

Wang Wen-ting and P'eng Wei-ts'ai. "Reform of the Taxation System has to be Taken in Two Steps," *Ta Kung Pao (Impartial Daily)*, August 11, 1957.

Wei I. "The Problem of Agricultural Investment under the First Five Year Plan," *Jen-min jih-pao*, August 19, 1955.

Wu Ching-ch'ao. "A New Approach to the Chinese Population Problem," *Hsin chien-she (New Construction)*, 102 (March, 1957), 1–9.

Wu, Ch'ing-yu. "Is the Socialist State Bank a Government Agency or an Enterprise?," *Hsueh-hsi (Study)*, 2 (January, 1957), 8.

Wu Shih. "An Exploration of the Food Problem during the Period of Transition," *Hsin-hua pan-yueh-k'an*, 10 (May, 1957), 104–109.

Wu Ting-ch'eng. "Explanation of Certain Problems Related to the Proposal for Computing the Social Purchasing Power," *Chi-hua ching-chi (Planned Economy)*, 9 (September, 1957), 27–29.

Wu Tsiang. "The Development of State Capitalism in the Initial Stage of the Transition Period," *Ching-chi yen-chiu (Economic Research)*, 1 (February, 1956), 84–116.

———. "The Transition from Capitalist Economy to State-Capitalist Economy," *ibid.*, 2 (April, 1956), 54–99.

Yang Ch'ing-wen. "Two Problems of Industrial Location," *Chi-hua ching-chi (Planned Economy),* 8 (August, 1957), 13–15.

Yang I-po. "An Explanation of the Proportion between Consumption and Accumulation in China's National Income," *Hsueh-hsi (Study),* 20 (October, 1957), 24–26.

Yang Pei-hsin. "The Problem of Accumulation of Funds for the First Five Year Plan," *Ching-chi yen-chiu (Economic Research),* 4 (October, 1955), 12–35.

Yang Po. "Has the Peasants' Level of Living been Raised or Lowered?" *Kung-jen jih-pao (Workers' Daily),* September 12, 1957.

———. "Planned Purchase and Planned Supply and the Socialist Construction," *Ching-chi yen-chiu (Economic Research),* 1 (February, 1956), 33–42.

———. "Preliminary Analysis of the Process of Socialist Transformation of Private Trade in China," *T'ung-chi kung-tso t'ung-hsin (Statistical Bulletin),* 15 (August, 1956), 7–10.

———. "An Understanding of the Proportion between Consumption and Accumulation in the Disposal of China's National Income," *Hsueh-hsi (Study),* 20 (October, 1957), 24–26.

Yeh Chien-yun. "Changes in the Living Conditions of An Industrial Worker's Family," *Jen-min jih-pao,* April 20–21, 1957.

Yeh Feng. "How to Compile Properly the Educational, Cultural and Health Plan for 1958," *Chi-hua ching-chi (Planned Economy),* 9 (September, 1957), 18–19.

Yen Ts'ui-yu. "The Standard of Fixed Assets and the Authority of the Enterprises," *Chi-hua ching-chi (Planned Economy),* 6 (June, 1957), 23.

Tu Tsing-chuan. "Development of Hydroelectric Power in China," *Hsin-hua pan-yueh-k'an,* 15 (August, 1957), 16–17.

Yueh Wei. "The Method of Computing National Income," *Ching-chi yen-chiu (Economic Research),* 3 (August, 1956), 48–66.

———. "On the Methods of Estimation and Interpolation, *T'ung-chi kung-tso t'ung-hsin (Statistical Bulletin),* 18 (September, 1956), 25–27.

I. EDITORIALS:

"Carry Through the Principle of Diligence and Economy in National Construction," *Chi-hua ching-chi (Planned Economy),* 12 (December, 1957), 1–3.

"Industrial Development Requires Simultaneous Development of Agriculture," *Chi-hua ching-chi (Planned Economy),* 10 (October, 1957), 1–2.

"The Need for Birth Control," *Jen-min jih-pao,* March 5, 1957.

"People's Livelihood Can Only Be Improved Gradually," *Jen-min jih-pao,* November 27, 1956.

"The Proper Understanding of the Present Problem and Difficulties of People's Livelihood," *Ta Kung Pao (Impartial Daily),* December 14, 1956.

"Repel the Rightist's Attack on the System of Planned Economy," *Chi-hua ching-chi (Planned Economy),* 8 (August, 1957), 1–3.

"Rightist Ta Chen Plots to Eliminate the Communist Party," *Kuang-ming jih-pao (Kuang Ming Daily),* September 10, 1957.

J. EDITORIAL SECTION:

"A National Survey of the Labor Force and Wages in 1956," *Chi-hua ching-chi,* No. 3, 1957, reprinted in *Hsin-hua pan-yueh-k'an,* 10 (May, 1957), 115–116 and 74.

"State Economic Support of the Agricultural Economy," *Jen-min jih-pao,* September 14, 1957.

II. ENGLISH-LANGUAGE SOURCES

A. GOVERNMENT PUBLICATIONS:

Government of India, Ministry of Commerce and Industry. Department of

Industrial Statistics. *Report on the Seventh Census of Indian Manufactures, 1952.* New Delhi: 1955.

———. Ministry of Finance. Department of Economic Affairs. *Final Report of the National Income Committee, February 1954.* New Delhi: 1954.

———. Ministry of Food and Agriculture. *Report of the Indian Delegation to China on Agricultural Planning and Techniques.* New Delhi: July–August, 1956.

———. Planning Commission. *Second Five Year Plan.* New Delhi: 1956.

U. S. International Cooperation Administration. *Survey of East–West Trade in 1955.* Washington: October, 1956.

———. *The Strategic Trade Control System, 1948–1956.* Washington: June, 1957.

B. United Nations Publications:

United Nations. *Direction of International Trade.* Statistical Papers Series T. Vol. VIII, No. 7, New York: October 16, 1957. A joint publication of the United Nations (Statistical Office), International Monetary Fund, and International Bank for Reconstruction and Development.

———. Department of Social Affairs, Population Division. *The Determinants and Consequences of Population Trends.* New York: 1953.

———. Economic Commission for Asia and the Far East. *Economic Survey of Asia and the Far East, 1956.* Bangkok: 1957.

C. Books:

Adler, Solomon. *The Chinese Economy.* London: Routledge and Kegan Paul, 1957.

Bergson, Abram. *Soviet National Income and Product in 1937.* New York: Columbia University Press, 1953.

Buck, John Lossing. *The Chinese Farm Economy.* Chicago: University of Chicago Press, 1930.

Chang, P'ei-kang. *Agriculture and Industrialization.* Cambridge: Harvard University Press, 1949.

Chen, Ta. *Population in Modern China.* Chicago: University of Chicago Press, 1946.

Cheng, Yu-kwei. *Foreign Trade and Industrial Development of China.* Washington: University Press of Washington, D.C., 1956.

Gerschenkron, Alexander. *A Dollar Index of Soviet Machinery Output, 1927–28 to 1937.* Santa Monica, California: Rand Corporation, 1951.

Holzman, Franklyn D. *Soviet Taxation: The Fiscal and Monetary Problems of a Planned Economy.* Cambridge: Harvard University Press, 1955.

Jasny, Naum. *The Socialized Agriculture of the U.S.S.R.; Plans and Performance.* Stanford: Stanford University Press, 1949.

Leibenstein, Harvey. *Economic Backwardness and Economic Growth.* New York: Wiley, 1957.

Lieu, D. K. *China's Economic Stabilization and Reconstruction.* New Brunswick: Rutgers University Press, 1948.

Liu, Ta-chung. *China's National Income, 1931–36: An Exploration Study.* Washington: Brookings, 1946.

Rostow, W. W., et al. *The Prospects for Communist China.* Cambridge: Technology Press of Massachusetts Institute of Technology, 1954.

Wu, Yuan-li. *An Economic Survey of Communist China.* New York: Bookman Associates, 1956.

D. Articles:

Biehl, Max. "The West and Trade with China," *Far Eastern Economic Review,* XXII (February 14, 1957), 208–211.

Hoffman, M. L. "Problem of East–West Trade," *International Conciliation,* Carnegie Endowment for International Peace, No. 511 (January, 1957), 257–308.

Jasny, Naum. "Intricacies of Russian National Income Statistics," *Journal of Political Economy,* IV (August, 1947), 299–322.

Kaser, M. C. "Estimating the Soviet National Income," *Economic Journal,* LXVII (March, 1957), 83–104.

Nove, A. " '1926/7' and All That," *Soviet Studies,* IX, 2 (October, 1957), 117–130.

Kuznets, Simon. "Proportion of Capital Formation to National Product," *Proceedings,* American Economic Association (May, 1952), 507–526.

———. "National Income and Industrial Structure," *Econometrica,* XVII, Supplement (July, 1949), 205–241.

Shabad, T. "Counting 600 Million Chinese," *Far Eastern Survey,* XXV, 4 (April, 1956), 58–62.

Sun, Ching-chih. "Food Resources and Population Growth," *People's China,* V (May, 1956), 4–10.

E. MISCELLANEOUS:

China Handbook 1950, New York: Rockport Press, 1950.

Twanmo, Chong. *Production of Food Crops in Mainland China: Prewar and Postwar.* Santa Monica, California: Rand Corporation, 1956. (Mimeographed.)

III. JAPANESE- AND RUSSIAN-LANGUAGE SOURCES:

"The Development of China's Export Capacity," *Ajia Keizai Jumpo (Asia Economic Bulletin),* Tokyo, 316 (March, 1957), 6–13.

Krotevich, S. "Vsekitaiskaia perepis' naseleniia 1953 g." (The All-China Population Census of 1953), *Vestnik Statistiki (Bulletin of Statistics),* Moscow, V (September–October, 1955), 31–50.

Ma, Nai-shu [sic]. "Vneshniaia Torgovlia Kitaiskoi narodnoi respubliki" (Foreign Trade of the People's Republic of China), *Vneshniaia Torgovlia (Foreign Trade),* Moscow, V (May, 1956), 8–13.

Index

Afforestation, 54, 60, 67, 74
Africa, 186, 187, 189, 190, 194, 258
Air transportation, 170n, 236
Albania, 169n
Animal raising (*see also* Livestock): defined, 56; 59, 60, 67, 69–70, 71–72, 74, 76, 87, 113n, 248, 249, 257
Anshan, 11, 49, 51, 52, 203
Accumulation
    national: capital formation and, 113
        components, 113–114
        defined, 80
        rate, 114–115, 118, 139, 206
    private: agriculture, 133–135
        industry, 14, 126, 150–151
        the public, 156
Administration, government, 102–106, 151
Agricultural Bank, 131n, 133n, 146n
Agricultural collective (*see also* Collectivization of agriculture)
    accumulation, 113, 133–135, 139, 221
    cost of production, 87, 134
    defined, 17
    development, 16, 23, 243, 244
    livestock, 69–70
    lots retained by peasants, 17n, 22n
    productivity, 68n
    size, 68
    statistical reporting, 63
    welfare reserves, 210
Agricultural credit, 67, 69, 131–133, 163, 166
Agricultural primary producers' coöperative
    defined, 12–13
    development, 16, 243, 244
    net savings, 133–135
Agricultural value product
    coverage, 59
    defined, 56, 61
    gross factor, 57
    growth, 9, 55–61, 86–89, 106, 130, 134, 227, 242, 257
    industrial value product and, 30, 34–35, 109–111
    net, how derived, 76

    pricing, 56, 108, 109
    valuation problem, 57
Agricultural year, 58, 59, 65, 135–136, 165, 178–179, 219–220
Agriculture (*see also* Collectivization of agriculture)
    area, 60, 64, 66–67, 68, 71, 73–74, 204, 245, 257
    defined, 55–56
    development program, 65–68, 70–71, 219, 221
    effect on capital formation, 135–136, 219
    on light industry, 48–49, 51n, 219
    on the whole economy, 219–220
    food drive, 68, 71
    growth rate, 55, 61, 71–74, 108, 220–221
    investment, 9–10, 53–54, 66, 67, 69, 71, 117, 130–135, 139, 221–222
    mechanization, 8, 62, 249, 250
    population growth and, 204–205
    production, 60, 246
    relative importance, 30–35, 39, 109–111
    socialization, 16–17, 243, 244
    statistics: Indian Delegation's observations, 62–64
    nature, 64–65, 198
    yield, 60n, 62, 63, 67, 68, 71, 247
Asia, 186, 189, 190, 194, 258
Atomic reactor pile, 169n
Australia, 188n–189n

Balance of international payments
    defined, 179, 184, 185n
    estimate, 179–185
    freight and insurance, 179, 189–190
    grants to foreign countries, 183, 184, 185n
    imports and exports, 178, 184
    interests on foreign debts, 170–171, 180, 184
    national income and, 80, 85, 107, 182, 185n
    official data, 176

overseas-Chinese remittances, 85, 107, 179, 180–182, 184
remittances of foreign businesses and immigrants, 13n, 85, 107, 182
repayments of foreign loans, 179, 180, 184
settling agency, 145
Soviet credits, 147, 171–173, 184
Bank check, uses of, 155, 156
Bank deposits
rural, 158
savings, 113, 131n, 146n
total, 155–156
Banking and finance
investment, 9
national income and, 79
net value product, 102–105
socialization, 14, 146n
system (*see also* People's Bank and Credit Coöperatives), 146n
Basic construction investment (*see* Investment)
Basic construction unit, defined, 11n
Black market, 22, 24, 28, 213, 215, 216
Bonds
accumulation and, 113
issues and terms, 151, 152, 258
peasants' purchases, 130
policy, 151
servicing, 151, 180, 181
Budget, state
balance: meaning, 144–145, 146
net, 146, 164, 258
note circulation and, 162–166
expenditures, 151–154, 258
revenues: fluctuations, 219–220
foreign-loan proceeds, 147n, 148, 171–173, 183, 217, 258
local-government collections, 152
national income and, 81–83
sources, 147–151
total: central and local governments, 152–154
pricing, 142–144, 154n
source data, 141–142
Bulgaria, 169n
Burma, 187, 188n–189n

Cambodia, 183
Canada, 189
Capital (*see also* Investment)
fixed: defined, 112, 130
working: defined, 80, 112, 113n, 114, 130, 137
estimate, 127–128, 130–135, 136
investment rate, 140

planned investment, 9, 128
source data, 115
supply, 24, 144, 145, 162–163, 166
Capital asset, fixed
defined, 113, 172
industrial, 51
nonproductive, 76
Capital coefficient, 136–138, 202
Capital formation (*see also* Investment)
accumulation and, 113
agricultural year and, 135–136, 219–220
basic construction investment and, 29n
by private industry, 125–128, 136
by the state, 116–125, 136
consumption and, 205, 216, 221, 222
defined, 112, 115, 185n
financing, 163
in a capital-scarce country, 139–140
in a totalitarian economy, 141, 166
in agriculture, 130–135, 136, 139
population growth and, 202, 204, 205, 218
rate, 84, 112, 115, 118, 136, 138–140, 202, 206
savings and, 206
Soviet aid and, 174
state role, 140
"Centralized purchase" scheme, 22, 129, 131
Ceylon, 183n, 187
Chemical fertilizers, 10, 41n, 57, 67, 74, 87, 108, 175, 221, 259
Chungking, 52, 215
Cities
employment problem, 79, 203, 204, 205
growth, 207
housing, 123, 128–129, 139–140, 215
labor force, 24, 203, 204
services, 207–209
Coal
commodity, 10, 18, 41n, 44, 211, 256
industry, 11, 41n, 47, 169, 256
Collectivization of agriculture (*see also* Agriculture)
agricultural credit and, 69
agricultural taxation and, 149n
budget deficit and, 166n
commercialization and, 209, 210
consumption and, 210, 213, 214
development, 12–13, 16–17, 63, 243, 244
effects, 68–71, 73
employment and, 204, 210

foreign trade and, 220
harvest losses and, 62
investment and, 133
land market and, 24
peasants' attitude, 61, 62, 69
planned, 13
productivity and, 61, 63, 68
state and, 73
statistical coverage and, 61, 63
Commercialization
consumption and, 209–212, 217
defined, 56n, 209
net national product and, 209–210
note issue and, 159n, 161
real income and, 157
speed, 209, 210–211
Commodity control
"centralized purchase" scheme, 22, 129, 131
"planned purchase and planned supply" scheme, 20–22, 131, 166, 200, 209, 220
state allocation, 18, 19, 20, 155n
trade volume and, 16, 26, 27, 239
Commodity reserves and stockpiles, 9, 21, 46n, 80, 114, 115, 127–128, 137, 185n, 206, 214, 216
Commodity unit, composite: defined, 17n, 152n
Communications
defined, 78
development, 236
investment, 9, 10
value product, 78, 97–100
Construction (see also Projects)
by the masses, 66–67, 76, 102, 105, 108–109, 139
by state security agencies, 77n
defined, 76, 112
gross value product, 77
investment, 117, 123–125, 128–129, 136, 140
net value product, 77, 97–100
Construction materials, 18, 28n, 40, 41n, 47, 54, 116, 117, 128–129, 172
Consumer- and producer-goods industries (see also Industry)
accumulation, 150–151
bottlenecks, 47
defined, 7n, 32, 39–41
development, 30, 34, 41–48, 229, 256
investment, 10, 48, 49n, 222
location, 49–52
mechanization, 39, 50, 235
planned, 8
taxes and profits, 42n

Consumer goods
composition, 219
export, 217
market availability, 205, 206–207, 210–212, 215, 219, 222
money income and, 28, 213, 215, 216
Consumer money income, aggregate, 28, 158–159, 163, 213, 215–216
Consumers' tolerance, limit of, 204, 205, 216, 217, 222
Consumption (see also Per-capita consumption)
collective: defined, 208, 217
national: commercialization and, 209–212, 217
defined, 80, 113, 185n, 205, 206
population and, 201n
urbanization and, 208, 209
Cotton, raw
commercialization and, 210
control, 18, 20, 21n
import, 71, 175
price, 28n
production, 58, 60, 61, 68, 71, 246, 257
Cotton cloth
classification, 3
control, 18, 20, 21
market supply, 210, 214–215, 216n
production, 45, 48
unit, 3, 45n
Cotton textile industry, 30, 31, 39, 47n, 49, 50, 71
Cotton yarn, 18, 20n, 44, 48, 256
Credit coöperatives, 131, 133n, 146n
Crop production
defined, 55, 61–62
development, 60, 246, 257
Cropping index, 60, 66, 257
Currency (see Money)
Czechoslovakia, 169n

Daily necessaries, 18, 23, 27, 210, 216n
Decentralization of control, 11n–12n, 145n, 152, 154
Depreciation, 75, 76, 77, 79, 80, 102n, 113, 134
Depreciation reserves, 149, 150
Domestic material product (net)
defined, 75–80, 85
estimate: ECAFE, 81, 82
official, 75, 81, 83, 107n, 147n
present, 93–97, 106
growth rate, 100
Domestic value product (net), 85

East Germany, 169n
Economic development: defined, 1, 7, 103

Economic structure
  effect on national product, 207–212
  material sectors, 75
  nonmaterial sectors, 102
  transformation, 109–111
Education and health
  capital formation and, 112
  development, 105, 196, 200, 204–205,
    208, 252–254
  expenditures and investment, 9, 117,
    153
Egypt, 183, 188n–189n
Electric power industry, 11, 41n, 44, 47,
  102n, 169, 256
Emergency economic and financial regulations, 13, 18, 154–156
Employment
  industry, 97–99, 129, 233
  material sectors, 101n
  problem, 79, 203, 204, 205, 210
  seasonal fluctuations, 24, 97, 233n
  social prejudice and, 79, 105
  state policy, 204
  trade, 241
Enterprise
  commercial, 13, 241
  defined, 33, 34, 140
  industrial, 13, 232
  profits, 13–14, 14n, 28, 34n, 76n, 80,
    116, 147, 150, 191
  quota (annual), 34n, 35, 46
  types: coöperative, 12, 15–16
    joint, 12, 14–15, 16n, 116, 126
    private, 6, 12, 13–14, 15n, 18–19,
      77, 126
    state-operated, 12, 15, 116
Export (*see also* Foreign trade)
  amortization and, 180
  composition, 185–186, 187, 188n,
    192n, 194, 217
  drive, 179, 184–190, 194–195, 217–218
  importance, 175, 177
  policy, 175, 177, 185–186, 217
  pricing, 179, 191
  quantum, 179n
  value, 178, 184, 258

Factor markets, 24
Factory (*see also* Enterprise)
  clandestine, 215, 216
  defined, 34n, 37n, 232n
  modern (*see* Modern factory industry)
Factory industry (*see also* Modern factory
  industry)
  development, 37, 40, 43, 91, 228, 229
  location, 49, 50, 51

net value product, 89–92, 110
planned, 8, 12
socialization, 6, 12, 13n, 16, 20, 23,
  126–127, 230, 231
structure, 233
Farms
  investment, 130
  types: collective (*see* Agricultural col-
    lectives)
    peasant, 68, 130, 131, 134, 135, 139
    primary producers' coöperative (*see*
      Agricultural primary producers'
      coöperatives)
    state, 62, 66, 67, 249, 250
Financial control, 6, 13, 18, 146n, 154–
  156
First Five Year Plan
  agriculture, 8–9, 64–65
  foreign-exchange cost, 175–176, 177,
    179
  foreign trade, 177–178
  industry, 8, 10
  meaning of fulfilment, 46–47
  objectives, 7–8
  planning work, 5n
  private agricultural investment, 130
  private industrial investment, 125–
    126
  socialization, 12–13
  state investment program, 9–12
  targets, defined: 7, 12
  why started in 1953, 6–7
"Five anti" movement, 6–7, 14n, 19, 32,
  126, 135, 147, 162, 165, 197
Food
  staple, defined, 21
  subsidiary, 22, 23, 26, 73, 185, 214
Food grains
  consumption, 72–73, 213–214
  control, 20
  defined, 55, 61–62
  effect of control on restaurants, 77
  export, 72, 185
  government-purchase quota, 20n–
    21n, 69, 71, 209
  markets, 18, 21–22, 24
  production, 60, 61, 71–74, 246, 247,
    257
  ration, 21–22, 73, 200–201
  value product, 58, 61n, 73–74
Foreign enterprises (private), 13n, 18, 85,
  107, 182
Foreign-exchange cost of the Plan, 175–
  176, 179
Foreign-exchange depreciation, 5n, 255n

Foreign-exchange and conversion rates, 5, 171, 172, 176–177, 181, 254, 255
Foreign-exchange reserves, 185n, 190
Foreign trade (*see also* Export, and Import)
   agricultural year and, 178–179, 219–220
   development, 177, 184, 189, 190, 258
   free world, 188–190, 193–195, 258
   geographical distribution, 186, 187
   policy, 175, 177–178, 185–186, 217
   quantum, 179n
   short-term credits, 190n
   socialization, 13n, 175
   Soviet bloc, 186, 187, 190, 192–193, 194–195
   state apparatus, 18n, 22n

General Agreement on Tariff and Trade (GATT), 190
Gestation period, 29–30
Grants to foreign countries, 179, 183, 184, 185n
Gross agricultural and industrial value product, 8, 30, 31, 163–166, 227
Gross factor (*see* Industrial value product, and Agricultural value product)
Gross national product, 79, 103
Gross social value product, 8n, 80, 100–102, 113

Handicrafts
   composition, 8
   employment, 233
   market, 20
   production, 8, 37, 43, 46
   socialization, 12, 15–16
   value product, 33–34, 37, 39, 43, 92–93, 228, 229, 230, 256
Heavy industry (*see* Consumer- and producer-goods industries)
Heavy-industry complex, 10, 51–52
Highway motor transportation:
   development, 30, 31, 49, 236, 238
   socialization, 16
Hired domestic help, 79, 99, 100, 108
Hong Kong, 5n, 181, 188n
Housing
   national income account, 76, 102–106, 112
   net disinvestment, 129
   per-capita space, 215
   pricing, 124–125
   state investment, 125, 139–140
   volume, 123
Hungary, 169n, 183

Import (*see also* Foreign trade)
   composition, 175, 188n, 194
   fluctuations, 179, 216
   pricing, 179, 216
   quantum, 179n
   value, 178, 184, 258
Income period, 159
India
   compared, 63–64, 68n, 84, 90, 103, 105, 110–111, 127, 137–138, 198
   trade, 187, 188n–189n
Indian Food and Agricultural Delegation, 60n, 62–63, 67n
Indonesia, 187, 188n–189n
Industrial location:
   centers, 12n, 49, 50, 51, 52, 234
   planned, 12, 51n
   policy, 49, 50
Industrial production
   fluctuations, 219–220
   major commodities, 44–45, 47–49, 256
   new products, 36, 37n
   planned, 10
Industrial value product
   agricultural content, 33n, 42n
   gross factor: enterprise, 30, 33, 34, 39, 42
      industrial sectors, 39
      industry, 33
      material sectors, 79
      plant, 34
   gross product: defined, 8n, 30
      growth, 31, 38, 94, 227, 256
      growth rate, 30, 37
      statistical problems, 32–35
   net product, 94, 96, 106
      how derived, 76, 93
      meaning, 34n
   pricing and, 30, 107–108
Industrialization
   accumulation and, 114
   balance of payments and, 185n
   commercialization and, 209–210
   consumption and, 205, 209
   economic structure and, 109–111, 207–212
   food consumption and, 72, 213–214
   foreign trade and, 175–176, 185, 194–195
   gross social product and, 101–102
   gross value product and, 33
   indicators, 31
   investment and, 120–121
   natural resources and, 52n, 194
   pace, 7, 30–39

policy, 7, 8n, 37, 216–217
population growth and, 202–203, 203–205
prospects, 217, 222
skilled labor and, 24, 196
social and cultural factors and, 198
Soviet aid and, 10–11, 194
Soviet experience and, 169
urbanization and, 207–209
Industry (*see also* Consumer- and producer goods industries)
agriculture and, 30–35
components, 8
defined, 30, 56, 102n
employment, 233
growth rate, 35–37, 39
investment, 9, 10, 11, 29, 117, 123, 124–128
location, 12, 49, 50, 51, 52, 234
mechanization, 39, 90, 235
planned increase in capacity, 10
socialization, 12–16, 126–127, 230
structure, 232
utilization rate, 50n
Inflation, 6, 17, 165–166, 213, 215–216
International Bank for Reconstruction and Development, 188
International Monetary Fund, 188
Investment (*see also* Projects)
agriculture, 9–10, 53–54, 66, 67, 69, 71, 117, 130–135, 139, 221–222
basic construction, 9, 29, 113, 115, 116, 117, 119, 120, 123, 153, 163, 165, 185n, 215, 216, 258
basic development, 9, 137
construction, 117, 123–125, 128–129, 136, 139–140
geographical distribution, 49, 50
gestation period, 29–30
heavy and light industries, 10, 48, 49n, 222
industry, 9, 10, 11, 29, 117, 123, 124–128
measurement, 116–119, 124–125
private (total, 1956), 15n
trade, 9, 117
transportation and communications, 9, 10, 117
state program, 9–12, 117
supervising agency, 146n
working capital, 127–128
Iron and steel industry, 11, 29–30, 40, 41n, 44, 49, 169, 256

Japan, 10n, 161, 188n–189n, 204

Joint operation (*see also* Enterprise), defined, 14–15

Kao Kang, reason for liquidation, 154n
Kerosene, 41n, 175, 211–212
Korean war, 6, 135, 142n, 161–162, 165, 174, 197

Labor (*see also* Employment)
market, 24
mobility, 24, 203, 204, 207
productivity, 51, 96, 218
shortage, 129
skilled, 24, 196
supply, 196
wages, 166n, 208
Latin America, 189
Liberal professions, 102–106
Light industry (*see* Consumer- and producer-goods industries)
Livestock (*see also* Animal raising), 17n, 22n, 28n, 59, 60, 64n, 69–70, 71, 113n, 120, 257

Machine-making industry, 11, 40, 41n, 44, 47, 169, 256
Malaya, 188n–189n
Marketing coöperatives, 13n, 240, 241, 242
Market (*see also* Black market)
agricultural products, 18, 23
free, "reopening" of, 23, 24, 26, 27, 28, 216
industrial supplies, 19, 20, 155n
manufactured goods, 23
open, 18, 19, 23
staple food, 18, 21–22, 24
Metal-working industry, 40, 41, 47
Middle East, 188n–189n, 189, 258
Mining (*see* Coal, and Industry)
Modern factory industry
composition, 39
defined, 8n, 37n
planned, 8
value product, 37, 38, 39, 228
Monetary control measures, 154–156, 163, 166
Money
controlled circulation, 155–156
demand, 156
foreign-exchange values (*see* item)
hoarding, 159n
income velocity of circulation, 159, 166n
new unit introduced, 5, 165

volume in circulation: estimate, 159, 160, 258
   reasons for increase, 161–166
   seasonal fluctuations, 159–160
Municipal utilities
   defined, 207
   investment, 9, 117
   national income account, 102

National income (*see also* Domestic Material Product): prewar estimates, 102–103
Natural resources, 51–52, 52n, 194
Nepal, 183
Net national material product, 80
Net national product
   agriculture and, 219–220
   balance of payments and, 80, 85, 107, 182, 185n
   budget and, 111
   commercialization and, 209–210
   defined, 84, 85, 182n
   estimate, 102–107
   growth rate, 107–109, 110, 138, 205–206, 221
   urbanization and, 208, 209
Net value product
   agricultural, 76, 86–89, 108, 110
   construction, 76
   factory industry, 89–92
   handicraft operators and coöperatives, 92–93
   industry, 76, 93, 107–108, 110
   new-product pricing and, 107–108
   nonmaterial sectors, 102–106
   other material sectors, 97–100
   pricing and, 34n, 109
North Korea, 183
North Vietnam, 183
Note issue (*see also* Money), 144, 145, 159, 160, 215, 258

Oceania, 188n–189n
Oils
   crude, 10, 41n, 44, 47, 175, 256
   fats and, 20, 21, 21n, 22n, 45, 68, 211–212, 214, 216n, 256
Outer Mongolia, 183
Overseas-Chinese remittances, 85, 107, 179, 180–182, 184

Pakistan, 187, 188n–189n
Paotou, 11, 52
Peasant (*see also* Farm)
   attitude toward collectivization, 61, 62, 69
   consumption, 205, 209–212, 213–214

income, 69, 69n, 130, 157, 210, 211
   lots retained, 17, 22n, 216
   savings, 130–135, 139
   tax burden, 150–151
Peiping (city), 11n, 27n, 50, 129n, 211, 215, 234, 251
People's Bank, 24, 131n, 144, 145–146
People's Construction Bank, 146n
People's Insurance Company, 146n
Per-capita consumption (*see also* Consumption)
   capital formation and, 221, 222
   cloth, 214–215
   disparity between rural and urban, 205, 212
   housing services, 215
   market supply and, 206, 210, 211–212, 219
   national consumption and, 80, 205
   official claims, 205, 206–207
   peasants, 209–212, 213–214
   staple food, 72–73, 208, 213–214
   subsidiary food, 73, 214
   urban workers, 205, 208–209, 213–214
Per-capita cultivated area (of farming population), 66
Per-capita national product
   per-capita consumption and, 205–212, 217
   population growth and, 202
Philippines, 188
"Planned purchase and planned supply" scheme, 20–22, 131, 166, 200, 209, 220
Poland, 169n
Population
   census (1953): results, 197, 198, 202, 251
      validity, 197–198, 202n
   "consuming," 201n
   effect on economic development, 196–197, 202, 218
   employment and, 79
   "farming," "rural," and "urban," 201, 202
   food production and, 71–73
   mobility, 24, 203, 204, 207
   natural rate of increase, 198–202, 218
   "new theory," 218
   overseas Chinese, 180n
   policy, 218, 219
   prewar and postwar, 161, 199
   rural, 130, 202–203, 204–205
   size, 197–198, 201, 251
   urban, 202–203, 207
Prices (*see also* Pricing policy)
   black market, 28

constant, 25, 32, 42, 79
control, 6, 18, 19
import and export, 177n, 179, 190–193
nonagricultural products, 109
official market, 19–20, 22, 25–28, 211
open market, 17n, 19, 26, 27–28
prewar compared, 42, 161
producer goods, 13, 19, 28n, 32, 116–117, 142–144, 172, 191, 192
retail, 25–26, 27–28
wholesale, 25–26, 27
Pricing (*see also* Pricing policy)
national income account, 79:
agriculture, 56
construction, 77, 124–125
industry, 30
new products, 36, 37, 107–108
restaurant services, 77
state budget, 116, 142–144
Pricing policy
agriculture and, 20n, 130, 150n
consumer demand and, 21, 22, 141
consumption and, 73
private enterprises and, 13, 19, 20n
production and, 21n, 67, 68, 69–70
profit margin, 18, 20, 28n, 191
state revenue and, 150
Producer-goods industries (*see* Consumer- and producer-goods industries)
Profit (*see* Enterprise)
Projects (*see also* Construction)
agricultural, 9, 66–67, 76, 102, 105, 108–109, 131, 137, 139
basic construction, defined, 11n
defined, 11
industrial: geographical distribution, 51, 207
number, 9, 11, 12, 29
number, 9
planned productive capacity, 10
Soviet aid, 10–11, 12n, 29, 36n, 171, 172, 174, 193
water conservation, 53–54

Railways
development, 30, 31, 49, 236, 238
investment, 9, 10, 117
Rationing (*see also* Commodity control)
cloth, 21, 214–215
food grains, 21, 73, 200–201
oil, edible, 21–22
Reclamation, 66, 71
Rehabilitation, 1, 5, 10n–11n, 30, 49, 51, 52, 120, 139
Repair, extensive, 9, 11n, 76, 120

Restaurants
development, 77, 99, 213
value product, 77, 99, 100
"Retained funds" of industry, 116, 145n, 146n, 149n
"Retained lots" of peasants, 17, 22n, 23, 216
Rumania, 169n
Salt, 18, 48, 214, 259
Sanmen Gorge area, 52
Second Five Year Plan
draft: degree of self-sufficiency in equipment, 8, 193–194
investment policy, 216, 221
population control, 219
proposal, 2, 8
Soviet-aid projects, 171n
possible trend: bond policy, 151
decentralization, 154
per-capita consumption, 216
population movement, 203–204, 219
Soviet aid, 193
statistical adjustment, 35, 37, 37n, 59, 76n, 157n
Shanghai, 11n, 13n–14n, 49, 50, 143n, 203, 211, 215, 234, 251
Shipping
development, 236, 237
foreign trade and, 179n
socialization, 14, 16, 238
wooden junks, 16n
Silver exchange standard, 161
Sino-Soviet joint-stock companies, 170, 182n
Social purchasing power
consumers' money income and, 158–159, 166
defined, 156
magnitude, 157–158, 215, 258
sources, 156–157
Social services, 203, 208, 217
Socialist industrialization, defined, 7
Socialization
development, 13–17, 230, 238, 239, 243
economy, 17, 18, 111, 147
objective, 7
plan, 12–13
process and technique, 13–17
Source data (*see also* Statistical problems)
agriculture, 25, 62–63
balance of payments, 2, 176
banking and finance, 2
evaluation, general, 2–4
foreign trade, 2, 176

industry, 3–4, 25
national income, 25, 84–86, 100
note circulation, 159, 160
population, 197–198
prices, 2, 25
state budget, 141–145
Soviet economic aid
    capital formation and, 174
    grants, 169
    imports and, 177
    interest rates, 170–171, 180
    joint-stock share transfers, 170, 173,
        180, 183
    loan agreements, 170–171
    loan proceeds, 147, 148, 171–173, 177,
        183, 217, 258
    projects, 10–11, 12n, 29, 36n, 171,
        172, 174, 193
    repayments, 179, 180, 217
    technical assistance, 10, 169, 182, 194
Soviet military aid, 170, 171, 173, 174
Soviet Union
    compared, 4, 8n, 29n, 30n–31n, 34n,
        35n–36n, 62, 75, 103, 105, 108n,
        111n, 113n, 118, 141n, 172, 177
    trade, 177, 186, 192, 258n
Special companies for joint operation, 15
State capitalism, stages, 13–14
State Economic Commission, 11n, 19, 47
State Planning Commission, 47
State Statistical Bureau (organization), 3,
    4, 26n, 64, 75, 226
Statistical problems (*see also* Source data)
    comparison: international, 4, 5, 84,
        176–177, 181, 188
        prewar, 4, 64n
    constant prices, 7, 25, 32, 35, 36, 42,
        56, 118
    coverage, 4, 59, 78, 79
    gross factor, 33–34, 35, 39, 42, 43, 51n,
        57
    measuring investment, 117–119, 124–
        125
    new-product pricing, 35–37, 39, 43,
        107–108, 110
    1952 as base, 4, 7, 65, 84
    subjective valuation, 57, 63–64, 197–
        198
Subsidiary work in agriculture, 56, 57, 58,
    59, 69, 74, 87, 111, 132, 204, 209, 210,
    212, 216
Steel (*see also* Iron and steel industry), 10,
    36n, 44, 47, 175, 256
"Supply and selling coöperatives," 13, 18,
    67, 131, 150

Taxes
    accumulation and, 113
    agricultural, 130, 134, 149
    current prices and, 109
    industry and trade, 14, 42n, 147, 150
    national income and, 80
    system, 141, 147n
Technical assistance
    given, 116n
    received, 116, 116n, 194
Terms of trade, 190–193, 194–195
Test-manufacturing cost, defined, 36–37
Tientsin, 49, 50, 234, 251
Tractor stations
    development, 57n, 67, 257
    services, 57, 74
Trade (internal)
    control, 13, 18, 126
    defined, 78
    development, 18–19, 239, 240, 241
    fluctuations, 219–220
    geographical distribution, 242
    socialization, 6, 12, 13–14, 16, 19, 26,
        239–241
    state investment, 9, 10, 117
    value product, 78, 97–100, 102–106

United Nations, 188
United Nations Economic Commission for
    Asia and the Far East (ECAFE), 81, 82
United States
    compared, 5, 84, 103, 111, 121, 140
    trade, 189
United States International Cooperation
    Administration, 187–188
Urban workers (*see also* Labor, and Per-
    capita consumption)
    consumption, 72–73, 205, 207–208,
        212, 217
    cost of living, 27–28
    state control, 24, 204
Urbanization (*see also* Cities)
    consumption and, 207–209, 217
    net national product and, 208, 209
    population growth and, 202–203, 204

Velocity of circulation (income), 159, 166n
Vital statistics (*see also* Population)
    data and estimates, 199–201, 203,
        204–205, 218
    system, 199

Wages, 14, 166n, 208
Water conservation, 53–54, 66–67, 69, 102,
    105, 117
Western Europe, 188n–189n, 189, 190, 258

Workers' insurance and welfare fund, 14, 144n
Wuhan, 11, 52, 215

Year, defined
    cloth ration, 21n
    food, 72n
    livestock census, 70n
    population census, 197
Yuan (*see* Money)

www.ingramcontent.com/pod-product-compliance
Lightning Source LLC
Chambersburg PA
CBHW021510210326
41599CB00012B/1196